THE CROMWELL STREET MURDERS

THE
CROMWELL
STREET
MURDERS

THE DETECTIVE'S STORY

JOHN BENNETT
WITH
GRAHAM GARDNER

SUTTON PUBLISHING

This book was first published in 2005 by
Sutton Publishing Limited · Phoenix Mill
Thrupp · Stroud · Gloucestershire · GL5 2BU

This paperback edition first published in 2006

British Library Cataloguing in Publication Data
A catalogue record for this book is available from the British
Library.

ISBN 0 7509 4274 6

Typeset in 10/11.5pt Goudy.
Typesetting and origination by
Sutton Publishing Limited.
Printed and bound in Great Britain by
J.H. Haynes & Co. Ltd, Sparkford.

CONTENTS

1735.

5.30pm 4/3/94
Gloucester police
station

I Frederick West
authorise my solicitor
Howard Ogden to
advise Supt. Bennett
that I wish to admit
to a further (approx)
9 killings expressly,
Charmaine, Reena,
Linda Gough and
others to be identified.
F West

Note to Superintendent Bennett from Fred West confessing to approximately a further nine killings.

PREFACE

In the years since those cold, dark days of February 1994, much has been said and written about Fred and Rose West and their despicable crimes. Some of it has come from people who knew them well, including members of their own family, the rest from others further removed. Some accounts were well researched and informed, others less so, but nearly all included considerable speculation about the extent and nature of the crimes the couple were involved in and as the dreadfulness of what took place at 25 Cromwell Street over more than twenty years became apparent, it was equally clear the Wests would secure their own place in the black museum of British crime.

Since then, I have been asked many times to give my side of the story, to correct the inaccuracies of other versions and commit to print a true account of what really took place. Although I could see some merit in doing so, I shunned all previous advances partly because as the Senior Investigating Officer I felt it a chapter best left to rest and partly because I did not want to experience again the media attention I felt such a project would attract.

So why the change of heart? And why now?

Perhaps naively, I thought the public's interest in the West Inquiry would diminish over time. In fact, every conceivable anniversary of the investigation and the events associated with it has brought fresh approaches from news organisations, whether to comment on, correct or put into context what had been said, written or reported by others. I hope this book will answer any future questions. Furthermore, I have also come to appreciate that not all senior investigating officers, and especially those involved in the more high-profile investigations, enjoy the same level of support afforded to me by my chief officers and that the rigours and challenges of real police investigations, let alone those with all the twists, turns and complexities of the Cromwell Street Inquiry, are rarely depicted to the public, for never was the expression that 'truth is stranger than fiction' more apt than here.

Let me be clear, this is not another book about Fred and Rose West, though they are obviously key elements. It is rather an attempt to document what I and my family experienced as well as other officers on the case and especially the courageous people who gave evidence, also the members of the organisations that became involved in the battle to bring the Wests to justice. It is hoped that now their true effort and commitment will be better understood and appreciated, and that the record finally will be 'put straight' concerning an investigation that owed its outcome to so many and from which many lessons have been learned. Who knows, perhaps this will be of some help to anyone unfortunate enough to go through a similar experience.

While I have been faithful to the truth and to make this as accurate an account as possible, I have tried not to betray the confidence entrusted in me, particularly by the families of the victims. They will forever remain uppermost in my thoughts. Neither would this book have been completed without the encouragement and support of Gloucestershire's current Chief Constable Dr Tim Brain, his Deputy Craig Mackay, former Gloucestershire County Council and Gloucestershire Constabulary solicitor Richard Cawdron and especially the assistance of Inspector David Griffiths, for which I express my sincere thanks.

I would also like to thank Graham Gardner who, since joining me in this endeavour, has worked tirelessly alongside me throughout the past twenty months and to Sutton Publishing, and especially Christopher Feeney, for considering the final work worthy of publication.

Finally, and most of all, I must thank my wife and family for their never-ending understanding and uncomplaining support throughout my career and into my retirement, which has always meant so much to me.

John W. Bennett QPM
August 2005

ONE

The unmistakable stench of death hung heavy in the air.

Not the customary mix of bone and rotting flesh. The gut-wrenchingly distinctive smell rooted several feet beneath the surface was the result of decomposed flesh and body fat coming into contact with water, and there was plenty of that, either from the broken sewer main or the natural water-table.

Senior Investigating Officer Detective Superintendent John Bennett recognised it straightaway. Fourteen years as a police frogman had honed his senses.

He had sampled it the first time as a fledgling police cadet in Stroud.

A suicide on the main rail line to London. Body parts, not found for a week or so, strewn along a quarter-mile stretch, were collected in the paper bags that were all they had in those days and stored in the boot of the patrol car. By the time the coroner and then an undertaker had arrived the bags had all but disintegrated.

'You'd better get used to it,' the Sergeant told the raw recruit.

Thirty-two years later in that dingy back garden, the Sergeant's words came back to him. He knew there were human remains somewhere. He could smell them. Not for nothing was it said in the force he had missed his vocation, that he should have been a scenes of crime officer, a mortician, a pathologist or even a doctor. Dead bodies, human biology and forensic science had always fascinated him, unlike most other policemen for whom attending a post-mortem examination was little more than one step along the investigative highway – an important step, but not one to linger over and certainly not to dwell on.

Often as not, though, it was a duty and sometimes a requirement for identification purposes for police to attend before, during or after a post-mortem. Most did what they had to do and left the rest to a scenes of crime officer, the exhibits officer, senior investigating officer or deputy. Not so John Bennett, or 'JB' as he was widely known. JB loved this side of the job and given the chance would be at the pathologist's side from the first incision to the last. Throughout his career, right from seeing that first death on the railway line, the way the body worked and the clues it offered up in death intrigued him.

Though just why John Bennett was there anyway was a curiosity. Some might call it destiny.

Promoted Superintendent Subdivisional Commander in 1989, he thought his return to uniform after more than twenty-two years meant the end of his days as a detective. Not many were given the opportunity to flit from plain clothes to uniform then back again, certainly not when they'd been in the job as long as he had. What's more, he'd enjoyed his time in charge of the Gloucester City Subdivision. It had given him responsibility for all aspects of policing the city rather than just focusing on crime as a detective, and everyone agreed he'd done a good job, but the opportunity to return to CID was too good to turn down and in any case, a detective was all he ever wanted to be. Now, after more than three decades in the job, he was at the peak of his powers. What's more, given his interest in forensic science, fate could hardly have chosen a better man to take charge of what lay ahead, for this was some time before DNA had assumed the importance it has now and if dead bodies could provide a clue to their killer he had always been prepared to exploit any advantage on offer.

It was Saturday 26 February 1994 and the team of police diggers had already been hard at it for a couple of hours. JB checked his watch and mentally marked the time at just after 2.50 p.m. as he and Detective Chief Inspector Terry Moore walked towards a narrow dirt track off St Michael's Square in Gloucester. It was spotting with rain again, just as it had been the previous afternoon when the digging began, and it looked like there was more on the way. It would make an already testing job even more difficult, Bennett thought to himself.

Moore, whose job it had been to get the operation started, pointed the way across a public car park that was the centrepiece of the square to where a constable in uniform was stationed at the entrance to the path. The constable saluted and made a point of noting both their names on his log sheet. It was no more than Bennett expected but this show of discipline and control of the crime scene pleased him. Acknowledging the constable distracted him from the small number of local news reporters gathered close by.

Walking on another 20yd, he could see off to his right the roofs and upper floors of what he guessed were the backs of some of the odd-numbered houses in Cromwell Street, a terraced row of three-storey Victorian houses now largely given over to flats and bedsits that had clearly seen better days. Many of the tenants were either on low incomes or benefits and didn't tend to stick around very long. In the ten years or so Bennett had worked in Gloucester he had occasionally gone along Cromwell Street to the city's main open space – known locally as the Park – but he had never had cause to call at any of the houses and had never realised the path he was now walking along even existed.

To his immediate right, above some fencing, he could see a line of conifer trees about 15ft high that formed a natural boundary between the end house and the adjoining property which was vacant. He realised this was where he was being taken as Moore had already mentioned the trees to him. It was also where the narrow, dirt pathway opened out onto a small piece of waste ground. Parked in the centre of this was a mini digger, scoop down with shovels and waterproof clothing draped over it. Several paving slabs were stacked against a fence.

Looking into No. 25, Bennett's immediate impression was one of surprise at how small the garden was for the size of the house. He reckoned it could only be 25–30ft long by no more than 15–20ft wide, although the combined effect of a high wall on the left, the trees on the right and the height of the house itself all made it feel more closed in and claustrophobic. His view was also obscured by a pile of brick debris from a home-made barbecue and wood from a shed, as well as more of the paving slabs that once covered the garden but which had now been lifted and stacked against the base of the trees. Some members of the Gloucester Police Division Support Group, a sergeant and six constables who were all specially trained in crime scene search techniques, were slowly digging in that area, every spadeful carefully scrutinised by Acting Detective Sergeant Bob Beetham and Detective Constable John Rouse who were both scenes of crime officers. Other members of the group were removing the remaining slabs by hand.

Peering into where the digging had already begun, Bennett could see what they were up against. Less than a spade-depth down there was a crusty layer made up of solid ground and gravel. About a foot down, this gave way to a thick, black and brown treacle-like mud, which had the smell of sewage. Even worse, it seemed that the deeper the hole was dug the more this liquefied mud began to seep in until it found its own level. Bennett knew the water-table in the Gloucester area may have been partially responsible and that the conditions weren't helped by a further layer of dense, dark, impervious grey clay that existed some 6ft below the ground – left there when the River Severn receded thousands of years before. The reason for this water, or where it was coming from, was not important, but to remove it most definitely was. Some form of pump was needed as well as a tent to cover the whole of the area. This would not only protect the men from the weather, it would also mark it out as a crime scene and block out the prying eyes of the media, for he realised now that some reporters had already got into neighbouring properties overlooking the garden in order to get a better view of what was going on. Bennett called over Sergeant Tony Jay, who was in charge of the support group, and told him to contact the fire service, while at the same time instructing Bob Beetham to make arrangements to get the crime scene tenting brought over.

While all this was taking place Bennett said little but his eyes were everywhere. If his outward expression gave nothing away his mind was alert, carefully considering what other problems might have to be faced. As Detective Superintendent Operations, he was there to give advice and take over serious crime investigations when it was appropriate. Today, as before on this investigation, he was acting in an advisory capacity for this was Terry Moore's case and one that Bennett knew he was perfectly capable of handling. After all, when they analysed it coldly and factually, this appeared to be just another domestic murder. Tragic, of course, like any other, but while the circumstances might be different, it was the sort of thing that happened all too frequently and it was beginning to look like an investigation that would be resolved quickly – once they'd found what they were looking for.

Turning back again towards the house, Bennett saw there was a shanty-looking flat-roofed extension made of brick, built on to the back. Piled on top of it were some old wooden boxes and other sizeable odds and ends and bits of building material. The extension was wider on the left than the house and appeared to be joined to the wall of the adjoining property that towered above it. A pair of double glass doors led into the back of the house and opened out onto concrete slabs, some of which had been removed. The right half of the extension had one window and jutted out onto the patio. Altogether, it was as wide as the garden and went right up to the row of trees, but it was a really ramshackle affair and Bennett doubted whether planning permission had ever been given for it since the work would never have passed inspection.

Moore had already mentioned that the initial removal of the slabs and early digging had uncovered a quantity of small bones and bone fragments. A local anthropologist had examined them and decided they were from dead animals. Some of it could even have been leftover food. In any event they appeared insignificant – unlike one large bone that was uncovered when a slab was raised immediately below the window of the extension. The discovery was made just before Bennett and Moore arrived. One of the diggers saw it sticking up through the ground at an angle. The two scenes of crime officers, Beetham and Rouse, had already had a look and thought it human, but what was puzzling was that it was as far away as it could be within the garden from where they had been told to search.

Bennett and Moore went across to the marked area and saw for themselves the protruding bone just as it had been described to them. Resting just below the surface, it was dirty, on the face of it old, and yes it did look human – maybe from an arm or leg. Then again, many times down the years Bennett had been called out to nearby streets by builders and householders who had discovered human bones in gardens, on wasteland and on construction sites only to find they were Roman in origin. His first thought, therefore, was that the bone they had just uncovered might not be relevant. Nevertheless, it would still have to be checked out.

As the fire service arrived and began pumping, it was clear that the machine would have to remain in place until the search was completed because although it was not a large volume of water that was hampering them, as soon as it was pumped out back came more, probably from a spring or some other source. If that wasn't bad enough, as the diggers made the hole bigger the foul-smelling treacle substance thinned to a custard consistency.

Bennett turned and went over to where the main excavation and pumping work was going on. The edge of the hole was rimmed with planks. The detective found a spot and peered over, quickly identifying the smell that was now emanating from inside as adipocere. It was little more than a whiff but it was there all right, faint yet unmistakable.

Adipocere is a sickeningly repugnant, nose-clinging stink. It is associated with human decomposition, especially in watery conditions. It results partly from the decay of body fat and is a smell that, once experienced, is never forgotten and one he had encountered many times when recovering decomposed bodies as a police diver. But there was no time to dwell on it. The diggers, who were working with Rouse, had uncovered what looked like human hair.

All the moisture that was around was making the hole very unstable and the sides of it were gradually crumbling and caving in. Even so, more bones were clearly visible now, including a sizeable one that looked like it came from a leg or possibly an arm. The stench of adipocere had intensified considerably. Everyone could smell it right to the pits of their stomach and it made the discovery of the bone near the extension seem even less important.

It was a sickening experience yet one countered by adrenalin as the investigation gained a new momentum.

First they had to notify the coroner for the city, David Gibbons, who would decide whether he or one of his officers needed to attend. Either way his authority would be sought to call out a Home Office pathologist. The man they were expecting was also the man they wanted on the job. Professor Bernard Knight, colloquially and respectfully known as 'the Prof', was the head of a consortium of Home Office pathologists based at Cardiff University. Sensing his skills might be needed, Moore had already been in touch with him.

The site was now definitely a crime scene and had to be made secure until the Prof arrived. Only then could all the officers involved, diggers and supervisors, return to Gloucester Police Station for some food and rest. There was nothing more they could do at 25 Cromwell Street for the time being.

Acting Detective Sergeant Beetham had decided to remove the bone found near the extension. He put it in a brown paper exhibit bag and took it to the station so that the Prof could take a look at it before they did any more digging at Cromwell

Street. Showing the complete bone to Bennett and Moore before the pathologist's arrival, it was evident to them all it was a human thighbone – a femur.

As promised, Professor Knight arrived at Gloucester Police Station within an hour and a half and there, over coffee, Moore, Bennett and Beetham outlined what had taken place so far, including the conditions he would find at Cromwell Street. Beetham then handed him the bag and asked him to look at what was inside. The professor removed the bone and, holding it in both hands, first made as if to smell it, though it was known he had all but lost this sense years before, then turned it in a circle at arm's length. Within seconds he confirmed it was human and almost certainly female. His initial view was that it had not been in the ground that long – and certainly wasn't there in Roman times! The slight curvature, which was a recognisable feature, meant it probably came from a young woman – at least that's what he thought. To be sure and in order to age it more accurately he would need to take it back with him to his laboratory at Cardiff and do more tests. Measuring the bone as he spoke he added that he thought it came from quite a young person who was possibly aged 15–25 when she died.

It was a startling revelation and not at all what they had expected to hear. The likely age of the bone raised new questions.

Darkness had started to fall and the rain had turned to a drizzle when Bernard Knight was taken to Cromwell Street just before 7 p.m. Entering from the rear pathway, he paused to pull on his wellington boots but refused the overalls offered to him, preferring his own anorak.

The garden area was now covered in well-used, crime scene tenting that formed a canopy over the pathway. Power for the bulbs that hung from the ceiling of the tent came from a generator. The more intense light that illuminated the area where the professor was headed came from movable electric arc lamps.

It was damp and cold. A mist of condensation formed around the lamps which was added to by the condensing breaths of all those in the hole and looking on. No one spoke unless spoken to first by the professor. A video camera operator had been arranged to work alongside the scenes of crime officers and the Prof, who would each take still photographs and video as the work progressed so that between them they would produce a complete record of the excavation and what was removed.

Bennett and Moore had positioned themselves alongside the video cameraman on the relative dryness of the wooden boarding from where they had a clear view of what the pathologist was doing. Crouching to examine the excavated area, he immediately confirmed the presence of what appeared to be human skeletal remains. In the wet and filthy conditions, the 'grave' parameters and its sides formed a sort of small quadrangle, the sides falling away to where the remains could be seen. Working to instructions agreed beforehand by Bennett and Knight, the video camera recorded and stopped as the painstakingly slow and methodical operation of excavating and removing the remains continued.

It was a grisly task carried out in the most relentlessly appalling conditions.

Each bone was handed to a scenes of crime officer to be recorded and prepared for removal so it could be examined again in greater detail later. The visible part of the remains was found around 2ft below the surface and had been pushed down to a depth of another foot or so.

Knowing that Bennett and Moore would appreciate it, the Prof gave a running commentary as to what he was finding and his initial opinions. As he continued, the smell of adipocere was even more evident – not that he was concerned, having lost his sense of smell many years before. This time, though, he didn't have to smell it because he could see it in the form of traces of a soapy, off-white liquid and traces of it were easily visible. The surrounding mud was also darker, no doubt due to further decomposition.

While the leg bones they had recovered were in some semblance of anatomical order, they appeared to have been separated from the torso and placed on it. Further down in the ground, a black polythene bin liner was found partially underneath the torso. Close by were two lengths of cord. The head also seemed to have been separated and was found with its hair still in place, though by now heavily matted in mud. According to Knight, the ground conditions must have somehow helped preserve it. By the time he had completed recovering what bones there were, there appeared no evidence whatsoever of any clothing. No material, no buttons, no zips. It seemed the girl had been buried naked.

Bennett and Moore watched intently, detached from emotion by their professionalism. Each stood on the boarding, hands in their anorak pockets, a posture they had both learned to adopt over the years, not out of slovenliness but because it helped to preserve the integrity of evidence by removing the temptation for them to touch things. On this occasion, too, both had their collars turned up, more in a vain attempt to keep warm than anything else.

Warm, cold or otherwise, they were about to get another shock to their senses.

Professor Knight leaned forward and pulled out another bone. It was part of a left thighbone – another femur. He could see it was obviously broken, though how he couldn't readily tell because of all the dirt that covered it. Then he pulled out another, longer portion that had a number of cuts near to where it had been broken. Moments later, another bone, this time a complete right femur.

'Well,' he said dryly, 'either we have found the world's first three-legged woman or there's another victim around here somewhere!'

TWO

Some say it was down to one, maybe more, of the Wests' children telling social workers their sister was buried under the patio in the back garden.

Others credit the dogged work of one woman detective who pursued a missing person case to its grim conclusion.

Both made good reading in the newspapers and an enticing sub-plot.

But while both played a key role in the unravelling of 25 Cromwell Street's dark secrets, the truth is it was that vanishing icon, the British bobby, the natural descendant of Dixon of Dock Green, who first lit the blue touchpaper.

It was 3 August 1992. Police Constable Steven Burnside was patrolling the part of his beat that took him along Cromwell Street when two young girls approached him. One of them told him she had a friend who was being sexually abused by her father and that there was pornographic material in her friend's home where there were also younger children.

And that's how it all began – though it was another two years before the full extent of Fred and Rose West's evil came to the surface, by which time they would have managed to slip through the court's fingers twice.

The first time was twenty-one years earlier when they appeared before Gloucester Magistrates Court on 12 January 1973, charged with assault occasioning actual bodily harm and indecent assault on their children's former nanny. For although the £25 they were each fined on each charge meant a total overall of £100, worth far more then than now, the punishment hardly fitted the crimes they had committed and which seemingly became their template for later acts that led to murder.

The second occasion, incredibly, involved their children.

Fred West had been charged with three offences of rape and one of buggery against one of his daughters, while Rose West was charged with cruelty and causing or encouraging the commission of unlawful sexual intercourse with a child. On 7 June 1993 they both appeared before Judge Gabriel Hutton at Gloucester Crown Court pleading not guilty. Just before the trial began the main witnesses refused to give evidence against them. The case collapsed as a result and the judge had no other option but formally to find them not guilty. Clearly overjoyed with this, the couple presented quite a picture sitting side by side in the dock, passionately embracing one another and laughing.

John Bennett, by now appointed Detective Superintendent after more than two years in uniform as Superintendent in charge of the Gloucester City Subdivision, was driving from the constabulary's county headquarters in Cheltenham to another divisional HQ in Cirencester. That damp, bright morning it had been a good run, straight through Leckhampton on the outskirts of the town, rising east into the countryside and on towards the Cotswolds along the old Roman route. Arriving early he began going through his notes and papers ahead of a series of joint management meetings, the first with Fred Davies, Gloucestershire County Council Social Services' Deputy Director.

In Gloucestershire, police officers and social workers had long moved on from the shared cynicism of the 1960s and 1970s, when most social workers were 'drug-taking hippies' and police officers 'fascists'. Fred Davies, though, was more than just a good ambassador for his profession. His quiet but amiable personality and his grasp of problems often encountered by all of the caring agencies and by the police in particular, ensured he and his opinions were readily accepted. His openness was refreshing and he was someone Bennett knew he could work with from their first meeting.

Today, the two men had arranged to meet prior to a full meeting with the Crown Prosecution Service special caseworker Withiel Cole and the members of a special investigation team, which for some months had been investigating a number of allegations of physical and sexual abuse by members of staff on residents at a privately run care home within Gloucestershire – the first investigation of its kind in the county.

Fred Davies arrived for the meeting.

'Hello, John. How's things?'

It was his usual greeting, though today the normally brisk stride and friendly smile were overshadowed by tiredness and overwork.

Over coffee the two men quickly dealt with the few apparent management problems and as they did Davies posed the question that would change Bennett's life forever – though at the time it appeared little more than a routine inquiry.

'Do you know about a sexual abuse disclosure to the police in Gloucester?'

As Bennett listened, Davies explained how a joint investigation of police and social services, working out of Gloucester Police Station, had been agreed and that the police had obtained a warrant to search a house in the city. As a result, the social workers on the investigation had taken out an Emergency Protection Order to have the five young children living there taken into care.

Emergency Protection Orders (EPOs) are always invoked if children might be at risk, even when the allegations are under investigation and yet to be proved.

Davies said that the investigation now involved several allegations of rape as well as physical and sexual assault and that as a result of the 'disclosure' the search warrant had been granted specifically to look for videos, pornographic literature and anything else relating to sexual abuse – which was just what they found. Not only that, they also discovered a large quantity of pornographic videos, film, photographs, papers and sexual paraphernalia, and, more strangely, intercoms and peepholes to bedrooms. All his staff involved had mentioned a similar feeling – that there was something strange, something wrong, which no one could put their finger on. This, he said, applied to the house, the children and the general circumstances – though at that point neither the address, 25 Cromwell Street, nor the names of the couple who lived there, Fred and Rose West, entered the conversation.

Soon the full investigating team joined them and the scheduled meeting took place, after which John Bennett returned to Cheltenham thinking nothing more of the Gloucester case Fred Davies had mentioned.

In October 1993, John Bennett was at Gloucester Central Police Station to discuss another joint police and social services child abuse investigation. There he saw the familiar face of Detective Inspector Tony James. James knew the reason for Bennett's visit and wanted to discuss a missing person investigation being conducted by another detective, Hazel Savage. Bennett said he would call back before leaving.

Bennett had known Tony James for most of his time in CID. Popular, loyal and reliable, he was an outgoing, energetic officer who always preferred to be out on the street doing the job rather than penned up in an office, which was where he was when Bennett returned.

Sitting at his desk James handed over a report that had been submitted to him by Detective Constable Hazel Savage. Bennett took a seat but before he could begin reading James asked if he recalled a child abuse investigation from just over a year ago, where the father of a Gloucester family was charged with rape and the mother with aiding and abetting and abuse. Bennett said he couldn't, so James explained that the witnesses and victims were the parents' children or stepchildren who, on the day the trial was due to begin at Gloucester Crown Court, refused to give evidence and the hearing was stopped. Some of the children of the family were juveniles and were still in care, but one of them, a daughter named Heather who by then would have been about 23 years old, could not be traced.

'From what you'll see in the report, she may even be dead. What's more, her parents may have had something to do with it.'

It appeared the girl had never been reported missing and that the investigation only came about because a uniform patrol officer, Police Constable Steven Burnside, had been approached by two young girls in Cromwell Street in Gloucester and told by one of them that one of her friends was being sexually abused by her father and that there was pornographic material in her friend's home where there were younger children. The police constable had returned to the station shortly after and reported everything he had been told to the sexual offences unit. Three days later, on 6 August 1992, armed with a warrant, police and social services went to Cromwell Street and knocked at the front door of No. 25, a three-storey, end-of-terrace house next to the Seventh Day Adventist church.

The five children who were there were taken into care, their mother, Rose West, was arrested for aiding and abetting rape – though after being interviewed, she was released on bail – and their father, Fred West, a jobbing builder, was arrested on a building site in Stroud and later charged with three offences of rape and one of buggery and remanded in custody. Rose West was arrested again on 11 August, interviewed once more and charged with an offence against one of her daughters – cruelty and causing or encouraging the commission of unlawful sexual intercourse with a child – but was subsequently released on bail.

It was around this time, according to James, that a chance remark with chilling implications surfaced for the first time, one that would come back to haunt both the Wests and their investigators.

Apparently, the day before, one of the young West children, while being interviewed, told a social worker that it was a sort of family joke that 'Heather was under the patio'. It was only a passing comment and in the way it was said and who was saying it, not really taken seriously. The social worker, however, did not forget it.

During the course of the search of the Wests' home, the police found commercial pornographic videos depicting bondage and other hardcore sexual practices; home-made 8mm film and photographs, obviously taken by Fred West, which showed his wife performing explicitly sexual acts with just about anything she could get her hands on – domestic implements, fruit – and having sex with a number of Afro-Caribbean men viewed through peepholes in doors with the aid of an intercom that linked the bedrooms. Clothing and a variety of trappings and items likely to be used for perverse sexual pursuits were also uncovered.

As Tony James went on, Bennett began to realise that this was the investigation Fred Davies had talked about many months previously when they were at Cirencester. By the time James mentioned the peepholes and an intercom he was in no doubt.

While Bennett read the report, James went to fetch its author, Detective Constable Hazel Savage, who had been involved in the investigation almost from the beginning. Her principal job had been to interview the West children and then Rose West. There had been some discussion then with the Crown Prosecution Service over why Heather West could not be traced, as she could have been important to the inquiry. However, after consultation with the Crown Prosecution Service, it was decided not to pursue this as her brothers and sisters had already made several serious allegations and the investigation was already complicated enough.

Even so, Heather had not been totally disregarded. As part of the process of finding out whether she, too, had been abused, both Fred and Rose West were asked in some detail about their eldest daughter. Very soon after they were arrested, the couple had been questioned separately about when and why she had left home and when they had last seen or been in contact with her. Both said she had gone to Devon to work in a holiday camp after some family disagreement around 19 June 1987, some four months before her seventeenth birthday. The only way the police could be sure if their version was true would be to find Heather and ask her, yet despite exhausting all the normal avenues of enquiry there was still no trace of her. Not only that, there was no indication of where she'd been or anywhere she'd worked from the time she left home. As far as official records went, from the day Heather West left home she simply ceased to exist.

Ever since the trial that never was, Fred and Rose West had made it abundantly clear they intended getting the care orders lifted so they could have their children back and be a family again, but the fact that the children had refused to give evidence did not in any way diminish the concerns of those who knew their background and who had seen in black and white and colour, in photographs and on film, their parents' perverse sexual interests and how they indulged them.

Although, from a police perspective, the 'West Abuse Case' was now over, a meeting was held on 20 August 1993 to consider the children's future welfare. It was attended by representatives from Gloucestershire Social Services, a legal executive representing the department and the residential social workers caring for the West children who had been living apart all over the country.

During a break, when most of those attending the meeting had broken up into small groups, the residential care workers began to talk to one another in general, discussing how the children were progressing and how they had coped with what had happened to them. It was then a truly staggering new line emerged. A piece of information that, if true, would give the investigation a completely different emphasis, and staggering because of the seemingly random way it came to light.

Comparing stories, the social workers noted how the patio at home seemed to keep cropping up in conversation with the children: how it had been laid at the time their sister Heather had left and how it had become 'a family joke' she was buried underneath. It appeared that the children had only mentioned it briefly and did not seem to take it seriously, though it did appear to be on their minds. Thinking back, members of the group reckoned at least one of the children had mentioned it the first time when the inquiry began in 1992 and that it had then arisen again around April or May of that year and had kept cropping up ever since.

There were no police at that meeting and the conversations concerning Heather were not discussed or minuted formally, but both Gloucestershire Social Services staff and the legal executive there had become sufficiently concerned to make contact with the police. Later that day the legal executive had telephoned Gloucester CID to speak to Hazel Savage but as she was not available had left her a message covering the conversations and comments made during the break.

On 23 August 1993 the detective returned the call and was given more details. At her request, concerns now emerging about Heather West were set down in a letter from Gloucestershire Social Services while she renewed her efforts to trace the girl.

Tony James and Hazel Savage returned to the room where Bennett stood, holding her report. It was Savage who spoke first.

'Hello sir, what do you think about this then – what are we going to do?'

John Bennett had known Hazel Savage since they were both young detective constables. In fact, she had joined the police in 1964, only a couple of months after him. In those days, most female officers remained in the policewomen's department and were almost a separate entity from the rest of the force, supervised by other women and dealing mainly with missing persons, absconders from care homes, child abuse and sexual offences. Policewomen did not work nights and were paid less than policemen.

Hazel Savage, though, was an exception – a career detective who had chosen early on in her police life not to take the path to promotion but to direct her considerable energy towards front-line operational policing. She had been stationed within the Gloucester Division, policing the centre of the city and its outskirts since her appointment to the CID. From those early days she had quickly gained the admiration of her colleagues, both within the CID and in other departments, in what was then a male-dominated profession. She had survived by learning over the years how to handle her male peers and supervisors, whatever their rank, often countering what today would be deemed as out and out sexism. Her bluntness was well known throughout the county, as was the fact that she was a most capable officer who could also be outspoken when necessary. She was an experienced officer who had been involved in many investigations and carried a heavy case load but who nevertheless always had time to help a colleague. She was equally capable of dealing with witnesses and, when necessary, their care, yet able to change to being an incisive, searching, tenacious and even aggressive interviewer as the situation demanded. Because of her length of time in Gloucester, she knew the city and its criminals better than most.

Of all the UK's police forces, Gloucestershire is among the smallest, both in terms of manpower and resources, and the three had worked together many times in the past.

Bennett asked if everything had been done to find the girl and Savage said it had and there was still no trace of her.

'There is always the chance, sir, she could have gone abroad, but if she has then she's managed it without having a passport in her name.'

Bennett made some minor suggestions along the lines of

further research of the Wests and their family tree, but Savage's solution was more radical.

'But once we've done that, sir, the only thing left is to go and search the garden.'

Bennett pointed out that the rather casual suggestion they should 'search the patio or garden' showed no idea of the huge amount of work involved. While he had no doubt something had been said in conversations between the residential care workers and the children, as far as the three detectives were concerned they were now listening to third-hand information. They needed to get something on the record, and to do that, Bennett said he would approach Fred Davies to get permission to interview the residential care workers and get access to any relevant information that might be of use. The police, meanwhile, would continue the search for Heather and if they still could not find her, or if the social workers confirmed the 'patio joke', he would get Davies's agreement to have the West children interviewed as well. If, after all that, everyone stood by what they were supposed to have said and there was still no trace of Heather, he would seriously consider a search warrant.

Bennett asked James to keep him informed of any developments and to be sure to advise Detective Chief Inspector Terry Moore, who was away on a course, of their meeting as soon as he returned. He also promised to bring it up with Fred Davies when the two men were due to meet later that week to discuss other child abuse investigations that were ongoing in Gloucester.

On the afternoon of 21 October 1993, the two men met in Davies's office at Gloucestershire County Council headquarters in Shire Hall, Gloucester.

Even if they had not been due to meet, the policeman's presence there would not have been a surprise. Child abuse investigations were becoming more frequent and it was work that brought them more and more into contact with the police; in fact,

John Bennett was in and out of their offices so often, a stranger might have thought he was a social worker not a policeman.

There had been several important and even dramatic developments in the child abuse investigations in Gloucester that week, which made that day's meeting necessary. Although none of them included Bennett's discussion with Tony James and Hazel Savage concerning the Wests and their missing daughter, he had made a mental note to raise it with Davies once the other matters had been dealt with.

Bennett began by asking if he could remember telling him about the West family and an investigation that had begun into what was going on at 25 Cromwell Street where they lived. He also enquired about the children who'd been taken into care and whether the failure of the prosecution against their parents had changed anything.

As expected, Davies was up to date with the case and had also heard something about what the children were supposed to have told their carers about Heather. Bennett explained how he had since been asked for advice concerning a further search for Heather because, despite all the enquiries at the time of the abuse investigation and since, she still could not be found.

Bennett asked if police from Gloucester could be given access to any notes the residential carers may have made since the children were taken into care. He also asked if detectives could interview them so that they could make written statements about what the children had said to them.

Davies agreed, and said that if necessary each child could be questioned separately, with a social worker and an officer from the Gloucester Police Child Protection Unit carrying out the interview jointly. Bennett also suggested the interviews be recorded on video so that whatever the residential carers had said could be fully explored with them.

Davies understood the reasoning behind Bennett's additional request and he agreed to have all the children brought to Gloucester at an agreed time and kept apart. All he asked for was as much notice as possible so that the appropriate arrangements could be made. As well as travel details to consider, some of the children might have to be housed as well. Bennett explained that Detective Chief Inspector Terry Moore, whom Davies had also got to know well, was on a course and that Detective Inspector Tony James was the likelier go-between, though Moore was due to return soon so it was possible he might be hearing from him as well. The two men parted knowing they were due to see each other on a number of occasions in the weeks ahead when this whole sinister mystery was bound to crop up again.

As Christmas came and went there was no respite, either for Bennett or the Gloucestershire Constabulary. The force was undergoing an initial review by its Chief Constable Tony Butler and the service nationally was looking at itself in light of the likely recommendations being made by an inquiry into the police service, its responsibilities and rewards known as the Sheehy Inquiry. It wasn't hard to anticipate what this independent, but government-arranged, inquiry was going to demand – more accountability locally and nationally, more performance targets and indicators, and an increase in responsibility and accountability downwards in the ranks with the eventual loss of overtime payments. All this had been widely reported in the press, as was the view that the service was considered 'top heavy' and needed fewer ranks. To this end, the Sheehy Report was expected to recommend the loss of the ranks of chief superintendent and deputy chief constable. For Gloucestershire, and the majority of police forces, this would no doubt mean altering its internal structure again, reducing divisions, and changing and increasing responsibilities of higher ranks as well as increasing the workload of the lower ranks.

The New Year dawned and Gloucester CID was as busy as ever, though by 15 January Heather West was moving up the agenda.

Hazel Savage had finished going over the old enquiries, and made some new ones, but there was still no sign of the missing teenager. Bennett decided it was time to investigate the patio claims on a more formal basis and told James to arrange to speak to the West children's social workers. Statements should be taken and if these supported what had been said earlier then the West children themselves should also be interviewed.

The suspicious death of a child followed and within the week a domestic murder, then a further suspicious death. Although these were each quickly resolved they increased the pressure further. In addition, the child abuse investigations were becoming more and more complicated and were constantly under review. It meant meetings between John Bennett and Fred Davies were more frequent and during one of them in mid-February, Davies mentioned that statements had now been taken from the West children's carers and that further arrangements were in hand for the children to be brought to Gloucester to be interviewed on the morning of Thursday 24 February, by coincidence the same date as a Child Abuse Investigation management meeting was due to start at 9 a.m. in Stroud. It was a significant date, too, for John Bennett, but for a more personal reason. Alongside this new entry in his diary was an earlier one from his wife Ann – in large capitals: DAVID'S 21st BIRTHDAY. David was their youngest son and there had already been a big bash for his eighteenth. For his twenty-first a more intimate gathering was planned.

Looking beyond to the next day's entries, Bennett could see that from 1.30 p.m. on Friday the 25th through to the late afternoon of Sunday 27 February he was committed to attending a live-in seminar at the Golden Valley Hotel on the other side of Cheltenham, which had been organised by the Chief Constable. This was an important meeting where the effects of change, financial constraints and the requirements of the force and departments were to be discussed fully in a no-holds-barred environment. During that weekend, the Chief Constable and his management team of chief officers would lay out his vision and strategy. No apologies would be accepted; it was a three-line whip. Bennett prepared one presentation on operational crime investigation, and another for Assistant Chief Constable Bob Turnbull on vehicle crime.

Thursday 24 February should have been just another working day, memorable only to the Bennetts because it was their son's twenty-first birthday. It was certainly a landmark but for very different reasons.

David Bennett was a chef and had set off for work at 6.30 that morning. Over a cup of tea, his parents had wished him happy birthday and helped him open some of the cards and presents that had arrived already. As David left he threw his father a knowing look.

'Now don't forget Dad. We're all going out tonight to celebrate so please try and be home early, can you?'

About an hour later, as Bennett prepared to leave himself, his wife Ann repeated the sentiment – with interest, 'Not that what I say will make much difference.'

It was a still, somewhat dingy morning. In the half-light there was a hint of something better even if bright sunshine was expecting too much. Bennett was early enough to miss the commuter logjam but still decided to take his preferred route up through Leckhampton to the top of Birdlip Hill then along through Cranham and into Stroud. Apart from being the prettiest drive, he knew it would cut out some of the traffic and bring him directly to the side of town where the police station was, without having to navigate its tortuous ring road.

As Bennett approached his destination, he tuned in to the eight o'clock news on the local BBC radio station and after hearing the headlines retuned to Severn Sound, the local independent station. Both carried similar international and national news headlines, but for local news the difference in

24

broadcasting styles meant the content often varied considerably. To Bennett's relief, there was nothing on the local radio news to worry him that morning as he travelled down through the narrow, winding hedgerows and soaring woodland and on into the Slad Valley, made famous by Laurie Lee in his book *Cider with Rosie*.

Parking his car at the front of the police station, Bennett made his way to the second floor from where two child abuse investigations were being run. It was shortly after 8.30 a.m. and some of the members of the investigation teams were already at work. Fred Davies arrived shortly after and at 9 a.m. they began their first meeting. This took rather longer than expected and the morning was half over by the time the second one could begin. As they prepared for it, Davies mentioned that the West children had been brought to Gloucester.

'I wonder how the interviews are going?' he pondered.

'I'd forgotten they were happening today,' Bennett replied. 'When we've finished this meeting I'll phone through and see what I can find out.'

It was some time after 12.30 when he picked up the phone and called Gloucester CID, asking for Detective Chief Inspector Terry Moore. Having received no reply from his office he was passed on to the general CID office on the ground floor where he was told Moore was somewhere in the building but not in that office. Eventually, Detective Inspector Tony James came on the line.

'Hello, Tony. How did the interviews go with the West children? I've got Fred Davies here with me.'

To Bennett's initial surprise James replied that a successful application had been made to Gloucester Magistrates Court the day before for a warrant to search the Wests' back garden for evidence in connection with Heather West's disappearance. Bennett was taken aback, not only because he was unaware of it, but also because the application had been made *before* the children had been interviewed. However, James explained that Detective Chief Inspector Moore, Hazel Savage and himself had taken the decision after reviewing the case and failing to find any trace of the 16-year-old. They'd checked and checked, he said, but could find no sign either of any national insurance number that surely she would have had. In addition, the residential care workers had put down in writing what the children had told them about Heather and the patio, confirming that it was a story they had heard repeated many times in recent months.

According to James, they had decided there and then they had reason enough to apply for the warrant. If the application was successful then the children could still be interviewed before the search was carried out. If the application failed, and more came out when the children were questioned, well, they could always try again. As it was, when the children were interviewed on video that morning, they more or less confirmed what their carers had said in their statements.

Bennett could understand the reasons for applying for the warrant *before* interviewing the West children even if he was a little uneasy at the timing. Yet, although he was relatively happy with the arrangements, and appreciated why they had asked for a warrant for the garden and not for the address, which would have included the garden, he was more concerned at the cost of the work involved and who was going to pay for it. The resources and finance to execute search warrants, which can take place any time up to a month after they've been granted, normally fell to divisional rather than headquarters budgets. However, if it turned into a long-drawn-out search or a serious crime investigation – and all the evidence they had pointed to that – they would have to ask the Chief Constable to dip into a contingency budget. Bennett also knew from experience that searching a garden for the reasons and circumstances that existed here would need a great deal of thought and preparation, and for that reason alone he was definitely taken aback when James mentioned that Moore was conducting a briefing as they spoke and that the warrant would be executed within the hour.

'It'll be Terry, myself and some other officers along with the Gloucester Support Group. We've also hired in some sort of mini earth-moving machine and other equipment.'

Bennett was aghast. He just could not understand what the rush was. Why do it that day? More to the point, at that *time* of day?

They were already into the afternoon and what had started out as a fairly bright morning had turned into a typically dank February offering, when darkness would fall before too long and definitely by 4 p.m. They would never be able to conduct and complete such a search within a few hours and certainly not in darkness, so lighting or guarding overnight would also become an issue.

'I understand what you're saying, sir, but we've planned for all that,' James replied.

'What about the lab?'

'We've been in touch with Chepstow' (where the South-Western Forensic Science Service was based) – *Bennett was reassured.* 'But they reckon our own SOCOs [scenes of crime officers] should be able to handle it' – *not so reassuring.*

In fact, Bennett was not sure about this at all. Searching a garden in the way he envisaged it being done would require more than just some thinking through, both before and once they were on site. He had also learned over the years that you can't turn back the clock once you've started or put back together what you have undone in investigations, and certainly not when it comes to scene-searching and gathering evidence. He knew you only got one chance to get it right. Make mistakes at the start and valuable evidence would be lost. Bennett's golden rule was always to 'slow down' the action wherever possible and 'take stock'. To his way of thinking it was the only way to obtain, preserve and make the most of any evidence they might find.

He asked about what vehicles were going to be used and how the officers carrying out the search would be clothed.

'Don't use the marked van, and leave it parked in the street, and have you got any plain overalls?'

'Yes, and we'll use an unmarked van.'

'Good, because we don't want to advertise this is a police operation. The media will get to hear about it soon enough, no point in making it obvious.'

Bennett knew the local reporters had their 'ears to the ground' and thought it sensible to have some plan or statement ready just in case. There was a 'story' in any police-generated search but the failed investigation and disappearance of a family member behind this one was bound to hype it up even more than usual.

James accepted his boss's instructions, adding that part of the operation of executing the warrant was to enable them to interview the mother and father again – Fred and Rose West – about Heather and especially about when she had left and when they had last seen her.

'OK, sir. I'll get Mr Moore to phone you later and we'll keep you up to date as things progress.'

Bennett put down the phone and told Davies what was happening. Soon afterwards they left Stroud, each promising to keep the other informed about his side of the investigation – Bennett on Fred and Rose West and the search of their back garden; Davies on the couple's young children, who were still the responsibility of social services.

Seeing no need to get involved any further at this stage, and knowing that either James or Moore would contact him later, Bennett set off back towards Police Headquarters. This time the lower, main road took him through the undulating beauty of the Painswick Valley, along twisting bends towards Brockworth to the east of Gloucester, before straightening into the final, built-up section through Shurdington and into Cheltenham.

Throughout the 45-minute drive, his thoughts centred more on what was said about the child abuse investigations and preparing the papers for the following day's management seminar. For now, events that were unfolding in Gloucester were the least of his concerns. Indeed, having spent the rest of the afternoon in his office, reading the advance papers for the seminar and sorting out other material he thought he might need over the weekend, he even managed to return home just after 6 p.m. – much to the family's surprise. They'd reserved a table at the King's Arms for 8 p.m. and as the pub was only 3 miles away he even had time to shower and change. In fact, there was still an hour to go when he emerged from the bedroom.

That's when the phone rang.

Before Bennett could answer, his wife had picked up the receiver in the hall. 'Hello Terry, how are you? . . . And how's Pat?' The formalities observed, Ann Bennett knew this was not a social call. 'It's Terry, for you.'

The Bennetts had known the Moores for over eighteen years. The two detectives had worked together often. Their career paths crossed continually. Moore became a detective constable at Stroud when Bennett was a detective sergeant there and both had young families. Later, Bennett was his detective inspector at Cheltenham when Moore was detective sergeant of the divisional drug squad. On Bennett's promotion to detective chief inspector at Gloucester, Moore was promoted detective inspector and they'd celebrated together. More recently, they'd worked together on a range of murders and other serious crime investigations in Gloucester.

Moore was regarded as an intelligent, conscientious and reliable officer. He had been appointed to the CID at a time when detectives were expected to work long hours with little financial return and his ability shone through. Although quiet by nature he could be a firm supervisor. Decisive rather than impetuous, he was another who held strong views which he was often able to support with well-founded logic when challenged. Both men shared a similar sense of humour, though Moore tended to wear his heart more on his sleeve. If something concerned or upset him, Bennett could usually tell from the tone of his voice or the look on his face. He had always been a keen and able sportsman and, as in his work, had shown himself to be a good team player.

While the rest of the family waited to leave for their birthday get-together, Bennett listened while Moore brought him up to date with developments at 25 Cromwell Street when they arrived with the warrant. Among the first things he heard was that the local newspaper, the *Gloucester Citizen*, already knew something was going on, possibly as a result of a keen-eyed paperboy realising it was a police operation. Not long afterwards, a photographer and reporter had been to the back of the house and were asking questions. Bennett guessed it wouldn't be long before the radio and television stations also showed an interest.

Moore then concentrated on the warrant and said Rose had been at home when they arrived. It was 1.25 p.m. but she answered the knock at the front door wearing little more than a nightdress.

'Apparently, her day for entertaining!' he quipped.

Fred was out at work, somewhere in Stroud. When they showed Rose the warrant she telephoned him straightaway but by the time everyone except the guard had left Cromwell Street, around 5.30 p.m., he had still not arrived home. Then, completely out of the blue, he turned up at the police station at 7.40 p.m. and volunteered to be interviewed on tape by Hazel Savage about Heather's whereabouts. Apparently he was saying he had seen her recently in Birmingham.

Moore added that Rose was also now being questioned on tape by Detective Sergeant Terry Onions and Constable Debbie Willats in her home.

As Moore continued with his account, something rang a warning bell in Bennett's mind.

'Rose rang Fred straightaway to tell him what was going on but he didn't turn up until much later. Where did he go? For he must have gone home first, then come to the station.'

As darkness set in, it had started to rain so Moore said they'd decided to call a halt to the search of the garden until the following morning, even though Fred West had not returned home by then. Arrangements had been made for a uniformed constable to stand guard overnight.

The garden was entirely covered by concrete and slabs to form a patio. A small excavator with caterpillar wheels and mechanical mini digger with a hydraulically operated scoop had been hired for the job.

In fact, it turned out that that was the reason why the operation had begun at what, to Bennett's way of thinking, was an odd time for around 1.30 that afternoon was the earliest they could get their hands on the machine. They were about to embark on what was to become one of the biggest, most complex investigations in British criminal history and it was a contract hire firm that was effectively firing the starting gun.

Once it arrived, the digger was used to help remove the slabs which were stacked to one side. Des Powell, a police constable in the group who said he had used one before, was given the job of operating it and instantly became known as 'Des the Digger'.

The patio was cleared of a shed-like structure and home-made barbecue made of bricks.

As the two men talked, Bennett's mind was full of questions. What was the Scenes of Crime Department doing? What samples were being taken? How were they digging the garden and how deep would they go? What effect would all this have on any buildings nearby? What would happen to the spoil and the slabs?

From the answers he received, it was Bennett's first impression the job had not been thought through properly, at least not in the detail he considered necessary. As his 'warning system' kicked in again he was at least consoled there was time to see the site for himself and review what Moore and his team were planning. For now, at least, it was time to slow things down and think things through.

Moore's quick call had turned into a lengthy conversation and ended with Bennett asking to be kept fully informed. Moore said he would go over the content of the day's interviews with Fred and Rose and compare them with what they had said earlier. He would also look again at the West family tree to see if they'd missed anyone. Bennett's immediate job was to inform his boss, Detective Chief Superintendent Ken Daun, and the head of Uniform Divisional Operations, Chief Superintendent Geoff Cooper, as well as the force press officer Hilary Allison. Even though he had things to do at headquarters the following morning, ahead of the Chief Constable's management seminar that weekend, Bennett told Moore he would be in touch to see if there were any new developments and he would definitely be over.

As the conversation ended, Bennett was oblivious to the fact that his family were gathered in the lounge waiting, some of them pacing, others seated, all of them impatient to go. His wife was in pole position in an armchair that looked straight down the hall and seeing the phone go down called out 'Come on'.

No one asked what the call was about or why it was so long. They were used to him not talking about his work. Even so, as they drove to the restaurant, Bennett's thoughts were on what Moore had told him, what they needed to do next and how it would be done. Only when they had reached their table was he able to put it to one side and enjoy the evening – blissfully unaware that it would be some time before he would be able to relax to that extent again or why he would always remember his son David's twenty-first birthday.

THREE

Rose West had not taken kindly to having police officers knock at her door.

Caught off guard by their unscheduled arrival she was not in control and Rose liked to be in control. She thrived on it.

Faced with a pair of detectives on her doorstep and a team of boiler-suited officers digging in her back garden she was vulnerable and her mood reflected her nervousness, swinging constantly between foul-mouthed aggression and jittery uncertainty.

But Rose West was not at the top of John Bennett's agenda – at least not then. It was the morning of 25 February and by now even his son's twenty-first birthday party the night before seemed a distant memory as he arrived at his office at about 8.15.

Ray Crabb, the office manager, was another early arrival and was about to embark on a tour of the CID and other departments to distribute the internal mail. As Bennett made himself a mug of coffee he reminded him that the Chief Constable's management seminar was now less than 24 hours away which meant that from later that morning and throughout the weekend he would be at the Golden Valley Hotel with the force's other senior managers. Before he could leave, though, he still had some work to do on the presentation he was preparing for the Assistant Chief Constable, Bob Turnbull, on the increase in theft of and from vehicles and what the police could do about it. Bennett's aim was to finish the report, slip back home to collect an overnight bag, then go via Gloucester to see how the search of the garden was progressing.

So far there'd been no news from Terry Moore, so Bennett decided to call him. Moore told him the support group officers had now returned to continue the search. In the meantime, he and some of the other officers had had a chance to review the interviews given by Fred and Rose the day before. As a result, it now appeared that the West family tree might not be as complete as they had first thought. Rose West's mother, it appeared, could still be alive although they had no idea where she was living. As she had not been interviewed before there was a possibility she might have some information about her granddaughter Heather. Consequently, Moore had sent Detective Constables Hazel Savage and Darren Law to 25 Cromwell Street to get the address and he was still waiting for them to return.

Bennett needed no further invitation and set off for Gloucester, but even before he got there the case had taken another unexpected twist.

At first glance the CID General Office was as he had expected to find it, no more than the usual everyday bustle and activity he was used to. Even a smiling Terry Moore was not unusual – though today there may have been just the hint of elation as he explained that Savage and Law had just returned with the news that Fred West had admitted killing Heather and he was in the cells.

Bennett's initial reaction was what Moore's had been earlier, that it must be a joke, until the two detectives related in full what had happened when they called at 25 Cromwell Street at around 11.15 that morning.

Fred had answered the door and when they told him what they were there for, he invited them into the living room where Rose was watching television. When they asked about her mother, Rose flew into a rage, shouting, screaming and waving her arms in the air. To prevent her hitting anyone, Fred took her into the hallway and shut the door behind him.

After a few seconds alone together, Fred came back into the room and said, 'Can we go to the police station?'

They took him out through the front door and put him in

the back of an unmarked CID car, which was when he admitted killing his daughter – adding only, in a matter-of-fact sort of way, that they were looking for her in the wrong place.

So it was, at around 11.20 – just 5 minutes after they had arrived to ask where his mother-in-law was living – Detective Constable Hazel Savage arrested Fred West on suspicion of murder and took him to Gloucester Police Station. Arrangements were now being made to interview him. He had asked for a solicitor and Cheltenham-based Howard Ogden, who was the on-call duty solicitor, was to represent him.

In Gloucestershire and most other forces a detective superintendent had to attend suspicious deaths. This had come about because in other parts of the country mistakes had been made early on in potential murder investigations which reflected badly on the professionalism of the police.

The news that Heather West really was dead saddened Bennett, but at least her father's prompt admission had vindicated the work they had done so far. That Fred West had owned up voluntarily suggested he would cooperate fully and the search of the garden was likely to take less time.

Things were shaping up well and it looked as though what was a divisional matter could remain so. All Bennett had to do now was to ensure that Moore had all he needed and wait to be told when the rest of the girl's remains had been found. Until then there was no need for him to be involved and he could make his way to the management seminar. Even so, in view of Fred West's confession, and what had happened just before he had made it – taking Rose out of the room to talk about no one knew what – Bennett knew they would have to bring her in too, not least because there were clear discrepancies between his confession and what she had said voluntarily when interviewed on tape the day before. As the conversation drew to a close, Tony James added that he had told Fred Davies of Fred West's admission and that Davies had asked if Bennett could call him.

Bennett found an empty room with a telephone and dialled the number for Gloucestershire Social Services. A voice on the other end answered and put the call through to Fred Davies's office.

'Hello.'

'Hello, Fred. It's John Bennett.'

'Hello, John. How's things?'

Bennett quickly brought him up to date, though the important part about Fred West's confession he already knew. Davies then took over.

'I've been looking at some probation reports that were compiled for both Fred and Rosemary West before the trial in 1993. They show that Fred was assessed as having a lower than average IQ and could be considered as bordering on the subnormal. As regards Rosemary, she had apparently taken an overdose of sleeping tablets during the time she was on bail. I thought you ought to know.'

It was as well he did because Bennett knew it meant that the police should only interview Fred or Rose West in the presence of what the law calls an 'appropriate adult'. An appropriate adult is always required under the codes of practice of the Police and Criminal Evidence Act 1984 when investigators wish to interview juveniles, though it's also a requirement for adults if the investigator becomes aware or believes that the person they want to question may have a learning disability or has previously or is currently suffering from some abnormality of mind or associated illness. This is the case whether or not a solicitor represents that person and a solicitor cannot object once the police have decided there should be an appropriate adult present. The idea is to safeguard the rights and welfare of such suspects.

Bennett was always one to err on the side of caution, especially in murder investigations. After all, at most trials the defence would suggest that an offender was not in control of themselves because of depression or emotional strain and that would be enough to warrant an appropriate adult anyway. He also knew from experience that in most cases anyone who kills is, either at the time or certainly soon after, not acting rationally. In the broadest terms, that made them psychopathic by definition, suffering from a form of mental illness. An appropriate adult was imperative, therefore, to ensure that all the interviews they conducted would be acceptable in evidence and not thrown out of court on a technicality.

The downside from the police point of view was that the allocation of an appropriate adult often delayed the progress of an investigation because first they had to find someone available from the list of volunteers. This was a job for the custody sergeant and could not involve any of the investigating officers, who could have no influence over the selection of an appropriate adult. Once someone had been contacted and agreed, they still had to get to the police station – all of which meant more time lost.

Returning to the CID office Bennett talked through what Fred Davies had told him with Terry Moore and Tony James. As they did so, Hazel Savage and Detective Constable Darren Law joined the group. When Rose was arrested it was agreed that she would be taken to Cheltenham and detained there, so the Cheltenham custody sergeant would have to make similar arrangements for her. They knew it had to be that way, but it was not what they wanted to hear, for the 'custody clock' was already ticking.

As he thought about heading back towards Cheltenham, time was not on Bennett's side. Not only would he be pushed to get to the hotel for the start of the management seminar, he had not yet got his accommodation sorted out and he would also need to find a moment to update the CID's Head of Crime Management, Detective Chief Superintendent Ken Daun, on the morning's developments. Even so, he told Moore he would return in the evening – or before if any trace of Heather West's remains were found earlier. With that, he walked out of

Gloucester Police Station, got into his car and headed out along the Ring Road towards the Golden Valley bypass, the 3-mile stretch of dual carriageway that linked the city with Cheltenham and by which most local people referred to the hotel where the seminar was being held. It was a journey he could have driven blindfold having travelled it probably more than twice a day most days during the last eight years.

Bennett joined the queue to register and after collecting his key took his bag to a room on the first floor, then went in search of his boss to bring him up to date with events at 25 Cromwell Street. Together, he and Daun briefed the Assistant Chief Constable, who Bennett then took to one side for a further chat about the presentation he had prepared for him – which at that stage was much more of a priority than an apparent 'domestic' in Gloucester, especially when the victim's father had just confessed to doing it.

The Chief Constable of Gloucestershire, Tony Butler, opened the seminar and explained how he hoped they would be able to agree the basis of the constabulary's objectives and business plan for the forthcoming year – one in which he knew that there would be the inevitable financial constraints. Looking around the table, Bennett thought it most likely that the CID would suffer the most from any squeeze. There had, after all, been a subtle shift in emphasis that had left the constabulary seemingly less concerned with rising crime figures and falling detection rates, and more focused on what the jargon called 'public interaction' and 'community policing'.

When they broke for their evening meal, Bennett made his way back to Gloucester to find that nothing more than a few animal bones had been found in the back garden at Cromwell Street. The almost constant drizzle meant that conditions there were deteriorating.

At 6.34, Detectives Darren Law and Hazel Savage had taken Fred West back to the garden, where he was able to indicate roughly where he had buried Heather. There was a cold indifference about him and he mocked the search team for digging near the roots of the leylandii hedge, saying he would not have dug that close in case he damaged the roots – a concern he had not extended to his daughter. Yet, despite switching the focus of their search, they were still unable to find anything. The work was called off for the night and arrangements made for the area to be guarded.

Rose West had been arrested at her home by Detective Sergeant Terry Onions almost 6 hours earlier and taken to Cheltenham Police Station. She asked to be represented by the Gloucester-based solicitor Leo Goatley, who had acted for her in 1992. However, the custody sergeant there had had great difficulty in finding her an appropriate adult and this resulted in her not being interviewed until just after half past four, more than 4 hours later. When she was told of her husband's confession – that he had killed Heather – she wailed hysterically, though her howling grief did not convince her interrogators, who thought she was putting it on. She continued to deny any involvement or knowledge of her husband's crime.

More interviews were arranged for both Fred and Rose West at Gloucester Police Station that evening. Where Rose was concerned, the police were still concentrating on the discrepancies between what she had previously told the 1992 inquiry about Heather leaving and the additional information she had volunteered to Onions when he interviewed her on tape the day before, when the search warrant was executed. They were keen to question her about her revelation that Fred had mentioned seeing Heather recently; that their daughter had telephoned home and spoken to her father; and that she had given Heather a substantial amount of money that she claimed she had saved before Heather left, which she hadn't told Fred about.

The custody clock the police had been concerned about was ticking on. By 11.20 the next day Fred would have been locked up for 24 hours, the same would apply for Rose at 12.25. They had to decide what to do next, especially if they were to keep them both in custody. To achieve that meant more rules to adhere to.

If the police weren't ready to charge them, they would need to convince the divisional superintendent that in order to prevent the loss of evidence – or obtain further evidence by questioning – he must authorise extending their detention up to 36 hours. Before committing to that, in the event that either or both the Wests objected to being held, he would have to listen to any representations from the couple's solicitors. Only then could he reach a decision.

If the police wanted to keep them in custody longer than 36 hours, an application would have to be made to a magistrate. Given the timescale involved this would mean arranging a court for the following day, which would take them up to Saturday evening! It was not an ideal prospect though one that was still a long way off and there was plenty to think about before then, not least whether to charge Fred West on the strength of his confession alone or wait until Heather's remains were recovered.

And the questions did not stop there. How to continue the search at Cromwell Street? What would be the best method bearing in mind the safety of the men carrying out the digging? How to continue the investigation? Would they need to set up an incident room based around a HOLMES computer (a Home Office Large Major Enquiry System)? Or could they get by with a paper-based system? What would be in the statement they would have to release through the press office? Media interest locally was intensifying.

One thing was certain. There was not enough time left that evening for them to finish questioning Fred West about the many inconsistencies in his story. No time either to examine his claims that Rose knew nothing about what he had done or even how his account differed from hers. Soon the custody sergeant would demand that Fred be allowed to rest so there was no need to rush the job. The same applied to Rose.

Instead, Bennett continued his boomerang existence between Cromwell Street and the Golden Valley Hotel, reassuring Moore that he would definitely be back in the morning to check on progress and that he would update the bosses when he got back to the seminar.

Twenty minutes later and he had reached his destination. The clock behind the bar showed just after 10 p.m. The seminar had only recently closed but Bennett had unfinished business. Finding Ken Daun, he set about bringing him up to speed. Over a pint of lager they pored over the problems of the search as well as the resources that were now becoming involved and what effect this was likely to have on other policing in the city.

When the Assistant Chief Constable joined them, Bennett repeated the message for his benefit. He in turn briefed the Deputy Chief Constable Nigel Burgess, who passed it on up the line to the Chief Constable, Tony Butler. With anyone who was anyone in the Gloucestershire Constabulary there, at least it didn't take as long as normal to get the message to the top. Not that that appeared to be to Bennett's advantage. When the Chief came by shortly afterwards, he threw him a smile and quipped, 'Some people will do anything to get away from a seminar.'

And the Chief wasn't the only one, for by now just about everyone there had heard about what was happening in Gloucester, but at least Bennett was able to unwind in the relaxed atmosphere even if he was the butt of some predictable jokes.

Sleep did not come easily. It never did the first night in a hotel. Sure, there was time to think, but nothing more to think about. All that could be done had been done, for the time being. Instead, Bennett's thoughts drifted ahead to what the morning might bring – perhaps the recovery of Heather West's remains? More information from Fred? Maybe even an admission from Rose about her involvement in the girl's death, for the likelihood of her not being involved, or not even knowing, did not seem plausible.

At the very least it appeared she had lied to cover up for her husband. After all, despite all the evidence of the couple's obsession for depraved sex, Heather was their first child. How could he have killed her, buried her under the patio and kept it from Rose? And what about the 'family joke' that had started it all? Everything the young West children had said pointed to their mother knowing all about what had happened.

Breakfast over, Bennett was back in his car and on his way to Gloucester. Moore had ensured the search was under way once more and arrangements were in hand to resume questioning both Fred and Rose, though by the time their solicitors and appropriate adults had arrived that was unlikely to begin until later that morning. The 24-hour detention time limit was approaching which meant they would have to get in touch with the division's acting superintendent so they could set about extending it to 36 hours. Scenes of crime Acting Sergeant Bob Beetham was also worried about how they were going about the search. Bennett and Moore reassured him they would talk about it when they returned to Cromwell Street.

At 11.19 a.m. the formal request to extend Fred West's detention in police custody up to a maximum of 36 hours without charge was granted by the acting superintendent. Once that was done, he repeated the procedure and signed the custody record in respect of Rose West. This gave the police another 12 hours in which to question the couple. They would then have to decide whether to charge them, release them or put them before a court to get permission to keep them even longer. Either way, they might only have until early evening to find answers to their many questions.

FOUR

There was no question of the professor being mistaken.

Professor Bernard Knight was a man of many parts who excelled in all of them. Highly respected not only by police officers but also by his fellow pathologists both locally and nationally, coroners and the medical and legal profession as well as by journalists and authors. For among his other talents he was an avid writer of medical reference books as well as crime novels and television dramas. If that wasn't enough, he was also a qualified barrister and his reputation as a pathologist went before him throughout the United Kingdom and abroad.

So, if the Prof's initial explanation of how Fred West had disposed of his daughter differed from her father's there was no question whose version carried greater weight. After all, West had first denied the killing then he had admitted it. Then he said it was an accident, only to change his mind again when her remains could not be found. He then went back to saying he'd killed her 'by accident' during an argument and then dismembered her – but that was only *after* the police had told him they'd found her remains. That was when detectives thought the remains they had discovered were those of Heather West – and only her.

This all meant that West could now be asked about the 'extra' femur – like how it had got into his garden – while the Prof continued excavating and removing any remains that were still to be found in the area now considered to be the main search site. For there was still much more to be done, both in the hole and around the surrounding area, removing the odorous mud and earth, finely sieving and searching through it. That, though, was work for scenes of crime officers and did not need the supervision of the professor, who agreed to take a look at the area underneath the extension window where the first femur had been removed earlier. It was already apparent that the ground conditions there would be the same and more preparations were necessary before he could start.

The support group officers had continued removing the paving slabs throughout the time the professor was working, loading them into wheelbarrows and passing behind the Superintendent and Chief Inspector, pausing only to watch the meticulous work that went into removing the remains.

As well as moving the lamps so they would illuminate the new hole where the professor would be working, they also had to put down more boarding to make a dry area from which to work. This gave the support group officers a new task that was willingly and quickly undertaken. Even though it was late, by this time everyone there was aware that the remains already recovered had shown definite signs of dismemberment.

'What a bastard: how could he do that to his own daughter?' said one of them. It was a view shared by everyone there but Bennett saw it as an added reason to call a halt to the search for the night. It had been a long and exhausting day and apart from being tired, dwelling on what they had found and personalising it did not help the operation and could lead to mistakes.

Before leaving it was agreed that the scenes of crime officer Bob Beetham would make arrangements for the recovered remains to be cleaned, photographed again, recorded and transferred to Knight's laboratory at Cardiff University.

It was the evening of Saturday 26 February and they were three days into the investigation. Detective Inspector Tony James, who was supervising the interviewing of Fred and Rose West at Gloucester and Cheltenham Police Stations, had been kept up to date with what was happening at Cromwell Street. The discovery of another thigh bone away from the specific area West had indicated meant there was almost certainly another set of remains – another victim. James briefed the interviewing officers who were already experiencing some of the obstructive, hostile and devious ways Fred and Rose West would adopt from now on.

Rose West, in her interviews, continually maintained Heather was alive, though as the questions became more pointed and searching she became more and more abrasive and foul-mouthed, as Detective Sergeant Terry Onions and Police Constable Debbie Willats knew from experience when they asked her about the £600 she claimed to have given her daughter before she left home.

'I was upset at the time. I was upset . . . What do you think? I'm a fucking computer . . . in the last eighteen months I've had fucking hell. What more do you want?'

When Onions explained he was just trying to find out if Heather was still alive she bit back with 'If you had any brains at all, you could find her. It can't be that difficult!'

Later, when he asked why she hadn't reported Heather missing, the astonishing reply was 'So I have got to snitch on my own daughter?'

At 18.45 that evening, the record button was pressed and Detective Sergeant Terry Onions with Detective Constable Neville Smurthwaite began a further interview.

The interview room was laid out to Home Office specifications. The walls had an extra skin of metal panelling to make them soundproof, though by now the original off-white paint had yellowed through the combined effects of age and nicotine. The door was also soundproofed and the windows double-glazed. A dark, varnished wooden batten ran around the walls to prevent damage from anyone leaning back in their chair. A free-standing, wooden table topped with formica was positioned in the centre of the room with an NEC twin-recording tape deck on it and a black microphone fixed on a matching backing plate just above. Interviewing officers sat with their backs to the door, the interviewee opposite them and their legal representative alongside – together with an appropriate adult when necessary.

The detectives questioned Rose West closely about when she had last seen her daughter; the last time they had had any contact; how she felt about her; and what she thought about her disappearing in the way she had. By now Fred West had confessed to killing Heather though Rose was unaware of this and remained sullen and generally unhelpful, intimating only that her daughter could be awkward and that she 'liked to be different to everybody else'.

Then Onions moved towards the news they had been holding back, that her husband had confessed to killing their first child.

'Why do you think you have been arrested today?' Onions asked.

'That's what I'm hoping to find out – I don't know.'

'We've gone over a lot of ground about last night – there has been a major development this morning. A major development.' Onions continued calmly, slowly emphasising each word, 'Fred has confessed to murdering Heather.'

This time Rose West's response was immediate.

'What!'

Then seconds of silence until she snapped, 'So you know where she is?'

Onions confirmed, 'He has told us where she is.'

Rose West's head rocked and from out of her mouth came a banshee wail that rose to a crescendo until it filled the room and then ceased abruptly almost as if it had never happened.

'So she's dead. Is that right?'

To the detectives it seemed a pre-planned response, acted out and insincere. Onions responded: 'I'm telling you Fred has confessed to murdering Heather.'

'What?'

'That automatically implicates you.'

'Why does it automatically implicate me?' anger now obvious in her voice.

'Our suspicions are that you are implicated.'

'It's a lie.'

Onions asked whether Fred had told *her* where Heather was, or if he had told her anything, but he got no reply and the interview was ended.

In another interview that had begun almost three hours earlier, Fred West – who at the time was accompanied by one of Ogden's clerks and Janet Leach who'd been appointed his appropriate adult – was told that the search had so far failed to find Heather's remains. After mocking his interrogators for a few minutes he ended the interview. The gap-toothed grin that he had worn before his admission returned.

Then, about half an hour later, he agreed to be interviewed again and completely retracted his earlier admission to killing Heather, proclaiming he had made it all up.

'Heather's alive and well, right – she's possibly at this moment in Bahrain. She works for a drugs cartel – she's got no identification that's why you can't find 'er – and there are more of them recruited from the Gloucester area, for drug runnin'. They're looked after like queens. I've got no idea what 'er name is as I won't let 'er tell me. She contacts me whenever she's in this country. Now, whether you believe it or not it's entirely up to you.'

The exotic picture he was creating didn't end there. He had 'seen her recently – had lunch with her. She had a car – a chauffeur – had changed her name', though before his claims could become even more fanciful, the interview ended with West challenging the police to carry on digging as 'nobody or nothing's under the patio!'

Shortly after, when the remains of what were later confirmed as those of Heather West were found, the information was given to Ogden's clerk so that he could inform Ogden and a further interview be arranged.

Howard Ogden worked out of an office in Cheltenham. He was well known within legal circles, principally as a defender of local criminals who had built up his caseload over a number of years while working for a firm of Cheltenham-based solicitors specialising in criminal defence work, and he often acted as a duty solicitor across the county. Tall, bespectacled, he was by nature pleasant and approachable, veering towards the flamboyant in manner. In the courtroom his delivery and enunciation were precise.

West was interviewed again by Detective Constables Hazel Savage and Darren Law and by now he had been told what the police had at last unearthed in his garden. Just as he had appeared overconfident and smug before, now he was showing signs of stress and had to be given a dose of diazepam prescribed for him during an earlier visit by a police surgeon. Knowing what was coming he apologised to Hazel Savage.

'I got nothing against 'er at all,' he told the room. 'Heather's where I told you she is.'

When the detectives told him of the conditions under the patio and the difficulties the diggers were experiencing, West offered a number of theories for this, including an underground spring. Then, before asking him once again about the circumstances of Heather's death – to see whether his story would change again – Hazel Savage asked if there were any other bones there.

West paused. 'That's a peculiar question to ask ain't it? Heather is in there but there ain't no more.'

The interviews with Fred and Rose West were being conducted in police stations about 10 miles apart and slightly staggered, so when Terry Onions told Rose that they had found human remains and asked if she knew anything about them, she not only denied all knowledge but also expressed her anger towards her husband: 'He's a dead man if I ever get my hands on him.'

Back at Gloucester Police Station, they were desperate to find out more about the third bone for it definitely wasn't Heather's, so another interview was arranged with Fred West, starting at 7.17 that evening.

Hazel Savage and Darren Law let West talk again about how he had buried his daughter, and just as before he rambled on over the same old ground, frequently straying off the point. The detectives let him carry on for some time until Savage told him they had found another bone – a third thigh bone on top of the pair recovered along with the rest of the remains he said belonged to his daughter.

'Heather didn't have three legs. Is there anyone else buried in your garden?'

'Only Heather,' he replied.

West's confidence had been shattered and he could no longer babble on about irrelevant detail. This was something new, something he hadn't planned for. Once again he was lost for words as only the barely audible sound of the cassette whirring in the tape machine broke the silence in the room until the solicitor's clerk, seated next to him, asked if he had any idea where this bone might have come from.

After a pause West answered. 'Yes. Shirley,' he said softly.

'Shirley who?'

'Robinson. The girl who caused the problem!'

If the third bone had pointed towards another victim, the introduction of another name was the first indication that Fred West was capable of killing more than just one person. This meant it was more than simply a 'domestic' murder and was also the first inkling of what lay ahead.

On their return to Gloucester Police Station, Bennett and Moore were quickly updated with the latest developments.

They were told that a woman had telephoned in the previous day claiming that as long ago as 1972 she had been abducted and then physically and sexually assaulted by the Wests who as a result had appeared at Gloucester Magistrates Court. With all that was happening, little relevance had been placed on her story and Bennett, who still knew little about the Wests' background, was surprised why, if she was telling the truth, no one had mentioned it before.

As they talked it through they reflected on the 1992 investigation and how Fred and Rose West seemed to be so close, making the likelihood of Rose not being involved even less credible. West's past record already marked him out as a petty criminal, now he was revealed as a cold-blooded and sexually perverted killer who had got away with murdering his daughter for more than six years. A man who had cut her up and buried the pieces in his garden, a place where he went every day, where his other children played, and just across from the patio slabs where he'd built a barbecue and where the whole family often came together. In short, he was ruthless, cunning and a liar.

His current explanation, the one with which he had started and now seemed to be favouring, was that he and Heather had had an argument over their concern that not only was she showing lesbian tendencies but she had also given her young brother LSD which made him want to jump off the church roof next door. As caring parents, it had made them even more concerned for the safety of their younger children – not that Rose had said anything about this. In fact she was saying very little at all about Heather.

Discussing it further, the three detectives agreed that during the 1992 investigation it had become clear that Rose was bisexual and that Fred knew and seemed to approve of this. It had also become apparent during that investigation that both of them had been fully involved in sordid and horrific sexual and physical abuse of a number of people over a prolonged period of time. Fred's explanation of how Heather had met her death just did not make sense, the reasoning being that what if, in 'West World', Heather *was* showing lesbian tendencies? Would it have mattered? And if it was the case, was it any surprise? Indeed, in the light of the 1992 allegations, was it any wonder she might be experiencing difficulty with her sexuality?

As they moved on to the conditions at Cromwell Street and how difficult it was recovering the remains, they recalled the two pieces of cord found in the burial area. One was almost 2ft in length, the other over 1ft. What, if anything, did they have to do with Heather's death? The cord seemed to have been buried with her. Fred had not mentioned this though he never missed an opportunity to point out 'Rose knew nothing of this and would kill him given the chance, now that she knew.' He even expressed fear of 'seeing her or being near her'.

And yet, the detectives pondered, how could Rose not be involved or, at the very least, not know? Apparently she had only been out of the house a relatively short time when it all happened – the argument, the death, the dismembering and the burial. Fred was saying he had cut up Heather in the bath then dug the hole to put her in. The idea that Rose might not have known seemed even more ridiculous when a scornful Bennett reminded his colleagues, if that was necessary, of the amount of blood and body fluids that would be involved as well as the effort and time needed to clean up afterwards in a small bathroom.

'If ever I spill a cup of coffee at home, my wife would know straightaway – no matter how hard I try to clean it up!' he remarked. 'Cutting up a body, and his own daughter at that, in his home, in the way and circumstances he's described without Rose finding out is just unbelievable.'

The 1992 investigation had also told them that Fred and Rose did *everything* together; their partnership and everyday lifestyle, bizarre and sickening as they were, were built on this. Suspecting Rose West's involvement was one thing, proving it would be quite another, for they also knew that if Fred West was charged with murdering Heather now there would be legal restrictions on the questions they could ask.

Rose still had many questions of her own to answer but she was now showing signs of clamming up. While Fred was happy to 'talk for England', Rose rarely answered any question fully.

Nevertheless, she had to remain in custody, as did Fred – certainly until he gave them an explanation for the third femur.

There was nothing else for it. A court would have to be set up that evening so they could apply for a warrant to keep him in custody for up to another 36 hours and a little while later Rose would have to be put through a similar process. Perhaps by then, they hoped, Fred would open up even more and maybe even implicate his wife.

The custody sergeant was given the news and told to arrange a court for extended detention applications for both Fred and Rose – not what he wanted to hear at the beginning of a Saturday night in Gloucester. The cells were always busy but even more so at weekends when pub and club revellers added to the workload.

While this and the further interview of Fred West – to tell him about the find of the third femur – were being arranged, Bennett made his way to the police canteen on the second floor. As he climbed the stairs, ignoring the lift as he always did, his mind drifted back to the management meeting he was missing. He would hear all about that soon enough – once the court had sat and hopefully agreed to their applications.

Bennett made sure that Fred West's solicitor Howard Ogden and Rose West's lawyer Leo Goatley were up to date. Ogden indicated that he would not object, pointing out that in view of the admissions already made by Fred he would sit in on the interviews.

Goatley, like Ogden, worked for himself and acted as an on-call duty solicitor on a regular basis. Tall, slightly hunched, with a good head of sandy-coloured hair swept straight back, he was softly spoken though perhaps more extrovert than his appearance suggested, and took his role as a defence advocate very seriously. Not for the first time, he emphasised that Rose strongly maintained she knew nothing about the death of Heather and that she was not involved in any way. Given that she was prepared to make herself available for further questioning, he would argue it was unnecessary to keep her in custody any longer.

The Crown Prosecution Service's on-call solicitor was briefed to make the application at Gloucester Magistrates Court at 8 p.m. A similar application in respect of Rose would follow soon after.

Bennett was curious now to see Fred and Rose in the flesh – especially Fred. He really knew very little about either of them and what he did know already concerned him – as did the unsatisfactory explanations and unanswered questions that were increasing all the time. Like other senior investigating officers, he would not involve himself in questioning suspects other than from a strategic level. In reality, the days of such officers personally questioning suspects had long since passed and only happened now on television or in the cinema. In fact it would be considered unprofessional as junior officers were trained in the latest techniques and were more regularly involved in interviewing suspects. Senior investigating officers were responsible for the management and direction of the investigation, its overall strategy and integrity and its staff – not to mention its financial implications.

Interviews had been tape-recorded as a matter of course in Gloucester since 1986, making it easy to listen to an interview or read an accurate summary of it shortly after it had taken place. So apart from the time involved – as you cannot 'fast hear' a tape – it was relatively easy to direct or produce an interview strategy – providing you could keep up with the pace of the interviews. In 1994, video recording equipment for everyday or serious crime interviews had not been installed in any interview room in the county. It was in use in a few other parts of the country but cost a lot of money. Gloucestershire did have two specially prepared suites away from police stations for the purpose of recording interviews with victims of sexual abuse or attack. They had been in use for some time and it was where the West children were interviewed in 1992.

Just before 8 p.m., having briefed the Crown Prosecution Service solicitor, Bennett and Moore made their way through the police station to the Gloucester Magistrates Court building.

Court 1 was about the size of a tennis court with rows of varnished benched seats for the public and press, leading to a tabled area where the lawyers and clerk sat facing one another. Behind and above on another level sat the presiding magistrates. If a case was being heard this would comprise a chairman and two other magistrates. This evening, just one would be enough. The dock, which held the prisoner, was on one side, the witness box on the other. Prosecuting and defence solicitors addressed the court from the centre.

Moore and Bennett entered the court and sat at the side, facing the dock at an angle. The Crown prosecuting solicitor came in first, Howard Ogden arriving shortly afterwards. The clerk entered and checked they were all ready before advising the waiting magistrate, by which time the cells had been told to bring Fred West to the court.

Bennett looked across to the dock, awaiting the prisoner's appearance. When West arrived he was talking to his guard, a uniformed constable who immediately signalled across the court that he wanted to speak to either of the detectives. Bennett and Moore had been totally preoccupied with the hearing and were blissfully unaware of the latest revelations concerning the 'third femur' and the killing of 'Shirley Robinson'. After all, West's latest interview had only begun some 45 minutes earlier and had to be cut short to allow him to come to court. So, as they made their way between the narrow rows of benches they had no idea what he wanted to tell them and nothing could have prepared them for what they were about to hear.

To their amazement the constable informed the two detectives that in an interview that had just ended West had now admitted there was another person buried in the garden. As well as his daughter Heather, West had mentioned another girl whom he had even named as 'Shirley Robinson'.

The information was quickly passed on to the prosecuting solicitor and magistrate's clerk. If they were surprised, their professionalism prevented them from showing it.

West stood round-shouldered, his hand clasping the dock rail. Looking around he spoke briefly to Ogden then turned to the guard again just before the magistrate entered. Bennett's first impression was of a short, stocky man with black, curly hair and a somewhat egg-shaped head, shirt-sleeved and muscular. He looked a little tired and disorientated, otherwise his face was expressionless. As West continued to talk to his guard, the clerk offered Howard Ogden the opportunity of a short adjournment due to the change in circumstances and West then left the dock to go back to the cells, under escort.

Bennett and Moore looked at one another with a sense of satisfaction; after all, this seemed to answer the conundrum of the extra thigh bone.

Shortly after half past eight West was brought back to the court. He looked pale, almost green, but now had a sort of fixed shallow smirk. The guard motioned, wanting to speak again. As the detectives drew alongside, he whispered that West was now saying there was yet another person buried in the garden! Heather and *two* others!

Their heads were spinning. What they had expected to be a routine court appearance had triggered unimaginable results. And yet these new disclosures had emerged in such a random way the true ramifications did not immediately hit home. Had it done so, they might not have felt quite so satisfied.

Looking at West, Bennett remembered that Hazel Savage had said that West wore that smirk most of the time and especially when he was being questioned. He spoke in a broad rustic accent born of his Gloucestershire/Herefordshire roots. Anyone who saw him in the months to come would get used to it but seeing it for himself for the first time Bennett did not like it. After all, the man whose features he was now studying across a court room had killed his own daughter, another young girl and now someone else – he should be showing some remorse, some feeling of pity, if only for himself. Other than his sickly pallor there was nothing, just an air of smugness.

Although Bennett was neither a psychologist nor a psychiatrist, his experience told him this was an early indication that West was a psychopath, someone who could kill without thinking, someone devoid of conscience who could put the taking of a life to one side and move on, acting as though nothing had happened. What West was, though, other than a murderer, was not the main concern at this stage for there was much to do before they could allow themselves to be sidetracked on issues like that.

This was becoming an investigation like no other Bennett had ever experienced and so far, he had failed his own first golden rule of slowing things down. Instead, events were overtaking him and dictating what was to be done next. This had to change if at all possible. Furthermore, he was finding it unusually difficult to temper his own emotions with his professional thoughts, another sure sign he too was becoming tired, though that was hardly surprising given the day's unforeseen events and the stress inflicted not only by the requirements of the law but also the pressure of time.

To Bennett it did not matter what West was saying, either now in the court or before. It all had to be explored fully and in detail, in properly conducted and recorded interviews, and that could only take place now he had been remanded back into police custody.

Leaving the court, Bennett and Moore hurried back through the police station to the CID offices where they told everyone what had happened in court. In return they heard that Rose West's latest interview had accomplished nothing more of any significance or even interest, and that her attitude had hardened to the extent where 'no comment' had become the standard reply to most of the questions put to her.

Even so, they could not rest yet. For some reason, Fred West had decided to confess knowledge of another victim and even, perhaps, another, and it was vital they interview him again soon.

While the question of *why* West had chosen to do this now was important in terms of how to conduct the interview and the overall strategy for later interviews, it was now even more important to establish precisely *what* he wanted to say – before he could change his mind. After all, having continually denied all knowledge of the third femur, now he had performed a quite spectacular U-turn by adding a further admission in a way no one could possibly have anticipated. Most important of all, if he was now telling the truth, who were these women he was talking of, and why and how did they die?

There was no need for a long and detailed briefing. The points that needed covering were more than obvious to officers of the calibre of Hazel Savage and the less experienced but equally astute Darren Law who had been her interview partner since West's arrest.

At 9.11 that night Fred West was interviewed again – for the fourth time that day. The custody sergeant would soon demand that he have time to sleep so there was no time to waste and quite apart from West's welfare to consider they also had the defence solicitors and the appropriate adults to think about as well as themselves.

West was again invited to explain himself. He had volunteered that there was yet another person buried in his garden so best to let him talk about that first.

He did so in a flat, matter-of-fact way. There was no emotion in his voice and no signs of emotion in his face or mannerisms either. To Savage and Law it even appeared he was enjoying recounting the past – perhaps in his sick and perverted way he was.

Shirley Robinson, the second victim he had confessed to, he claimed was a lesbian with whom he had had an affair and made pregnant. She wanted to marry him and was going to tell Rose but West said he couldn't let that happen as he was frightened of what his wife would do so he killed her. Strangled her, dismembered her body and buried her under the patio.

As for the third victim, West described her as 'Shirley's mate . . . Shirley's lesbian lover from Bristol.'

West explained that she had come to Cromwell Street looking for Shirley. She showed him a photograph of the two of them together. West told her that she no longer lived there and she seemed to accept this explanation and went away. However, the girl returned a few weeks later and said she knew that he had killed Shirley and she was going to the police. West said he had persuaded her not to go to the police and offered her a lift back to Bristol in his van. As they drove out of Gloucester along the A38 he stopped in a lay-by, strangled her and took her back to Cromwell Street where, just as he had with the other two, he cut her body into pieces and buried them in the garden.

Whether West was telling the truth this time only he knew. The police could only go on what he was telling them and at this early stage they were still not to know what a compulsive liar he was. All they could do was review his latest version of events and decide where their priorities lay.

From a quick check around the assembled group, it was apparent no one on the case had ever heard the name of Shirley Robinson. Who was she? Where did she come from? Where in the garden of Cromwell Street was she buried and when? As for 'Shirley's mate', it was a vague description to say the least. Hopefully, West would be able to provide more information the next day when they could take him back to Cromwell Street and he could show them exactly where he had buried them. Now, though, it was time to concentrate once more on Rose.

The deadline for the application to detain her in custody for a further 36 hours was looming. At this stage she was completely unaware of her husband's latest confessions. Now it was time to let her know and arrest her on suspicion of the murder of 'Shirley Robinson' and the other unnamed girl her husband had referred to. Perhaps she knew who 'Shirley Robinson' was – or even who they both were?

Fred West's latest revelations made it even more important to keep Rose as long as possible even though they knew she would almost certainly continue to deny all knowledge of any of the deaths. Unless she had a complete change of heart and/or Fred involved her, Bennett knew he would not be able to hold her for much longer. Of course, if she was released she could always be rearrested for further questioning on the same evidence, though he knew it would be better to bail her back to the police station for a future date. Then, if further information came to hand, they would have more time to question her.

Rose West was escorted into the Gloucester Magistrates Court and sat in the same seat her husband had occupied not long before. Seeing her arrive, her solicitor Leo Goatley turned and leaned towards the dock to talk to her. Although Bennett's view was momentarily obscured he reckoned she was around 5ft 5–6in and at least a little overweight. She had a round face framed by a crop of dark brown to black, somewhat lank, greasy hair. Her eyes stared out from behind a pair of large, clear, almost square-framed glasses. Clearly not used to her surroundings she cast her eyes around the courtroom nervously, then, perhaps not knowing where best to look, tilted her head down towards her lap as she waited for the magistrate and the application to be made. As she looked across the court Bennett thought her expression sour and cold.

To some people, the likelihood of this woman having committed any of the sexual offences that were discovered in the 1992 investigation would have been unbelievable, let alone that she could have been involved in the murder of her daughter and maybe the other girls. To a policeman like Bennett, everything was possible and nothing should or could be discounted. There was nothing in his mind that human beings would and could not do to each other. What's more, he had seen this for himself many, many times.

The magistrate entered and everyone present stood at the clerk's direction. Rose West raised her eyes – a penetrating look, which even from behind her glasses and from his position some distance away across the court, Bennett thought portrayed contempt, even hatred.

The application was made and granted, despite Goatley's protest of his client's innocence and willingness to help by making herself available for questioning if she was released.

Bennett, Moore and James knew there was a multitude of things to do now; most importantly it was time for the officers involved in the interviews to be quickly debriefed then told to go off duty. They needed the rest for it was essential they were fresh for the next day, which was likely to be just as demanding as the last three. Before leaving they would be told what their next tasks were and when to expect a further briefing. Tony James was left to make these arrangements.

Bennett's first move was to get the investigation onto the HOLMES system. There would, inevitably, be a problem with getting staff to run it but that could be sorted out in the morning. Moore would have the job of maintaining the policy log – a complete record of every decision made along with when and why it was made – which the Senior Investigating Officer would sign and he would countersign as a witness whenever possible.

And, there was the media to think about. Local reporters had already been sniffing around Cromwell Street, especially now that Fred West's revelations about Heather had somehow already reached them. Soon, interest would spread through the regions to the national networks.

Then there was the site itself at Cromwell Street. Bennett was still not happy with the existing set-up and now that even more digging had to be done he wanted to look at it all again and discuss with Bob Beetham and a police search adviser how best to progress. His first instructions were to slow down the work and to have West taken back there before any more digging was done in earnest. Leaving Moore to get on with these arrangements, it was time for Bennett to return to the management seminar where he would be able to update the Head of CID Ken Daun and the other chief officers.

It was just after 10.35 p.m. as he walked into the hotel's lobby. Hardly noticing the random mix of greetings and jeers coming from the bar and the small groups seated around the tables, he quickly sought out the Detective Chief Superintendent. As expected, day two of the seminar had finished late again and Bennett's colleagues were now winding down and enjoying what was left of the evening. Having bought himself a pint of lager at the bar he sat down with Ken Daun and began by telling him that the investigation was now one of multiple murders – West was a serial killer.

Daun listened intently as Bennett went through the twists and turns of the day. When the story was complete Daun set off down the small flight of steps to the adjoining lounge where Chief Constable Tony Butler was seated along with Deputy Chief Constable Nigel Burgess and, nearby, Assistant Chief Constable Bob Turnbull. After a few minutes Daun beckoned to Bennett to join them.

'Ken tells me you've had a busy day, John. Are you alright?' asked the Chief Constable.

Having assured him he was, Bennett again went through what had happened at Cromwell Street and how the day's events had unfolded until they were all completely up to date.

'Are you sure it's Heather or could it be someone else?' asked the Chief.

'Is West making up the murders of the other two as he said he did about Heather?' enquired his Deputy.

Bennett explained that where West was involved, anything was possible and that they would have to check everything he said down to the last detail. Soon after, he left the group and headed for his room.

Making his way up the stairs he realised that he had not

spoken to his wife since the Friday, which was completely out of character for him. Entering his room he closed the door behind him and switched on the light before scrolling through to 'home' on his mobile phone. It was after 11.30 but Ann Bennett answered almost immediately. Clearly, she had been asleep but as she said 'Hello' her husband began to speak and she gathered her wits almost immediately.

'I was wondering about you. How's it going?' she asked.

Ann Bennett was referring to the management seminar as she had no idea he had not been there for most of the last two days. He replied that he didn't know much of what had taken place as he had been at a murder inquiry at Gloucester, but she didn't pursue it as she was used to him not telling her about his work unless it was already in the news by some means or another. Instead, they concentrated on the usual domestic priorities – everything okay at home? How were she and the boys? Any problems in the family?

As tiredness began to get the better of him, Bennett told his wife he would be in touch the following day but would not be home at the time he had expected – when the seminar was due to end – as he was sure to be tied up in Gloucester. The words came as no surprise to her. She was used to the unpredictable demands the job made on their lives. Once you've had your husband leaving you to get home from a wedding anniversary celebration meal alone in order to take control of an investigation into an unexplained death, there was little in comparison to complain about.

No sooner had Bennett wished his wife goodnight, than his thoughts returned immediately to what lay ahead.

How could they find out who 'Shirley Robinson' and her 'mate' were if Fred West could not or would not help any more and if Rose either refused to help or just did not know? Had they recovered Heather, and if they had, how were they going to identify her? What to do with the excavated spoil from Cromwell Street – retain or dispose of it? How near to the house extension and church wall could they excavate the patio and garden, and to what depth in safety? (This really concerned him.) What were the forensic needs and had they got it right so far? How many inquiry team officers would he need? Bennett decided he was far too tired to give any of these important questions the thought they demanded and that for sure there were many more questions to consider.

And anyway, things were always better in the morning.

FIVE

The night passed quickly. Perhaps it was the heat of the room, subconscious thoughts about the last few days or just his normal body clock that woke Bennett way before his travel alarm sounded. Lying in his bed, hands clasped behind his head, he looked towards the window. Through the closed chintz curtains, the lights of the occasional vehicle negotiating the roundabout outside flickered on the ceiling – but not enough to disturb his concentration.

This was thinking time. His mother had told him when he was a teenager: 'Sleep on it. Things will always be better in the morning.' It was a piece of advice he had come to rely on down the years, to such an extent that some of his best ideas and solutions came in those first waking moments of the day when he could think through a problem in relative solitude.

This morning he was quietly reflecting on what had happened at Cromwell Street from the time Terry Moore, Tony James and the Gloucester Support Search Team had first executed the warrant. He was worried he had not concentrated hard enough on what was happening. If the excavations were not being carried out to the standard he expected, it would soon be too late to put things right.

So much had happened on the Saturday. Finding what were almost certainly Heather West's remains and their removal, the discovery of that other femur and now West's latest admissions and the decisions that followed. It was easy to forget what had been done and what was going to be done, but, more importantly, what else *needed* to be done?

Putting his feet to the floor and turning on the bedside light the impromptu bleeping meant his alarm clock had caught up with him at last. He leaned over, turned it off and then reached for the briefcase on the table next to his overnight suiter.

Opening it up, he removed the well-travelled folder from inside, unzipped its contents and began making notes in the form of questions – another habit that had served him well in the past. He would make sure he got answers to them as soon as he arrived at Gloucester.

1. What photographs had been taken of the patio and garden area before excavations had begun?
2. Had he made it clear that it was necessary to have someone available to video record when it was judged appropriate, as they had arranged with Prof on Saturday?
3. What samples had been taken as a control of what was there before digging had started, to show the strata of the ground?
4. How deep to dig now?
5. What plans were there of the garden, and had the accident investigation unit been asked to use their computerised plan drawing system as he had directed earlier?
6. What about the search and excavations – had they got a police search adviser (POLSA) yet and more importantly had the city council or elsewhere been able to provide someone who could properly advise as regards the safety aspects?

This last question really worried him. Before West's latest revelations he knew that the whole garden area had to be completely excavated and the spoil searched, but now it was even more important to get this right – there was only one chance. Apart from losing or harming evidence, it would be even worse if the house or next-door church subsided. Professional engineering advice was essential.

He continued with his list.

7. When would the HOLMES system be up and running? (He knew there would have to be an early meeting with

'Scriv', Detective Sergeant Roger Scriven, the HOLMES manager, when they could discuss the structure of the system as well as the parameters of the search and scope of the investigation.)

8. Was it necessary to search 25 Cromwell Street again now?

9. What could be done at this stage to establish whether it was Heather's remains they had found and who the others were?

10. What staff did he need now? If he needed more, where were they to come from – the constabulary was already fully stretched with other investigations, not to mention its everyday policing requirements?

Bennett's mind raced on but he was conscious of the time. He had to get moving. Shave, shower, have breakfast, then make his way to Gloucester.

It was drizzling with rain, the sort of fine, misty drizzle that soaks without you realising it. Cursing their luck, he knew that even if the whole of the garden at 25 Cromwell Street were covered the work there would be affected – both inside the tent and out.

These were some of the thoughts occupying his mind as he put his bags into the boot of his car. Among them his 'go bag', a holdall he kept in the car containing all manner of items that might be of use when he was called to a crime scene. It was a collection he'd built up over the years from when he was a detective inspector and one that he still added to. He never went anywhere without it, even when he had become a uniformed superintendent. He reckoned that if *he* did not need it then someone else might be glad of it and so it had proved many times. It was part of his 'boy scout' mentality.

Apart from his wet-weather gear and the pair of green wellington boots, the bag also contained several other items including POLICE chevroned armbands and POLICE magnetic car stickers; plastic and paper evidence bags and exhibit labels; exhibit list; house-to-house enquiry proforma; a plastic sheet and a blanket; statement forms; plastic handcuffs; safety helmet; forensic-style paper overalls; disposable plastic overshoes and rubber gloves; and a good torch. He was sure he was going to need his wellington boots and overalls if nothing else.

Before driving off he called Terry Moore on his mobile to warn him of the impending visit of Daun and the Assistant Chief Constable, and check if there was any news. Moore confirmed that most of what had been directed the day before was in place and that Detective Sergeant Roger Scriven was setting up HOLMES as quickly as he could, although monitor screens and keyboards, as well as extra furniture, had to be collected from its store at the traffic and operations divisional headquarters. He also confirmed that Scriv had already asked for an early meeting and that the local and regional news media were asking for statements and whether there would be a news conference.

As he drove along the Golden Valley bypass that spans the greenbelt between Gloucester and Cheltenham the rain seemed to get heavier. It crossed his mind that waterproof clothing would be needed for the team at Cromwell Street and they would also need feeding. Then there was the thorny issue of maintaining 24-hour security of the area – a considerable manpower problem all of its own, which, although essential to prevent the loss of evidence and unauthorised intruders, would not in itself progress the investigation any further whatsoever.

His last thoughts before stopping at the rear of Gloucester Police Station and asking through the intercom for the electronic doors to be opened revolved around what he could do to satisfy the media. His preferred option was a holding statement that said little until he had decided when and with what to charge Fred West and what to do with Rose West.

Climbing the stairs two at a time as normal, Bennett quickly reached the fourth floor where he sought out Terry Moore and together they went through Bennett's prepared query list. Moore confirmed that Gloucester City Council had offered the services of a member of their engineering department and that Police Constable Andy 'Snowy' Ewens, an accident investigator, had made his first visit to Cromwell Street and would be preparing plans. Sergeant Pete Maunder, a POLSA (police search adviser), was working with Sergeant Tony Jay and the Gloucester Support Group to progress the search of the garden area when directed – though for the time being they were tidying up and making preparations. Bob Beetham and John Rouse, who were both SOCOs (scenes of crime officers), were at Cromwell Street and would be there to discuss their requirements that morning. Detective Constable Malcolm Wood was earmarked as the video recordist and had been told to await further instructions. Scriv had assured him that HOLMES would be up and running properly later that day, repeating their previous conversation that an early meeting was imperative.

Bennett was not surprised that things were settling down and becoming more organised. With Moore to oversee his instructions, anything to the contrary would have been out of character. Yet although much of Bennett's query list had been covered in conversation and directions the day before, there were still some decisions about the forensic side of the search that needed addressing.

Moore then went on to detail the arrangements that had been discussed in outline the previous night, to take Fred West back to Cromwell Street in the hope he would show them where he had buried the other two victims he had admitted killing – Shirley Robinson and her 'mate'. This would all be recorded on video. Afterwards, both he and Rose would be interviewed again though the two detectives agreed that whatever happened during the visit to Cromwell Street, West had to be charged, at least with the murder of his daughter. As for Rose, her immediate future would be dictated by what her husband said and, just as important, by what she admitted or denied.

As for the increasing manpower demands, Moore said that although the division was at full stretch they were managing to keep a 24-hour guard on Cromwell Street by using a combination of regular and special constables, though the weather was causing problems. He added that normal contingency plans for feeding at special events had been put into operation and the canteen staff had willingly turned out as ever and were preparing the emergency main meal menu – which was always a combination of chips, eggs and ham with maybe some salad, followed by ice-cream!

At 10.15 a.m. a small convoy of vehicles pulled out of the security compound at the back of Gloucester Police Station and headed for 25 Cromwell Street. Inside were Fred West, his legal representative, the appropriate adult Janet Leach and the interviewing officers Hazel Savage and Darren Law. The video recordist was already there along with scenes of crime officers Beetham and Rouse and the seven-man Gloucester Support Group.

Approaching his home from St Michael's Square along the dirt path, West saw for the first time how the work was transforming the rear of his garden and patio – and not, in his eyes, for the better! A pile of earth now lay on the unused land off to the left with the mini digger parked alongside. The whole of West's 'pride and joy' was now covered by white tenting with access into it where the back gate had been. The patio slabs had gone and in their place a narrow strip of planking to provide a runway for the wheelbarrows that were, for the time being, parked alongside. The step-roofed garden shed – the playhouse he had built in which the children had played – and the brick barbecue were also gone. Opposite, he could see a hole, its edges marked but with its sides crumbling into the dark water. To the side were the leylandii trees which had now been trimmed back.

West knew this was where the remains of Heather had been found and he must also have realised then that things were not going to plan, in fact, far from it. Now he was there to show where the two other young women were buried.

West had seen on the night the digging had started how the search team was operating. First, removing the slabs, and then working inwards from both the alleyway and the house. This was why he had admitted killing Heather before they could find anything else for he considered the police to be stupid – unable to match his cunning. He knew only too well how he had got away with so much in the past. He could carry this off, no problem.

What West hadn't accounted for were the changes in police procedure and, precisely because of past failings and learning from previous mistakes, how searches of crime scenes were now conducted. That's why his attempt to stop them looking other than where he had said he had buried Heather was bound to fail – though he would never have considered this at all. He would have thought it just plain bad luck that they had found that other thigh bone. Now he knew it was only a matter of time before the garden gave up its other murky secrets. There was nothing else he could do. He had to try and take control again, limit the damage. Tell them what they would find and admit to these further killings. That would satisfy them; after all they only came looking for Heather!

West was reassured. He had found time to get his story together and he was confident he could still protect Rose. She would be freed soon and could look after the house and the children and wait for him – he wouldn't be long inside, only a few years. Okay, so he hadn't got away with killing this time, but if he couldn't get away with murder he could get away with manslaughter.

When West had first admitted killing Shirley Robinson he had insisted, just as he had when first admitting killing Heather, that Rose knew nothing because at the time she was in hospital giving birth. He believed the police would never sort it all out or even bother to go after Rose. Once they had him, they would be satisfied. So, to tell them he didn't think Rose knew Shirley Robinson and hadn't even met her seemed a good plan, especially since he would say he never intended to kill her, just strangled her by accident.

The other girl – 'Shirley's mate' – was more of a problem though. Could *he* remember who she was? He had to make something up that would satisfy the police, make them understand how he had to cover up the death of Shirley.

The idea he came up with was to say her 'mate' had come looking for her once but went away again. Then she returned and said she was going to tell the police that she thought Shirley had been killed. That meant he then had to kill her too to stop her. To some extent he thought he could be excused for that and the court would accept it too. The police would not be able to find out who she was if he didn't help them and he only knew what Shirley had told him about herself: that her father and mother were divorced; that her father was probably living in Germany and her mother somewhere towards the north of England; and that she had been living in a care home in Bristol. Even if they could identify Shirley it would not help them with her 'mate'.

Of course, West knew that once he had shown the police where he had buried the two women he would face another grilling, though that was nothing to worry about. He would just talk about what he wanted to rather than what they wanted him to. The police would be really busy now and he had made this happen. Soon his home would be rid of them and his family could get back to normal – even though he would not be there for a while. Rose could look after herself, he was sure of that, and she would be waiting for him.

With the video officer recording every footstep, West led the assembled group of police and legal representatives along the planking. Then he stopped, looked around and pointed to an area immediately in front of the back door to his house. The spot where he had buried Shirley Robinson.

Moving to his right, towards the extension, he pointed again to just in front of the bathroom window. That was where they would find her 'mate'.

And that was it. No words of regret, no remorse, but then it had been the same the last time he was there to show them where he had buried the daughter he had butchered.

Once Fred West was on his way back to Gloucester Police Station it was time for those left to get their heads together before the Assistant Chief Constable and Head of CID arrived.

Taking Bob Beetham to one side, Bennett asked the scenes of crime officer if he was happy with the arrangements that were being made and how the search was going. Beetham took little time in asking for a firm guarantee that the mechanical digger would not be used again unless he agreed to it. It was not a difficult request to agree to, for Bennett shared his concern that evidence could be lost if its use was overdone.

Bennett had worked on a number of cases with Beetham over the years and liked and respected him as an experienced professional. He told him that he wanted a 'slice' or 'control trench' dug away from where West had indicated, that samples should be taken at regular depths of about 1ft and that where the samples were taken from should be marked and photographed. In this way the strata of the ground in the garden could be established. He added that excavations should go down to Severn clay as this was the level above which Heather West's remains had been removed, his reasoning being that without mechanical means no one could dig into the dense clay, making it a natural parameter to the depth of search. This, of course, meant the whole of the garden would be excavated to this depth though exactly how and when would depend on engineering advice. Beetham replied that an expert from the city council was available and he had already sought his advice.

Before leaving, Bennett told Beetham that he had it in mind to put him in overall charge of the work at Cromwell Street as crime scene manager and that while Sergeant Pete Maunder would be in charge of the search arrangements and Sergeant

Tony Jay the search team, they would have to work to his direction once safety procedures had been fully considered. Bennett promised to make sure everyone knew of his decision soon and that if there were any problems as a result to contact him direct.

They also knew they would have to bring Professor Knight up to date with developments surrounding Shirley Robinson and her 'mate'. Both men agreed that once evidence of further remains had been found, he should be asked to remove them himself rather than another pathologist and that if he wasn't readily available they would just wait until he was.

Bennett was being introduced to Syd Mann, the adviser from Gloucester City Council, when Assistant Chief Constable Bob Turnbull and Chief Superintendent Ken Daun arrived. They were taken to the hole where Heather West's remains had been recovered to see the conditions for themselves. By now the pump was struggling to remove the water that had once again begun to fill it, for it had been turned off for a while before West had arrived and only turned on again when he had left.

Mann told them they should not dig within 4ft of the church unless he was there to supervise. If these areas needed to be excavated then he would advise how this should continue at the time as it would involve smaller excavations which would have to be properly infilled with concrete. It sounded a daunting prospect.

With one last lingering look to take in the grim reality of what was developing into one man's home-made burial ground, the Assistant Chief Constable and Head of CID turned to leave.

Back at Gloucester Police Station Bennett told Turnbull and Daun that the HOLMES system would soon be operating and he asked, if not pleaded, that on their return to the management seminar they impress upon the Chief Superintendent in charge of uniform operations, Geoff Cooper, and all the other divisional commanders the need to release whatever staff he asked for without resistance, as he had enough to contend with already. Having been a divisional commander himself, Bennett found the normal negative response time-consuming, frustrating and to his mind unnecessary.

He already knew he could rely on Gloucester Superintendent Phil Sullivan for support as apart from the fact that all this was happening within his division, and he was already fully aware of what was going on, he had promised the previous night that he would help in any way he could.

Even so, despite assurances he would keep staffing to a minimum, Bennett knew he would soon require around eight teams of two officers, HOLMES room staff, search officers and 24-hour security for Cromwell Street – and that was just to begin with. He promised to come up with more precise requirements the next morning but he needed some officers now, to help get the incident room under way, and give a break to others who had been interviewing Fred and Rose West for the last three days.

Conscious of Bennett's other workload, Ken Daun asked what he could do to remove some of the burden, as it was already apparent this investigation was not going to be over in 'a couple of days'. Bennett quickly thought it through and said that for the time being he felt he could cope but that he was sure that soon there would be a more than usual media interest and he was going to ask Hilary Allison, the force press officer, to make herself available from now on and base herself at Gloucester for the time being. In fact, she had been at the seminar and was already aware of what was developing, so it was agreed that as West was likely to be charged later and Rose either charged with something or released, then they would send her over as soon as they got back so she could prepare a statement for the media.

At 11.45 that morning Rose West was questioned once again. When it was over, just as in all the previous interviews with her and her husband, attempts were made to inform Bennett and Moore of what she was saying, but already this was proving to be more difficult than anticipated as they had much to do and were not always together. If finding them was difficult, getting them together was even more time-consuming and time was not on their side. Unless there was a breakthrough soon, they knew they would have to release Rose.

Apart from an initial and essentially concise verbal briefing, both Bennett and Moore tried to read the summaries that were prepared by the interviewing officers as soon as possible after each interview. Although this was becoming more difficult it was regarded as essential since it would keep them up to date until they had the time to listen to the interview tapes and read a full transcript. Yet with so little time available even the verbal update was proving a luxury, let alone the tapes, while no arrangements had even been made to transcribe any of the interviews.

From her latest interview Bennett learned that Rose West had once again been asked to give details of what her husband had told her about Heather leaving and what contact he was supposed to have had with her since. In response, she questioned her husband's confessions, suggesting the police were just trying to make up for their earlier failures.

While this was taking place in an interview room at Cheltenham Police Station, in a separate interview in Gloucester that had begun at 12.02 Fred West was being questioned along the same lines, though in his case he was being asked specifically about what Rose knew of the circumstances leading up to his killing Heather, as well as how he had disposed of the body and kept it all from her mother. By now his answers were well rehearsed and rather than going into any detail about what happened he made it clear both off and on tape that Rose knew nothing and was not involved in any of it.

But they weren't about to give up and it was decided that Fred West should be interviewed yet again in an endeavour to get more specific detail of how Heather had died and try to get him to lower his guard over Rose. Bennett knew he could not hold off charging him with his daughter's murder for much longer, especially as he had confessed to two other murders, about which he knew very little since he had been concentrating their efforts on Heather.

Bennett left them to get on with that and drove back to Cromwell Street. Soon they would be setting up the HOLMES system and they had to decide how it would be configured. The parameters of the search and how it was to be conducted from now on would have to be properly documented and he needed to look at the area more closely and have another word with Bob Beetham in the process.

As it was a Sunday, St Michael's Square car park had plenty of spaces and as he manoeuvred into one he noticed a number of local television and news reporters gathered together some 20yd away. As he reversed he saw in his wing mirrors they had begun to move towards him. Bennett was not there to talk to the media; he had not yet decided what he was going to tell them. Instead, he moved hastily towards the tape at the beginning of the lane that would take him to the rear of 25 Cromwell Street and sanctuary.

Just as he was about to enter the cordoned area his attention was drawn to a middle-aged man who was approaching from the rear of one of the other houses in Cromwell Street. He was smartly dressed in an open-necked white shirt and dark trousers, but before Bennett could work out whether he was a reporter it became clear he was someone who knew Fred West and lived nearby.

'Are you in charge here?' he called out.

'Yes,' replied Bennett.

'This is a scandal. It's all your fault. We've been pestered all day,' he thundered, angrily pointing to the reporters who were now about 25yd away. 'The Wests are a lovely family. He's done nothing and there's nothing in the garden. All this is being done out of spite.'

Bennett was taken back and, unusually for him, lost for words, though the lapse was only momentary. 'It will soon become clear that what we're doing is right and necessary. We're making every effort to carry out what has to be done with as little disruption as possible.'

The words tripped off his tongue like a politician, though he meant every one of them. He also knew that because there were likely to be another two sets of remains in the garden, the task of removing them would go on for some time, perhaps a week or so, and the media interest would not reduce.

Bennett turned and quickly walked away through the cordon, pretending not to hear the calls of 'Mr Bennett' from the reporters who were now held back at the tape.

Instead of going to the garden of No. 25, Bennett decided to make his way through the garden of the adjoining house next door, No. 23. It was vacant and the garden overgrown. The pathway was broken but visible and led to a wooden gate and out into the road. Looking up, the house was clearly in need of a lot of work and had been neglected. By comparison, No. 25 with its ornate number plate looked like a palace.

As he turned right and walked towards the park he smiled to himself as he remembered that he had checked out this street shortly after he was married and it looked like he might be transferred to Gloucester. He remembered his wife had not liked any of the flats or the areas in Gloucester he had taken her to that would have been in their price range.

Turning and crossing the road between the cars that were parked nose to tail on either side, he walked back towards No. 25. This time the white-painted rendered front of No. 23 looked smarter than the caramel of No. 25, which surprised him. He thought the houses looked as though they were built in the Victorian era when they still had small front gardens and access to below-ground-level cellars which had long since been turned into living accommodation and let out as flats. All in all it was just an inner city street, no different to many others in

Gloucester or elsewhere. Some houses were smart and clearly well cared for, others not so. No. 25, he thought, fell into neither category – just mid-range.

As he looked at the Wests' home from the opposite side of the road, he could see three windows rising vertically above one another, all with net curtains and lime-green paintwork. These, he thought, were quite new and certainly not the original sash windows, as it appeared they opened only at the top. At pavement level, there was a black-painted, wrought-iron railing on top of a two-course brick wall. Between the railing and the front of the house was a concreted area that held a number of dustbins. A pillar in line with the corner of the house held one of a matching pair of tall, round-topped, scrolled wrought-iron gates, the other was fixed to the seven- or eight-course brick wall that formed one side of the church of the Seventh Day Adventists. As he stood there his eye was drawn to the unusual wall plate fixed some 8ft from the ground that announced you were outside '25 Cromwell St'. Not plain number 25, but '25 Cromwell Street'. The plate was ornately sculptured in black wrought iron to match the gates. The letters and figures that made up the address were in white and fashioned in joined-up writing. It was an example of another of Fred West's skills and its maker was proud of it.

Looking down between the church and No. 25 there was a concrete path about 8ft wide that appeared to belong to No. 25, but did it Bennett wondered? It led from the address plate, down the side of the house to a glass-partitioned door painted white and set in white surrounds and above which were two oblong transom windows under a corrugated-iron roof. This effectively connected 25 Cromwell Street to the Seventh Day Adventist church and appeared to be the front part of the extension to No. 25 he had seen from the back. The detective doubted whether the door was anything to do with the church, whose red-brick front and architecture looked much younger than the houses in the road. Once again he questioned how

West had gained permission to use the wall of the church as part of his home.

Walking further along Cromwell Street, past the church, he realised how the rear alleyway from St Michael's Square abutted the grounds of the Gloucester College – which reminded him he had not yet decided what to do with the earth sludge and debris that had been excavated from the garden of No. 25 and left in no man's land. Making a mental note to deal with it that evening he turned and walked back to the side entrance at No. 23 and then into the enclosed garden of No. 25.

Catching Beetham there, he broached the idea that once he was satisfied that everything likely to be of relevance had been removed, he would have the spoil taken away by contractors rather than storing it. Under the law covering the disclosure of evidence Bennett knew the soil and debris could be described as 'exhibits', and that a decision not to retain it could be criticised in court. However, if he was sure it had all been properly searched and everything relevant removed, the scene and process recorded and Professor Knight satisfied with how it had all been done, he felt his decision vindicated.

Bennett left the garden and headed towards the cordon. The constable on duty came out to note his departure and lift the tape. Over where his car was parked Bennett could see a small group of reporters and television crews. He knew he could not avoid them this time so instead of making straight for his car Bennett walked in their direction, meeting them on the edge of the car park then strolling back to where the reporters had left their camera crews.

He was pleased to see he knew all the reporters and cameramen that were there and they him. He had never been afraid to face reporters and their questions whatever the situation.

'So, Mr Bennett, what can you tell us?'

. . . A relatively easy one for openers . . .

'All I can say is that a man and a woman are in custody on

suspicion of murdering their daughter. Human remains have been recovered from the garden area of 25 Cromwell Street and the coroner has been informed.'

'Are you expecting to find any more victims? How long will the search take?'

'Excavations will continue tomorrow and that's all I can say at this stage. If there are any new developments, we'll issue a press release.'

Bennett knew he could not mention Fred West's latest admissions or that he would soon be charged with Heather's murder, but then no one had asked him directly about any of that so he could not be accused of misleading them. He headed for his car little knowing that soon he would have reporters from all over the world beating a path to his door.

SIX

Fred West was taken to the first-floor interview room at Gloucester Police Station for the eighth time.

All previous interviews with West had delved into *how* he had killed his daughter. Now Detectives Hazel Savage and Darren Law wanted to explore how he could have done it *alone*, without Rose or without her even knowing or being involved in some way, either then or later.

West was happy to be interviewed and more than willing to answer the officers' questions. Stopping his mind wandering off into irrelevant detail was the biggest problem and one they would grow accustomed to in the weeks to come.

It was the afternoon of 27 February 1994. Twelve minutes past two, about the time most people would have been settling down after their Sunday lunch.

West heard the bleep of the warning tone signifying that what he was about to reveal was being recorded onto tape.

From outside came the intermittent wail of the city's circling seagull population. Inside, West explained in his own words when, why and how he came to murder his daughter in cold blood, then cut her into pieces which he buried just a few feet below the grass where his other children played, close to the home-made barbecue where they gathered as a family.

It was June 1987.

A Friday morning.

Fred West and Heather were alone at 25 Cromwell Street. Rose was out, shopping. Heather was upstairs.

It should have been a big day for the West's eldest daughter. It was the day she planned to leave home. On her way to a new job in a holiday camp near Weston-super-Mare – the beginning perhaps of a new life? Except that the job had fallen through.

She had a telephone call the night before. Even so, all of her clothes and personal belongings were gathered up in a suitcase and plastic bags and lined up ready to go by the front door.

'I called 'er into the 'allway,' West told his interrogators, 'and I said to 'er, now what's this about you leavin' 'ome? You know you're too young. You're a lesbian and there's AIDs and all that. I'm not going to let you go.'

No one interrupted. Everyone just listened.

'Anyway, Heather's standin' by the washing machine. In the 'allway then but it's not there now. Enterin' the 'ouse through the front door the washin' machine and dryer used to be there.

'So she's standin' there against the dryer by the washin' machine like that, doing the 'big lady' business.

'And I said to 'er about gettin' a flat up the road if 'er wanted girl friends up there. It would be no problem to us, which was what we'd 'ave done for the other two. And she said, "If you don't fucking let me go I'll give all the kids acid and they'll all jump off the church roof and be dead on the floor."

'I already known she 'ad given it to Barry as 'e 'ad already jumped off the church roof for that reason – which we didn't know for some time after the school reported 'im.

'Well, we knew 'e was walkin' a bit funny. 'E jarred all 'is 'ips and 'is speech was gone funny and anyway it was traced back to Heather who'd given him acid on sugar or summat and then 'e'd met 'er and 'er told 'im to fly off the church roof: so that was it.'

As his story unfolded, it was clear West had been in no mood to discuss his daughter's plans and as Heather West tried to go past him he grabbed her roughly.

'She stood there and she 'ad a smile with a sort of a smirk on 'er face that said summat like "you try me and I'll do it".'

Real or imaginary, it was a look that sealed the teenager's fate.

'I lunged at 'er and grabbed 'er round the throat and I 'eld 'er for a bit. 'Ow long I held 'er for I don't know, I can't remember 'cos for that few minutes I can't even remember what 'appened to that extent. I just remember lunging for 'er throat and next minute she'd gone blue. I looked at 'er and I mean I was shakin' from 'ead to foot. What the 'eck had gone wrong?'

West said he had tried to revive his daughter by giving her mouth-to-mouth resuscitation and pressing her chest, just as he had 'seen on the telly', though with no proper training it was a wasted effort.

'I put 'er on the floor, blowed into 'er mouth and that, and she just kept goin' bluer.'

Seemingly frantic now, he dragged the 16-year-old into the living room and put some wet cloths on her face. Again there was no response, as was the case when he tried to force a drink of water into her mouth. Nothing.

'By this time I'm panickin'. I'm literally a nervous wreck at this stage because of what 'ad 'appened. I mean, I 'ad no intention of 'urting Heather because I think the world of 'er.'

If Fred West hadn't yet recognised his daughter was dead he must have known she was perilously close to it and yet he still persisted with his own DIY form of first aid. Taking a brass mirror off the living room wall to check for any sign of life he put it over her mouth but, he told the detectives, 'there was nothin' on it'. He then dragged her body into the bathroom and bundled her into the bath.

'I ran cold water on 'er but still couldn't get no life out of 'er. I can remember standin' there and thinkin', 'ow do you know when somebody's dead?'

Having already removed his daughter's clothes, West dragged her lifeless body out of the bath and set about drying it. He described how he put something, a pair of tights he thought, around her neck because he didn't want to touch her while she was alive.

'I mean, if I'd started cuttin' 'er leg or 'er throat and she'd suddenly come alive? That's what I was thinkin'. I tried everything to try and get 'er to breathe again, but she just couldn't.'

His solution was to stash his daughter in a dustbin, which he brought in from the garden and tipped onto its side so he could slide her inside. He folded her at the waist but she didn't fit.

'No way you'd get the lid on. I mean, she was a good foot or two out. 'Er legs were even farther up than that.'

So, he cut her into pieces that *would* fit.

Then, in that same casual tone, as if what he was describing was the most natural thing in the world, Fred West explained to the two officers how he dismembered his eldest daughter.

How he had first closed her eyes because he didn't want her looking at him while he went about his task.

How he planned to use an 'ice knife' but when that wasn't sharp enough discarded it in favour of a much bigger one, more like a saw that he used for cutting big blocks of ice.

How he twisted off her head.

'I remember it made an 'eck of a noise when it was breakin'. I 'ad my eyes closed. I couldn't look 'er in the face and do it to 'er. 'Ow I cut round I've no real idea.'

West was now in full flow and seemed to be relishing the opportunity to relive in detail the events of that day, detailing how he cut off his daughter's legs, separating them from the groin with a knife and twisting her foot until the leg came loose with 'an almighty crack'.

Leaving the legs to one side, he lifted what he called 'her main body' into the bin.

When his interrogators asked him how he felt, West told them 'I was absolutely dead. I was tremblin'. I couldn't think of nothin'.'

And yet, he was able to place the lid back on the dustbin and roll it like a beer barrel into the garden where he found a length of rope hanging from a tree which he cut in half and used the two pieces to secure the lid to the handles of the bin. He then rolled it down behind the Wendy House, covered it with a sheet and returned to the house to clean up.

By the time he had finished there was, he claimed, no blood

anywhere, no marks either. Heather's suitcase and other belongings, still lined up by the front door ready for her planned departure, he stuffed into black plastic bags and put outside for the dustman.

West completed the job later that night, when the rest of the children were in bed and he'd sent Rose out for the evening. Under cover of darkness, he set about burying Heather in the back garden where the two other girls were also entombed.

According to his account it was a wild night. The wind was 'blowing a gale' which probably drowned out the sound of the water sloshing around as he dug down through the soil of Cromwell Street. In fact, he'd only gone down about 4ft when he decided the hole was deep enough to conceal Heather's naked, dismembered body parts. When he had finished backfilling the hole, he concealed it with a blue plastic sheet to cover up the digging.

When asked if there was any sexual motive for the killing, he replied, 'No nothin' like that.'

And Rose?

'She was out shopping.'

For police officers more used to interviewing shoplifters and burglars, this was an encounter with evil way beyond anything they had previously experienced. Similarly, for West's solicitor Howard Ogden. What the civilian appropriate adult Janet Leach made of it, only she could say. What is certain is that when the interview had formally ended and the tapes were being sealed, everyone present knew they had experienced an event they would remember for the rest of their lives.

Of course, West had already shown himself to be a habitual liar, though surely not even a mind as deranged as his could have concocted a story like that, so sickening in its detail, so chillingly indifferent in its delivery – unless it was true. Especially when it centred on his own flesh and blood.

Perhaps with the possible exception of Rose's involvement,

surely this must have been the way it happened. Even so, to be really sure, they would need Professor Knight's forensic insight to get to the truth.

Yet, no matter how remarkable the event they had just witnessed, whether true or false, no one in that room apart from West had any inkling that what they had just heard was only a sliver of what was to follow.

SEVEN

Fred West's continued insistence that his 'wife knew nothing' about the murders to which he himself had now confessed, along with the laws of evidence, left Bennett with no option other than to charge him with the murder of his daughter without further delay.

There was little doubt that the couple had agreed on a story – probably at 25 Cromwell Street on 24 February, the last night they had spent together – and that part of the plan was that 'Rose knew nothing'. Equally, there was no hint that Fred was likely to change his version even though it had been put to him how improbable that was, how Rose *must* have known what he had done or at the very least found out about it – even if she was not actually involved or had been there when it happened.

Whatever the truth, Bennett and Moore knew the charging of West with his daughter's murder could be delayed no longer and at 4.13 that afternoon, reading from the typed charge sheet, Detective Constable Darren Law formally charged Frederick Walter Stephen West with the murder of Heather West between 28 May 1987 and 27 February 1994 contrary to common law.

Surprisingly, given his earlier tendency towards verbal diarrhoea, West said nothing in reply. Perhaps he just considered it inevitable, though it was certainly an event the young officer was unlikely to forget, as it was the first time he had ever charged anyone with murder.

As for Rose West, they'd still not been able to obtain any evidence that would link her to the crime. They'd held her for as long as they could and questioned her as often as the law would permit in the hope of extracting either an admission from her or uncovering a flaw in her husband's story that would implicate her in some way. Now, they had to accept neither was going to happen. All of which meant that as far as she too was concerned, Bennett's next course of action was clear. He would have to release her on bail – albeit with the provision to bring her back to the police station should the need arise.

Although this was unavoidable in the circumstances, it was not the formality it should have been for Bennett knew that Rose West was not as tough as she liked to appear. He knew, as a result of the conversation with Fred Davies, that during the 1992 investigation she had tried to commit suicide and he was concerned she might try again. It was why he had directed she be interviewed in the presence of an appropriate adult. Now his thoughts switched to where she would go and who would care for her – and if necessary prevent her harming herself again. So, while the bail forms were being typed, he confided his concerns to Hazel Savage and asked her to accompany him to the cell block where they could raise the issue with Rose's solicitor Leo Goatley.

At first Goatley argued that there was no need to tell the police of her plans. Bennett replied that he would release her for the matters for which she was under arrest but would immediately detain her for her own safety until he was satisfied that a responsible person would be with her – at least in the short term. At that the solicitor revealed she intended going back to Cromwell Street and promised to make sure her family would be there to look after her when she did.

At half past eight that night, the custody sergeant at Gloucester formally released Rose West on bail but, just as Bennett had instructed, she remained in the police station while Goatley checked out her domestic arrangements. Another 51 minutes elapsed before he returned to collect her.

Detective Sergeant Roger Scriven had spent most of the day collecting equipment and installing it in the lecture room that was in the process of being converted into a major incident room, usually referred to as the 'MIR', the hub around which any major incident, including murders, train or plane crashes, could be managed. This one was freely referred to as the Cromwell Street Inquiry or West Inquiry. Already adorned with computer screens and keyboards, some of the other essential furniture like chairs, tables and filing cabinets were brought in from the operations store though most of it was 'borrowed' from offices around the police station. What's more, they also had a water boiler and a plentiful supply of tea, coffee, chocolate, soup and paper cups – luxuries that signified it was already regarded as a serious investigation!

Scriven contacted British Telecom to get more telephone lines installed. They already had a few screens which they used for identification parades, but they would need more of those too, both to block out prying eyes and the heat of the afternoon sun which, when magnified by the huge, plate-glass windows, could make working there unbearable.

Even so, preparing the room on this occasion was less difficult than normal, as the equipment had been used up until the Friday for a HOLMES indexers' course. Indexers were the specially trained people whose job was to load information into the computer and for once their training could hardly have been better timed. Skills just learned would be sorely tested in the weeks ahead.

Before HOLMES – the Home Office Large Major Enquiry System – incidents and investigations that required administration on a scale larger than those encountered every day were managed through a paper-based system – one that had evolved over the years mainly through the experience of the Metropolitan Police and the Murder Squad of Scotland Yard. In the 1960s it was normal for county forces all over the country to call in 'the Yard' to lead an investigation when it was not immediately apparent who the offender might be, or where an offender was not quickly arrested and charged. Calling in the Yard also appealed to forces like Gloucestershire because it meant their paymasters, the local council-funded police authority, would designate the inquiry as a 'special occasion', allowing them to dip into the emergency contingency fund to meet the extra costs.

But while HOLMES reflected the more forensic approach of the 1990s, in terms of the buzz and *Boys' Own Paper* appeal of 'calling in the Yard', it was a poor substitute. It was, however, born of necessity, its development accelerated by the failings of the paper-based system that dogged the hunt for the 'Yorkshire Ripper'.

The Ripper Case was among the most high profile investigations of the twentieth century. Because detectives were dealing with a number of murders and serious assaults across a wide area, all of which appeared to be connected, a number of different forces were involved in the investigation. It was a logistical nightmare with the potential for cock-up immense. For such was the vast quantity of information being collected and the time it took to process it, there was always a delay in getting it to the officers whose job it was to follow it up. In other words, the system could never be relied upon because it was never up to date. As a result, the detectives were always at least one step behind the Ripper.

Even so, Gloucestershire Police had not purchased the HOLMES system immediately it became available. Apart from financial considerations, they had not had that many occasions when they needed to use it, for the paper-based system had always been good enough to get the job done. Not only that, there were a number of HOLMES systems available, some offering different options and all matching Home Office specifications. However, they didn't want to pay a higher cost for something that was not truly tried and tested, even if it appeared to have the best facilities.

So, they took their time, saw how they all worked in the field and eventually favoured the American-made McDonnell Douglas Information System that came into operation throughout the county in 1989. It had an easy to use 'free text search' facility which allowed searching across the system for a word or string of words immediately – or at least as fast as the host computer could work – with no delays due to overnight searches as was the case with some of the others.

Bennett had first been introduced to the paper-based system during his initial detective training course with the Met in 1967. By the time he was made a detective inspector in 1979, the Gloucestershire Constabulary was regularly using this method for major crime investigation, especially as the frequency in the need to set up incident rooms mirrored the increase in more serious crime.

When Gloucestershire bought into HOLMES, Bennett was the Detective Chief Inspector in charge of the divisional CID at Gloucester. In those days, 'Scriv', as Roger Scriven was best known, was a detective sergeant, hard-working, discreet and a stickler for detail, all qualities Bennett respected. They had worked together closely over several months on an internal investigation into a 'supergrass' operation in South Wales that had collapsed, and got on well. Both were family men and experienced detectives. Scriv was Gloucestershire's first HOLMES manager and, along with another experienced detective constable, Jill Field, was responsible for introducing the new system to the force and training people how to use it. Although not completely in command of its complexities, Bennett had put himself through the month-long indexers' course and was an eager convert to the new technology. Using it on a number of other serious investigations had helped improve his skill and knowledge of it by the time the West Inquiry had begun, but he would be the first to admit that he was far from being an expert. Bennett considered it essential to be able to understand the demands that he placed on an incident running on HOLMES and its staff. To him, knowing how to be an indexer, the most difficult role, was the only way.

Bennett went into the incident room where Scriv was sitting on a table facing the door. The room was by now almost ready to be put into full operation and would be the following morning.

Bennett told him the investigation would pursue and explore not only the three deaths already unearthed but also any more that might be uncovered. They would also delve into West's background, together with that of his wife, their families and associates, and try to fill the gaps in the couple's 'family tree'.

Bennett was also pleased that Terry Moore had already been trained on HOLMES and was a faster, more experienced user than him. It meant that rather than relying on others to keep them informed, both could review all actions and reports on the system individually before Bennett, as Senior Investigating Officer, could sign them off. This, he reasoned, would reduce still further any chance of error. Scriv, as HOLMES manager, would oversee and monitor it all to make sure all their work was up to the mark. Bennett knew that this would mean extra work and be time-consuming but he had a feeling the weeks ahead would throw up all sorts of problems and he wanted the system to be as reliable as it could be right from the very beginning. He did not like going back over old ground to correct bad police work.

Next came the potential nightmare of who would staff it all.

Scriv looked at Bennett quizzically. He had already experienced difficulties in getting divisional commanders to release their officers to incident rooms in other investigations, especially since the uniformed rank had become responsible for their own criminal investigation departments and their own budgets, a move that had enhanced their power and influence within the force. As a CID man at heart, even during his time in uniform in charge of the Gloucester Division, Bennett had always been sympathetic in similar situations and if Scriv could not get who they wanted, he promised to intervene if necessary.

Scriv was not convinced – especially as some of Gloucestershire's most experienced HOLMES indexers had been seconded to other investigations for something like the last twelve months and their bosses were unlikely to want to lose them again. Bennett reeled off a list of the people he wanted, at the top of which were, among others, Constables Chrissie Mannion, Tina West and Debbie Willats. All of them were good all-round officers with considerable HOLMES experience. The expression on Scriv's face showed that he knew this would be a hard call for him and he was relieved when Bennett agreed that, for now at least, they would try to keep down costs by doing without an office manager, though he was considering a disclosure officer who would be responsible for marking all material in the investigation so that it could be properly disclosed to both the Crown Prosecution Service and the defence. He knew he would have to decide on this soon as it was time-consuming for someone to backtrack once the volume of material started to increase – and this could happen very quickly. They already had to go back over all the information gained since the investigation began in earnest on 24 February, not to mention everything they had done before. Bennett knew he must not let this element of his housekeeping get out of control.

As regards inquiry teams – officers who would actually follow up leads and work to instructions laid down by the senior investigating officer – they would start with four teams of two officers working together with supervisors, which would mean at least a couple of detective sergeants. Transport, radios and mobile phones would have to be borrowed from whichever department or division could spare them and if necessary they would hire in. It would be up to Scriv to fill all the other positions in the incident room, though Terry Moore had already suggested that Detective Inspector Tony James, with his knowledge of the investigation so far, should be the 'action allocator' who would be responsible for running the inquiry teams. Moore had already given one of his detective sergeants, Neil Gavin, who had just completed the HOLMES supervisors course, the role of receiver and it was decided that Detective Sergeant Howard Barrett, who had also just completed the course would be the statement reader. These were important appointments as the receiver often had the responsibility of working with the senior investigating officer and deputy in putting together the prosecution file. Equally the statement reader would scrutinise each statement raising actions for clarification along the main lines of enquiry.

Scriv asked Bennett if he wanted to use the 'exhibits' package – a separate piece of computer software for logging the origin, receipt and tracking of all exhibits and creating documentation for when they were ultimately returned or disposed of. Few other forces had this and Bennett knew how important this system was, for it could transform the management of a task that was not only time-consuming but also vital to get right. Equally, he knew that there were only a few officers who could work this package really well, among them Detective Constable Paul Kerrod. Here, he sensed another possible problem as he had used Kerrod recently and had only just returned him to his division, who wouldn't want to lose him again. Still, if Bennett was going to search 25 Cromwell Street, and that was definitely in his mind, there could be a huge number of exhibits. Property, as well as exhibits, their seizure, retention and location were the bane of police officers' lives, and loss or wrongful handling had caused the downfall of many investigations and police officers over the years. Gloucestershire was one of the first forces to purchase this type of software and use it. Kerrod would do a good job and he had to have him.

As Bennett left he reminded Scriv to use his name whenever necessary to get the staff he wanted, including Detective Constable Mark Grimshaw the headquarters' criminal intelligence analyst who should be told to report to the incident room. They also agreed that the handwritten policy log, which was already under way, should be entered into HOLMES.

All the key positions in the incident room had now been identified. They were either in place or soon would be, except for additions to the interviewing teams.

Initially, it was agreed that all officers on the investigation would work 12-hour days each, beginning with a briefing at 8.30 a.m. or as indicated on the incident room or inquiry team noticeboards. This would take effect as soon as the room was properly staffed and up and running. In the meantime, briefings would be 'as required', as other staff would arrive throughout the day. There would also – certainly in the first few days – be an evening briefing for everyone.

A 'briefing book' would be used to keep a handwritten record of briefings. Recordings on tape and/or video were ruled out as an unnecessary drain on resources because of the time they took to review and transcribe, and they could prove embarrassing and even inappropriate if they were ever made public. Bennett knew only too well that police officers were human and when working under stressful conditions as a team were liable to come out with remarks about virtually anything or anyone. So-called 'black humour' could be moderated by discipline without affecting morale – but there was no need to record it.

However, on the afternoon of Sunday 27 February 1994, four days after Gloucester Police began digging in the back garden of 25 Cromwell Street, they did go public for the first time.

The carefully worded press release read as follows:

MEDIA RELEASE 27/2/94
Police investigating the disappearance of Heather West have charged a 52-year-old Gloucester man with her murder. He will appear before city magistrates tomorrow (Monday), accused of killing Heather between May 28th 1987 and February 27th 1994.

A 40-year-old Gloucester woman who was arrested on Friday in connection with Heather's disappearance is still being questioned by officers in the city.

Late yesterday police search teams searching a house and garden at 25 Cromwell Street discovered what appeared to be human remains. As a result Prof Bernard Knight has visited the scene and confirmed that they are the remains of a young female.

The remains were removed with the authority of HM Coroner Mr David Gibbons and are now undergoing examination at Gloucester Police Station. They will later be taken to Cardiff University to be examined by forensic experts.

The search of the house and the garden in Cromwell Street, Gloucester, has continued today and will continue tomorrow. We will seek further advice from the city council's engineers and surveyors department in connection with excavations there.

We would like to appeal to anyone who knows anything about Heather's whereabouts since May 28 1987 to contact us at Gloucester Police Station.

An incident room has been set up in Gloucester Police Station led by Detective Supt John Bennett and Det Chief Insp Terry Moore.

The word was now 'officially' out.

EIGHT

A briefing had been set for 5 p.m. but Bennett decided not to go. He was behind and, as nothing much had changed, decided Moore could fill him in afterwards if anything new emerged. Right now he was more taken with something Hazel Savage had mentioned earlier in the day.

Apparently, back in the 1970s she and other detectives – as well as other officers in the then women's department who, in those days, mostly dealt with young people, female offenders and sexual offences – had become aware that runaways from local children's homes, or absconders, had turned up at 25 Cromwell Street. In those days the Wests took in lodgers, many of whom were known to the police. This had given the house a reputation that made it attractive to rebellious teenagers who saw themselves on the fringes of the law. So, when Shirley Robinson was talked about, the fact that their enquiries revealed a girl of that name, or one using it, had lived at Cromwell Street and had 'left' when she was heavily pregnant, was of considerable interest, as was Fred West's claim that she came from Bristol where she was in care.

It was obvious that they would need to get help from social services and possibly the Department of Health to try and identify her. It might also lead them to 'Shirley's mate', the third victim. Perhaps she, too, was an absconder, either from Gloucester or Bristol, as that was where West said he was taking her when he had killed her. Maybe officers who had visited Cromwell Street all those years ago would still have their pocket books or remember finding absconders there or in the vicinity? It was something else that needed to be followed up.

Roger Scriven had mentioned to both Bennett and Moore that statements had now been taken from the woman who had phoned in on Friday saying the Wests had been convicted of physically and indecently assaulting her after picking her up in their car. The couple's criminal records were being held at Scotland Yard but it seemed she was telling the truth.

It was Sunday afternoon but Bennett decided to call Fred Davies, not because he had promised to keep him up to date with any new developments, because there hadn't been any, but because he needed him to do some research and the sooner the better. The detective knew that as deputy director of social services Davies would be able to get some of the information he needed much quicker than *he* would be able to.

Taking his digital diary from his briefcase and punching the access code into the keyboard to access the 'secret memory', Bennett looked up Fred Davies's home phone number and dialled it. Within seconds he was pleased to hear Fred's voice.

'Hi Fred, it's John – sorry to disturb your Sunday afternoon.'

'Are you still there – how's it going now?' was the response.

'We're getting ourselves organised – gradually – and nothing much more has happened since Fred said there are two more women buried in the back garden, which you have already been told about. I'm phoning because I really could do with your help tomorrow. I thought if I phoned you now it would save a call in the morning and you could think about it. I know you will be busy then anyway and we are pushed for time.

'We are trying to find out who Shirley Robinson is. We know a girl of that name was at 25 Cromwell Street and that she was pregnant and may have been in care at some time in Bristol. She must have seen a doctor in Gloucester, she may have still been in care for all we know – it may not be her real name.

'Apparently, she was quite young, not more than 17 or 18 so we think. As well as this we don't know whether Fred is making up that he killed another girl. He says a friend of Shirley but it seems that in the past some absconders from

Gloucester care homes have been either found at 25 or have been known to be there.

'It would be a big help if you could get your records of everyone in care homes in Gloucester, especially the names of any outstanding absconders, and also find out anything about a Shirley Robinson.

'Can you also get in touch with Bristol Social Services and give us an introduction in case we need to make enquiries there?'

Davies gave his answer without a moment's thought. 'I'll get on to it now. Should be able to find out those still outstanding but over what time? As you don't know who the girls really are perhaps you need to look at the records of all the Gloucester care homes?'

'We don't know yet when the Wests came to Cromwell Street, we're working on that, but best to go back as far as we can – certainly into the 1970s as that's when I'm told that girls from the care homes had been there. We may need to contact some of them now to see what they can remember – or even to see if they are safe and well!'

'Ok. It will be a lot of files and records but I think you will need to have access to them.'

In the deepest recesses of Bennett's mind an alarm bell sounded. Davies's instant compliance recalled an incident two years ago when the two men's special relationship had got the detective into trouble. That was when he had tipped off the director that an employee who was about to begin work with young people had just been cautioned for a sexual offence. He had acted without first clearing it with the Assistant Chief Constable; had he done so it would have been all right. Instead, the social worker was suspended and retaliated with a formal complaint. At the end of an investigation lasting several months the Police Complaints Authority decided Bennett should be 'given advice' rather than face a disciplinary tribunal – in other words, a slap on the wrist. As the main witness,

Davies had always deeply regretted what had happened, even though his friend had never held it against him.

Even so, Bennett was cautious. 'Maybe, but there's the issue of confidentiality on your part – you have to think of that.'

'John, if you need the information to do your job and I can help, whatever I can do I will – we have overcome bigger problems than this in the past.'

It was a green light to another request.

'I would also like to know more about the involvement of the caring agencies with the West family over the years. I'm sure I will need detailed information to progress the investigation and whatever involvement there has or hasn't been, it will be important and will become an issue.'

'I've got most of that, or at least I think so, but whatever you need just ask. We will work something out. What time will you be there to tonight?'

'Don't know, quite late – lots to do still. Tomorrow will be worse – there's the press to think about as well. I expect they will be on your backs as well. Will your press office have a statement ready if asked?'

'I'll make sure they have something for the morning or before. I'll give you a call later.'

'Great, thanks Fred – bye.'

Bennett put down the phone thinking how fortunate he was to have such an ally – and at this time.

The 5 p.m. briefing over, Terry Moore came back to their office and told Bennett that in further interviews with Fred West, which had not yet been copied, he had confessed to using a spade on his daughter and that this accounted for the marks on her bones! Bennett doubted whether she had been cut up using a spade – maybe he had struck her limbs when he was putting her in the ground – and he was becoming more of the view that West was changing his story to fit what he was told rather than telling the truth. Moore agreed, saying that while West's sickening accounts were no longer shocking to his interviewers, as Hazel Savage and Darren Law gave their summaries new members of the team freely expressed their disgust in both looks and words.

His wife still maintained she didn't know Shirley Robinson but conceded she might have been to Cromwell Street to visit other tenants who lived there at that time.

At just after 7 p.m. the telephone rang in the Senior Investigating Officer's office. Bennett answered to find it was the clerk at the front desk.

'Hello, sir. Social services are unloading a number of cabinets from a van for you. They're being taken through to the lift area. Could you send someone down to take care of them?'

Completely taken aback, Bennett and Moore quickly made their way down the stairs to see what the delivery was. On reaching the ground floor Bennett was amazed to see a number of filing cabinets positioned outside the lift door with a note attached to one with his name on it. Each bore a sticker indicating the name of a different care home in Gloucester.

As the two detectives stood rooted to the spot, two members of social services came through from the public lobby. Both were well known to Bennett and explained they had been contacted by Fred Davies and told to collect all the immediately available records of residents of care homes and any other documentation they could find and take it all to him that night. There were probably other records buried away in Shire Hall or elsewhere. These would follow as soon as they had been found.

Bennett opened the top drawer of one of the cabinets and took out a file. Quickly looking through it he realised it was the complete school and background file. 'Are you sure Fred meant me to have this? They look like complete files.'

'They are and Fred says you needed them – and as soon as we could get them to you. So we've been round and collected all we can get tonight and we'll be back in touch tomorrow.'

Arrangements were made for the cabinets to be put into the lift and taken up to the incident room on the fourth floor for safekeeping. Back in the Senior Investigating Officer's office, Bennett phoned Fred Davies at home again.

'Fred, it's John again. I have just had a delivery . . .', but before he could continue the voice on the other end of the line interrupted him.

'I know they are not all there. There will have to be a further delivery. Tomorrow. After a proper search, though it may take longer – a few days – sorry.'

'I had no idea you were going to arrange this today – but do you know that these cabinets contain complete files?'

'Yes. Can't see how you can do what you said you wanted to do without all the information. It would take weeks to extract limited information from those files and then you would be asking for more. It would tie up your staff and us. We are just doing what we should be doing, *working together* – like it says in the Children Act.'

Bennett, though, was still concerned about confidentiality.

'Fred, you appreciate that now I have these records – the fact they are here and how they arrived – will be documented and disclosed to the defence in any prosecution that may follow. At the very least it could be embarrassing for you.'

'I know but we have been here before. Maybe, it's my turn now.'

'Thanks Fred. I really appreciate your help – speak to you in the morning. Let us know what your press office is going to say.'

'Will do. You and Terry take care.'

The cabinets, filled with files and records of local care homes and the youngsters who had absconded from them, were carried from the hallway outside the Senior Investigating Officer's office into the incident room and put to one side. They contained a huge amount of paperwork and the task of reviewing it all was a daunting one. Bennett and Moore were clearly taken aback by the gesture and wondered how many other forces would have received such help from a social services director and on a Sunday?

As regular as the dawn, Ann Bennett woke at 6 a.m. and went to make their early morning pot of tea. When she came back he confided that the 'job at Gloucester' was now likely to involve more than one murder and that because of this and other circumstances he could not go into it was 'turning out to be complicated'.

There was real concern in Bennett's voice but his wife had heard it all before. What he was really telling her was 'I'm going to be really busy again so don't expect me home until I arrive – but if you need me, then you know how to get hold of me.' To Ann Bennett it was just another form of words; he didn't need to make a preamble about a murder.

At that time of day, the drive to Gloucester Central Police Station took just over 25 minutes. As expected, getting CID staff from headquarters was not that difficult, acquiring experienced HOLMES staff from divisions was proving more so, but Scriv had arranged for those he had to arrive as soon as they could and most would be there before 9 a.m.

There was a lot for Bennett and Moore to discuss before any briefing could take place, and as they returned to their office a HOLMES terminal was up and running on a desk behind them.

Standing against the window sill, looking out over the road to the Crown Court and the cathedral, swathed in scaffolding and silhouetted against the grey but gradually lightening dawn light, Bennett repeated the obvious that as things stood, instead of a straight application for a remand in custody for West – which would almost certainly result in him being held just over the road in Gloucester Prison – they would apply for a 'three-day lie down' that would enable them to keep him in police custody for three more days. They would base their application on his admission to two further killings and the need to make more enquiries. It was doubtful whether Howard Ogden would resist or the magistrates refuse to grant it. To achieve this, though, arrangements would have to be made first thing with the magistrate's clerk's office and Crown Prosecution Service to put West before the court as soon as possible – and before the 'media balloon' went up any higher.

Turning away from the window, he returned to the search of Cromwell Street. The overwhelming concern 'to be sure to get it right' had dominated his thoughts from the outset, so much so that when Professor Knight told him he had commitments for Monday and possibly Tuesday and had offered to send another pathologist in his place, Bennett declined, so important was it to have the Prof working on the case. Anyway, he reasoned, it would give them all some time and space to tighten everything up and really get a grip of the site and search as well as put together a proper strategy as to how to proceed.

Sitting now, Bennett said he would contact Withy Cole as he felt that he needed a special caseworker to advise on the case from a Crown Prosecution point of view. Normally, he had every confidence in the Crown Prosecution Service's Gloucester Office but he knew that no one there had dealt with anything like this. Withy, on the other hand, had considerable experience in complicated investigations, especially murder, and was well respected in wider circles.

'Gloucester CPS are no less experienced in this respect than we are – but they're not in charge of the investigation!'

It was said as a joke but what Bennett really meant was that from now on he wanted the very best advice from anyone and everyone, and especially those with more experience in dealing with a truly major crime investigation as this was clearly what they were facing.

Pausing for a moment to look out towards the cathedral again, he thought about what he had just said and realised that he was beginning to appreciate the enormity of the task ahead, one that was beyond his own experience. There was, however, no time to dwell on that. There was an interview strategy to work on and the interview teams would have to be briefed to carry it out and then debriefed after each interview so that the strategy could be continued or amended accordingly, which Bennett and Moore would do to ensure continuity.

They needed to establish how and when the killing and physical and sexual abuse within the family had started and whether Shirley Robinson and her 'mate' had been killed before or after Heather. While Bennett accepted he might have missed something, he felt they would need some help to analyse West and his relationship with Rose and how it all fitted in. On the face of it, this alone was bizarre and was unlike anything he had come across before – and he didn't know anyone who had. Free relationships and marriages were one thing but this was something else!

Bennett told Moore that he had recently sought the opinion of Paul Britton, a criminal psychologist who had advised on other serious crimes and murder investigations in the country. Britton's name had been mentioned in presentations at a *Serious and Series* crime course at the police college. Britton was regarded as one of the best in this relatively new field and was always in demand. Not only was it difficult to get hold of him and his services, it was, by all accounts, even more difficult to get a written report from him afterwards!

When they had worked together before, first on an unexplained death and then shortly after on a murder investigation, Britton had helped him by profiling the victims and offender and giving him a checklist to consider whether there were any lines of enquiry he had not followed or ones that he should. The detective had understood the advice he received to be constructive rather than prescriptive and if he did seek the profiler's advice that's all it would be. The buck, as ever, would stop with the Senior Investigating Officer, though involving Britton would certainly help ensure they covered all the angles.

Given the circumstances they had come across already, Bennett felt Britton might want to get involved and that his expertise would be another addition to his 'investigator's toolbox'. Even so, there was still time for Bennett to argue the pros and cons, not so much with Moore as with himself.

'I'm not sure whether anyone can really understand the mind of another person. If they could then there would be many people alive today as prisoners who'd previously been convicted of murder and would have been kept in custody rather than released as "no longer considered likely to be a danger to the public" principally on the advice of psychologists!'

In the end it came down almost to a case of nothing ventured, nothing gained while Moore, who had never met Paul Britton, bowed to his boss's knowledge and experience.

'Mind you, if we can get him, it'll be on the understanding he brings the written reports I'm still waiting for from the other times I've used him!'

If that was a joke, the fact that the police file of the 1992 investigation had been destroyed was no laughing matter. Bennett was keen to have a look at it and in particular the statements that the West children had provided.

Looking a little embarrassed, although he had no reason as it was way before his time and involvement in the case, Moore repeated what he had mentioned earlier, that the file had been destroyed in 1993 not long after the case had collapsed. Not only that, all the exhibits taken from 25 Cromwell Street had been inspected and either returned where appropriate to Fred and Rose West or in the case of the hard-core pornography destroyed with the couple's consent. Bennett was surprised but could vaguely remember being told.

'What sort of exhibits were returned and destroyed then?'

'All sorts of sexual paraphernalia – dildos, clothes, soft and hard pornographic videos, photographs and home movies. Some of it we destroyed – the more hard-core stuff and some of the items they didn't want anymore. We also destroyed photographs and film which Fred had obviously taken, some showing Rose performing various sexual acts in front of him alone and also with Afro-Caribbean men.'

Bennett found it difficult to understand why the papers and material had been destroyed and the items returned in such haste and said so. He doubted if the Crown Prosecution Service would have destroyed their files and was certain that Fred Davies and social services would still have papers and perhaps some evidence they were relying on to ensure the young West children remained in their care.

'Let's get all the remaining papers relevant to the 1992 investigation from whatever source we can and bring them to the incident room. If that's not possible, let's have a copy. Hopefully the file can be put back together, and as things have changed so spectacularly we can decide what action we need to take.'

'I've already started on that,' said Moore. 'I think social services have a video we might be interested in as well.'

The discussion continued regarding the material that had been returned to the Wests. Was it at 25 Cromwell Street? Was there anything there now that could help in this new investigation that might identify the victims? Would it provide information as to where Shirley Robinson came from and give a name to 'Shirley's mate'?

Because of Fred West's new admissions, the Police and Criminal Evidence Act would allow them to search 25 Cromwell Street itself, rather than just the garden for which the search warrant had been granted, but despite this Bennett decided that a further warrant should be obtained for the house. He knew this search would take a long time – perhaps a week or so – and that Rose and whoever else was staying there would have to move out while it was carried out. At the very least there would have to be a detailed forensic search of the ground floor and bathroom area to see if there was any evidence to support Fred West's account of where he had dismembered Heather and his other two victims. He also felt that everything in the house would now have to be gone through, especially any papers or photographs and anything that had been given back to them in 1992.

The search warrants would last for a month and so it was important to keep a record of when they were obtained as well as when they were executed, as it was possible they would need to be renewed if the work had not been completed in time. Terry Moore immediately began a record and placed it on the Senior Investigating Officer's office wall in front of his desk. He also entered them into the policy log together with the reasons for them, which Bennett dictated, such as:

- Pursue lines of investigation
- Establish identity of victims
- Ensure integrity of investigation.

It was obvious that with the changes in circumstances the Wests' grown-up children, as well as those in care, would have to be interviewed again. Apart from anything else, they may know about the other victims and who was at 25 Cromwell Street at the time they were there and/or murdered. It was vital to get some information about what went on inside 25 Cromwell Street from someone other than Fred or Rose – although so far she had not been very open about this or anything else; in fact, quite the contrary.

Terry Moore said that he had ensured that the adult West children – Anne Marie, Stephen and Mae – had been kept informed of the discovery of Heather's remains, adding that they were as much victims in this case as anyone. Both detectives agreed it was imperative they be treated as such and that only those officers they felt comfortable with – whom they felt able to confide in – were given the job of interviewing them or keeping them in touch with developments. This meant they would have to select experienced officers who not only possessed considerable interviewing skills but were also sensitive and compassionate and would not become emotionally or personally involved in the process. Few officers had all of these talents and most who did worked in the more complex areas of sexual and child abuse and were already involved in other serious investigations. They knew this would be another delicate staffing issue that would be difficult to overcome but it was one that had to be sorted out that day, either from the officers they had already or by asking for more. It would not be a popular request.

Then there were the Afro-Caribbean men in the films. They would have to be traced to see if they could add anything. Both sides of the extended West family would also need to be interviewed, first about what they could say about Heather and what Fred and Rose had told them about her leaving, and about the other two victims – had they ever known them, seen them or visited Fred and Rose and seen who lived there with them? In fact, anything and everything about the family had to be looked at, checked and double-checked and properly indexed into HOLMES.

The West family tree would have to be looked at again.

When the history of Fred and Rose was mentioned Moore reminded Bennett that he had already told him that when he was a young constable in uniform stationed in the village of Bishop's Cleeve near Cheltenham, Fred West was living in a caravan there and was regarded as a 'ne'er do well' whom he had 'chased around Cleeve' and whom he had booked a number of times for traffic offences. Since then he had acquired a number of relatively minor convictions for theft and had served at least one short prison sentence. Rose West was formerly Rosemary Letts who also came from Cleeve and he knew her family from his time there.

Already there was a massive amount to 'back convert' – updating HOLMES and incident room records, as well as directing research and what to do next. Both would eat up manpower but keeping on top of it all was a priority.

The application to remand Fred West – his first public appearance in court – was approaching and with it the breaking news that they were investigating more than one murder, meaning an immediate escalation in media interest.

'I have a feeling that dealing with the media will be a major problem,' Bennett remarked with a grimace.

As they spoke behind their closed office door – something that was a rarity, for both operated an 'open door policy' as often as possible – they could not help but be conscious of the general noise and chatter from the corridor outside and the rooms on either side. At least some staff were arriving!

NINE

As Bennett pored over the papers on his desk, picking up from where he'd left off the night before, he was a troubled man. It was 6.30 a.m., the investigation was into its fifth day and soon he would have to break off again and concentrate on the briefing as well as that morning's press release and he didn't like being behind with his work, forced to play 'catch up'. Of course, he could have made do with a verbal update but that was not his style. In conversation it was all too easy to overlook something and there was never a definitive record of what was said. This was one investigation where there could be no room for error.

As he scanned copies of the officers' reports and interview summaries he and Terry Moore had been desperately trying to keep pace with, it dawned on him once more that he still had no idea how long the Wests had lived at Cromwell Street. This was now vital, as was compiling a complete history of both Fred and Rose, as it would narrow down the period when the other victims could have been killed. Hopefully, they would soon be able to establish the identity of Shirley Robinson and her background – whether she had been in the care of a local authority and if she was pregnant when she lived at No. 25. If so, she would have left a trail and if the police investigations were unable to come up with the truth he was pretty sure Fred Davies would.

From reading the summaries it also appeared that Fred West was beginning to enjoy the experience of being questioned; he was certainly not lost for words. What's more, those who were either representing him or there to support him – solicitor, solicitor's clerks and the appropriate adult – seemed just as interested in getting him to open up and tell his story and even went as far as asking their own questions when the detectives were interviewing him on tape, which was not something he'd come across before. Bennett also recalled being told that the appropriate adult, Janet Leach, would often remain with West when either the solicitor Howard Ogden or one of his clerks was discussing matters with him between interviews, which all seemed unusually cosy and hardly normal for an everyday investigation, let alone one of multiple murders. More than ever, it seemed to Bennett, they needed advice on how to pursue these interviews and he decided to phone Paul Britton immediately after the briefing in the hope he would be able to come down later that day.

He also made a note to find out more about Janet Leach. He didn't have to; it was more out of personal curiosity for he knew nothing about her and like the others involved in the interviewing process, she too was undergoing a unique and potentially traumatic experience.

As Bennett's thoughts moved on, he made a note to emphasise at briefing the importance of making the best of the next three days – not only in the hope of formally identifying Heather West, Shirley Robinson and her 'mate' but also extracting new information from Fred West. Then there was 25 Cromwell Street itself. They'd already decided it had to be searched again after Fred West had admitted killing Heather there. With Rose West offering no help at all, the property and what was inside it, might hold evidence as to how Heather died. It could also provide clues to what happened to the other victims and who they really were. The problem was, Rose was living there along with her son Stephen and daughter Mae. Any one of them could, by accident or design, remove or destroy something that might be relevant. In other words, they had to get on with it for to complete a proper search would take days, possibly weeks. Rose and her family would have to move out.

It was not Bennett's responsibility to find Rose West somewhere to live but he couldn't abandon her either. He knew the gathering media would soon be on her trail and in any case he might want her brought in at short notice. Not only that, it was always preferable to maintain the best possible relationship with the family of anyone charged or in custody. Since Rose had already appeared quick to express her contempt of the police, it was best not to give her an excuse to harden her attitude, especially if, as he suspected even at this early stage, she was involved in the crimes they were investigating.

With staff still arriving and everything else they had to prepare for – Fred West's court appearance, the warrant and a separate briefing for the interview teams – the major morning briefing was moved back to around 9.15 a.m. with Bennett imposing a maximum time limit of 40 minutes.

Hilary Allison, the force press officer, appeared in the passageway and was beckoned in. Media interest, she said, was growing and she was getting more and more requests for interviews. So far she had been able to fall back on the statement released earlier but faced with an increasing number of questions she was unable to answer, a news conference had to be considered.

Bennett and Moore went to the adjoining office where Tony James was marking his boards with his teams of inquiry officers and their personal contact details – vehicle, pager and mobile phone numbers. Bennett told him they were making arrangements to have Rose moved out of 25 Cromwell Street to somewhere unknown to the media.

'Will we be doing anything to keep her under surveillance?' asked James.

Bennett immediately took this to mean would they be bugging the house, either with some form of listening device or camera, and he was surprised he had not thought of this himself for covert surveillance was one of his key responsibilities and if such methods were to be used, now was the time to get things rolling, not after she had moved in.

'Good thinking,' was Bennett's response for it could provide some indication or even evidence as to what Rose West knew about the murders or even her involvement in them.

His first inclination was towards a listening device rather than cameras, even so, this was not a decision for Bennett to make; he could only request authority to use this type of intelligence-gathering. Approval would have to come personally from the Chief Constable and that was never given lightly. He resolved to give it more thought while they looked for a property nearby to move Rose into.

Leaving Tony James, he realised, too, that all the decisions he was now making would mean asking for yet more staff to be released from the divisions – a prospect he was not looking forward to. Not only would he have to explain over and over again why he needed them, but also give an indication as to how long for, and that was something he had no way of knowing. He still had a number of specialist CID staff at headquarters, but using them would reduce even further the force's capacity to fight crime elsewhere in the county. Even so, he knew he must look to them before calling on the divisions. His mind made up, the decision was duly noted in the policy log.

It didn't take long to find a place for Rose West. A couple of phone calls to the Gloucestershire Police Housing and Records and to Fred Davies at social services produced a property in Gloucester.

Social services took on the job of finding furniture and other essential household items to make the house habitable. The constabulary's headquarters' operations department was standing by to move Rose West and her family into the house as soon as it was ready. All that was left was to make the request to the Chief Constable for the use of a listening device and get legal advice on making Rose West a tenant of the property.

'Hello, John; everything all right over there?' asked Chief Constable Tony Butler as Bennett's call was put through to him.

'Good morning sir, yes lots to do. We are going to move Rose West out of 25 Cromwell Street and then search it. We are in the course of getting some accommodation for her.

'I would like to have a listening device installed in the house before she gets there so we can listen in to her from the time she gets up to going to bed. Her son Stephen and daughter Mae will almost certainly stay with her – it could provide evidence that we are unlikely to get any other way, especially of her involvement. Equally, it could help to show the opposite. We just don't know whether she is involved or what she really knows but this could help us to establish it one way or the other.

'We have the opportunity to do this now and it will be more difficult later on once she has moved in.'

Bennett expected his Chief to come back with searching questions. He always did when such applications were being made and it was right that he should, not only to satisfy the legal requirements but also to safeguard both his and the constabulary's reputation.

Tony Butler listened, quizzing Bennett intently on how it would be done, the likely results and implications, before giving the go-ahead – then asking for the written application and all other necessary documents to be brought to him as soon as possible. This was, however, one aspect of the investigation Bennett would need to keep relatively secret from most of the officers and staff on the investigation if it was not to be compromised. Difficult as it would be with all the incident room comings and goings, the reading and recording of summaries and transcribing of the tapes, knowledge of the bugging of Rose West had to be on a need-to-know basis.

Before he knew it, Terry Moore was pointing out it was almost 9.15 a.m. and time for the briefing. Together they made their way down the stairwell to the first floor and the social club where the briefing was to take place, just a few steps from the interview room where Fred West had been interviewed over the past three days and where he would continue to be interviewed if they were successful in getting him remanded back into custody in less than an hour's time.

Bennett entered the room with Moore close behind him. Members of the team were sitting in a sort of semicircle near the windows that overlooked the rear station yard and Gloucester Prison beyond. The general chatter quietened as they made their way towards the bar area, drew up two chairs and sat down to face the officers who would be the mainstay of the investigation.

Bennett was used to conducting such briefings and could usually get a fair assessment of morale and team spirit from the general atmosphere and look on the faces of those attending – that plus any information he'd gleaned from the supervisors. Morale was one thing, team spirit another. That had to be built and often took more than a few days to truly manifest itself, usually when the first moans and groans were openly expressed during the course of a briefing and taken up by the majority. It was a moment he looked forward to.

Looking around the room he couldn't help noticing they were sat pretty much within their own working groups – incident room, interviewing, search and enquiry. As their attention was drawn towards him Bennett sensed an unusual air of expectation – excitement even – that was accompanied by an attentive turn of heads, sombre looks and, uncommonly, an immediate silence on his command to 'Listen up'.

Bennett quickly brought everyone up to date with events of the previous four days, including the 1992 investigation and that Fred West would soon be in court for the three-day remand application.

The main lines of enquiry, he said, would be to identify the other victims that West had admitted to killing as well as finding and recovering them. No. 25 Cromwell Street would also be searched and the Wests rehoused. Completing the West family tree was most important in order to fill the gaps, as was tracing the rest of the West family to see if they were 'safe and well'. The immediate response from the floor was that they were already having problems finding West's first wife Rena and a daughter from the marriage named Charmaine.

Bennett then handed over to the detectives who had been interviewing Fred West so they could add their views and perspective. Detective Constables Geoff Morgan and Barbara Harrison, two more experienced detectives, had now joined Detective Constables Hazel Savage and Darren Law. They described how Fred West had made his confessions without emotion and in great detail, confessions which, they felt, lacked credibility, especially as to where and how the killings had occurred and his wife's complete lack of knowledge and involvement.

'After he had killed Heather and cut her up, he was more concerned about his hedge than anything,' said Hazel Savage, her tone a mixture of scorn and disgust. 'When we hadn't found her we took him back to show us where he had buried her – he said we were looking in the wrong place as he wouldn't have dug that close to his hedge as it might have damaged it.'

There was not a smile or comment from anyone, just the gentle shaking of heads accompanied by looks to one another of disbelief and after a moment or two Bennett broke the silence.

'The press are understandably getting interested in what we are doing and over the weekend it's gradually risen from local to regional to national level. We have given out a holding press release and Hilary Allison is handling this well but I expect we will have to have a conference later today. This should stem questions to the press office and the publicity may help us confirm the identification of Shirley Robinson.'

As he finished, from behind him came the resounding beat of a fruit machine coming to life, its lights flashing in tune to the music. It was randomly timed to come on automatically but for the first time that morning there were chuckles and smiles all round. Bennett and Moore saw the funny side of it and joined in, though the Senior Investigating Officer made a mental note to 'turn off the infernal machine' before the next briefing!

Sensing that time was moving on he turned to 'admin

matters'. Hours of duty would be determined as necessary and meals provided at Gloucester, where they would all be stationed from now on – another necessary move to cut down on travelling expenses and preserve the constabulary's finances. It was an unpopular decision but to his surprise there were no objections. Either they accepted it as inevitable or they realised, as he himself did, that this investigation was going to be different – one they would always remember – and they were all just pleased to be involved.

After a pause for questions and a warning not to discuss the investigation with anyone outside it, not least to avoid leaks to the media, the briefing was wound up and Bennett and Moore left the room. As they did so the intense silence gave way to a more relaxed chatter and somehow even the level of this seemed unusual to Bennett who overheard someone saying, 'What luck to be here, this is different'.

He wondered if everyone who was on this investigation felt the same way and if they did, whether they would maintain it and for how long. He knew it was his responsibility to get it right and yet he was totally reliant on everyone else there, not only to carry out instructions but also to keep him informed of what was happening, even when things went wrong. They would also have to think for themselves, just as Bob Beetham had over his concerns about the excavations, and Tony James had with regard to bugging Rose West. Bennett knew he could not think of everything himself and just had to make sure they all appreciated this and that their suggestions would be more than welcome. Worried he might not have made all this totally clear during the briefing he resolved to go over it all again the next time he called them all together, for apart from the legal processes, the heat from the media spotlight was also intensifying.

Next on Bennett's agenda was to contact the forensic psychologist Paul Britton who, he suspected, would already be aware of the discoveries at 25 Cromwell Street since they'd been reported in that weekend's newspapers. His expectations were well founded and after a few calls eventually Paul Britton came on the line.

'John, how are you? I see you have another interesting case.'

'I thought you may have read about it but the press are not aware of some developments yet – or at least they have not gone to print – so I doubt if you are fully aware of what we are facing.

'We have charged a father with murdering his daughter and released his wife on bail. I hope we'll have him for at least the next three days on remand.'

Bennett went on to describe the more gruesome details as he knew this would not only interest Britton but also give him some idea of the investigation.

'We found evidence of another victim during our search and he has now admitted that he killed another two girls and also buried them there – we haven't recovered them yet.

'I don't want to talk about it over the phone but really would appreciate it if you could come down and give us your opinions – especially as regards how we should progress the interviews. I'll tell you about the problems we're experiencing if you come.'

Britton thought about what he had just been told then asked, 'You arrested the wife and she's on bail now?'

Bennett replied that it was a long story and asked again if he could find the time either that day or the next to pay a visit.

Britton agreed to come down the following afternoon.

'Ask for me when you arrive – oh and please bring down the two reports you already owe me – I really need them – I can't put the files together without them.'

Britton apologised, blaming the volume of work, though Bennett noted as he put down the phone that he did not say he would bring them with him!

Fred West was due in court at 10 a.m. and appeared on cue. As he did so, Bennett noticed that he still had that smug grin. It was an expression that, together with his rounded features, resulted in something he had not felt so strongly before – that this was a truly evil man. As he looked on from his bench seat facing the dock he could see West's large hands cupped over the dock rail – hands that had seen hard work as well as killed. His patterned long-sleeved sweater under a navy-blue body warmer seemed to exaggerate his short stocky build.

West lifted his head and looked around the court, his expression changing slightly. His chin moved forward and his mouth dropped at the sides – perhaps an indication of stress or anxiety? If so, it was not before time Bennett thought. Was he, though, looking for Rose? His family? Or just to see who was there? Perhaps Paul Britton would be able to explain West's state of mind.

Unusually for a Monday morning, the court was almost full. There were no spaces on the press benches and many faces in the body of the court that Bennett didn't recognise, though their notebooks and general demeanour suggested that they too were reporters. As expected, the hearing was a formality and lasted no more than 8 minutes. West was only required to confirm his name – Frederick Walter Stephen West – which he did in a confident tone, distinctive for its Gloucestershire/ Herefordshire burr. The charge of murdering Heather West was read out, followed by the Crown Prosecution Service solicitor Malcolm Hayes informing the court West had also been arrested on suspicion of committing two further murders.

There was no objection from Howard Ogden, who acknowledged his client's admissions and asked for reporting restrictions to remain. As West was escorted back down the stairs to the cells he peered over his shoulder, a final act that sent all the reporters scurrying for the exit. If this investigation had not been very newsworthy nationally before, it was now.

Bennett and Moore paused to let the court clear then headed towards the waiting room and the interior door that connected to the police station. A handful of local reporters lay in wait but a court official was on the same wavelength and unlocked the door and ushered them through.

Back at the major incident room, things seemed to have settled into a more organised state of affairs than earlier in the day. This room was both the body and the heart of the investigation and was beginning to look and beat as it should; it just needed to be fed with the right diet of information and not overfed too quickly. If its health was regularly kept in check it would be of considerable help in every aspect of the investigation, if not it could have the opposite effect.

Bennett left the room and telephoned his headquarters' criminal intelligence office to ask if a list of missing persons from the force area was on its way. It was a logical place to start as it might contain the names and identity of West's other victims. Staff there were also searching the headquarters' basement archives for the ageing files of two of the force's longest unsolved missing persons cases, those of Mary Bastholm and Lucy Partington, who disappeared more than twenty years ago.

Checking HOLMES Bennett could see there were a number of actions out now and that these were increasing. Most important to him were those relating to 25 Cromwell Street, when the Wests' had moved there, who had lived there over the years and did they know Shirley Robinson and any of her friends. His concentration was interrupted by a call from Fred Davies.

'John, a Shirley Robinson did stay at 25 Cromwell Street. She had been in care and she was pregnant – no record of her having the baby though, not here anyway.'

'Thanks Fred. Some of our enquiries are confirming this. Have you got more details?'

'Yes – some – have you found her?'

'No, not yet, but it looks as though that at least he has told the truth that she is dead. We've just got to get on and find her but the conditions down at Cromwell Street are bad – and now to make matters worse the press are here in droves. I'll get actions created to get your information and will keep in touch. Oh, and thanks again, and for helping with the stuff for the Wests' house move, that's on.'

'More files are on their way, John, but we are still searching for some of the older ones.'

'Thanks, Fred. Bye.'

After checking on the progress of Rose West's tenancy agreement, Bennett left his office and asked if anyone had been in touch with Police Scientific Research Services about equipment they might need. He had it in mind to have the walls of Cromwell Street X-rayed and once the house was empty, searched from top to bottom. He wanted to know what equipment they had that could help and any advice they could give.

Detective Inspector Mike Wilson had been brought in as office manager to ensure the smooth running of the incident room and would also double up as the interview coordinator. This meant him debriefing the interview teams, directing them along agreed lines of questioning and regularly updating Bennett and Moore. It was a post invented for the unusual circumstances that they were now encountering and was designed to ease the workload of the Senior Investigating Officer and his number two.

The morning had almost slipped by and it was just before noon when Fred West was interviewed for the first time since his earlier court appearance. Once again the subject was Shirley Robinson and once again he confessed to killing her but little else, though with the work of the investigation and the information provided by Fred Davies it seemed only a matter of time before her remains would be uncovered.

TEN

The gabbled sound of chatter and greetings drifted up to the Senior Investigating Officer's office from the street below. Looking down from his window to the narrow parking area outside the police station entrance, Bennett saw an unusually large group that was growing by the minute. There were already around twenty people gathered there, some he recognised most he did not, but he didn't need to be a detective to know they were all reporters. Their notepads, folders and cameras gave the game away.

They were obviously waiting for something or someone. Some of the TV crews were setting up, others seemed to be filming already and the volume of conversation increased as hands were extended, greetings exchanged and old acquaintances renewed.

Bennett shrugged inwardly, for if they were waiting for him there was nothing more he could tell them.

They had been to court and seen Fred West remanded into police custody; they knew that Rose West was out on bail and that the search of 25 Cromwell Street was still going on. And in any case, what they could report was strictly limited by restrictions imposed by law, for although Fred West had admitted the killings, the how, why and whether it was accidental or intentional could be the basis of his defence and could not be compromised by wider exposure.

Besides, he had more pressing things to do. He'd still not secured the services of his preferred prosecutor Withy Cole, there was Rose West's tenancy agreement to chase up, the background check on appropriate adult Janet Leach and he had to go back to Cromwell Street – and sooner rather than later. Lunch would again have to be at his desk or on the move.

Withiel Cole was a special caseworker, one of a small number of highly experienced Crown Prosecution solicitors who advised senior investigating officers on, and prosecuted, the more serious and complex prosecutions. A round-faced, balding, amiable, precise and quietly spoken family man with a variety of interests, from football to classical music and heavy rock, he preferred a more casual open-necked shirt and fleece to the conventional suit, except when in court. He was considered throughout the sizeable area that he covered a most knowledgeable legal 'tactician and technician'. He had worked with Bennett on several cases and was currently involved in a number of child abuse prosecutions within the county.

The call to Withy Cole did not bode well. The solicitor was already aware of the case from what he'd read in newspapers and seen on television but there was a note of caution when asked if he could help.

'I would be happy to, John, but you will have to go through the Gloucester office and *they* will have to ask for me or a special caseworker. I am sorry but I just can't take this on without their request. It's the internal procedure and that has to be followed.'

Bennett understood, but if ever there was a need for input from someone of Cole's ability and experience it was now, especially in light of how the case was developing. He would take it up with the Gloucester office as suggested.

The role of the Crown Prosecution Service and its special caseworkers was, at that time, under revue. Control of Gloucester was soon to switch to the Droitwich office in Worcestershire. Times had changed and appeared to be changing yet again as to how cases were prosecuted. Until 1986 local police forces were responsible for deciding whether to prosecute and senior police officers made the decision. Under the Prosecution of Offences Regulations that were formulated in 1956 only the more serious or series of crimes were referred to the Director of Public

Prosecutions for authority to prosecute. In Gloucestershire, up until 1983, all prosecutions were authorised by a divisional or headquarters' chief superintendent or one of the chief officers, though as the volume of court work increased it was later delegated to a chief inspector. An inspector then, in some cases, would also act as prosecutor. Where a case had to be tried at the Crown Court or was more complicated or serious, the file would be referred to the police solicitors. If they were too busy then the work would be 'farmed out' to selected local solicitors. By 1994, the CPS local offices, governed by the London-based Director of Public Prosecutions, had the final say in whether or not all police cases were to be taken to court or dealt with in another way. Their decision was based on two questions: whether there was a 50 per cent or more likelihood of getting a conviction and/or if going to court was in the public interest.

By and large the police regarded the 50 per cent rule as financially motivated and certainly 'not in the public interest' for it meant CPS solicitors second-guessing what a jury would decide and that was something most experienced police officers had given up long ago. Too often, from a police point of view, CPS solicitors who were new to the job would err on the side of unnecessary caution whereas the police had always worked on whether or not there was a prima facie case – a case worthy of being put before the court – before deciding on a prosecution, which was a much broader test than that applied by the CPS.

The CPS's chief prosecuting solicitor in Gloucester was Roger Fry, a softly spoken and approachable man often prepared to listen to an opposite point of view, but he could hardly have failed to detect the disappointment in Bennett's tone when he ruled there was no need for a special caseworker to become involved in the inquiry. Bennett based his argument on the complexity of the case, that they would more than likely be investigating at least three murders with a husband and wife the prime suspects. Fry's response was to agree to meet Bennett to discuss the case further but that CPS solicitors

Malcolm Hayes, who had already dealt with Fred West's remand application, and Rita Crane, who was already involved in the case and knew about the failed 1992 investigation, would stay with it.

When Bennett told Terry Moore of Fry's decision he was equally disappointed, but at least there was better news elsewhere. County Legal Services solicitor Richard Cawdron had confirmed that the paperwork to make Rose West a tenant of the property she was being moved into was ready for collection and Fred Davies had also been in touch to bring them up to date with what social services were doing to safeguard the Wests' youngest children.

Bennett, though, was still intrigued by how the appropriate adult, Janet Leach, had been selected and phoned the cell block to find out from Fred West's custody record. West's interviewing team, Hazel Savage and Darren Law, had mentioned earlier that she was employed by a homeless project in Cheltenham rather than social services. Normally, in more serious crimes – and especially murder – social services would provide someone. Not only were they more readily available, they were also more used to hearing and dealing with the often bizarre and sometimes traumatic human behaviour that might come out in evidence.

It turned out that the custody sergeant *had* approached social services but they had refused due to their involvement in the case already through the care of the West children. The custody sergeant then looked up other likely agencies and contacted the Cheltenham Homeless Project, who more often than not provided appropriate adults for juvenile prisoners, and they and Janet Leach had agreed to the request. From what Bennett could glean, she was training to be a social worker and lived in Gloucester. What's more, the defence and Fred West were completely happy with her appointment and the way she was carrying out her role.

Having satisfied his curiosity, Bennett's only concern was whether she was a security risk due to the information she was now privy to, for, having sat in on interviews and been party to other conversations with Fred West and his advisers, the media would regard her as a very attractive source. In the same way, in terms of the integrity of the investigation and the rights of West, he had realised that Howard Ogden had in his employ two clerks who were now frequently sitting in on interviews with West, rather than Ogden himself. He knew he could not prevent this 'representation' unless the clerks acted criminally; the decision was Ogden's. Nevertheless, he found it hard to accept that they were involved in this way with someone arrested for such serious crimes. Bennett would mention his concerns to Ogden and while he accepted that West's legal team and the police interviewers were bound by their own rules of confidentiality, he could not discount the possibility of leaks coming from any quarter. As for Janet Leach, he decided to seek advice from Richard Cawdron at County Legal Services about some form of confidentiality agreement.

Things were moving now but the hours of the day were also quickly slipping by. Fred West had been interviewed again, mainly about how he had killed Shirley Robinson and how he had buried her. His version was strikingly similar to the explanation he had given of killing his daughter Heather. When pressed about her burial he again admitted cutting her up but went on to explain that he had done this to all three of his victims 'so as to be sure they was dead'.

His fear of burying someone who wasn't dead, he claimed, related to a story from years before when he was working on a farm with his father. Then, so the story went, someone had been accidentally buried when they were still alive and for some unexplained reason it was later realised and the coffin was exhumed. By the time it was reopened the person was dead but marks on the inside revealed the desperate struggle to get out!

By his own admission, Fred West could calmly throttle his own daughter and two other young women but he couldn't bear the thought of incarcerating them alive.

Whether West was telling the truth or simply fantasising made little difference to Bennett, who was losing patience with the inability of his police interviewers to stop him meandering off the subject and not taking their questions seriously. Occasionally, West's legal representatives intervened, yet he seemed able to control the interviews by his seemingly meaningless and never-ending stories.

Rarely did Bennett let this sort of thing get to him as he was used to suspects and prisoners not answering questions at all. Perhaps, then, it was the pressure of the last few days, the long hours of frustration he had encountered that day and because with Terry Moore out of the office he had no one to complain to. Whatever the reason, clasping a handful of interview summaries he marched down to the major incident room and let rip.

'These interviews are crap! He's taking over! We're getting nowhere and our time is running out!'

Everyone heard but no one said a word. From the astonished look on their faces they hadn't seen it coming either, so out of character was it.

Bennett lowered his head, a mixture of regret and embarrassment at losing his composure. The moment passed and he wandered between the desks picking out newcomers who'd just arrived.

Police Constable Debbie Willats, who'd interviewed Rose West during the 1992 investigation, would occupy the post of principle indexer.

'Hello sir. This seems to be a bit different doesn't it?'

Detective Constable Paul Kerrod, the exhibits officer, was also settling in, while Detective Constable Mark Grimshaw, the newly appointed criminal intelligence analyst, was also making his nest nearby, surrounded by not just a HOLMES terminal but his free-standing computer and a laptop, the desk in front of him against the wall transformed into a library of computer software cases. Grimshaw, tall, well built, with dark slightly greying hair, regularly made it clear that he 'enjoyed the company of a computer rather than humans'. In reality he was a very social person but played up to that image so he would be left alone to concentrate on his work. An early morning scowl would warn others off for a whole day and had earned him the nickname of Grumpy, though his love of Italy and preference for Italian clothes led to the much friendlier epithet 'Marco', which his colleagues used when they wanted his help! Which was just as well, for where Bennett was concerned, the post of analyst, though new to most investigations nationally, was imperative, even pivotal, to the success of the investigation. With his computer skills he could transform material that was fed into HOLMES into information that was clear and much easier to understand. He knew how highly Bennett valued the sequence of events and contact charts he could produce even though those who didn't understand dismissed them as his 'wheels of fortune'. The task of assembling the West family tree was quickly assigned to him along with a list of missing persons that was on its way from criminal intelligence. Detective Constable Nick Churchill, another experienced detective and talented indexer, was on his way to help with that.

After his brief outburst, Bennett's demeanour had quickly changed. He was pleased to see the room getting into its stride and keeping on top of everything coming in. Detective Sergeants Neil Gavin and Howard Barratt were settled into their roles of receiver and statement reader. Detective Sergeant Roger Kelland had now been appointed as the disclosure officer and they were working on how this could best be carried out. He hadn't got all the staff he wanted but he was happy with those he had.

A further interview of West had been scheduled for mid-afternoon to try and get more details of how and why he had killed Shirley Robinson, then disposed of her – this time to find out what the police wanted to know, not just what he wanted to tell them. It was also time to check on progress at Cromwell Street.

As Bennett drove into St Michael's Square with Moore in the front passenger seat he could not fail to see the large number of vehicles parked around the car park area, some with satellite dishes on their roofs. Four or five separate groups of people, some with cameras and microphones, others with notepads, were gathered at various vantage points, all facing the alleyway where he was driving. As his car approached the police control point the groups had merged into one and it was running in his direction, cameras flashing on arrival.

Even through his closed car windows he could hear the familiar questions.

'Mr Bennett, has anything more been found?'

'When is there going to be a press conference?'

'When are you going to speak to us?'

Their words fell on deaf ears.

Signing in at the control point at 1.45 p.m., he made his way along the alleyway that ran parallel to Cromwell Street as he had done before. Passing the rear entrance to the vacant No. 23, he noticed that its garden path, which led straight to Cromwell Street, was being used by the search teams and scenes of crime officers to get to the front of No. 25 without going round nearby streets.

As he approached the rear of No. 25 he was surprised to see a scaffolding tower had been erected in the garden of a property overlooking the rear of the house bearing a camera crew that was obviously filming. Seeing this he looked up and saw camera lenses of various sizes sticking out of most of the upper windows that overlooked the Wests' back garden, all pointed in his direction. It almost stopped him in his tracks for he had never experienced this sort of media interest in anything he had been involved in before. He'd always expected media involvement might pose a problem for the investigation, and this confirmed it. What he had no way of knowing was that this was just the start and the tip of a very daunting iceberg.

Still, he reasoned, they were within their rights to take

pictures and report what was happening and, besides, the garden area was now almost all covered in crime scene tenting so their view would be limited.

Inside the garden, the familiar drone of the water pump and the sucking noise it produced provided the soundtrack to the back-breaking task of reducing the garden to the level of hard, impervious Severn clay some 4–5ft down. The control trench that Bennett had ordered had been dug, and the marking points where samples had been taken were still evident. The filthy conditions they had first encountered where Heather was buried were now certainly due to sewage and broken drainage pipes as well as the low water-table. In one of the control samples they'd found some sort of blue clay-type material. It did not come from Heather's gravesite nor from where the other victims lay so not much was made of it. Its true relevance was only established later.

The city council's buildings expert Syd Mann was advising on how near to the church they could excavate, Sergeants Pete Maunder and Tony Jay hanging on his every word. As they suspected, the extension at the rear of the house had been built without planning permission or the authority of the church to use its wall as part of the construction. The front of the extension had been built on a frame of 4 × 4in timber, making it even more difficult to excavate nearby. Ever mindful of incurring unnecessary costs, Bennett directed that whatever support was necessary should be put into place – he was not sure of his legal position and didn't want the constabulary to be sued if it came down, either by design or otherwise!

Back at the incident room Bennett and Moore talked through the next steps.

Once Rose and her family were out of the way and the arrangements for bugging her new home dealt with, 25 Cromwell Street could be searched from top to bottom. The exhibits officer Paul Kerrod would have to supervise the removal of furniture and other property, all of which would have to be properly catalogued.

As one door closed another opened and Moore's departure coincided with the arrival of the Head of Gloucestershire's CID, Detective Chief Superintendent Ken Daun, and the two men made their way to a first-floor office. Daun was both liked and respected within the force. His strong Scottish accent meant he was often referred to as 'the Scotsman', though his sometimes bluff and blunt mannerisms masked an understanding and compassionate nature.

The first thing he wanted to know was how they were coping and Bennett assured him they were 'getting on top of it' and that Terry Moore's support meant 'a difficult job was being made much easier'. Next came the ever-present problem of staffing and releasing Bennett from some of the other cases he was involved in.

As the conversation drifted into general chat about the future, the phone rang.

Bennett picked up the receiver. It was Moore with the news that at 5.20, what looked like a human skull had been uncovered near the extension at 25 Cromwell Street in the area where the third femur had been recovered earlier. Bennett replaced the phone and shared the news with his boss. Neither expressed surprise, least of all Bennett, who'd been assured by the Prof that there was at least another victim. Soon they would know for sure.

The discovery would also lead to even more media interest and in a brief chat with Hilary Allison, Bennett learned something else he knew was coming. With the makeshift press office being overrun with calls and requests for information and interviews, she repeated the need for a formal news conference to reduce the pressure. She also warned him that Howard Ogden was already commenting about the way the local newspaper had ignored the court order by reporting Fred West's admission of guilt. Keen to avoid any suggestion the police were acting improperly, Bennett promised she too would get more staff to help her, while at the same time insisting all requests for information had to be channelled through the incident room. It was an unusually vague instruction he would come to rue much later.

The 6 p.m. briefing began on time, Bennett sitting in his normal position with Moore on his left and Daun, whom he'd invited along, on his right.

All conversations had stopped as they entered, though from the general noise and chatter beforehand it was clear everyone was now aware of the further discovery at Cromwell Street. Even so, there was a definite change in the mood, which Bennett found unsettling.

Getting down to business, he confirmed that Shirley Robinson had lived at No. 25 and that she had been pregnant, though there was no record of her either giving birth or being heard of since. There was a lot of discussion and information exchanged about her, where she came from and her family. Then with a mixture of rage and frustration, Hazel Savage complained that much of what she was hearing was new to her, that none of it was in HOLMES and this had put her at a disadvantage when interviewing Fred West earlier that afternoon.

Although Bennett knew that Hazel Savage couldn't work the HOLMES system and had not worked on an investigation run this way, he could sympathise with the reasoning behind her outburst. Scriv would have to train her, and others like her, on how to get into areas on the computer that would help their interview research. Even so, he pointed out that no matter how many staff they had or how efficient they were, there would always be information in transit, hence the need for regular briefings, and anyone who felt they had discovered something important – especially along the main lines of enquiry or for the purpose of interviews – should make it known to him or Terry Moore immediately.

The briefing over, Ken Daun left Bennett and Moore on the stairwell and promised to be in touch the following morning.

Back in the Senior Investigating Officer's office Bennett asked Moore whether he had detected a change in the mood at the briefing. Moore said he had and went off to see if he could find out what it was all about. Within minutes he had his answer. According to the grapevine, Daun's appearance and long discussion behind closed doors with Bennett was 'confirmation' he was taking over the inquiry. This had unsettled them because the more experienced detectives, of whom there were a number, who had worked in sizeable investigations before, knew that a change in senior investigating officer always meant a different way of working and a review of what had been done, leading to more work before moving forward. Bennett blamed it on the SRS, the 'serious rumour squad', and said he would correct it at the next briefing and make sure he fully explained everything in future.

If the media were still camped in Cromwell Street when Bennett and Moore returned there at around 7.45 that night, they were either well hidden or had decided not to bother them. The scaffolding tower was still there but empty and there were no 'snappers' anywhere. More likely they had all made for the many city centre pubs that were just a matter of minutes away, either to spend their expenses or see what they could find out about the Wests – especially Fred, as so far they knew little about him.

Bob Beetham looked up from his position near the back door of No. 25 as Bennett and Moore entered. Alongside him stood Detective Constable John Rouse, their faces fixed in a grim expression.

They showed the two detectives an area just in front of the extension's bathroom window, not far below the surface and certainly no more than 2ft or so down in the glutinous mud. Along with clear evidence of human remains there was the faint smell of adipocere. Where the mud had been moved back, an off-white to yellow area of bone and the mostly hidden but still recognisable features of a skull with hair matted in mud showed through. A somewhat irreverent but necessary scene of crime marker was planted nearby for the purpose of photographic records.

As always, Beetham had carried out his instructions to the letter, for once something of relevance had been found he had stopped the excavations, marked and photographed the find and reported back. As clearly there was evidence of further human remains the coroner, David Gibbons, had been notified and the Prof had also been told so that he would definitely return as soon as he could arrange it the next day.

Bennett and Moore peered through the artificial light of the arc lamps, though the tenting and the noise of the pumping covered what they saw from anyone on the outside. There would be much more and worse in the weeks that followed.

Bennett decided there and then that the finds should be numbered in the order they were discovered – convinced there would be a third set of remains soon. Heather would be number one, this find number two and so on. They would remain numbered, not named, until they were formally identified to the satisfaction of the coroner. In fact, they had only been able to charge Fred West with the murder of Heather West with the coroner's agreement, as she had not yet been formally identified. Still, she would remain victim number one throughout the investigation. To Bennett's way of thinking, this was simply the correct, professional way of doing things.

While all this was being discussed, Detective Constable Rouse and the support group were continuing their work, painstakingly removing the mud towards the area beneath the back door. Almost as fast as they cleared an area, water seeped back in, the pump doing its best to remove it as they worked. When they were at about the same depth as where Remains 2 had been found Rouse leaned forward and indicated that he had found something. Beetham went over and looked down as Bennett and Moore stared across from the planking nearby. Bennett again recognised the faint but unique smell of adipocere as both Beetham and Rouse declared there were certainly further human remains there.

It was just 9 p.m. and this was the third set of remains.

West had told the truth – or there were at least three victims in his garden.

Nothing more could be done that night. The Prof would come and do his work tomorrow when much more would be revealed.

Which one really was Shirley Robinson? Which one her 'mate'?

There would have to be a press conference and Paul Britton was coming so it was sure to be another hectic day.

There was no need for Bennett and Moore to stay any longer. They left at 9.30 p.m. to return to the incident room, update anyone still there and make up the policy log.

ELEVEN

When told of the new finds at Cromwell Street, Professor Knight promised to be there around 9 a.m. the next day – Tuesday 1 March. The building was now completely surrounded by reporters, the immediate area virtually under siege.

Bennett, Moore and the rest of the team had been at work since well before 7.30 a.m., preparing for the internal search of the house. With Rose West, her son Stephen and daughter Mae now out of the way, each room was to be photographed and all the family's belongings recorded before being stored in a Ministry of Defence building on the outskirts of the city. The listening device was up and running.

Fred West was due to be interviewed again during the day. This time they would focus on 'Shirley's mate' in the hope of finding out something, anything, that might help them establish who she was.

As normal, the Prof arrived on time, warning of the difficulties in identifying the victims. It was one thing Fred saying it was 'Heather' and 'Shirley Robinson' and her 'mate', quite another proving it. Dressed in his now trademark grey anorak, Professor Knight, with Bennett and Moore, arrived at the crime scene. Bob Beetham and John Rouse were standing by the window of the bathroom next to the hole the professor had come to inspect. The pump had now been removed to make it easier to get to, but the small pit was already beginning to fill with blackened slime. Sergeant Pete Maunder, the search adviser, already suitably dressed in his blue overalls, stood by as the new arrivals put on wellington boots, and the video recordist, Detective Constable Malcolm Wood, checked his camera. Powerful arc lights were available if needed; Beetham prepared his clipboard to take notes.

As this part of the search got under way the Gloucester Support Group diggers slowly removed the spoil from other parts of the garden, areas that the patio had hidden before 24 February. It was taken barrowload by barrowload and dumped on wasteland at the back, outside the tented area. Professor Knight, trowel in hand, looked into the shallow hole around 1½–2ft square, the sides of loose sand and dark-reddish subsoil gradually sinking into the blackened, liquid mud. The changing colour of the ground and soil was caused by the decomposition of what was buried there. As the hole was right up against the extension, it was clear what a slipshod piece of work it was. It also occurred to Bennett that where the victim was buried directly in front of the back door, anyone using it would have trodden on the area or at least part of it. The question was, had the remains been put there before the extension or after?

Either way, he mused, West must have walked there daily. How could anyone with any conscience remain indifferent to this? Then again, he had buried his daughter almost directly opposite a barbecue, which meant he and the rest of the family would have picnicked on the spot where her dismembered body lay.

What if, as he suspected, Rose West was involved in all this? She would have been at the house more than Fred and would have trod those paving slabs more often than him over the years. The thoughts were hard to come to terms with and distracted him from the job at hand.

His attention returned to where the Prof was now slowly removing small quantities of the thick treacly mud from around the partially exposed areas of blackened bone that resembled a skull on its side. More matted head hair became apparent as he set about his work. Apart from the even tone of Malcolm Wood's 'in the garden of 25 Cromwell Street' commentary, there was only the general noise of the other officers' footsteps and movements, and this came from inside the house rather than the garden and was typical of the respectful silence kept by those most closely involved in what was taking place.

They had already encountered the problem of removing the remains and cleaning them on site, so to prevent any loss of evidence a system had been devised. When he had removed an item, Professor Knight called for it to be photographed, noted, labelled and recorded in the order it was removed. If necessary, finds were put in plastic exhibit bins, appropriate containers or bags. If the remains needed cleaning again before they were taken away for closer examination, it would be done at Gloucester Police Station, where a garage had been commandeered for use as a temporary mortuary. A special filtration unit had been made to make sure no evidence was lost.

As Professor Knight began to remove the skull, its hair slid to one side and a squelching, sucking sound signalled the clinging mud's reluctance to release its hold. Everyone there could see there was something wound beneath the chin and up around the top of the head though it was still masked by black slime. With his every move captured on video and in photographs, the Prof gently scraped at the surface with his fingers until it was obvious it was a wide belt with a large buckle. Even though it was now quite loose, it would have prevented the wearer from opening their mouth, irrespective of whether they were alive or dead, because the presence of flesh and hair would have made it much tighter.

The video stopped to allow a short time for sombre reflection until Bennett put into words what they were probably all thinking.

'Well, unless Fred is telling another story today then he has got some explaining to do. He's made no mention of this belt, just that he used his hands to kill her like he did Heather – that's if this is the girl who came to find Shirley. It will be interesting to see what story he comes up with to get round this.'

The area the professor and Beetham were working in was almost liquid and it was obvious that water from one source or another, maybe drainage or the low water-table, was always there as in the previous area they had excavated, but this was worse. Progress was more by touch than sight as one bone after another was brought out and there seemed to be no order in the sequence that the dirt-covered, blackened bones were recovered in. The professor explained that this was probably due to the changes that would have taken place once the flesh and organs had decomposed into sludge, coupled with the movement of water. Over time, the combination would have gradually affected the position of the bones, even causing them to move and sink.

As each bone was removed the Prof first examined then identified it, occasionally using his own body to demonstrate where it had come from. When a second femur was found in this area, the professor confirmed from its slight curvature it was female and made a pair with the other found on Saturday, which had first raised the possibility of more than one victim – so at least part of what West had said was true.

By the time he had recovered all the sizeable bones, he was paddling around in 2ft of water. These would be called Remains 2. Meanwhile, the rest of the search would be left to Beetham. The area would be completely excavated to the level of the base Severn clay and then the entire spoil removed to the temporary mortuary for sieving. Unlike the bones at the first site the Prof had not yet seen any marks where dismemberment might have occurred, though they may be hidden by the dirt. As in the area of Remains 1, the pits were similar in size and depth and there was no evidence yet that either of the women were clothed when the burials had taken place.

Moving across the planks to where Remains 3 lay, he could see the dimensions of the hole were about the same as before. This one was wedged in between the wall of the Seventh Day Adventist church and the doorstep to the house. They were still trying to find out if planning permission had been given, which might help them put a date on when the burial took place. Maybe the older West children could shed some light; indeed, Bennett and Moore knew any information they could provide would be vital.

Squatting on his haunches, Professor Knight followed the same procedure as before. Here, though, the ground was not quite so liquefied and the bone and shape of the back of a human skull was just visible. There appeared to be no hair this time, possibly, according to the professor, because the slight change in conditions may have caused it to decompose. As he removed the face-down skull and gently smoothed the black mud from it, some parts of the bone were more blackened than others, another indication of the way the ground had changed since burial.

Delving into the treacly consistency nearby he retrieved some vertebrae, and then came some leg bones including a femur or thigh bone.

As the mud was scraped from this bone it exposed a number of deep black marks, some of which penetrated right through, along with a larger number of finer ones. The Prof's first impression was that these had been made with a sharp instrument; the deeper ones were more likely chop marks. He doubted they had been made by a spade but would examine them more closely back at the lab when they had been cleaned up.

As more of the larger bones were discovered, so too were some that were very small. They were all mixed together in the same area. The Prof examined these closely using clean water to wash them – before confirming that some were the remains of what looked like a full-term baby or a baby nearing full term.

Just as before there was little comment from anyone as the recovery process continued in near silence. The discovery of more 'baby' bones seemed to add to the poignancy of their task. Not even their professionalism could completely mask the sadness they felt. Once again there was no evidence of any clothing – no buttons, zips, thread or elastic. If Remains 3 was Shirley Robinson, she had been buried naked like the others.

It was early afternoon before they completed the search of the areas where the two sets of remains had been found, and once again they had turned up a new and unexpected dimension. This time it was the matter of the belt around the head of victim number two that would have to be put to West.

Back at the press office they were being overwhelmed with enquiries and requests for interviews. Bennett promised to issue a new statement in the hope it might produce fresh leads as to the victims' names – but he would not be mentioning the belt. Of more concern was press officer Hilary Allison's suggestion that a mole was supplying information to tabloid newspaper reporters – especially in view of the sensitivity of what they had uncovered.

The interview of Fred West that began at 11.30 that morning again focused on Remains 2, whom he referred to as 'Shirley's mate' or 'friend'. Once again he repeated in that same flat, emotionless tone how she had come to Cromwell Street looking for Shirley; how he had got rid of her by telling her Shirley had left; how she had then come back, first threatening to go to the police, then demanding money; how he eventually persuaded her that he did not know where Shirley was and agreed to take her back to Bristol in his van, and then as they travelled along the A38 he had changed his mind, turned the van around, stopped in a lay-by and strangled her in the passenger seat. When he had got back to Cromwell Street he used some straps to carry her into the rear garden where he covered her with sand near the window and then 'chopped her up' before burying her as he had Heather and Shirley. Again, he was adamant Rose knew nothing about any of it.

Whether or not he was telling the truth, it still didn't help them identify the girl or explain the belt looped around her head – unless he was suggesting it was one of the straps he used to carry her in. Perhaps they would get an answer in the next interview arranged for that afternoon.

As they made their way downstairs to meet the criminal psychologist Paul Britton, Bennett asked Moore to make notes, as it was unlikely they would get anything in writing from him quickly.

Bennett extended his hand, introduced his number two and couldn't resist asking Britton if he'd brought the outstanding reports from the last time he'd sought his advice. It didn't bother him it might compromise their relationship. Bennett was a stickler for detail for whom each case was just as important as another. Clearly embarrassed, the psychologist promised to get them to him sooner rather than later.

As the three men settled in the Senior Investigating Officer's office Bennett launched into a systematic presentation of the information they had. It began when a teenage Fred West was charged with incest, though the case collapsed, and then moved on to when he met Rose. It continued with the failed 1992 investigation and the allegations that, among other things, Rose helped her husband have intercourse with one of their daughters. Then there was West's belief he could produce a 'West master race' through a mixture of his intercourse and the added sperm of Afro-Caribbean friends. All this and the relatively large amount of pornographic material, sexual toys and implements seized from the Wests' home noticeably caused Britton's eyebrows to rise.

Bennett's discourse continued through Heather West's disappearance, how that investigation had begun, the events since and the search of 25 Cromwell Street that had begun the week before. Fred West's behaviour, demeanour, lack of conscience, admissions, denials and lies; Rose West's attitude, her release and her husband's repeated insistence she knew nothing, were all gone through before Bennett introduced the then still limited details of their convictions for assault and indecent assault on their former nanny Caroline Owens. Finally, he described how the remains had been found, concentrating on the way at least two of the victims, including Heather, had apparently been dismembered. In addition there were the 'artefacts' – the piece of rope with Remains 1, Heather, and the looped belt around the skull of Remains 2 – and the fact that all three appeared to have been naked when they were buried.

Britton listened intently. More than 6ft tall and heavily built, he was an imposing figure. As one of the few psychologists who specialised in advising the police and profiling crimes and criminals, some newspapers thought him the inspiration for the fictional TV profiler 'Cracker'. Round-faced and bespectacled, with a dark, receding hairline, he seemed to chew over every one of his softly spoken, well-pronounced words, which were delivered in a slow, even tone.

'He's a psychopath,' Britton pronounced gravely.

This time it was Moore's eyebrows that lifted, though it was Bennett who spoke, 'I think we worked that out for ourselves after we found he had murdered and dismembered his daughter, his perversions and how he was able to cover all this up, let alone the other two he's now admitted.'

Britton ignored the interruption and continued. 'West is a predatory sexual psychopath. He would not feel guilt. He plans things, is cunning rather than intelligent and likes to be listened to and talk about himself. He tries to control everything and everyone around him and it's this that's allowed him to stay one step ahead.'

'Rose West is out on bail now. There is just not sufficient evidence to think of charging her with anything,' added the Senior Investigating Officer. 'Terry and I are not alone; in fact there is no one on the team, especially those who have interviewed either Fred or her, who does not think Rose is involved in the murders rather than just knowing about them. What do you think?'

'You're right, she is the same as him. He would have taken her along a journey, a journey of sexual depravity and adventure where from time to time they would find the need to try something different to achieve satisfaction. Then the next time they would go further. Though it may not be that regular, they would find the need. Something may spark off the occasion. I'll try to help you find what this is.'

Britton pointed out how important Mrs West, as he referred to

Rose, was to Fred – she was his and now did what he wanted. He would likely have schooled her in his ways and have got her to enjoy what they were doing. They would then have sought others with similar sexual needs, keeping most of what they did either within their family or to themselves, for these were intimate secrets they dare not tell anyone. This, said the psychologist, was what bound them together. She would help him with his fantasies, involve herself in his games and even in experiments with their own children – and there would still be more the next time!

'John, is there a special food that you like? One that you do not have that often but from time to time you get a sort of craving to have and when you do you really enjoy it?'

Bennett appeared puzzled so Britton prompted him.

'For me its quails' eggs . . .'

To which Bennett replied, 'Fish and chips from a chip shop – cod and chips.'

Britton latched on to the answer, explaining how Fred and Rose might have tried their cod and chips with salt, then with vinegar, before moving on to tartar sauce and so on. But for them, sex was their cod and chips and they would have continued experimenting until they had found satisfaction, then experimented some more.

Bennett admitted, 'There's a lot we still don't know about West and 25 Cromwell Street but we will soon – like when he built these extensions near where the last two victims we found were buried. Who knows whether there is any more evidence or even victims there? I've virtually decided we have got to search this area – dig it up like the garden. As it is we are stripping the house.'

'You're right to think that way. You don't know when this started – it could have been many years ago – certainly as far back as their convictions in 1972.'

Britton had arrived late in the afternoon so there was little time left to discuss it further before both a briefing and a media conference. Instead, Bennett asked him to stay and meet the officers who had carried out most of the interviews and advise them on their interview strategy. When Moore had left the room he also said he would like an opinion on their mental state, for although he needed them to be on top of their job, he was also responsible for their well-being and was concerned about the effect on them of what they were dealing with.

Detective Sergeant Terry Onions and Detective Constables Hazel Savage and Darren Law were already in the canteen when Bennett and Moore arrived with their guest. It was somewhere that was immediately available and would make the meeting less formal.

After introductions, Britton took a seat at the table and asked if there was anything new from their interview with West that afternoon.

They explained how they had tried to get him to focus on when and how he had dismembered Shirley Robinson and her 'mate' and why the belt was there, but he had more or less just repeated all he had said earlier without giving any explanation of the belt, that he had killed Shirley after the rows they had had about her threat to tell Rose it was his baby she was carrying. He had also rambled on about Shirley writing to the other girl he had killed asking her to come and get her but he didn't know who she was.

Knowing West as well as anyone, Hazel Savage suggested this might have been 'just more of Fred's fantasies' and asked Britton if he'd been told of West's 'master race' experiments. Leaning forward and talking even quieter than normal, even though there were few others in the room, Britton said he had, but 'would like to hear more about both Mr and Mrs West'.

Savage described some of the rooms at Cromwell Street in detail, from the findings of the 1992 investigation.

The 'Black Magic' Bar – a wooden bar with bottles and optics – so called because that was the name on the sign above painted on a picture of palm trees.

'Rose's Special Room' with its mirror and four-poster bed

adorned with a bull having intercourse with a cow, the wrought-iron sign on the front unashamedly spelling the word 'cunt'.

The peepholes in doors and baby intercom system that enabled whatever was taking place to be seen and heard. The films taken of Rose having sex with other men and other sexual acts and the use of various 'things' in the process.

Britton listened while the detective reinforced how West seemingly enjoyed and even encouraged his wife in having sex with anyone and anything, and that it was obvious he was not the father of one of the daughters as she was clearly of mixed race.

'Perhaps he thinks his experiment worked?' said Bennett. 'We know he's cunning and perhaps not too intelligent; he must have believed it was possible, to go to the lengths he did to try it, unless of course he made it up to hide another of his fetishes?'

Savage replied that while he didn't seem to mind Rose having sex with women he apparently did not feel the same about homosexual acts and would not involve himself in that.

As Hazel Savage went into more background detail Bennett once again realised how little *he* still knew of Fred and Rose West's life history. It was coming to him in dribs and drabs, and with all the other aspects of the investigation to manage he was having difficulty remembering it all. At least it would all be in HOLMES and he was confident that his criminal intelligence analyst Detective Constable Mark Grimshaw had the computer systems and knowledge to get it sequenced properly and in detail.

It was approaching the time for briefing so Britton was left alone to read through the papers he had been given.

The psychologist's involvement was first on the agenda before Bennett launched into a forceful delivery of his concern that from the questions the press office was getting and articles that had appeared in newspapers there appeared to be a leak within the investigation. Unauthorised information could have come from somewhere else, possibly West's legal team, but it could have come from someone in the room.

'Everything that's said in these briefings and anything else you learn, is to be kept completely confidential and not discussed with anyone other than members of the team. Not any other officer, no matter what their rank, and definitely not anyone outside – not even family. Is that clear?'

It was a question that needed no answer and a brief period of silence followed until the sombre mood was broken once more – by the fruit machine bursting into tune! Even Bennett had to smile as a few uneasy smirks turned into a roomful of laughter.

Once they had composed themselves Bennett explained how numbers would continue to identify the remains until they were able to satisfy the coroner who they were. The only exception for now was Remains 1, who they were virtually sure was Heather West and whose name was on the charge against Fred – though she would still have to be formally identified. Officers who were investigating specific remains would update the rest of the team at each briefing. The Wests' children were also to be treated as victims and kept up to date with developments, and every meeting with them or any other victim's relatives or potential witnesses had to be logged into the HOLMES system.

Detective Sergeant Roger Kelland, who was trying to establish the identity of Remains 3, thought to be that of Shirley Robinson, said they were making progress towards identifying her father and tracing her mother, who, it appeared, were no longer together. Others who knew her had not seen her since May 1978 though she was never reported missing. Shirley Robinson's medical history and the discovery of the baby's remains made it even more probable Remains 3 were hers.

As for Remains 2, it was looking more likely she too may have been in care as 25 Cromwell Street seemed to be a magnet for girls with no real roots.

The meeting was now in full swing.

They already knew that Fred West's first wife was named Rena Costello and that she had at least two daughters, Anne Marie who was Fred's and the older Charmaine who wasn't. A priority now was to track them down and, even more important, find out if they were safe and well, an essential obligation for anyone linked with the house. An appeal through the media might help speed things up.

Before closing the briefing, Bennett reminded them how important it was to continue to share information in the way they just had and that whatever they had to say, even if it was criticism of the way the investigation was being handled, he wanted it in the open. Only by acting as a team would they get through the weeks and months ahead.

His relatively short 'state of the nation' speech delivered, he turned his thoughts towards the news conference.

According to Hilary Allison most of the questions to the press office centred on who the three bodies were and how they died. Apart from local journalists who'd been onto the story from the start, there were now reporters there from all the national newspapers as well as the national television and radio networks who looked like they were settling in for a few days at least. It was time, she said, for someone other than a police spokesman to answer the questions she could not. In other words him, for that was his style anyway and she knew it.

Three big blue background screens with the constabulary logo emblazoned on the middle one were dragged into place, then a top table of desks and in front of them a collection of bar stools and chairs in rows for reporters. A solid bank of TV cameras came next and the room was ready.

The press officer went to fetch Bennett and Moore to quickly outline how the conference should be run. A few reporters took the opportunity to ask if they could 'use the toilet', a seemingly innocent enough request that was hard to refuse, except that they were later found wandering around the first floor peering into interview rooms and offices, claiming they were lost or looking for where the press conference was being held. When told, Bennett was furious. Security was paramount but he had not imagined the investigation had brought to Gloucester a much more devious and cunning brand of journalist, the like of which he had never encountered before. It was another lesson on this very steep learning curve.

Seated in the centre directly beneath the force crest, Bennett began with a brief statement that covered the finding of the remains but he quickly moved on to taking questions as he preferred that to reading from a note. Terry Moore sat alongside him with instructions to kick or nudge him if he thought he was in danger of saying anything he ought not to. He would also do one-to-one interviews, with Allison making sure he didn't overrun.

Speaking directly to his audience he confirmed the find 'two further sets of remains, possibly those of young women, having been recovered from the garden of 25 Cromwell Street that morning'. Forensic examination of what had been found would take some time and identification would be difficult as would the search of the garden due to the condition of the ground that existed there.

It was all pretty inconsequential stuff and nothing that they did not know already but at least he was saying it.

Opening it up to the floor, Bennett was surprised at some of the questions.

'Who are these young women?'

'Can't you give us photographs, we might be able to help you find who they are?'

Bennett calmly reiterated that what had been found were 'remains' – resisting the use of 'bones' in deference to the victims' relatives. 'The state of the remains is such that any conventional means of identification like photographs are out of the question.'

'How did they die?'

'At present we do not know and factually we might never now.'

'You must know whether they were stabbed, shot or strangled? Any knife wounds, bullet holes?'

Trying not to show his growing exasperation, but somewhat comforted by the chuckles and hisses from some of the other reporters, he ignored that one.

'Human remains have been found, not bodies. We hope the media will report it that way so as to save unnecessary work and calls coming in to the investigation from those who have lost loved ones and want to try and identify them. What we are engaged in is similar to an archaeological dig.'

This seemed to do the trick as more sensible questions followed.

'How many officers are working on the investigation?'

'Has anyone else been arrested in connection with these murders?'

'Are you going to and when are you going to charge Fred West with these murders?'

The last two questions they knew Bennett couldn't answer for legal reasons but it didn't stop them asking anyway.

The 'one-to-ones' that followed took about half an hour and went over pretty much the same ground, but it was a necessary exercise to satisfy television and radio.

Back in his office, Bennett was reassured by Paul Britton that his officers were holding up remarkably well, commenting specifically on their commitment and Hazel Savage's depth of knowledge of the West family. When Terry Moore joined them his advice was to 'let Mr West talk'.

'Try to get him to take you through his life, through his first sexual experience. Let me know how you get on.' However, his final words were of little comfort to either of them: 'It can take years to do this and you only have a few days.'

As Britton prepared to leave he asked to be kept informed and promised to come back if they wanted him to. This did not stop Bennett making one last dig about the reports he was still awaiting.

TWELVE

When Bennett turned up for work the next morning, Terry Moore was already in his office, his head buried in a newspaper.

'Ah, is this the 'copper's copper' arriving? A strict disciplinarian – a methodical policeman of the old school?' enquired the Chief Inspector wryly.

Bennett was completely nonplussed. 'What?'

'More Wexford than Morse?'

After yesterday's press conference the regional morning newspaper the *Western Daily Press* was carrying a profile of the Senior Investigating Officer, comparing him to two fictional detectives.

'Who's put that out, where did they get all that from?'

Still laughing, Moore handed him the newspaper, which also had a large photograph of him and another piece about 'the Professor of Whodunits', Professor Knight, with the warning that other copies had reached the incident room.

'I could do without this and all these "informed insiders" and "sources close to the investigation" making comments. Still, I suppose there are much worse TV coppers than Wexford I could have been likened to!'

The HOLMES 'volumes' – the amount of information to be entered and followed up – were increasing, but under the supervision of Roger Scriven and Jill Field the team were just about keeping on top of it.

Among the day's priorities, the search of the inside of 25 Cromwell Street would continue; West would be interviewed further – again with the aim of identifying Remains 2 and getting any further information about Shirley Robinson and anyone else that went to Cromwell Street; and they would begin to follow Paul Britton's advice – if there was time. When this had been taken as far as it could they would consider when West should be charged. Before that Bennett would speak to the coroner David Gibbons to update him and ask if he objected to the charge naming Shirley Robinson. West said that was who she was and there was every reason to believe now that someone of her age who was using her name, fitted her description and was heavily pregnant, was last seen at Cromwell Street.

Attempts to trace Catherine 'Rena' West, née Costello, West's first wife, and her daughter Charmaine, were proving less fruitful as none of her close family had seen her for many years. West would have to be asked more about them, as would his family and especially Anne Marie.

Hilary Allison interrupted their meeting with the news that press interest was showing no sign of abating. The media realised that West would have to appear before the court again the next day and they were speculating that more 'bodies' would be found at Cromwell Street. Some of the papers and TV coverage still referred to the finds as 'bodies', which was putting even more pressure on her office. Not only was she being questioned about 'Shirley Robinson', local reporters were putting forward 'Mary Bastholm and Lucy Partington' as possible victims. Others were asking about Rena West and Charmaine, and some seemed to have quite detailed information about them and about Anne Marie – and she'd been asked to confirm that Paul Britton was advising the investigation when that was supposed to have been a secret!

None of this was a surprise.

Mary Bastholm went missing from Gloucester on 6 January 1968; Lucy Partington from Cheltenham disappeared on 27 December 1973. These were cases he knew well and had already asked for the files to be dusted down and sent over, for the dates could be significant, especially as they still did not know precisely when the Wests had moved to 25 Cromwell Street, only that they had moved there from a flat in 25 Midland Road, less than a mile away. Various dates had been suggested between 1971 and 1973 but there was nothing on paper to tie it down. Until there was it would be even more difficult establishing whether Remains 2 were those of either Mary Bastholm or Lucy Partington.

Personally, he doubted whether either of them were Remains 2 as a Shirley Robinson had definitely existed, had left Cromwell Street and disappeared just weeks before her baby was due. Professor Knight's first analysis and the last sighting of her around April 1978 corroborated this. While Bennett placed little reliance on anything West said, he reasoned that if the victim, Remains 2, was someone who had come to look for Shirley Robinson, she would have died five years or more after Lucy Partington had gone missing. For it to have been Lucy she would either have been held captive for all that time or gone off and changed her life completely, and both options seemed highly improbable.

Whether there was a leak from within the investigation was hard to tell. Officers on the inquiry had been asking many people about Shirley Robinson, some of whom, including members of the West family, they knew were talking to reporters. It all made the need to name her or trace her relatives more urgent – along with an appeal for Rena and Charmaine to come forward – but they still didn't have enough information for that.

To help the press office, it was agreed to issue another statement. No names or appeals, just confirmation that 'the search would continue and that a forensic psychologist had been asked to advise and that we are still trying to identify the two further victims'. Hilary Allison would also put reporters straight on referring to 'remains' rather than 'bodies'.

Arriving in the MIR, there were more 'Wexford' taunts to embarrass Bennett.

'What did you have to give them to print all that, JB?'

Those who knew him best were the loudest with their jibes,

but he took it all in good part and consoled himself it was good for team spirit and morale.

As the quips subsided, Bennett moved in alongside Mark Grimshaw whose eyes were now firmly fixed on his computer screen. He wanted charts prepared to help him understand what they had found, precisely where they had found it and what they were dealing with, as well as completing a sequence of events file. He also wanted side views of the house and extension, and overhead plans of the rooms inside, all to scale, and he wanted it all in the computer for future reference. If Grimshaw needed help, he could contact Police Constable Andy Ewens who had come up with the sort of thing he wanted using a theodolite.

Tony James said he had called the Scientific Research Branch, who had offered to X-ray the walls and floors. They could also get hold of ground-penetrating radar, a sort of sonar that might help establish if there had been any disturbance of the ground and any voids. Bennett thought it might help with the search beneath the extension and told James to find out how much it would cost to hire.

The Wexford jokes continued, and although it was wearing a bit thin Bennett knew he would have to put up with it for the rest of the day at least, and by the end of it he also knew they would have to charge West with the two other murders. At that point the interviews would have to stop as well. Their only hope was that the court would remand him back into their custody and not to prison.

The early results from the bug in Rose West's safe house were disappointing. So far she had said nothing to implicate herself in any of the murders, just lots of what she now thought of Fred and what she would do to him if she could get her hands on him. Although it was not what they were hoping for, it was giving them a better insight into her personality. She was certainly not very bright and not at all articulate. She had a quick temper and was as foul-mouthed as her husband, for there seemed to be no words or expressions that she would not use nor anything that embarrassed her, which all supported what Paul Britton had said.

Then, completely out of the blue, came a telephone call that would have a decisive effect on the investigation.

The Senior Investigating Officer's office had a direct line that was ex-directory and a few internal ones for calls that were normally filtered by the switchboard operators. When Bennett answered one of his internal phones the MIR telephonist apologised saying she had a male caller on the line who said he was a former fire officer and was asking to speak to him.

'He was sure you would agree to speak to him, Mr Bennett,' said the operator.

Bennett recalled the name and came on the line.

The pleasantries over, the caller asked if he could remember a fire officer called Gough who had worked in fire prevention at the Cheltenham fire headquarters.

'Did he ever mention that his daughter went missing some time ago?'

He then related how Lynda Gough had left home in Gloucester in the early 1970s when she was about 20 to live with a man and woman in the city whom he was sure lived in Cromwell Street. After a while, her parents went to the address and although they were told their daughter had left, they noticed that the woman who came to the door was wearing some of their daughter's clothes and that some of her other things were on a washing line. He had not spoken to the Goughs and wondered whether the police knew.

Bennett was sure that had this information already reached the MIR he would have been told immediately, but he went and checked just in case. There was nothing.

Returning to the phone, he asked if the girl's disappearance had ever been reported, concerned that he had still not reviewed the county's missing persons list. The caller was not sure though he thought that it had been mentioned to a police officer neighbour.

Clearly, the gaps in what the investigation knew of the Wests' history seemed to be widening but if what he had just been told was right, if 'Shirley's mate' was Lynda Gough, then she must have gone missing in the late, rather than early seventies. It would not take long to check this out. Mr and Mrs Gough lived on the outskirts of Gloucester and he would make it a high priority to have them seen – if they didn't get in touch themselves first.

It was too soon to get excited over this call, although the possibility of Rose West wearing this girl's clothing interested Terry Moore too, when Bennett told him a short time later.

When West was interviewed later that morning, Howard Ogden again protested at why he had not been charged. Even so, West was asked about his early life.

The Gloucester coroner had no objection to Shirley Robinson's name being included, so two further charges were put to him that afternoon: the murder of Shirley Robinson between 1 January 1972 and 27 February 1994 and the murder of an unknown woman between the same dates. In the High Court, a successful application was made on behalf of Gloucestershire Social Services restraining the press from identifying the West children who were in care. There was no doubt everyone involved in the investigation felt for these children who from birth had the potential to be unwitting victims. Now at least they had been spared that possibility.

Enquiries to establish the Wests' movements from a flat at 25 Midland Road to 25 Cromwell Street were still going on. West said they moved in at the end of 1972, but this had still to be checked. It was believed a man called Frank Zygmunt, whom West worked for in lieu of paying rent, owned both properties. They also knew that while he was living at 25 Midland Road,

West had served a short prison sentence though it was not yet known precisely what for. The couple's presence on the electoral roll meant both Fred and Rose were at Midland Road from October 1971 and they appeared on the electoral roll at 25 Cromwell Street exactly a year later. Zygmunt was now dead and his relatives were being sought to try and find out exactly when the Wests moved.

Information was also coming in from various sources – from people who had lived at Midland Road in nearby flats and in the same building, from others who had visited or lodged at 25 Cromwell Street – but still they could not pin down the precise dates. Many people were being asked by the police and the media to remember events from a long time ago, which would have seemed inconsequential at the time. Others could recall the Wests' extraordinarily open relationship, how they encouraged sexual encounters and invited others to join them in sex. For some it was a part of their lives they were embarrassed about and wanted to forget, others were happy to talk to the press, knowing there was money to be made. When reporters got there first it just added to police frustration, especially when people who refused to talk to them later appeared with their pictures in a newspaper alongside the 'latest explicit revelation'.

Within the MIR other actions had been raised to contact former Gloucester-based police officers who may have visited the Wests at either address. Between them they had been able to confirm 25 Cromwell Street as a place where young people, and particularly young girls, were drawn. These included many who had run away from home or absconded from care homes. Drug raids, too, were relatively commonplace, but not as frequent as some suggested. They also discovered Fred West had been an occasional police informant though his information was mostly about his 'lodgers'.

Clearly, many young people had drifted through and those who were traced remembered those they could by a combination of nicknames and descriptions, and accounts rarely tallied. Fred West was always changing the place, adding bits to the outside, making more rooms on the inside, so the more ex-residents and visitors were found, the more confusing it became.

The evening briefing was now becoming regular practice, as was the growing interest from the media. Not satisfied with the holding statement they had been given, they wanted more information about Fred West, his family and his first wife. Hilary Allison was finding it increasingly difficult to answer their questions and wanted Bennett to hold another conference. Reluctantly he agreed, though it was not a universally popular decision within the squad.

'They're getting in our way.'

'They get to some before we do.'

'We've even had to wait till they've finished before seeing some we've made prior arrangements and travelled miles to see.'

'Who's running this, the press or us? Why should we help them, we should just tell them to get lost.'

Bennett may have agreed with them but he knew he could not follow their advice. It was important to keep the media informed but they could not be allowed to compromise the investigation. At least there were no more Wexford jibes!

Detective Sergeant Roger Kelland, who had been working on finding Shirley Robinson's relatives, believed that by the next day he would succeed. Her father was thought to be in Germany, divorced from Shirley's mother, and there were new leads that would help him trace her, too.

Mr Gough had been in touch and confirmed much of what they were told on the phone. Meeting both Lynda's parents was now a priority.

At that evening's news conference there were many more reporters than before.

Some of the questions centred on Shirley Robinson but there were more about Rena West and Charmaine and the fact that neither had been seen for many years. This forced Bennett into saying, cautiously, that what appeared to be positive lines of enquiry were being followed up as regards Shirley Robinson's relatives. He also appealed for Rena West, formerly Costello, or anyone who knew her or had seen her, to come forward.

The conference only lasted about three-quarters of an hour yet it was time away from his real work Bennett felt he could ill afford. Satisfying the media was taking up too much of his time and everyone else's. He would have to find a way to handle it, to distance himself more.

THIRTEEN

Exactly one week on from the start of the search that marked the beginning of the investigation, Fred West was to appear again at Gloucester Magistrates Court. Now he faced three murder charges.

A queue began to form long before the court was due to start at 10 a.m. and by the time the doors opened the huge throng of people trying to get in far outstripped the number of seats. For once reporters outnumbered local miscreants there to answer for their crimes and no doubt a few were there 'just to have a look', while those who couldn't get in milled around the entrance kicking their heels.

A request for a further three-day remand to police cells was going to be made and although Howard Ogden was not expected to object it was thought he would complain about the way the case was being reported and, in particular, the one local newspaper that had ignored the restrictions by writing that West had admitted to murder.

When West was brought into the dock this time, he looked dishevelled and less confident. Dressed in a blue jacket and crumpled grey shirt he looked around before sitting. Janet Leach, the appropriate adult, was already at the back of the court and West smiled in her direction.

The magistrates entered and the proceedings got under way. After confirming his name, West listened while the charges against him were read out in full. As the clerk reached the second, the murder of Shirley Robinson, West's face turned white then green as the blood drained from his features. His knees buckled and he grabbed on to the rail in front of him until he was helped into his seat by the uniformed police officer who was guarding him. Seeing what was happening, the clerk paused for a couple of minutes until West had recovered his composure, then continued.

It was all over in 6 minutes. Ogden made no objection, the magistrates remanded West to police cells for a further three days and he was back on his feet, still gazing around the court as he was escorted down the steps and out of view. His face had coloured up and bore a slight smirk but there was none of the swagger of before.

Statements had now been taken from Lynda Gough's parents and they made interesting reading.

Lynda Gough had left home and later gone missing but before she actually went a woman had called at their home to take her for a drink. She left with her in a car that was waiting nearby.

Lynda had been telling her parents she wanted to move out to get some experience of life. Although they were not in favour they accepted she had to go and get it out of her system.

June Gough, Lynda's mum, was sure it was mid-April 1972 when her daughter left. She had taken everything she owned, leaving behind a note, which they had kept. It read, 'Dear mum and dad please don't worry about me, I have got a flat and I will come and see you sometime, love Lyn' – an abbreviation she often used.

In order to keep tabs on her, her parents found out where she was living in the city and checked to see if she had kept up her work as a seamstress, but when, after a few weeks, she did not return home as they had always hoped, June Gough had gone to the address where she believed Lynda was staying. She was sure it was 25 Cromwell Street.

She recalled it was on a Saturday morning and she saw the same dark-haired woman who had called for Lynda before she had left home. She was with a man who also had dark hair who, from the way he talked and acted, she thought was the woman's husband. When June Gough asked them about her daughter they told her she had 'left and gone to Weston-super-Mare' – a Bristol Channel resort some 50 miles away. As they spoke, she noticed the woman was wearing slippers that she recognised as Lynda's. She was also wearing a blouse or cardigan, she was not sure which now, that also belonged to her daughter, and on a washing line were other items of clothing she recognised as Lynda's. When she mentioned this the couple passed it off by saying, 'She just left this all behind when she left.'

Most, if not all, of what had taken place they had told a neighbouring police officer and friend, whom they thought had noted it but they hadn't formally reported Lynda missing because they accepted that as she was in her late teens and regarded as an adult there was little they could do to make her return home, and despite making enquiries through the Salvation Army they never heard from her again. Instead, the Goughs had lived every day since in the hope their daughter would contact them or better still return home. It was a sad reflection officers closely involved in the investigation would hear many times in the next few weeks.

So, it seemed the Wests were living in 25 Cromwell Street in mid-1972. June Gough had been certain of the year. This would have been before the offences against Caroline Owens, though the year still didn't fit in with what Fred West was saying about 'Shirley's mate'. If Lynda had known Shirley Robinson and had met her after going missing in 1972, would she have come back after 1978? No one had been able to place her there then; more likely she was at Cromwell Street in 1973 rather than 1972! Apart from that, there was little doubt June Gough was describing Fred and Rose West and 25 Cromwell Street.

While there was still some checking to do, it seemed that like Heather West, Lynda Gough had just vanished. Even the excuse that she had 'gone off to Weston' was similar to how the Wests had explained their own daughter's disappearance.

Why, though, if she had moved on would she not have taken all her clothes with her? She was earning very little as a seamstress and she didn't leave home with that much anyway. Rose wearing Lynda Gough's slippers, the blouse or cardigan and other items of clothing on the washing line made the Wests' tale extremely suspect.

Bennett and Moore discussed June Gough's statement with officers who were still working on the date they believed the Wests had purchased 25 Cromwell Street, which was based on the recollections of the lodgers and visitors they had traced. What June Gough was now saying would have to be put to Fred West, for it was information, perhaps even evidence, of the identity of Remains 2. Ignoring Paul Britton's advice, they decided to change their interview strategy and put these new allegations to him. They could go back to regressing West through his life later.

This change of direction did not go down well with Hazel Savage, who had made it clear from the start she did not agree with following Britton's suggestions, but now the decision had been made she felt they should stick to it. Once it was explained, though, it was clear how relevant this information might be. If Lynda Gough was Remains 2, how was Fred West going to explain his wife wearing her slippers and clothing and the date? If she was not Remains 2, where was she? Savage readily accepted its significance and how important it was now to find out exactly when Fred West bought 25 Cromwell Street and when they moved in.

If this was a possible breakthrough, West was not about to make it easy, totally denying knowing a Lynda Gough or ever having met anyone of that name. Adopting the same cocky, know-all attitude he first displayed when he turned up at Gloucester Police Station a week previously, he claimed someone was 'making it up', 'getting on the band wagon' to make money out of the press. Mocking his interrogators he argued he could not have been in Cromwell Street in April 1972 because he hadn't bought it then.

Perhaps thinking he had 'got one over' on Hazel Savage,

West had asked about the state of his home. When told it had been stripped bare, he threatened to sue if it fell down, though by then he had written to Rose, Stephen and Mae and agreed to pass on ownership to them so they could sell it.

CPS solicitors Roger Fry and Rita Crane sat in the Senior Investigating Officer's office, as Terry Moore closed the door to reduce the background noise of the MIR and officers talking and preparing their reports next door. It made the small room almost claustrophobic despite the large windows. Bennett stood facing them, his voice stern with conviction.

First, he went back to the beginning, covering every aspect of the investigation, including the failed social services inquiry. Then, how they had many witnesses to prove both Fred West and Rose had lied about their daughter's disappearance. Next, he detailed the couple's uncannily close and free relationship with its deviant sexual practices; Fred West's unbending assurances of Rose's innocence, for even when he had admitted there were three victims he quickly made it clear 'Rose didn't know'. As for Rose, she too denied knowing anything about any murders, Shirley Robinson or that Shirley Robinson was pregnant. There was their previous conviction for indecent assault, though Bennett admitted he could not understand why they hadn't faced much more serious charges, for it was undoubtedly a joint enterprise with Rose taking a major part. As for the recovery of the remains, how they appeared to have been dismembered and the use of the belt, he emphasised that it seemed to be more evidence of restraint and deviance, just like some of the witnesses and the indecent assault victim had endured.

Rounding it all off, Bennett stressed these were also the views of Terry Moore and the entire inquiry team, throwing in Paul Britton's analysis of the pair as 'predatory sexual psychopaths' for good measure. Britton, he said, was sure they would have shared and been involved in everything together, as confirmed by some members of their family and 'friends' who joined them in their sickening sexual practices. According to Bennett, the psychologist had also suggested there might be more victims and that as the team was looking back over the Wests' past life, there was growing concern for his first wife Rena West and her daughter, not to mention Lynda Gough, whose disappearance was now part of the investigation.

The lawyers listened intently, so when Bennett had finished and they said nothing he checked with Terry Moore in case he had missed anything. After a further moment's silence he reaffirmed his conviction that Rose West *was* involved in the three murders while at the same time reassuring them the aim was to get to the truth. Only when they were certain would she be rearrested, for although they could not yet prove her involvement, the amount of similar fact evidence to implicate her was building by the day. That was why he needed the guidance of a special caseworker, preferably Withiel Cole.

Bennett thought he had made a convincing case, not so Roger Fry.

'There does not seem, as you say, to be any real evidence to support what you think. I don't think there is any evidence in what you have said that can warrant her being charged with anything at present.'

Bennett knew that it was more or less what he had just said, but he couldn't believe it when, in a faltering voice and with just the hint of a smile, Fry announced, 'We will still continue as we are – but if more than five murders are involved then you can have Withiel Cole!'

The look of disbelief on the two detectives' faces was identical. Bennett implored Fry to reconsider but this time the reply was even more emphatic, 'Come back to me if there are five or more.'

That evening's briefing brought a similar story of a press office under siege and an incident room creaking under the weight of work. Only when everything was properly indexed into HOLMES would they regain control and for that they would need more staff.

At Cromwell Street the search was continuing and arrangements had been made to X-ray the walls. While men from the Gloucester Support Group continued digging in the garden, a similar team from Cheltenham would carry out the search of the interior. The property had now been stripped room by room, attic to cellar, floor to ceiling of more than 1,300 items, all of which had been recorded and put in storage until a thorough examination later. Any weapon, bloodstain, evidence of sexual perversion would be of obvious interest, but in such an ever-changing investigation no document, no item, nothing could be discounted. Who could say what relevance it might have, and the job was complicated still further by the finding of a record of the property confiscated, later returned or destroyed during the previous investigation into the Wests. The possible relevance of this and what it contained could not be discounted either.

The excavations that had unearthed Remains 2 and 3 meant there was now a danger of the extension falling down. They had done their best to shore it up, its weakness now more a reflection of Fred West's craftsmanship.

At the briefing there were more sighs and shaking of heads when in response to news that reporters were 'camping out' in pubs and bars close by, Bennett appealed to them not to go to their usual watering holes or socialise outside the investigation but to use the police bar instead.

At least there was some good news. Shirley Robinson's mother had been found and interviewed. Comments expressing how they had hoped she would be traced before hearing it through the media showed how they were bonding together as a team and that the collective spirit was getting stronger by the day.

In his later interviews, West talked of his time at Cromwell Street but still denied knowing Lynda Gough. Hazel Savage's earlier dissent at the decision to change tack not only earned her and Darren Law the chance of a well-deserved break and time off, it also confirmed the need to increase the interviewing pool. Detective Constables Barbara Harrison and Geoff Morgan had brought themselves up to date on past interviews and were ready to take a turn.

There was still no trace of Rena West or Charmaine and now it seemed that the marriage of Fred and Rose was bigamous, though this was yet another piece of information still to be confirmed.

FOURTEEN

With Fred West back in police custody there was a chance to take stock and clear up the uncertainty over precisely when he and Rose had moved into 25 Cromwell Street.

The information the police now had pointed to 1972 and long before 6 December that year, the date of the offences against their former nanny.

Caroline Owens, or Raine as she then was, had worked at 25 Cromwell Street in October looking after Anne Marie, Heather and Mae who was born that June. Rose had returned to 25 Midland Road after giving birth to Mae so they were still living there then. The likeliest explanation was that their landlord Frank Zygmunt had loaned Fred West the deposit for a mortgage on 25 Cromwell Street and that West then did odd building jobs for him as a means of repaying the loan and the rent that was due on 25 Midland Road.

Whether they were at Cromwell Street in the latter half of 1972 and not before August was critical, for June Gough said she had gone there when her daughter Lynda went missing in April of that year, though other 'tenants' claimed Lynda Gough was there in 1973.

As the list of young girls who had had contact with the Wests increased, establishing that they were safe and well became a priority. Every new name that came to police attention was traced and interviewed. Names were cross-matched and verified. Any name that couldn't be found was highlighted, names of anyone in care known to have visited Cromwell Street were at the top of the list of people to be found and questioned.

Mark Grimshaw had produced a plan of 25 Cromwell Street and the three burial sites. Bennett suggested a few modifications and told him to put one on the wall in front of his desk and another on a noticeboard in the main room. Grimshaw left him the original 'in case you think of anything else', but the chart reminded him that 'Remains 2 and 3' were found close to the bathroom and kitchen extension which West had built piecemeal while he lived there. It again begged the question he and Terry Moore had discussed many times: 'Were there any more victims under the floor?' The only answer was to dig it up, just like the garden, especially in light of Lynda Gough's apparent disappearance.

Studying the chart afresh, Bennett also noticed for the first time the icon that read 'Remains 1', possibly Heather West, Born 17.10.70'. It suddenly dawned on him that Fred and Rose's first child was born on the very same day as his first son Andrew. Then he remembered, too, that this whole investigation had stemmed from the execution of the search warrant on 24 February, his second son David's twenty-first birthday, and that he and his wife had looked at flats in Cromwell Street when it looked like he would be transferred to Gloucester much earlier in his career.

As the order of the day fell into place, there was again little spare time for keeping pace with developments. Despite the media coverage, there was still no trace of Rena West and Charmaine, though concerns over Lynda Gough now took precedence.

As the team were taking their places for the briefing Bennett switched off the fruit machine, which caused some laughter but that quickly fell away when he again voiced his concern that the media seemed to know more about the investigation than they should. At least they hadn't yet latched on to the Lynda Gough line.

When it was Hazel Savage's turn to bring them all up to date on the interviews with West, she too was irritated by not having specific enough information to counter his claims that he was not at Midland Road when he was at Cromwell Street. It put them on the back foot and West was revelling in it, she said. It was pointed out to her that this could not be helped when investigations had to look back in time for even a few days, and in this case they were delving back twenty-four years!

Bennett outlined their intention to search the whole of 25 Cromwell Street 'properly', which meant that once they had excavated under the extension they would move on to the cellar for, as he explained, 'It would be unthinkable for someone in the future to find evidence of more victims that we had not found.'

Savage and Law mentioned how West regularly asked about his home and what sort of condition it was in. News that the extension may have to come down and the floor dug up, said Law, might give him something more to think about and knock his confidence – especially when he learned of the ground-penetrating radar equipment.

The newspapers were reporting that since the investigation had begun, the National Missing Persons Helpline had been overwhelmed with enquiries. Bennett was unaware it even existed but it would need looking at – and so, too, information from their own CID about missing persons in Gloucestershire and the Bristol area, which had not yet been checked. If any of them fitted what West had said or what they knew about Remains 2 he was certain he or Moore would have been told. Nonetheless, Mary Bastholm and Lucy Partington had now almost been dismissed, while the combination of date and forensics they had so far gathered seemed to rule out Lynda Gough as well.

Controlling the media siege of Cromwell Street was now a major problem as it was not only obstructing the flow of traffic through the area but also having a knock-on effect on other parts of the city. Even walking the short distance from the police station to Shire Hall where social services were based had to be carefully thought out in advance in order to avoid being intercepted by reporters who seemed to be around every corner.

When Bennett and Moore arrived in St Michael's Square just after 4.30 p.m. the car park had been virtually taken over by the vast array of outside broadcast vehicles. The police caravan was now used more as a changing room, its floor covered in newspaper to counter the worst of the mud. As they changed into their wellington boots, they could see a group of photographers and camera crews at the taped barrier, though the officer who was logging all the comings and goings warned them it became much more intrusive the closer they got to the back garden, with crews hanging out of windows, on ladders and scaffolding.

The ground-penetrating radar was supplied by a Surrey-based company called ERA Ltd and having arrived that morning was already in use in the cellar. Although other police forces had tried it out, it was used mainly by the military to find buried plastic mines. Now it had been developed further to inspect pre-cast concrete constructions and archaeological sites, and could penetrate the surface to a depth of around 6ft and produce a graph or analysis of the structure of the ground below the surface. It was not, however, designed to detect bodies or skeletal remains and while Bennett was prepared to try anything he was not convinced it would take them much further.

Stripped of all the Wests' belongings, with the exception of a large fish tank that was too big to move out, the house was cold and uninviting. The upper floors had been cleared and every feature now exposed was being systematically logged. The narrow staircase leading to the cellar was steeply angled, making it necessary for most people to bend slightly to prevent banging their heads as they went down.

It was the same in the cellar where the two men from ERA dragged their machine to and fro across the bare, grey concrete floor, stooping slightly to avoid the low ceiling and beams that ran across it. One of them, Dr Richard Chignell, was taking notes. The floor extended throughout the cellar and was partially divided into three: a large area to the rear of the property, a smaller area in the centre partially enclosed by part walls and the stairs, and another larger area similar in size to that at the rear.

The entire floor was grid-marked with yellow paint that would eventually become a map of the equipment's soundings. It had already located the sewer and waste system which were marked on the map in green painted dots.

The walls of the rooms were almost bare of paper. Children's drawings and paintings on the plaster added to the eerie atmosphere.

Again, it was pointed out that it would take some time before the work produced any results and after watching for a short while Bennett and Moore decided to have a look around the rest of the house to get a better idea of the layout. The door with the peephole was still in place and it was obvious there had been a lot of alterations.

Less than an hour after entering the Cromwell Street checkpoint, Bennett and Moore were back on the fourth floor of the police station when Hazel Savage and Darren Law approached them.

Savage looked tense and annoyed, just as she had during the earlier briefing.

'Something's up. Now he says he doesn't want to be interviewed any more, at least not until he's seen Ogden. Canavan [one of Ogden's clerks] is with him now, and Janet Leach. We don't know whether he wants to make a complaint or what.'

Both detectives repeated that they felt let down by HOLMES not being accurate, especially over the dates Lynda Gough had gone to 25 Cromwell Street. They said that West now remembered her though she wasn't there in 1972 but a long time later and that she had gone off to Weston-super-Mare with another tenant called Terry. Even getting this, they said, had been difficult because he knew they were still confused and he was playing on it. He probably only remembered Lynda because other people had mentioned her name.

Looking just as anxious as his partner, Darren Law said they had told West that the floor of his house was going to be searched with special radar equipment and that it would be dug up.

Bennett and Moore left them and went into their office where a few minutes later Bennett took a call telling him that Howard Ogden was in the building and wanted to see him urgently. Bennett agreed and arranged for him to be brought up.

The three men met on the landing.

Ogden's face was pale, deadpan and serious. 'You may like to sit down before reading this,' he said as he handed over a lined piece of paper torn from a notebook.

Bennett took the note and turned sideways so that Terry Moore could read it at the same time. Ogden stood in the doorway looking on. As Bennett's eyes focused on the handwriting he could hardly believe what he was reading. He read it once quickly to himself and then again much more slowly, hanging on every word.

5.30 p.m. 4/3/94
Gloucester police station
I Frederick West authorise my solicitor Howard Ogden to advise Supt Bennett that I wish to admit to a further (approx.) 9 killings expressly Charmaine, Rena, Lynda Gough and others to be identified.

F. West

As the thick handwritten words sank in, Bennett began to feel a little cold. First he looked at Moore who appeared equally shocked, and then he turned to Ogden and asked, 'I take it this is West's signature?', for it was obvious the wording was that of the solicitor not his client.

Ogden confirmed it was and Bennett handed the note to Moore who jotted down the time '17.35' on the top left of the note.

Bennett asked Moore to find Hazel Savage and Darren Law and within seconds there were five in the office. Bennett read out the note once more and both he and Moore put an arm on Savage's shoulders, perhaps to support themselves as much as her for this was a revelation none of them had envisaged and none of them would ever forget. It seemed that for whatever reason West had given up trying to outwit them.

Ogden said that West would go into more detail later but that the victims had been buried in Cromwell Street and Midland Road and included, he thought, Lucy Partington.

Little more was said and to observe legal requirements Bennett photocopied the note and returned it to Ogden. Arrangements were made to interview West about it later.

There was no briefing scheduled but they had to tell the rest of the inquiry team as soon as possible and everyone who could be contacted was summoned to the social club. The Chief Constable would also have to be made aware but Bennett also needed time to think things through. The note had so many ramifications and he had not even begun to think what they might be; it had come completely out of the blue and such a short time ago it had barely sunk in.

As he wrote out an exhibit label for the note before putting it in a polythene bag he wondered who it was, apart from Rena, Charmaine and Lynda Gough, that West was admitting to 'killing' and where he had put them. The note was vague, what did '(approx.) 9 killings' really mean? And what would he now say about his wife's involvement?

It also meant the size of the investigation would have to be increased both in outside inquiry teams and within the MIR, no matter what West said. Once the news got out, the press office would have to be staffed up even more for it would create a media frenzy which they had to try and control.

There were bound to be questions asked about every aspect of every murder now. If he had thought they were under the spotlight before then it was nothing to what he knew was coming. There were also legal implications to think of and the possibility of having to move out the people who were now living at 25 Midland Road.

When Moore returned they began to mull over how to take the investigation forward. As far as Bennett was concerned, it had to be regarded as a major incident and reorganised along the lines of a small plane or train crash with multiple victims. The force already had a draught plan for such an incident that only needed to be slightly modified to handle murder. With the Chief Constable's approval, they would introduce a 'Gold, Silver and Bronze' command structure.

Bennett and Moore made their way into the police club where not more than half of the officers working on the investigation had gathered. It was unusual for briefings to be arranged on the hoof unless there were major developments and there was an air of expectancy.

Stern faced and in a low voice, Bennett said the allegations from Lynda Gough's mother coupled with the extended search of his house had unsettled West who had given a note to his solicitor.

Holding a copy, he hardly had to read it, as he now knew its contents off by heart.

For a second or two you could hear a pin drop, then heads turned and the silence gave way to excited chatter as everyone realised they were now involved in something quite unique, maybe to some an adventure.

It didn't last long as Bennett reminded them of the work that lay ahead – identifying the victims and breaking the news to their families – and the sombre mood returned almost immediately as everyone pondered on what their role might be.

'We will go through this together. Everyone must put forward their thoughts and concerns, your collective brain power and experience will come up with the ways and ideas to make this an investigation to look back on and be proud of, despite the sadness of it all.'

And he repeated, more forcefully than ever, the need to keep everything they heard and knew within 'the team'.

Questions now arose over whether 25 Midland Road or any other locations should be guarded and whether Rose West should be rearrested.

Each point was discussed as it was raised. They would get a warrant to search the Wests' former home, and while Rose would always be a consideration, they had to concentrate on Fred. Now that he was talking, they needed his help to show where he had put his other victims, find out who they were and when and how he had done it all.

He closed with a reminder that stress counselling was available for anyone who wanted it.

Fred West's next interview began at 6.10 p.m. He was talkative, unruffled and completely unemotional, and as far as he was concerned, back in control of himself and the situation. Now, though, in contrast to his four-line confession of less than an hour before, he was unable to say – or just would not – how many victims he had buried at Cromwell Street. His memory had failed him!

Hazel Savage was having none of that and pressed him for details but he was determined to do it his way and his answers were vague.

Lynda Gough, he said, was underneath the bathroom. The others were in the cellar.

He talked glibly of burying young women and dismembering them, denying that anyone else was involved. He identified them as they came to him.

There was 'the Dutch girl', 'a girl from Newent' and 'Lucy Partington'. He said that Rena was buried 'at Dymock' and 'Charmaine at 25 Midland Road'. He gave slightly more detail about these, saying how he had first 'strangled' Rena then 'strangled' Charmaine.

Hazel Savage's task was to confirm the content of the note

with West and get as much as she could from him without prolonging the interview unduly. They wanted to hear what he had to say so they could prioritise what to do next. Once West had indicated that he was 'not sure' how many victims there were or where each of them was buried the interview was ended. Due to his previous mood swings – admitting and denying, helping and then trying to frustrate the investigation, even trying to control and run it – they could not waste any opportunity to get as much information from him as he was willing to give up, for who knew how he might feel the next morning? They would have to take him to Cromwell Street that night so he could show them where he had buried the girls he was now admitting to killing.

With West, Ogden and Janet Leach in agreement, Terry Moore made the arrangements. As before, West would be covertly conveyed to his home dressed in overalls, with Ogden and Leach and as few other police officers as possible led by Terry Moore. Bennett could stay behind to get on with his briefing notes for tomorrow's meeting with the Chief Constable and make a list of what needed to be done.

Terry Moore waited in the police station backyard along with the rest of the 'convoy' until policemen guarding 25 Cromwell Street were certain there were no reporters still around and gave him the all-clear to go. West's home bore little resemblance to how it was when he had last seen it, when he was taken there to show them where he had buried the last two girls whose murders he had confessed to.

He went inside to what was now little more than a shell and was handed a tin of red spray paint. Watched by the video recordist and representatives from both sides he sprayed red circles onto the floor, pinpointing where he 'remembered' he had buried the girls he had killed there.

At times he appeared lost and out of himself as he looked around. Whether this was due to the stress of his plight or him wondering what was going to happen to his home, his family or himself only he knew.

When the exercise was over the convoy pulled away as quietly as possible and headed back to the police station, hoping more than anything that the media had not got wind of what had taken place.

By the time the policy log was brought up to date, the last job of the day, it was approaching midnight on Friday 5 March, a day just like 24 February that anyone who was there would always remember.

His wife was asleep in bed when the phone rang.

Bennett said he would be home within 45 minutes and asked if she would be up when he arrived because he wanted to talk to her. He had not eaten much during the day so he asked her to get some cheese and biscuits ready and to open a good bottle of red wine.

As he drove away from the city the complexities of what was now unfolding began to dawn upon him. He never doubted that with the help of the team, and Terry Moore in particular, he could handle the investigation, though that evening's incredible and quite unexpected developments made him wonder what else might be in store, a thought that festered in his mind and made him question whether he might not be up to the job. There was just so much to get to grips with and he still wasn't satisfied he was completely across what had happened so far.

All these thoughts were spinning around in his head as he arrived back home to find his wife sitting at the kitchen table with a mug of coffee. Where he normally sat there was a glass, a plate and an uncorked bottle of Châteauneuf du Pape, together with the cheese and biscuits he had asked for.

'You look tired out,' she said, though she didn't ask what merited wine at that time of night.

'The Gloucester investigation has got bigger and more complicated and there are now more victims,' he said, pouring himself a large one and cutting into the cheese. 'I'm not sure I'm up to this. I've never dealt with anything like it.'

She knew not to ask him to explain more. He had told her as much as he could. Even so, she was surprised, for it was not like her husband to doubt himself.

'I can't see that. What's brought this on? You always meet problems head-on, everyone knows that. One thing after another, you always do. What's different with this?'

Before he could answer, another question followed, 'What time do you have to be in, in the morning? If it's early again you better not have any more of that wine. Come to bed. You're just tired. It will seem different after you've had some sleep.'

As his wife left to go to bed he finished his glass, corked the bottle and cleared the table, hoping that she was right and her confidence was not misplaced.

FIFTEEN

The atmosphere in the briefing the following morning was electric. A good night's sleep had dissipated any self-doubt Bennett had had.

New teams of officers were allocated to each of the new victims and they had another look at who was involved with victims' families, the West family in particular, and what appeared to be the more important witnesses. Only those guarding Cromwell Street or working in the main office or press office were missing.

There was no need to go over much of what had happened the day before. A copy of West's note said it all and that was displayed in the MIR for all to see. Those who had missed the previous night's briefing had, by now, heard all about it on the grapevine.

Laying out the order of the day, Bennett said he would soon be briefing the Chief Constable and asking for the investigation to be managed under the contingency plans for a major incident. If agreed, more staff would arrive, including extra help in the press office, and the command structure would change – though he would still be the Senior Investigating Officer and Terry Moore his deputy.

Mr and Mrs Gough, he said, had now been told that Fred West had admitted killing their daughter, Lynda.

Terry Moore explained what happened when West was taken back to 25 Cromwell Street, for although West claimed to be still unsure of exactly how many he had killed, he was able to indicate where he had buried four of his victims in the cellar: 'Lucy' (Partington), 'a Worcester girl', 'a girl from Newent', 'a Dutch girl', and another under the bathroom – 'Lynda Gough'.

He also told them Charmaine, the other missing daughter, was buried at 25 Midland Road in Gloucester, and Rena, his first wife, in a field at Kempley near the village of Much Marcle on the Gloucestershire–Herefordshire border.

This made the number still to be found seven and, with the other three already recovered, ten victims in all.

The biggest question now was what was to happen to Rose West. Would she be arrested again?

Bennett, though, was unwavering.

Nothing would be lost, he said, by biding their time; to arrest her now would add unnecessary pressure when they still weren't fully sure what they were dealing with. Rose West, he promised, would be arrested but he would decide when and that may not be for some time.

As the briefing drew to a close Bennett made a special point of publicly praising Hazel Savage for the way she had followed up the story of Heather West being buried under the patio. Many, he said, would have just ignored it even against the background of the 1992 investigation, but Hazel Savage had shown tenacity in following up her enquiries and insight in bringing it all forward, which now, sad as it was, would end the uncertainty for a number of families.

Perhaps embarrassed by this tribute, Savage said she hoped those who had lost their loved ones could now grieve, though she didn't feel she had done anything more than many others would have.

Now that Fred West had admitted ten killings, detectives had to draw more information from him to help them identify his victims, trace their relatives and then get him to explain how they died. This would not be easy, for he had not been very forthcoming over Shirley Robinson and even less her mate, never mind Lynda Gough.

Back at Gloucestershire Police Headquarters, Bennett was explaining to Ken Daun how he saw the investigation developing under the Gold, Silver and Bronze command structure. They also discussed how to get the extra staff he needed.

Joining Bennett and the Head of CID for this crucial planning meeting were Chief Superintendent Geoff Cooper, who was in charge of the county's three policing divisions, Chief Superintendent Colin Stabler (Operations and Traffic Division), Assistant Chief Constable Bob Turnbull and the Chief Constable, Tony Butler.

Tony Butler had become the Chief Constable of Gloucestershire in August 1993 on promotion from the Leicestershire Constabulary, where he had served since 1987, first holding the post of Assistant, then Deputy Chief Constable. He had a joint honours degree in sociology and psychology from the University of Birmingham and had continued his study of the psychological implications of police work to obtain a PhD. He was on the Association of Chief Police Officers' crime committee, had written two books on police management and regularly contributed to professional journals on child abuse.

In the six months since Tony Butler's arrival, Bennett, as a member of his senior management team, had got to know him. While he left no doubt as to his rank, he was amiable, easy to speak to and his usual greeting of 'Right, right, come on in, mate' or 'What are we up to today, matey?', though taking some getting used to, was endearing.

His mood could change though when he felt he had been let down and he did not like being caught unawares.

The Chief Constable listened to Bennett's presentation and, having sought a second opinion from Daun, agreed the investigation should now be classed as a 'major incident' and managed along the lines of the force plan.

As 'Gold Commander' the Detective Chief Superintendent would be responsible for the wide-ranging overview of command and policy. In this case he would more likely advise chief officers on issues of concern and ensure a two-way flow of strategy and policy between them and the investigation.

Bennett would be the 'Silver Commander' responsible for everything to do with the direction and everyday running of the investigation, with Terry Moore his deputy.

The 'Bronze' command, the operational level, responsible to 'Silver' would be split into four. Inspector Richard Bradley, a headquarters-based police search adviser who had already been involved at Cromwell Street, would be the search coordinator; Hilary Allison would be responsible for media relations with Chief Inspector Colin Handy, the force press officer before the post had been civilianised, to assist her; the logistics officer would be Inspector Wayne Freeth-Selway who would provide staff and equipment; the incident room manager would be Detective Inspector Mike Wilson.

Using a flip chart to explain, Daun went through the wide-ranging implications this would have on CID. Some departments would be deployed completely to the West Inquiry, other investigations would be shelved and, if necessary, extra staff would have to come from headquarters and the divisions, for what Bennett was asking for was only the minimum requirement and no one knew whether it would be enough. Certainly, more uniform staff would be needed once the media got wind of the other areas that may be searched.

Agreeing with the proposed structure, the Chief turned to Bennett and asked him how everyone was coping, telling him to pass on his thanks for the work they had done and the way it was coming over in the media. Then he told the meeting, 'John can seek all the advice he needs, I've no problem with that, it's essential. We will supply him with the staff he needs to deal with this, everyone left behind will just have to work harder to cover. I'm not going to have it suggested we should be amalgamated and cannot cope because we are too small by asking for mutual aid [help from other forces]. I'm not going to be the last Chief Constable of Gloucestershire!'

The Chief then said he would talk to the chief executive of the county council and discuss the issues with the Area Child

Protection Committee. As there were deaths of children (Heather and Charmaine) within the West family there would need to be a review, as required by the Children Act. It was also becoming apparent that children from care homes had visited Cromwell Street, and there would have to be an investigation into how this had gone on for so long. An independent body would have to look into it and it was not long before a Chief Officers' Strategy Group was set up and the Bridge Consultancy contracted to undertake these reviews.

Less than 30 minutes later Bennett was back in Gloucester. Fred West was being interviewed again and arrangements were being made to take him out to where he said he had buried Rena.

The media still appeared unaware of West's latest admissions but Janet Leach had commented to officers that he had suggested she ought to sell her story to the newspapers. As the appropriate adult she had sat in on all the interviews and knew as much about his confessions as anyone. This immediately rang alarm bells with Bennett. He was still worried about how secure she might be and while it reminded him to get her tied to a confidentiality agreement, he was also concerned the effect of being so locked in to such a unique and stressful investigation might have on the rest of her life. He would ensure that she was given the opportunity to stand down. Apart from that he could do little more. Her role and her appointment were based on impartiality, to ensure that West was treated as he should be. It was not something that he could interfere with and neither he nor the police service owed any more responsibility of care to her than they did to West's solicitors.

But Janet Leach was not his only media-related problem.

Detective Sergeant Roger Kelland was part of the 'Shirley Robinson' team and had been contacted both by relatives of the dead girl and police officers from the force where they lived. They were angry that despite his assurances the police would not reveal their whereabouts it had got out and reporters had been to their home. On top of that, it looked as though the press office was responsible. Despite his apology, they were going to complain. Worse still, they had lost confidence in him and that would be hard to regain.

Hilary Allison explained that information about the area of the country where they lived had been taken from the press log rather than the agreed press release. She also told him of renewed speculation about more 'bodies' at Cromwell Street. How they had picked this up she had no idea though it seemed that the Mirror Group newspapers' reporters were the best informed, closely followed by the *Sun*, *News of the World* and *Daily Star*.

There would be no more news conferences at Gloucester Police Station and certainly not in the club where the briefings were held.

Mr and Mrs Gough had been brought up to date but it now appeared that Lynda did not go missing in 1972 but 1973. June Gough had looked at the pedigree certificate of a dog they bought when Lynda was with them, and a photograph. The dog was born and collected in 1972. Mrs Gough recalled Lynda had gone on a Thursday, 19 April. This date fell on a Thursday in 1973 not 1972. She had been a year out.

Whether this inaccuracy had encouraged West to deny he knew Lynda or that she had been at Cromwell Street no longer mattered. It was the realisation that the police were not put off by his denials and would eventually get to the truth that forced him to change tack. His wife wearing Lynda's clothes was something he could explain only if he 'remembered' Lynda's mother's visit. If he denied it took place then he could not.

Relatives of Lucy Partington were also contacted and told that West had admitted killing their daughter. Ever since Lucy went missing in 1972 her parents had maintained a dignified approach to everything that followed. It was their way of dealing with their sad loss, and, when reporters tracked them down, they offered only guarded comment and support for the police.

At Cromwell Street, the ground-penetrating radar was being trawled across the areas where West had painted the red-circle markers. Initial soundings indicated the earth beneath the concrete was different in composition to other parts of the cellar.

In the MIR they were still trying to work out how best to categorise all the information pouring into the HOLMES database. Following up queries from the public regarding the identity of Remains 2; checking social services files, tracing missing people and establishing they were safe and well all generated more work; tracking back down the years, going over not just the Wests' background but that of anyone who had been at Cromwell Street or Midland Road. Bennett wanted to see 'every milkman, postman, neighbour, workman, friend, anyone and everyone that had passed their doors or knew them'. He wanted to know 'every vehicle the Wests had owned or had access to, and everywhere he had worked or visited socially'. On the face of it, this was an indexer's nightmare – but they had to keep on top of it.

Just before midday, Bennett was told that the excavation in the cellar had turned up further evidence of human remains.

The work was stopped as the same procedure they had used on the three previous discoveries kicked in. The conditions beneath the concrete were similar to those in the garden. These would be Remains 4.

So far West had been unable to say who was buried where. He had even changed his mind on where he had buried them. This could have been due to stress, tiredness or a combination of both. Then again, he had never expected to have to tell anyone and to him murdering and burying was not something worth remembering, just something he did when necessary. Another of the areas he had marked would be penetrated soon and another search begun.

By now West had made some drawings of the cellar and marked on them the names of girls he remembered and where he had hidden them. He was rambling again so although it looked like he was helping, he might have thought he was regaining control.

He was asked to go over where Charmaine was buried in the flat in Midland Road and went into great detail about how he had killed her after killing Rena. He said he did it soon after being released from Leyhill Prison, but he didn't dismember her body and he buried her in her clothes wrapped in a blanket.

The arrival of Bennett and Moore, this time on foot, caused a flurry of activity in St Michael's Square among reporters and news crews who were gathered around just waiting for something to happen, for they still seemed unaware of how the search was going. Approaching from the rear of Cromwell Street the sound of drilling got louder as they reached the stairs and headed down into the cellar. The air was filled with concrete dust and small chips were flying as an officer disguised by his protective clothing continued to attack the concrete floor with a pneumatic drill. He had just broken through in front of an open fireplace. Almost opposite on the floor on the other side of the room was a hole approximately 3ft × 2ft in front of a false fireplace. In it they could make out a thick, black, waterlogged clay-like sludge.

The drilling stopped and Beetham showed them what seemed to be remains in the hole. There was no need to look further, the unmistakable smell of adipocere was there, not masked at all by the stagnant liquefied substance. Bennett commented upon this as Beetham pointed to an area in the hole where what looked like bone protruding could just be seen.

Bennett had intended to give the diggers Sunday off, but not now. While the media remained in the dark they could get on with the work without that added pressure. If what West had told them was true they might be able to find all his victims by Monday when it was hoped the Prof could visit again.

They were now well and truly on a treadmill.

With no time to see what was in the second hole, Bennett and Moore headed back to the MIR to continue planning for the next few days. When they got there it was to be told that Beetham had phoned in to say more remains had been found – and there was more disturbing news from the press office.

Questions were coming in from reporters, principally Howard Sounes of the Mirror Group, who said the following day's *Sunday Mirror* would report that the investigation had found five more bodies and that the police were going to search at places other than Cromwell Street. Hilary Allison suggested a press conference later in the day would reduce calls to the press office and give them the chance to correct any inaccurate speculation. Bennett was not sure. He knew there was not much he could say and he did not want to cause unnecessary suffering for families already anxious about missing relatives. But he knew the sort of story he envisaged going out would have that effect and there was nothing he could do to stop it. And any conference would have to be in the police station because they had not yet been able to find anywhere else!

It was obvious to Bennett there was a leak – possibly someone who was in on the interviews, though it could in fact be almost anyone involved in the investigation.

That afternoon Fred West was taken out to Kempley on the Gloucestershire–Herefordshire border. There'd been a slight delay because reporters had staked out the backyard exit to the police station. Once there, in a field named after the nearby letterbox, not far from the village of Much Marcle where he spent most of his childhood, 20–30yd uphill from the road, he pointed to the spot where he had buried his first wife Rena West, and marked it with a piece of wood.

The evening briefing began with Detective Constable Malcolm Wood, the video recordist, showing pictures of West being taken back to Cromwell Street. It was the first time many of the team had seen him and witnessed for themselves his mannerisms, how he talked and his unaffected way of describing what he had done. From their expressions it was clear they could hardly believe what they were seeing.

Bennett told them of his meeting with the Chief Constable earlier in the day and that the media now knew West had admitted more killings, though he decided this was not the time to dwell on his fears of a leak.

Team spirit was good and they were making more progress than they could have hoped. The different teams were also gathering information about their allocated victims:

- The 'Worcester girl': there was a girl outstanding from a children's home and West said he knew where this girl lived in Worcester.
- The 'Dutch girl': West said she was a hitch-hiker. She came from Holland. She had a badge with a truck on it so he called her 'Truck'. They would follow it up through Interpol on Monday.
- The 'Newent girl': from what West had said, she was living there, had a father in America and relatives in Gloucester. There was a possibility her name was Juanita Mott. It wasn't definite but a sister had been found and she was being seen.

Someone also mentioned that West regularly talked about a girl he knew and referred to as Annie, an Ann McFall who had apparently been living with him at Much Marcle in the midsixties, near where he said Rena was buried.

West had also said that Charmaine would not be found as she might have been removed when the foundations were dug out for an extension at Midland Road. He was there then, and had looked for her, but had been unable to find her.

The short briefing had covered a lot of ground. Next was the news conference that Bennett was far from looking forward to.

At about the same time, in another part of the building, West had asked to see Hazel Savage and Darren Law and was telling them of two more victims, one of them another girl from Worcester.

By 7.30 p.m. all the television crews, radio and newspaper reporters had gathered in the police station social club. Once again there were more there than the last time.

Bennett looked down at the carefully worded statement he had written with a few alterations from Hilary Allison. She was seated on his left, Moore on his right. There was sadness in his voice as he read the following:

This afternoon, police searching 25 Cromwell Street Gloucester, discovered what they suspect are the remains of two further human beings. Excavations will stop shortly (in about half an hour) and will begin again tomorrow.

Home Office pathologist, Professor Bernard Knight, will not be attending the scene until Monday at the earliest, when the latest findings will be confirmed or otherwise.

While the identities of these suspected remains haven't been established, we have contacted relatives of two people who we believe may be able to help us if the remains are identified as human. Both of these families are from Gloucestershire and only one of the two people has been officially reported to the police as missing. At the request of the families, we are unable to elaborate further on the question of identification at this time.

With reporters hanging on his every word, he explained that the specialist equipment had indicated a number of readings in the ground-floor area but the results were still to be analysed. The ground radar only detected disturbances in the ground, things like pipes and sewers, and was not 'a body or skeleton detector'. The whole of 25 Cromwell Street would be methodically searched, though how long that would take was impossible to tell. Only when that was done would they search in two other, for now unspecified, areas of Gloucestershire.

Some of the questions that followed had already been asked at previous conferences, some he had only just answered. As far as Bennett was concerned, this was irritating, time-wasting and unnecessary, and once again he had difficulty in hiding his true feelings. It took over an hour but at least he had managed to hide Fred West's note, West's visits to Cromwell Street and Kempley and the number of victims he had now admitted killing – though exactly how much was known by the press would be revealed the next day.

SIXTEEN

It was the *Sunday Mirror* that told Bennett what he wanted to know, or at least some of it. The newspaper was not only reporting for the first time how many victims were buried at 25 Cromwell Street, it also published a detailed diagrammatic plan of the three-storey house, pointing out exactly where each of them was buried.

It also coined the headline 'The House of Horrors' – the first time the Wests' home had been described like that and a name by which it became universally recognised from then on.

That the *Sunday Mirror* had the story did not surprise Bennett. Its reporters had always been ahead of the rest. Any lack of detail, he thought, was probably intended to protect their source, for now there could be no doubt someone was leaking information and it would only be a matter of time before the media would be on to the other places they were planning to search. From now on they too would have to be guarded, using resources the force could ill afford.

By contrast, the huge amounts of money the media was prepared to throw at potential witnesses was an even bigger headache, as were rumblings from some reporters questioning his and the force's ability to handle such a complex investigation.

There was concern, too, at the pressure the media was exerting on the West family.

Rose, Stephen and Mae may have been under police protection but that did not stop reporters trying to track them down. Their safe house was more like a prison. Contact with the outside was restricted to the telephone or Stephen and Mae's liaison officer, Detective Constable Clive Stephens. Rarely did either of the children venture out and never at the same time for fear their mother might harm herself.

It was clear to the police listening in that all this was putting a considerable strain on the family unit, but if the police were hoping it would lead to Rose letting slip more about what she knew, it had not happened yet, and when the stress boiled over into a violent argument between Stephen and Mae, and Stephen could be heard remonstrating with his sister, they were in a real dilemma: how to check if Mae was all right without giving away how they knew what had happened. They got around it by sending local officers who said a neighbour had reported the row. Neither Stephen nor Mae was visibly injured, nor did they suspect the truth.

The occupants of 25 Midland Road would soon have to be told their property was going to be searched below the extension and they would have to move out. Another warrant would be needed to search Letterbox Field.

The National Missing Persons Helpline, the charity that none of the team had heard of before but which regularly featured in the media, had been contacted and was overrun by enquiries, especially since the reports were of more 'bodies' rather than 'remains'. The charity had offered to help in tracing both Charmaine and Rena. It had an artist and age progression computer software that could be used to produce a picture of how they might look now. The police were convinced Rena was dead but also knew they could not rely on what Fred West was telling them. If she was alive and living with her daughter, great, but very embarrassing if the police had already said they thought she had been murdered. Issuing an image through the media might not find her, but it could flush out others who knew her.

It had become an investigation like no other, not least because everything was the reverse of how events normally developed. Most murder inquiries begin with a body. That has to be identified and its killer sought through a combination of police work and media appeals for witnesses and information. Here, they already had a killer who was telling them where his victims were. The police just had to establish who they were and how they died. As for the media, instead of helping it just seemed to be frustrating the investigation at every turn and causing the police more work.

An early morning briefing had been scheduled, shorter than usual but just as revealing:

- When mentioning Ann McFall, West had talked about her being somewhere in the same field as Rena – and that it was Rena who killed her not him!
- It was decided there and then that Mcfall should be the subject of further detailed investigations and 'owned' by an inquiry team – just like all the other victims.
- West also said he was wrong about the 'Dutch girl', she was still alive. The dead girl might be German.
- He accepted that Juanita Mott was one of his victims as he could remember a girl with a distinctive name like that.
- As for his admission there were 'two Worcester girls', West Mercia Police had records of three young women who were missing, though they could only find details of a girl named Carol Cooper who had disappeared in 1973.

While all this was being discussed, the digging team from Cheltenham continued their excavation of the areas in the cellar at 25 Cromwell Street that West had marked in red paint, first drilling through the floor, then slowly removing by hand what was beneath. At 9.02 a.m., they were working near the left wall, in between the partial dividing centre walls, when John Rouse spotted what was to be Remains 6. Bennett and Moore were told on their return to the MIR.

To add to the workload, letters were now flooding into the office, some addressed to the Chief Constable, some to Bennett personally, and others simply to the 'Cromwell Street Murder

Investigation' or a version of it. If any contained information helpful to the inquiry, the relevant action was taken and noted but that was rarely the case. Some of the letters offered prayers, support or thanks to the officers involved in the digging. Some offered advice on how best to continue the investigation. Others were from professional gardeners and gravediggers with views on how best to dig and clean spades, even suggesting they might be of help.

And, of course, there were the saddest letters of all – from families desperately trying to trace relatives, now believing them to be victims of Fred West.

Bennett had already replied to some and made it a policy to answer them all personally within two days.

A contingency plan for moving out the occupants of 25 Midland Road and all that entailed was now a priority and, under the newly implemented major incident plan, would be the responsibility of Chief Superintendent Ken Daun at 'Gold', Inspector Wayne Freeth-Selway, logistics, and Inspector Richard Bradley, the search coordinator. Bennett had already briefed Daun who would brief the others.

For Bennett, double-checking reviews of the missing person files on Mary Bastholm and Lucy Partington was even more of a priority since West had confessed to killing Lucy. Uppermost in his mind was whether the investigation in 1973 had made any mistakes and missed something that connected the young student with Fred or Rose West or Cromwell Street. The similarity in both girls' disappearance was obvious and one the media had already picked up on, though West himself had not, as yet, admitted knowing Mary Bastholm.

Lucy Partington's relatives, as expected, had kept what they had been told completely confidential. To reporters they confirmed only that the investigation had been in contact with them, reaffirming their confidence in the police and that they were being kept informed of developments, all of which was true. Similarly, Mary Bastholm's brother, her only surviving close relative, had been told of the lines they were following, although it was extremely unlikely his sister was buried at Cromwell Street since the Wests didn't begin living there until some years after her disappearance.

At 11.50 a.m., Bob Beetham phoned in with news of another set of remains, Remains 7, underneath the cellar floor beneath the stairs where conditions were the same as in the other cellar holes and not much dryer than those in the garden. West's 'memory' of where he had buried these victims was proving to be quite accurate, though recovering Lynda Gough's remains from under the bathroom would be much trickier. According to West, this part of the extension was built over an old garage pit. When he put Lynda there he filled it in with dirt and debris. Excavating her remains without making the building even more unstable would be more difficult and dangerous than anything they had done before.

Early that afternoon there was a flurry of activity among reporters outside the police station.

Officers had been watching 25 Midland Road and the Fingerpost Field at Kempley for some time when suddenly the area around the entrance to the police station, normally awash with journalists and cameramen, emptied. Moments later, the constable on guard at Midland Road reported a convoy of reporters turning into Midland Road, stopping to look at No. 25 then after a short while moving off again en bloc. Within half an hour there were similar scenes at Kempley. Bennett's worst fears had been realised. A round-the-clock guard would now have to be positioned at both locations, *more* expense the investigation could ill afford.

As expected, Howard Ogden carried out his threat to lodge a formal complaint of contempt of court against the *Citizen* newspaper for reporting that Fred West had admitted killing his daughter Heather. As far as Bennett was concerned, it would be up to the Attorney-General to decide what action to take, but he knew that first an investigation would have to be conducted by the Gloucestershire Constabulary, and by officers not on the murder inquiry. It seemed an appropriate time to see Ogden about the leaks to other newspapers.

Ogden had just finished seeing his client when they met at the cell block. With nowhere else available they settled for a converted cell normally used to interview juveniles.

Bennett got straight to the point. He accepted information might be coming from the police or the appropriate adult but he was also concerned that Ogden's clerks could be to blame.

Perhaps the solicitor took it as a personal attack for his manner switched from pleasant and easygoing to rather arrogant and pompous. He defended his clerks and claimed that Janet Leach had been more responsible for West's confessions than the police, a suggestion Bennett thought strange coming from a defence solicitor. Visibly rattled, the solicitor told Bennett to 'look to his own' before accusing the defence.

By the time they got around to discussing Fred West's next appearance in court, the atmosphere between the two men had more or less returned to normal and Ogden said he would not be objecting to a further remand in custody.

With that they went their separate ways.

By just after 9 p.m. that night Bennett had had enough.

As he reached his car in the dimly lit rear yard, he could see how dirty it was, something he never allowed to happen and an indication of how little time he had had to himself since the inquiry began. He *never* used a car wash – but tonight was different. He was tired, it was dark and he was low on fuel. The petrol station on Westgate Bridge was just around the corner and pretty much on the way home; he could do it all there.

The wash and wax package took about 5 minutes and was probably the first time he had felt relaxed all day, but as he left the forecourt he noticed a man in a raincoat with a yellow scarf suddenly dart out of sight. As he pulled onto the main road two sets of headlights appeared in his rear view mirror.

Approaching the Longford roundabout he realised the vehicle that was behind him when he left the garage was still there and another vehicle was immediately behind it. Was he being followed? Surely not? Pure paranoia.

He negotiated one roundabout and then another and still both vehicles followed, dropping back only slightly. Convinced they were following him he accelerated and then slowed for about half a mile until he reached the Elmbridge Court roundabout, which he took at a virtual snail's pace. The first vehicle was, by then, so close the driver could do nothing but follow. The second waited to join the roundabout as Bennett went round for a second time before branching off and accelerating – with both vehicles in pursuit!

It was obvious they were following him and he was annoyed. It didn't matter who they were, though he suspected they were reporters, for they were no match for his anti-surveillance skills and local knowledge, which took him up a side road and into the rear entrance of a local hospital where he stayed for a quarter of an hour until he was sure the coast was clear. If they thought he was on the job that was bad enough; if they were trying to get to his home and family that was unacceptable – and was it just him or could others on the investigation expect the same treatment?

He would have to tell everyone what had happened at briefing the next morning. That would go down really well with those who had already made it clear they thought they were doing too much for the media.

SEVENTEEN

Fred West's confessions had broadened the scope of the investigation considerably, increasing the pressure on the inquiry team's ability to analyse all the information it was collecting.

Within the MIR Scriv continued to wrestle with the complexities of the HOLMES system, reconfiguring indexes, categories and sub-categories, creating files from files, all of which was designed to meet the ever-changing needs of the investigation.

Witnesses receiving payment for their stories required a sub-category of 'Witnesses paid/signed up to the media'. There was a sub-category for those who 'Lived in 25 Cromwell Street', another for those who 'Visited 25 Cromwell Street'. One for those who had 'Sexual relations with Fred', one for 'Sex with Rose', another for 'Sex with both'. The list just kept on growing and included everything that was known about the Wests; previous investigations like those involving Caroline Owens, Mary Bastholm and Lucy Partington. The complete record of everything taken from Cromwell Street then and before, more than 1,300 items in all, had to go on the exhibits system in the user-friendliest way, for who knew what information might be needed or when?

Bennett's insistence on up-to-date charts became a standing joke as every morning, before doing anything else, he made straight for Mark Grimshaw's 'computer corner'. Grimshaw's familiar cry in mock anguish of 'Oh no, not another dream?' was based on the Senior Investigating Officer's normal opening that he had a new idea, one that had come to him that morning in the shower, and he would then describe a chart or some aspect of one he wanted him to create.

Producing charts was not a problem for Marco but because there was no software readily available that would transfer the data from HOLMES into his software, the huge volume of information had to be entered manually. It was an extremely meticulous, time-consuming job, which was why Detective Constable Nick Churchill, from the Force Intelligence Bureau, was enlisted to work alongside him as a researcher. He, like Bennett, came from Stroud and had worked many times before with the Senior Investigating Officer and his deputy. While Grimshaw's interest was more in software, Churchill's was directed to programming and they became two complementary parts of an important team.

Another significant addition was Detective Sergeant Dave Griffiths, the transcript reader, another post made necessary by the number of tape-recorded interviews with Fred West. Each had to be transcribed and checked. The tapes of the bugged conversations of Rose also had to be checked against their summaries, although for now they would not be transcribed. Griffiths, or 'Griff', genial in manner, was also very experienced in HOLMES-based investigations and had worked with Bennett before. Among his talents was an astute eye for detail and accuracy. He was earmarked to take over the key role of statement reader and then receiver, whose job would include preparing the papers for court, a major task in itself. It was not long before he realised that he was, coincidentally, involved with the Wests, as in about 1991 Rose West had rented a flat at 56 Stroud Road in Gloucester, where he had rented a flat in 1978, and also that his aunt and godmother had helped the parents of Fred West to move house in 1941.

Joining them in the MIR were Detective Constable Tina West and Police Constable Chrissie Mannion, both experienced officers and HOLMES indexers who were always in demand for major inquiries.

The updated charts Bennett had ordered now adorned the walls and screens around the room. Some showed how and when the outside of 25 Cromwell Street had been extended down the years, others revealed changes to rooms, the cellar and garden, with numbers marking where the remains were found. A copy of the master chart, which was constantly being modified in line with Bennett's latest thinking, hung on his office wall so he and Moore could see it whenever they sat in their chairs.

The pace of it all was remorseless.

The number of 'missing' people they needed to trace continued to grow. The vast amount of property taken from the Wests had to be checked to see what leads it might produce. Processing the information coming in so that it was ready for the interviewing teams when they wanted it was a near impossible balancing act and one which officers not used to the HOLMES system often questioned. There was so much research to be done yet it had to be readily available if West's interrogators were to extract the maximum detail of the murders and his victims from him. It was imperative that the indexing in the MIR was up to speed, but equally that the transcriptions of West's interview tapes kept pace, for only then could there be proper analysis of what the investigation had uncovered.

The only answer was to farm out some of the work to other parts of the force. Gold command would have to sort it out, which was why the Gold, Silver and Bronze structure was put in place.

With all this going on, Bennett had almost forgotten he had to call the CPS. Its chief prosecutor Roger Fry had made a promise and he was about to hold him to it.

'How many do you think he's killed? Is it more than what you've found?' the lawyer asked.

Bennett could only tell him about West's note and that what he had put in it seemed to be accurate.

True to his word, Fry at last acceded to Bennett's request to use his special caseworker Withiel Cole and promised to make the necessary arrangements. Bennett was already expecting to see Cole that morning to review a long-running child abuse investigation. To say he was pleased to get his man at last was an understatement.

The sound coming from the police social club as Bennett and Moore made their way to briefing that morning was noticeably louder. This was now the largest team of officers the Gloucestershire Constabulary had ever committed to an investigation and those in front of him were still only the tip of the iceberg, for there were many more regular and special constabulary officers and civilian staff involved in other parts of the county – and the numbers were likely to grow.

Apart from all the new arrivals, he had asked for as many as possible to be there.

Bennett began by welcoming the newcomers and praising again the efforts of those still involved and the few who were about to return to their normal duties.

What happened next he hadn't planned yet it seemed to strike a chord. He compared them to 'troops on the front line' and said they were engaged in a 'war' with 'enemies on all sides'; some they would quickly become aware of, others were disguised. There may even be 'agents' within – a reference to all the leaks.

'You are all in the front line, every rank. You are not alone and will all stay together. There will be casualties and these will be on all sides, but if you do what you are told and act properly then it will not be you.'

Intelligence, accuracy and communication up and down were the keys to success. So far they had 'attacked all of the known enemies and defended, or were defending, some counter-attacks. We have also invaded some areas and are advancing, in others where we are in unknown territory we are still on the beaches.'

He finished with a warning they may need to dig in from time to time, to get reinforcements or re-equip themselves, and that without their total and combined commitment, loyalty, effort and ideas on how to succeed they would quickly lose ground, battles and the war.

As he spoke, it was clear he had not only captured their attention but what he said was going down well – except that just as he finished and the room fell silent for a moment, the mood was shattered by a tune from . . . the fruit machine. The smiles changed to laughter. It was a moment of light-hearted relief they would often recall, though not again that day.

Once order was restored, Bennett again stressed their duty of confidentiality. The *Sunday Mirror*, he said, had revealed details that should have stayed inside the investigation. It had talked of 'Shirley's friend' being her lesbian lover, terms used only by West, as well as gaps in the West family tree he had been asked to fill.

He then went on to being followed the previous night and how he thought it was the media, warning them all to be on their guard. The story did not go down well, just as he knew it wouldn't.

'We should stop telling them anything.'

'Tell them it's *sub judice*.'

'Shut the press office.'

'Let the "scumbags" find out everything for themselves.'

'Scumbags' was not a term Bennett would have liked the media to know was being applied to them, not then or at any time, not least for fear of a backlash. Even so, he, too, was of the opinion the actions of a few reporters made it an apt description and one that would stick.

Now that Fred West was maintaining he had killed 'two Worcester girls' and not just one, it looked like a 15-year-old named Carol Ann Cooper who had gone missing from a children's home in Worcester on 10 November 1973 might be one of them. She was last seen catching a bus to her grandmother's at 9.10 p.m. that evening but never arrived and, despite a long and full investigation by West Mercia Police, she was never seen again.

Details of the investigation were on their way, along with information about another young girl missing from the same area.

Shirley Hubbard had disappeared on 14 November 1974, almost a year to the day after Carol Ann. She was a 15-year-old schoolgirl on work experience at a department store in Worcester, who vanished on her way home. West Mercia Police carried out another big operation but she, too, had not been seen since. Now, apart from limited personal details on a list of outstanding missing persons, there were no papers regarding her or the investigation, not even a photograph.

Fred West was saying both 'his' Worcester girls had been hitch-hikers whom he had picked up, he wasn't sure when, on the road to Tewkesbury, a small Gloucestershire market town. Either he was lying yet again, or only one or neither of these girls were the victims he was describing.

A large gathering of public, reporters and camera crews was blocking the entrances to Cromwell Street and parts of St Michael's Square. Extra barriers had to be put up to control the crowd. The interest in 25 Cromwell Street and the work that was going on there was so intense the police removed the street sign for fear it would be stolen as a souvenir or sold on the black market, for such examples of public enterprise were already commonplace.

Some house owners in the area were not only charging news crews for the use of their gardens or windows, but their toilets as well. Others were selling hot and cold drinks, sandwiches and bacon rolls from their doorways to anyone who would buy.

Officers with many, many years of service had never seen anything like it.

There was a lot to cram in that morning.

Bennett would be at Cromwell Street when the Prof explored each of the newly exposed areas showing evidence of human remains. It was possible that the work on the former garage pit where it was thought Lynda Gough was buried would be completed so he could examine those remains as well. That would make eight sets so far, though because of West's claims to have killed two Worcester girls instead of one, there was now some confusion about whether he was saying there were eight or nine victims buried there. They might just have to take him back again to refresh his memory. In any event Bennett had long ago decided to excavate every part of the ground and cellar to the depth of the Severn clay, so with or without his help they would find out eventually.

Knowing that the Prof was due at Cromwell Street, the media was clamouring not only to film him arrive but also inside the house. Bennett was happy to agree to the first request but definitely not the second, and not until the afternoon – give them what they wanted too soon and they would be baying for more.

Such was the interest in this story, reporters were now coming from all over the world and there was nothing he could do about that, or the particularly unhelpful and devastating speculation over who the victims were, how many there were or where the search would focus next. On top of that, some of the British tabloid newspapers were publishing free telephone numbers asking anyone who knew the Wests to contact them.

It was an intrusion into an investigation the like of which he had never encountered before and begged the question of who was conducting this inquiry, the police or the media?

Policing the media was more the Attorney-General's responsibility but Bennett was worried much bigger contempts than Howard Ogden's complaint against a local newspaper had been committed and these could play right into the hands of West's defence. Just because he had admitted the killings now did not mean he couldn't change his mind later. It all had to be settled through trial by jury, not by the media.

As Fred West was smirking his way through his latest appearance before Gloucester Magistrates Court, another routine hearing that lasted barely 2 minutes and saw him remanded back into custody for another three days, Professor Knight was being taken to Cromwell Street via St Michael's Square and in through the back – leaving the front door for his photo opportunity later.

The work in the bathroom cum washroom area was well under way.

A hole drilled through the concrete floor then widened had exposed soil and rubble and some brick walling, just as West had said. Getting this out safely without the sides collapsing was proving difficult and once again posed the question whether the extension should be completely demolished. Keeping it up was not only slowing down the work, it was also expensive. Bennett had already made up his mind; he just had to check the legal position.

With extra lamps to light up the claustrophobically cramped conditions next to the imitation fireplace, the Prof began his work in the hole thought to contain Remains 4. As before, only essential personnel were present: the video recordist, scenes of crime officers Beetham and Rouse who were overseeing the operation, Sergeant Pete Maunder and Inspector Richard Bradley, the Gold search coordinator, who was taking notes to help him plan for the search at Midland Road.

Again, the hole was full of semi-liquid mud, just as it was when it was opened the day before, though bigger now than when the remains were put there. Carefully, the Prof felt inside the black mud, gently clasping the bones within. The sodden conditions made it difficult to tell precisely how they had been buried.

Scraping some of the bones as he went along and identifying them as before, he pointed out cut marks on both femurs, some quite fine, saying they were definitely female and that dismemberment had probably occurred there. Next, he brought out a blackened, waterlogged, mud-soaked knotted loop approximately 14in in diameter, which looked as though it was made of cloth. This was carefully placed in an exhibit bag and labelled without further examination. Then, and obviously from close to where the cloth loop had been removed, he produced a skull and some hair, pointing out actual signs of decomposition in its cavity. Some of the foul-smelling adipocere could be seen, though they all knew it was there from the moment holes were drilled in the concrete the day before.

There was little doubt that although it had not been found around the skull like the belt in Remains 2, the cloth loop had been used for the same purpose. It had either come off the skull during decomposition, had moved in the mud or been thrown in with the remains – forensic examination would decide which. Whatever the conclusion, it looked like more evidence of the victim being bound to stop her from opening her mouth.

Two vertebrae, which the Prof said were from around the neck, also seemed to have cut marks on them, making it likely that decapitation had taken place there.

With all the main bones recovered, Bennett and Moore left the professor to his work and returned to the station, where they were to meet the parents of Lucy Partington.

Although there was little more Bennett could tell them, he knew they had always appreciated the way the investigation into Lucy's disappearance had been handled and being kept informed. Caring for all the victims' families, and keeping them up to date with developments, was high on his list of priorities, though finding the right words was always difficult and that morning even more so, for Lucy's parents had waited more than twenty years for news of their daughter, no doubt fearing the worst but always hoping for the best. Now the waiting was over, could there have been a more distressing outcome?

If Bennett was finding it upsetting after all his years in the job, how would his younger, less experienced officers cope?

The warrant to search for human remains in Letterbox Field at Kempley had been obtained and, like the others, would remain in force for a month. If it wasn't executed by then, they would apply for another, for although guarding three sites was costing money, Bennett did not want to start a new search before finishing the previous one.

Demolishing the extension at 25 Cromwell Street and rebuilding it if West successfully sued was likely to cost around £33,000. Just making it habitable could set the force back £20,000. The Chief Constable would have the final say but Bennett was still pondering the figures when Moore, Griffiths and Grimshaw arrived in his office for a meeting. Half turning towards them, with Gloucester Cathedral, swathed in scaffolding, visible through the window behind him, he blurted out, 'It's just got to come down.'

'Why?' protested Moore as the three of them burst into laughter.

It didn't take Bennett long to figure out that while he was referring to the Cromwell Street extension, they were winding him up about the cathedral.

Professor Knight's photo opportunity was fixed for his return from lunch. He would arrive via St Michael's Square, walk through the pathway of No. 23, turn left into Cromwell Street, then walk the few yards to No. 25 and pause at the front of the house. Terry Moore would lead the way. Once it was confirmed, there was even more frenzy as reporters, photographers and camera crews jostled with the public for the best vantage point. The crowd behind the metal barriers which lined the centre of the road from past No. 23 to beyond No. 25 stood four, six, even ten deep in places.

Bennett, on the other hand, decided to work on in his office and join the Prof at Cromwell Street later. He was becoming increasingly irritated by the costly, time-consuming extra work caused by pandering to the media – though he was equally determined never to give them an opportunity to complain about any lack of cooperation. In that way he knew he could justifiably point out their wrongdoings without them being able to complain it was because he had withheld information or kept them in the dark – which he knew they would if ever the need arose.

Having survived the media gauntlet, Knight's normally unruffled air was momentarily disturbed as he walked through the front door of 25 Cromwell Street and into the sanctuary it offered. It was not surprising. Moore had warned him what to expect but the size of the crowd, the flashing camera bulbs, the demands to 'turn this way', 'that way', 'hold up a hand', 'a thumb', 'smile', 'don't smile', was much more intense than he had envisaged.

At 2.25 p.m. the diggers from the Cheltenham Support Group uncovered clear evidence of human remains deep below the bathroom. It had been the most physically demanding find so far and brought the number of sets of remains to eight, four of which the Prof had yet to see.

'Which one do you want me to do next?' he asked, his composure restored.

A more difficult question to answer was whether they had found everything, for while this search had uncovered more remains, another area West had marked in the cellar had not. Now that he was saying there were two Worcester girls instead of one, did that mean eight in total or was there another one? Whatever the number, the truth would be revealed in time as the entire area was going to be excavated, though before they could do that, they had to fill the holes they had already dug with concrete to ensure there was no danger of the house moving or collapsing. The same process would have to be carried out systematically for each subsequent hole until the search was complete.

Within minutes the Prof was back in the hole in front of the open fireplace. He went about his work with pictures of Marilyn Monroe gazing down from the wall, his soft Welsh voice describing what he found as he came across it.

These were Remains 5.

The conditions were now barely worth a mention, so similar were they to every other hole excavated so far. The difference in clay tone marked out the exact spot where the remains were buried. Again, there were some fine cut marks on the upper part of the femurs and a deeper mark on one. Next came bones from the trunk along with some of the vertebrae, together identifiable as belonging to a young woman.

Slowly, Professor Knight moved more sludge until the top of a skull came into view. It was facing the wall. The victim had been dismembered into three parts, just like all the others, but something else had caught his eye.

Stooping, staring, using both hands to get at it, the Prof was puzzled. From his position, he could see something that for the moment no one else could. There seemed to be something around the skull. Slowly, ever so slowly, he lifted it free of the black, cloying, liquid mud. What it was still hadn't registered and as he turned and gently cleaned the outside he had to change his grip to get a better hold, as what appeared to be light-coloured tape was becoming dislodged. Even the Prof had stopped his commentary and the room was perfectly silent as everyone watched in sombre stillness. Slowly the sad realisation of what it was, told in their faces.

The skull was completely encircled in a mask made of overlapping tape – from around the forehead to down below the jaw. Every part of the head and face was covered, making it a blindfold as well. Sticking out from between the lower layers was a length of discoloured plastic tube about 1ft long.

Even the Prof was momentarily lost for words. As he turned the skull around to examine it from all angles the mask moved too. It was loose now, he explained, due to decomposition. When the victim was alive it would certainly have been tight against her skin. Keeping the mask in position, he turned the skull so that he could look up and inside from the base, pointing out as he did so that the tube went through the tape into the area where the girl's nostrils would have been, making it another 6 or 7in long and just under 1ft 6in all told.

No one could have anticipated finding anything quite as horrific.

Even with their combined years of experience, it visibly shocked everyone, from the professor, who as a pathologist had seen death and murder in the raw on countless occasions, to the seasoned old hands among the detectives and scenes of crime officers.

While the skull and mask were being preserved for closer examination later, Professor Knight got back to work and almost straightaway, from close to where he had just retrieved the skull, he brought out another piece of plastic tube which matched the tube in the mask and looked about the same length, 16–17in. There was little doubt that this one also went through the tape to act as a crude breathing pipe but had become dislodged.

When he had recovered all the main bones, the Prof climbed out of the hole, leaving the rest of the search to the scenes of crime officers.

'I wonder what we will find in the next one,' he commented solemnly.

There was no doubt everyone harboured similar thoughts.

Remains 6 were next. They were in the alcove on the main wall. Here, the Marilyn Monroe wallpaper was replaced by children's nursery figures. It was on the other side of the cellar directly below the ground-floor entrance hall Professor Knight had walked along when he arrived.

The hole was roughly the same size as all the others in the cellar. The mud around the side was slightly more solid, but not by much. Slowly once more, the filthy, fluid mess gave up its secrets – leg bones, femurs, all in the right order, some with fine cut marks, all belonging to a young woman. Other bones followed and then a 6-in black-handled kitchen knife.

Having recovered some vertebrae the Prof then found the skull, with its jaw facing upwards out of the hole. The truly appalling conditions made it difficult to see whether there was a mask or anything else, though close by was a length of thick cord made from two pieces knotted together in the middle, about 1ft long in total.

After slowly removing the skull he produced a 16–17-in loop of light-coloured tape, which had been wound round and round until it was about 4in wide. As he gently removed it he pointed out hairgrips and what looked like hair inside the loop where there would have been adhesive. Satisfied there were only small bones and teeth left in the hole, the Prof climbed out and left the rest of the work to the scenes of crime officers.

No one there doubted this was further evidence of another mask. It may not have been in place now but the grips and hair showed it had almost certainly been wrapped around the head at some time. The rope was probably used to tie her and, like the others, she appeared to have been dismembered.

Professor Knight climbed out of the hole and moved directly across to the opposite wall to the matching alcove under the stairwell to begin the retrieval of Remains 7. Everything else – lights, exhibit bags, labels, the video cameraman – were also moved into position. By now, nothing the Prof was likely to find would surprise anyone who'd been there throughout this grim operation and there was still the discovery in the bathroom to work on. If they found any more, he would have to come back.

As he leaned forward, his face betrayed the effort needed to free whatever it was he had hold of. Slowly some bones emerged, pulling with them others connected by something. Searching with his fingers, he delved further into the hole and gradually pulled out an upper arm bone which had some knotted plastic-covered rope attached, like a clothes line. It was wrapped around the bone near the elbow and at the other end, close to where it would have met the shoulder. It continued under what would have been the trunk, where there were two small loops about 18in apart, across to the bones of the right arm, around to the right knee and back around the femur in a loop. There was another piece of rope with loops but not now attached to anything.

The conditions made any immediate analysis virtually impossible, though the Prof could tell from the thigh bones this was yet another young girl and that her remains had either been folded or dismembered. No cut marks could be seen; she appeared to have been hog-tied, arms to legs, and the plastic rope bindings were only loose now because the flesh around the bones had decomposed.

As the professor slowly removed the skull, he found even more evidence of restraint. Despite the ever-present, foul-smelling, black runny mud it was obvious that a loop, made by entwining a number of different pieces of material, was wound around the skull from the top, down under the jaw then round to the back. Nearby was the last sizeable find, which although discoloured was obviously a pair of panties. Examining the skull more closely, he pointed to an area below and behind the right ear that looked like a depressed fracture. Whether it occurred before or after death would only be established through closer forensic examination back at the lab.

While the scenes of crime officers moved the equipment upstairs to the bathroom, it gave the Prof the chance to discuss what they still had to do.

Every burial site in the house had still to be checked to recover any more bones or other remains. The Prof was as sure as he could be there were no sizeable bones left. Some teeth may have been lost during decomposition but they should be found during the search that would be conducted after he had left. He would find out much more from his work at the laboratory in Cardiff. On the vital issue of identifying the remains, he would talk to Dr David Whittaker, an odontologist, and make the skulls and the restraints he had found available to him. DNA would be of little help due to the conditions in which the remains had been found.

As for everything else he had recovered, such as the various bindings that created the hideous home-made masks, he would leave Bennett to decide what he wanted examined in detail.

With Beetham and Rouse watching from above, Professor Knight climbed down the metal ladder into the narrow oblong pit. The hole in the bathroom floor was about 6ft deep and contained Remains 8 – according to West, those of Lynda Gough.

Earth, stone, household rubbish and other debris had been carefully removed, not only for closer examination, but also to give the diggers more room to work, for this rubble seemed to form the sides of the pit along with what was left of the brickwork. The council buildings expert Syd Mann was worried this 'sideways mining' had weakened the construction and that it could cave in at any minute. It also meant the men had all but bypassed what they were searching for as bone was found to the side rather than below them. To remove these remains would require even more careful 'mining' which the Prof would have to do himself. Even the slightest danger of collapse and Mann would order him out straightaway.

It had been claustrophobic and exhausting work for the Cheltenham Support Group Search Team but at least it was dry. They had worked in twos, changing over every 30 minutes – a system the Gloucester team working outside had adopted earlier. Now it was the turn of the professor, and the scenes of crime officers and everyone else there stood transfixed as Knight began slowly removing one bone after another from the side of the pit.

There was little room for him to move but he did not complain, identifying the bones as he found them. They did not seem to be in any anatomical order and were possibly even more jumbled than the other remains he had removed that day; many of them were missing, including some vertebrae – more, in fact, than elsewhere.

For the first time he was able to see what he was doing and what was there before removing it. The leg bones and femurs were slightly curved, confirming this was another young woman. Both had many fine cut marks around where they would have joined the hip so almost certainly she was dismembered and, as he delicately brought out the skull, there were more signs that she too had been gagged and possibly bound. There was an oval-shaped ring of overlapping tape around 15in in circumference, which seemed to be made up of a mixture of parcel tape and some other type of tape. A piece of material about 2in wide and 5in long was also found nearby.

And the day was not over yet.

West would have to be asked about these bindings, for his stories so far had not made any mention of masks or tying up. Perhaps that would move him to tell them who the girls were, as naming them was still their priority. Daun would have to be told the extension 'had to come down' and they needed to check on arrangements for searching 25 Midland Road. Finally, there was the briefing that the Deputy Chief Constable and Professor Knight had agreed to address.

Leaving Cromwell Street by the back entrance, the poignant events of the day and what they had seen were on the minds of everyone who had been there. Soon they would be going all over it again for the rest of the team. The question was, how much of it would get into the media? The sinister masks and bindings would top any story that had come out of the investigation so far. If it did get out the repercussions hardly bore thinking about. Inevitably, it would lead to more wild speculation in the press that would mean more work for them and more heartache for anyone missing loved ones. Of course, it was something that would have to come out at some time, preferably during the court process. If it came out now they would know for sure they had a leak within the team.

It also posed an additional set of questions.

What, when and how would Bennett tell the victims' families about their relatives and what had been found with them and what it all might have meant? And if the news did break before he was ready, what would he tell them then?

Though this thinking may have been professional, and more than troubled him, when he focused on what had happened to these young girls his mind turned to the awfulness of their plight. To them death must have been a welcome release; contemplating how any of them had suffered was unbearable.

Arrangements were made to take Fred West out to Letterbox Field again, once they were certain there were no reporters or photographers around. West needed to confirm where he had buried his first wife and elaborate on his ramblings about a former girlfriend named 'Ann McFall' – not that he had 'killed her mind, that was Rena!'

By the time Bennett arrived for the briefing with the Deputy Chief Constable and Professor Knight, he could tell by the looks on everyone's faces that news of what they had discovered that day had got around.

Most of them only knew the Prof either by sight or reputation. Few had heard him speak and they hung on his every word. Even through his soft Welsh tones there was a noticeable sadness as he referred to each of the remains by numbers for the benefit of the individual teams assigned to them. Many there looked down and momentarily closed their eyes as he described in detail his day's work.

As Bennett again mentioned his concern for everyone's health and welfare and reminded them of the availability of stress counselling, the tall, slim figure of the Deputy Chief Constable Nigel Burgess approached. He made his way to where Bennett and Moore were sitting and acknowledged them before turning towards the rest of the team. He complimented them on behalf of the Chief Constable, who, he said, was full of admiration for them and the work they were doing, as was he, though he also reminded everyone of their duty of confidentiality, warning them that as the investigation progressed media scrutiny would at some point switch between the police and social services and focus on how these murders could have occurred.

It was a mixed message but one Bennett welcomed. It also

brought the briefing to an end and as everyone got up to leave and he scanned the room, he couldn't help pondering on the long, testing and no doubt harrowing road that lay ahead of them all and that had he known what was in store, there wasn't a single person there he would not have wanted on this inquiry.

EIGHTEEN

Not content with eight victims, the media went into speculation overdrive.

Depending on which newspaper you read, the predicted body count rose from ten, to twenty, to forty and more. If some of the figures appeared fanciful, they were supported by equally fictitious 'informed sources close to the investigation'.

From published reports, the number of sites soon to be searched by the police appeared limitless and included a caravan site at Bishop's Cleeve near Cheltenham – because the Wests once lived there – and countless building sites and other locations around Gloucester where West had worked. Reporters found local residents now 'living in fear' their properties might be excavated because Fred West once did some building work there.

The ground radar equipment, which Bennett had stressed from the outset was not a body detector, was being written up as a 'wonder weapon'.

Of most concern were photographs of the cellar at 25 Cromwell Street that found their way into the newspapers. It was little consolation they had somehow come from the 1992 investigation. It was a breach of confidentiality, a possible contempt of court and another sign that very little if anything could be kept from news organisations prepared to throw unlimited sums of money and manpower at the story.

It was unlikely, therefore, that the 'official' release detailing Fred West's latest court appearance, the discovery of the eighth set of remains and the need to guard a field at Kempley would satisfy reporters and film crews who now arrived daily from America, Europe, the Far East and just about every other corner of the globe.

The extent and scope of the coverage was also the talk of the MIR. That, and the revelations of the day before, left them in no doubt – if indeed they ever were – of the volume of work they faced.

'I've just said to Grumpy, shall I ask JB if I should book the Christmas do?' joked Tina West.

'You might as well, there's no doubt some of us are going to be here longer than that.'

Mark Grimshaw had upgraded the master chart and the plans of the cellar and garden. This, plus the photographs they had, would be used to get West to show them in more detail what he had done and exactly where he had done it. They could then match that information to the nicknames and descriptions he had given of his victims in the hope it would help them find out who they really were.

Inside the actual cellar and bathroom, the search went on. The concrete cavities surrounding the pits where the remains had been recovered were widened so that the fine searching of the sludge could continue, though the most they expected to find were small bones, maybe some teeth, and toe- and fingernails. Even if they found nothing, the sludge would still have to be sieved just in case West's defence wanted to query their work.

The one remaining area in the cellar West had marked with red paint had so far revealed nothing so the diggers were having to go deeper.

Bob Beetham and John Rouse had been arranging for the remains found in the cellar and bathroom to be taken to the temporary mortuary at the police station where they would be cleaned up and photographed before being transferred to Cardiff. The main bones recovered by Professor Knight were preserved in numbered exhibit bins and boxes. The many smaller bones, teeth and nails recovered in the 'fine' search later were in smaller exhibit boxes. All of them were stored inside the house in an area specially set aside for the purpose. Everyone moved around it with reverence for it was a poignant reminder of the tragedy that was unfolding and all the work that had gone in so far.

The larger exhibits were due to be removed early that morning and Bennett felt the smaller containers should be treated with equal respect when they were taken out later, so he sent Detective Constable Sarah Morris to a haberdashers in the city with instructions to buy enough black material to cover them all. When she returned, he took the cloth to Cromwell Street and told Acting Sergeant Jim McCarthy he wanted it cut into large enough pieces to cover each of the boxes so they could be carried with dignity to a police vehicle.

Not everyone there was instantly comfortable with the idea. They were worried what the media might make of it, but Bennett argued it was the right thing to do and eventually they agreed. McCarthy, a big, burly officer, volunteered to carry out the boxes himself.

The press office was told to liaise with Cromwell Street before informing the media when it would happen and early that afternoon the solemn photo opportunity got under way.

Slowly and with as much dignity as he could muster, his head slightly bowed, his face fixed in sorrow, McCarthy carried the first of the remaining exhibit boxes, now draped in black, from the front door of 25 Cromwell Street to the waiting vehicle. As he passed, the uniformed officer on guard outside spontaneously bowed his head and saluted. The process was repeated for each of the boxes and became one of the most enduring images of the entire investigation.

Yes, it was a photo opportunity for the media, but the thought behind it was to show how everyone on the inquiry felt about the work they were doing and how they were going about it, for they had families of their own and wanted to show respect for these murdered young women whose true identities for the most part were still not known.

As the victims may have been killed any time in the previous twenty years or more, many dental records were no longer available. Practices had closed or relocated. Records were now on computer or had been misplaced – and, all the while, the list of possible victims was getting longer. Now it was made up of 'those most likely', based on the work they had done so far, and 'other names' suggested by the public and the missing persons helpline charity. In addition, names appeared in the media either directly or in news reports and they too had to be considered.

According to Professor Knight, Dr Whittaker had perfected an identification method that combined video photography with his expertise as an odontologist. It enabled him to identify a person from a skull with teeth in place even if there were no dental records available. To do this he needed a photograph to superimpose over the skull. That was it in a nutshell; Dr Whittaker could give the more detailed, scientific explanation later.

David Whittaker had been keen to help as soon as he was contacted. Like Professor Knight, who was both a colleague and a friend, he was highly regarded in his field, both at home and abroad. He was a reader in oral biology at the University of Wales College of Medicine Dental School in Cardiff as well as being a consultant. He had more than twenty-five years' experience in forensic dentistry behind him and had been involved in many police investigations as well as assisting with the identification of disaster victims. He had not only kept his own skills up to date, he was also a pioneer who had perfected new methods.

Neither Bennett nor Moore had met him before and they were keen to do so. Without the help of DNA, he seemed to offer their best hope of putting names to the eight sets of remains.

Short and wiry – ideal for mountaineering, which he loved – Dr Whittaker spoke in a quiet northern accent and in a disarming way that endeared him to the two detectives immediately. To their delight he was confident he could help them. More than that, he was eager to get down to work. In short, he was a dental version of the Prof – easy to talk to, easy to understand, someone for whom nothing was too much trouble either to explain or do.

First, he wanted to know if there were any 'possibles' – remains they were close to naming. The difficulties were explained to him, which included West changing his stories, altering times and locations.

He was told Heather West was thought to be Remains 1, Shirley Robinson Remains 3, Lynda Gough Remains 8 and Lucy Partington another, though there was confusion as to which. The others were being worked on and in some cases they were approaching the 'probable' rather than 'possible' stage. On the rest they had little information.

Dr Whittaker, or as he quickly became known to the team, 'Doc Whittaker' or 'the Doc', gave them a list of what he wanted from each of the names suggested to compare with 'their' remains. He was aware that Professor Knight would look at the remains first and he would tell him about things like healed broken bones and how they compared with medical records. For his purposes, he would like any dental records that were available and as many photographs of the missing person as possible – the more recent the better. Ideally, he wanted close-up, full-face, portrait-style photographs with teeth showing, and for each one he would like the negative – though they had to be careful not to send reverse photographs or negatives. Also important was the date the photograph was taken, proved if possible or estimated if not, with some level of proof as to any estimation. He also wanted to know the camera that was used, and if an additional lens was fitted, what it was and what speed and focal settings were used. Finally, he wanted to know what film was used, its make and speed and if the negative was not available, where the film had been developed.

The way the Doc had reeled off his list made it seem a simple exercise, though he made it clear he would happily settle for as much as they could get, accepting that might be less than half, especially in view of the time that had passed since the women had gone missing and been killed.

In truth, getting anywhere near that amount of information was a formidable task, though copies of the list were made and given to each of the individual remains' inquiry teams to do the best they could. It was agreed they would pass on any information they found straightaway and in return the Doc would contact the MIR every other day to keep them updated.

Forensically, all that was left was for Bennett and Beetham to decide which items would be sent to the forensic science lab at Chepstow and what they hoped to learn from them. Forensic science was an expensive part of any investigation and there was no point having items examined just for the sake of it.

Someone else had the idea of putting together a photograph album of each of the missing girls. These photos would be shown to West in the hope he would identify them. Also a police artist would draw the victims, based on West's description. This would be done before the photographs were shown, just to make sure he didn't end up describing one of the photographs. It was another example of this 'upside down investigation' – the offender trying to identify the victim rather than his investigators.

Although identification was their first priority, and trying to find any more victims, they would soon be moving to other locations. Rose West's involvement was never far from Bennett's thoughts, or those of the rest of the team, but there was still so much to find out about the Wests' lives together and Fred West was about to be remanded to prison, where his availability for interview would be greatly reduced. To get around this, Bennett decided to try and have him treated like a supergrass or as the prison service referred to them 'resident informer'.

The system had been used in the 1970s and 1980s for both terrorist and serious criminal investigations but it was fraught with pitfalls and was now rarely considered. By invoking section 29 of the Criminal Justice Act of 1961, Gloucester Police Station could become a virtual extension of prison, at least as far as West was concerned. This would mean he would be subjected to the same rules but not the prison regime's strict daily timetable. If he were in Horfield Prison in Bristol or Winson Green in Birmingham – two possible destinations – the regime would leave little time for any police interviews. If he was remanded to police custody, providing his solicitor and appropriate adult were available and he was given proper rest in between, then interviews could take place at any reasonable time and any day 'in house'. There would be no 70–100-mile round trips to Bristol or Birmingham, no time-consuming security checks and the minimum upheaval for police, lawyers and the appropriate adult.

Certainly, they needed to make the most of every opportunity, for time was not their ally. With West's propensity for storytelling and so much still to learn about his victims – who they were and how they had met their deaths – it was obvious they would need to conduct more interviews than could be crammed into the next three days at Gloucester Police Station. Running against and beating the various legal clocks that existed to ensure the care and custody of prisoners was the bane of most police investigations, but in this inquiry, with its almost daily contortions, it was even more of an occupational hazard and one that had dogged them since the beginning.

The whole thing depended on Fred West agreeing and the Home Office granting the application, but Bennett knew that Gloucester Police Station cells met the Home Office criteria for long-term detention of prisoners. If there was a problem Cheltenham and Stroud were both only 9 miles away and the cells there were suitable as well. If Ogden and West accepted the proposition, he could make the application straightaway. Given the nature of the investigation and its growing notoriety he might even get it rushed through for Friday.

Bennett decided to discuss his idea with Ogden to enable the solicitor to take it to his client. Bennett had purposely distanced himself from West, who had enquired many times when he could expect a visit. Interviewing officers had reported that he often asked, 'How's Mr Bennett?', as well as, 'How's the investigation going?' Much as the Senior Investigating Officer would have enjoyed interviewing him, he knew it was all part of West's games. Once he had tired of him he would have wanted the next rank up, so Bennett had decided right from the start to remain an unknown quantity.

Bennett explained to Ogden what he had in mind and the benefits to both sides. Ogden was sure his client would agree and on that basis he had no reason to object.

In the late afternoon, Bennett received an unexpected call from the officers guarding Cromwell Street. The Chief Constable had turned up in full uniform and was besieged by reporters. Bennett was a little annoyed at this, not because the Chief had decided to pay a visit but because he had failed to tell anyone he was coming. Bennett knew he wasn't trying to catch them out, but had they known, the media could have been given a photo opportunity. Instead, the Chief had presented them with their first opportunity to say they had not been kept informed, and although Bennett could see the visit had done wonders for morale, he still made the point in as diplomatic a way as possible.

Back at the MIR, the Chief showed the same interest in everything that was going on, studying the charts on the wall, the photographs on display and listening intently to what was said. At that evening's briefing, he echoed what was said the night before, that he was receiving lots of messages of support both from the public and from other forces, all complimenting them on their work and the professional and caring image they projected.

As the Chief sat down, their attention turned to more pressing matters.

The number of 'possibles' for the 'Dutch girl' was increasing dramatically. Interpol had come forward, mainland European police services as well as members of the public were making contact and, as ever, the press were making suggestions of their own. The full missing person file on Carol Ann Cooper contained dental records and photographs but they had still found out nothing about another 'possible', Shirley Hubbard, nor did it appear were they likely to. West was now saying that Remains 4 were those of Juanita Mott.

At 7.10 that evening, not long after the briefing had ended and the Chief had bade his last farewell, the first indication of a ninth set of remains was uncovered at 25 Cromwell Street. Remains 9 was found in the hole that had been made bigger during the day – the last area in the cellar Fred West had marked in red paint. Now he would have to be brought back again in the hope he might 'remember' more about this or any others.

Bennett and Moore did not stay long at Cromwell Street that evening. In less than 20 minutes, they had spoken to the search teams and Bob Beetham, and seen what looked like a leg bone protruding from the blackened mud at the bottom of a hole towards the rear of the cellar almost opposite a washbasin. As they left, so did any lingering reporters, and with that the covert convoy operation swung into action, taking the blue-boiler-suited West back to what remained of his house.

If he appeared upset, it was more to do with the state of the building and his family than the plight of his victims, for the police were now systematically destroying everything he had done. He could no longer speak to Rose, and his family was distancing itself from him. If he felt sorry for anyone, it was only for himself. Yet for all this he was still claiming to be confused or had difficulty remembering, looking around as though he was trying to get his bearings. Or was he just seeing what had been done, taking it all in and wondering what he should do or what he should tell the police and anyone else next? He might have been thinking of new ways to confuse them even more, perhaps tell them more tales. He had plenty of time on his hands to let them sort it out.

At least he had kept them away from Rose. He had told them she knew nothing of what he had done and she had told them the same. They were the Wests, they thought and acted as one. They were invincible. They had to believe him.

Paul Britton had said Fred West had schooled his wife to be like him. A team, far better than that which was investigating them. No one knew precisely whether these thoughts were going through his head and no one ever would but the smirk on his face and the tone of voice said 'I know what I know and you'll know what I tell you, when and not before.'

That night he maintained there were two Worcester girls, and that this latest find might be one of them.

But that wasn't all. West had a feeling there was still another victim in the cellar, though he couldn't be sure where. It mattered not. The whole of the ground floor was going to be dug up, of that he could be in no doubt.

NINETEEN

Some of the media thought that Letterbox Field at Kempley could be the next search site; others were sure. The field where West had put down a wooden marker showing where he had killed his first wife Rena and his previous address at 25 Midland Road in Gloucester were now being guarded around the clock. There was no doubt the police would begin searching one of them soon.

It made sense, then, to carry out a preliminary survey of the field using the ground-penetrating radar. The police didn't need it at Cromwell Street any more and it was still costing them money even while it was lying idle. This, though, presented Bennett with a new dilemma, for having promised to keep the media informed of any developments this would confirm Letterbox Field as a possible burial ground.

Still, the work had to be done and one thing was certain, it would be carried out when he decided, not the media.

'Other sites' had become a favourite topic for reporters, who either sensed the work at Cromwell Street was coming to an end or were just keen to move the investigation on. Some continued to speculate on possible locations in Gloucester and Cheltenham, others even linked them to victims who might be found there, with Mary Bastholm still the most talked-about. This, inevitably, led to further conjecture over the final body count. Popular estimates now ranged from fourteen to more than twenty and although there was never any substance to these claims, some reports were saying that articles had been found that showed how the girls had died. Was it lucky guesswork or more evidence of a leak?

Bennett wanted to use the ground radar to search the area in Letterbox Field, but he also knew it would give the game away to the media, who were desperate to know about any further search sites. Once they knew, they would trample all over it if it was not properly secured and to do that would require a large number of officers the force just could not afford. The best compromise, he decided, was to treat it as a photo opportunity. News crews could film the equipment at work and talk to the operatives if they wished, after that they would be warned to keep their distance. If they did not then he would halt the search and it would be their fault and he would tell them so. That way both sides would get what they wanted without the need for huge numbers of officers to police it.

It would all take place the following day.

Kempley is a little more than 15 miles from Gloucester, deep in the countryside and within sight of the border with Herefordshire. Two miles outside the village, Letterbox Field was in the middle of nowhere, not on a main road or one you would travel unless you had a specific reason.

'No waiting' signs were placed along the roads leading up to it, forcing the media to park in a field opposite where the photo opportunity and ultimately the search for Rena West's remains would take place. The similar incline, however, gave them a good view of what was happening. By now the number of camera crews and reporters had become predictable rather than acceptable. Even so, the array of cars, vans and satellite-dish-mounted vehicles that had set up camp seemed out of place in the green rolling landscape.

The gathering did not take long. Bennett pointed out to reporters the boundaries of where they were allowed to go and the implications of them trespassing onto the site. They got as much as they wanted, knowing this was just a preamble to the more serious business that would come later.

Of the nine victims Fred West had said were at Cromwell Street, eight had now been recovered. What was almost certainly the ninth set of remains would have to wait until the next day when Professor Knight returned.

It now seemed that Remains 1 was almost certainly Heather West and Remains 3 Shirley Robinson, who were both in the garden. In the cellar, according to West, was Remains 4, Juanita Mott, along with possibly Lucy Partington, Carol Cooper and maybe Shirley Hubbard, though he was not sure where. Remains 8, found under the bathroom, he still claimed were those of Lynda Gough.

Even allowing for West's conception of the truth, they still had no positive leads for the other set of remains in the garden – Remains 2 or 'Shirley's mate' – or the 'Dutch girl' who was another of the cellar victims. The number of probable identities for both seemed to increase by the day and this was making the job more complicated, but there was no way of reducing the list until they had more specific information either from West or some other source. Instead, the phone calls to the MIR, the police press office and the missing persons helpline charity kept on coming, and even though it was made clear the investigation centred on the remains of young women, it did not stop people enquiring about male or elderly relatives missing in the UK or abroad.

Detective Constable Nick Churchill had been following up many of these names and had created a simple but effective matrix grid that he could quickly update when any new information came to hand. Yet, so reliant was he on cooperation from outside organisations who often worked long hours on his behalf, he could never keep pace with the requirements of the investigation. His catchphrase to those who thought he should be doing better was 'It's not as simple as that'. Others who appreciated the work he was putting in gave him the new nickname of 'Finder'.

Despite all this, he still managed to 'find' many of the names of those who had reputedly stayed at 25 Cromwell Street, had lived in Gloucester care homes, been reported to the police as missing or put forward by the missing persons helpline. In the process, he had also uncovered a disturbing anomaly in how the police recorded missing people. 'How many missing persons are there from Gloucestershire?' seemed a straight enough question. 'On the PNC [Police National Computer] ten, but the National Missing Persons Helpline charity have recorded seventy-five', was not the reply Bennett was expecting.

Churchill explained that the PNC only recorded missing persons thought to be vulnerable by the police when they had been reported missing. The charity, on the other hand, recorded all missing persons no matter how they had disappeared. Bennett was far from happy with this and could see already as an aftermath of the investigation embarrassing questions being asked about police procedure. He asked Churchill to find out more and arrange to visit the missing persons helpline charity.

From the very beginning the investigation had set out to handle the families of the victims with sensitivity, and even more so as the death toll had risen. At the same time, Howard Ogden had made it clear to the media on more than one occasion his concern about how they were reporting the case and the effect it could have on his client's chances of a fair trial. Bennett, too, was continually asking for restraint on both these counts but there was no stopping the speculation and, it seemed, no appealing to the better nature of some reporters whose attitude seemed to swing between couldn't care less and downright uncompassionate.

If he ever thought he had half a chance of softening their approach it ended with news of their latest and, to his mind, sickest ploy yet. Families were getting calls from reporters telling them the police had found remains which could be their lost relative and suggesting they call the station to see when they were going to be told.

Bennett was incensed. This was not news. How could they justify it? All it did was to cause unnecessary upset and undermine the investigation. It seemed to him the media was now so obsessed with the race to see who could identify the victims first, who would uncover the exact body count and get exclusive interviews or contracts with anyone involved in the investigation, that all rules or ethics had gone out of the window. Having a notebook or microphone thrust in their faces as well as numerous phone calls had become a daily ordeal for families. Even the relatives of 'probable' victims could expect no time or space in which to grieve.

He decided to raise the issue once more, and in the strongest possible terms, at the following day's news conference.

Fred West was about to be charged with five further murders, making a total of eight, and there would be a big media presence for that. The Chief Constable, too, would have to be told of the problems the media were causing. Withy Cole said he would see his concerns were conveyed to the Attorney-General.

It was looking likely they would soon be able to match names with at least six sets of remains. They just needed forensic confirmation. Blood samples for DNA comparison would be taken, though that was thought to be an exercise for the future as DNA matching had all but been ruled out by the condition of the remains. Estimates of age and height were expected from Professor Knight and Dr Whittaker at any time.

The review of the Gloucester care homes and their residents was also bearing fruit. The name of one girl in particular kept cropping up. Alison Chambers was born in Germany but had lived with her mother in South Wales until she was placed into care and became a resident at Jordan's Brook House in Gloucester. While there, she had worked on a youth training scheme at the office of one of the city's solicitors. She came to Gloucester sometime around 1979 when she was 16 and disappeared soon after. Earlier that year she wrote to her mother saying she was living in a flat with a family with five children, but gave no address. The envelope was postmarked Northampton. She had been reported to the police as an absconder from care when she had first gone missing.

After she had reached 17, and in view of the letter to her mother indicating she was safe and well, the West Glamorgan

Authority released her from care, but when nothing more was heard, her family recorded her name at the Metropolitan Police Missing Persons Bureau. That was 1991.

Alison Chambers was rising from a possible to a probable and the South Wales Police had been asked to make urgent enquiries.

As for the 'Dutch girl', there was nothing new on her.

Thursday 10 March marked two weeks into the investigation.

The major incident structure had settled down but problems of identification, Fred West's ever-changing stories and the media's blatant aggression were still hampering progress.

People with information were going to newspapers before the police. When officers tracked down a potential witness, they found they had already been seen by a reporter or had contacted the press through free telephone numbers in the tabloids. If they hadn't, they would do so as soon as the officer left. This was affecting police research into West's background although, thanks to the police in Scotland, they were beginning to find out more about Catherine 'Rena' West and Ann McFall, and arrangements were being made to search in another field at Kempley. One warrant would cover Letterbox Field where Rena was buried; a second for the adjoining Fingerpost Field, named after the signpost at its entrance gate, where West 'had a feeling' Ann might be.

A news conference was arranged for 11.30 a.m. at the Brunswick Road Campus of Gloucester College of Art and Design, not more than 200yd from St Michael's Square and Cromwell Street. Bennett would deliver a short statement covering the murder of five unknown females between 1 January 1972 and 27 February 1994 that West had now been charged with, and he would again outline his concerns about how the media was operating.

By the time he and Terry Moore arrived, the room was brimming with news crews from North and South America,

Canada, Australia, New Zealand, South Africa and all across Europe. Their number did not improve his mood. Simmering feelings of anxiety and annoyance were evident on his face.

The vast array of microphones on the table in front of him meant their owners had to move them as he sat down. Others were then produced, pushing those already in place aside. There was even more jockeying for position in the aisles and the seats before everyone settled down. If he had not faced a media circus before, he was now and he did not much like it. If ever the team's favoured term 'scumbags' applied, it was never more so than now, he thought.

The fact that he looked more gaunt than at any time in the past fortnight gave added emphasis to his words. There were few questions from the floor. The one-to-one interviews that followed were restricted to two questions per reporter.

He wasn't sure whether his warning would have the desired effect and he certainly wasn't confident. It would probably need the Attorney-General's intervention or whoever was regulating the press at that time. What he did know was that most of those his anger was aimed at were in that room.

An hour and a quarter after they had entered, Bennett and Moore were on their way out again. Even by recent standards it had been unusually draining.

Professor Knight was due late afternoon and would remove Remains 9. Before that they would discuss where they were with Remains 1–3 which he had already received and begun examining. Remains 4–8 would be available for him the following day.

These five sets of remains were now in the temporary mortuary Bob Beetham had prepared in the police station garage. Bennett wanted to see them now they had been cleaned up, as he had with Remains 1–3, before they had been taken to the professor. He also wanted to scrutinise the method being used to clean the bones and sieve the earth that had been taken from the areas where they were buried. Arrangements were made for him and Terry Moore to meet Beetham, John Rouse and Pete Maunder outside.

Additional garage space had been set aside to house the later finds. It was far from ideal and possibly irreverent but it was the only accommodation available with a water supply nearby.

Five trestle tables were draped in white. On each of them were the skeletal remains and the artefacts found with them.

Witnessing their recovery and the conditions where they lay had been both distressing and unforgettable. Now they were cleaned and laid out anatomically they appeared more human. Everyone there bowed their heads, their expressions the same as when the remains were taken from the ground.

The moment of silent respect over, it was time for work.

It was now even more apparent that the remains were different in colour. As Bennett walked around, he noticed some of the bones were missing, most noticeably kneecaps. Looking at Remains 6 it was obvious that one of the largest bones in the body, a shoulder blade or scapula, was missing. Anxiously, he pointed this out to Beetham and Rouse, who already knew but had held back from mentioning it, and asked them to explain.

The two scenes of crime officers showed him, and the others, the system they had put into place since Remains 1 had been found. It was a sort of mining sluice with a series of filters, the final one a pair of women's tights stretched across. The mud and earth had been poured into the top and raked down while being washed with running water. They believed some other bones were missing – especially finger and toe bones – but they had recovered a lot including teeth and nails. There was no way that a bone the size of a shoulder blade would have escaped their search, or the sets of kneecaps or patellae that were missing from other remains.

They confirmed that the area surrounding every recovery had been properly searched as agreed and all the liquefied mud brought for examination. No site had been infilled by the time it was realised the shoulder blade for Remains 6 was missing and when they went back, they found nothing. Clearly, it was not there to be found, neither were any of the missing bones. Some of these would have been sizeable and could have been buried elsewhere, but they were not at Cromwell Street, that was certain.

By late afternoon Professor Knight had arrived to discuss the way forward and the missing bones. The professor was well aware of the method that had been used to follow on his search. In effect, he had done most of the work himself as he only moved to another area once he had come across a change in the colour of the mud that indicated the boundary of decomposition. He dismissed the likelihood of large bones decomposing though he accepted some of the smaller ones might have, adding that some of the vertebrae were missing where decapitation had taken place. Some remains even had the same bones missing. He would do a complete bone count for each set of remains and put it in his report.

The discussion continued, with the Prof giving as much information as he could about the remains he was yet to receive, which he, too, was seeing laid out for the first time. Just confirming they were young and female meant some of the names could be removed from the list of possible identities.

Then it was time to go to Cromwell Street to begin the recovery of Remains 9. No one could forecast what he would find but given the unbelievable discoveries a few days before, more evidence of tying up and gagging seemed likely.

The hole in the room at the garden end of the cellar was near a sink. The search team had gone some 3ft down before they made their discovery. This time the hole was larger, an indication of how difficult it had been to find what they were looking for. The sticky, liquid mud had changed from brownish clay to black, once again marking out the parameters of putrification and the original area where the body was buried.

Setting himself in the pit, the Prof slowly pulled out, one by one, lower leg bones and then a femur, again belonging to a young woman. They were in line and appeared to have been buried that way. Next came the pelvis and trunk, each carefully handed to a scenes of crime officer. As before, everything was video recorded under the gaze of Bennett and Moore.

A short time later a skull was recovered with some black hair still intact. Wrapped horizontally around what would have been the lower face, mouth and jaws was an elasticated cloth band, about 3in wide. Knowing looks, rather than words, passed between the onlookers. The skull was upright and from where he had found it the Prof concluded it had been decapitated. Then came shoulder bones.

Painstakingly the professor searched through the sludge with his fingers, delicately removing one bone after another until he brought out two separate pieces of cord. One was around 6in long, the other over 1ft with a 3-in knotted loop. They looked similar to that found earlier with Remains 6. The looped cord appeared to be near the arm bones but not around them.

Climbing out of the pit, the Prof cleaned off some of the larger bones with his hands to reveal deep cut marks on both femurs – the victim appeared to have been severed in three as before. To no one's surprise now there was more evidence of restraint and muzzling.

Everyone there paused for a few moments to reflect on this latest grim discovery before their professionalism kicked in once more and they carried on with the work.

The Attorney-General decided to curb the press by issuing a warning through the police, though he considered it 'unlikely' that any of the reporting so far would prejudice Fred West's chances of a fair trial. Bennett decided the best person to present his words was the Chief Constable, in full uniform, to show how seriously they regarded it. Tony Butler said he would be over the next day.

Leaks to the press were now of such concern that the Deputy Chief Constable Nigel Burgess and Chief Superintendent Geoff Cooper turned up at that evening's briefing to get the message across, and when the fruit machine made its customary, spontaneous contribution to the meeting no one, especially the Deputy Chief, saw the funny side.

He sat stone-faced as they were told the Home Office's Prison Department appeared sympathetic to the request to have Fred West remanded to Gloucester Police Station. The Friday deadline, just 48 hours away, even seemed a possibility.

West, it appeared, had not been looking forward to going to prison and had greeted the news with near delight. Bennett, however, assured them that once he was on a 28-day remand they would be able to organise themselves much better. It would give the interview teams time to prepare and gain the control they had been trying to achieve but had struggled to do so because of the legal restrictions they were operating under.

Nigel Burgess got to his feet and reminded them in no uncertain terms of the need for loyalty and confidentiality, warning them of the disciplinary consequences of anyone leaking details of the investigation, though his injunction that they guard against being the 'senior or well-placed (police) source' quoted by newspapers touched a nerve with Bennett. He was not sure if the Deputy Chief was referring to him or Terry Moore but he knew he had spent the last fortnight battling with these very issues and he was not going to let this pass. Whoever was responsible for the leaks he knew it was neither him nor his number two, and in any case 'senior source' was often used to hide the real source of a story, even if the quotation was entirely made up.

The point was made and realising he may have gone too far with his delivery if not his message, the Deputy Chief Constable repeated that the force was watching with pride the work they were doing and that he hoped that what he had said would not affect their efforts.

With that the two uniformed officers left the room, followed shortly after by Bennett and Moore.

The atmosphere was not the same as at the start of the briefing. Perhaps it was not a bad thing for them to think about what had been said.

TWENTY

The Chief Constable of Gloucestershire, Tony Butler, stood in front of Gloucester Police Station, a semicircle of camera crews and reporters before him. Although they knew he was to address them, surprisingly few had asked why. Those who had were told he would be making a statement on behalf of the Attorney-General and nothing more.

The Chief Constable, in full uniform, delivered the words forcefully:

> Following a formal complaint to the Attorney-General by Mr West's legal advisers concerning press coverage of this investigation the following warning is considered appropriate.
>
> Our attention has been drawn to the extensive media coverage afforded to the circumstances leading up to and surrounding the arrest and subsequent court appearances of Frederick West. We have noted that in particular, background material relating to Frederick West includes reference to the nature of the evidence said to be available against him, and alleged past misconduct towards members of his family. There has also been much speculation about possible offences going well beyond those with which he is charged. Frederick West was arrested on 25 February 1994 and at that point the proceedings became 'active' within the meaning of paragraph 4 of Schedule 1 to the Contempt of Court Act 1981. We would like to take this opportunity to remind editors of their obligation not, at any time, to publish material which gives a 'substantial risk' of serious prejudice in the proceedings.

Most of the questions that followed focused on how the force was coping, to which the Chief replied he had the utmost confidence in the investigation team and that the entire force was committed to the task. It was the first of many public endorsements.

Just around the corner Fred West was due in court again. Members of the public started queuing over an hour before in the hope of catching a glimpse of the country's most notorious murder suspect. Reporters who had been at the Chief's news conference and didn't have a colleague saving a place had no chance of getting in.

West appeared more smug than ever, confident he was on his way back into police custody rather than prison. He was comfortable there and although he had been to prison before, the sort of crimes he was charged with this time would be a completely new experience for him. *He* may not have considered himself a sex offender but other prisoners would and who knew what that might lead to? At least for the time being he could fall back on Howard Ogden and Janet Leach while still considering himself more than a match for 'Policeman Plod'. Surveying the court with an air of 'Look at me', he even seemed to be enjoying the attention he was getting, nodding slightly to acknowledge his appropriate adult when he saw she was there.

As the eight murder charges were read out to him, he gazed expressionless into the middle distance, his crumpled, blue, padded body warmer covering a grey and navy patterned jumper that made his short, stocky frame appear larger than it was. Again there was no objection and within 5 minutes of entering the court he was on his way back to the police cells where he was remanded until 7 April.

The Home Office Prison Department had pulled out all the stops to visit the Gloucester Police Station cell complex that day. West was kept there, too, in anticipation of Home Office approval, which was rubber-stamped by telex later. Howard Ogden had agreed on behalf of his client, so everything was in place for Superintendent Phil Sullivan to become the pseudo-governor of the Gloucester Police Station wing of Gloucester Prison. West was being kept in what was normally the female cell area, with a more frequent turnaround of guards – to prevent him worming his way in with his police custodians.

Warwickshire Constabulary had agreed to allow their artist, Detective Constable Bob Wilcox, to assist in the investigation. A trained artist who had often been used to produce impressions from descriptions by witnesses, he was to get West to describe each of the unknown victims in detail so that he could compose a likeness. With a legal adviser and appropriate adult present, the two would work together until West was satisfied the final image was as accurate as it could be. Wilcox was shown how to record the process on tape.

Later that morning, on Bennett's instructions, the whole investigating team, including searchers, scenes of crime officers, everyone working on the MIR interviews and outside enquiries as well as the press office, gathered in the social club to be given advice on stress management by force counsellors. Everyone, including the Senior Investigating Officer, was expected to sit through the session and listen in silence to what was said. Whether they took any notice of the advice given was up to them. Relaxing music was played and the sound of waves lapping on a beach. Everyone closed their eyes and within minutes some were asleep, the unmistakable sound of snoring mixing in with the waves and music.

For Bennett it was also a chance for some self-analysis. He liked a drink but had not had much of an opportunity to overindulge even if he had wanted to, and although he enjoyed a small cigar he was conscious he was now smoking them more regularly. As for sleep, he was so physically and mentally tired at the end of the day, morning came too soon. Only the adrenalin-fuelled demands of the inquiry kept him going – as they did the others. The remedy was to make sure all the officers had a break, himself included. He had neglected his family again, especially his mother, who was 80 and due to go into hospital for a hip operation the following Monday. He would try and find time that weekend to take her to lunch on Sunday – Mothering Sunday.

Saturday 12 March was the first day that no work was done at Cromwell Street since the investigation had begun, though the MIR and investigation team continued their work over the weekend. Bennett was planning to read up on West's background and the files on Mary Bastholm and Lucy Partington, but any hope he had of the media taking notice of the Chief Constable's warning was short-lived as newspapers continued to speculate over other burial sites and were again linking West with the disappearance and murder of Mary Bastholm, all of which would again have to be referred to the Attorney-General.

Dealing with this took most of the morning which meant that once again Bennett had been diverted from what he intended doing by the media. So much for shoehorning breaks into the schedule. He would not now finish early and would have to come in the next day as well. Still, he decided there and then that come what may he would call a halt by Sunday lunchtime and take his mother to lunch. To make sure, he phoned his wife and asked her to book a table at a restaurant in Gloucester and get his sister to meet them there with their mother.

The files on Mary Bastholm and Lucy Partington related to two of Gloucestershire's longest-standing, unresolved missing person investigations. Sad stories that for Bennett contained an element of nostalgia.

The investigation into the disappearance of Mary Bastholm in 1968 had been taken over early on by Detective Chief Superintendent William Marchand of the Metropolitan Police

Scotland Yard Murder Squad. With no computers then, it was run on the old card index and paper-based system.

Bennett was in no doubt that Mary Bastholm was not one of the nine found at Cromwell Street but her disappearance was similar to that of Lucy Partington and possibly some of the other victims. Yet the investigation had revealed that Fred West had worked in Bristol Road where she disappeared and the Pop-In Café may have been a regular haunt for both of them. Certainly, the media had latched on to this and made it the basis for speculation connecting West with the café, her disappearance and the victims. Bennett accepted they might well be right for the theory had been discussed in briefings, but there was no evidence yet and they already had enough on their plate. Her disappearance had to be looked at but only to make sure they hadn't missed any glaring connections in light of what they had uncovered in the last two weeks.

Mary Jane Bastholm went missing on the icy, snow-covered evening of Saturday 6 January 1968 when she was nearly 16 years old. She had left her home in Gloucester well dressed for the cold in a knee-length coat, jumper and cardigan over a mini skirt. She was carrying a blue umbrella and a white carrier bag containing a game of Monopoly and intended to catch a bus from Tuffley Avenue to see her boyfriend, who lived in the village of Hardwicke about 5 miles away. Her boyfriend had arranged to be at her stop but when the bus arrived she was not on it so he got a friend to take him to her home only to find she wasn't there either.

Mary was reported missing to the police that night and a local search for her began. When she had not been found the following morning concern increased and the search was widened. It soon became apparent that this pretty girl, who measured around 5ft 3in, was slim with blond, shoulder-length hair and who came from a well-respected local family, was just a normal teenager of the time. She had the occasional under-age drink with friends of her age and often went to the local Pop-In

Café in Bristol Road close to the city centre, but otherwise she did what her parents asked. She was thrifty and spent her pocket money on make-up and stockings. There was no reason for her to go missing that night and every reason for her not to.

Bennett remembered it well. He was a newly appointed detective constable and had returned from his initial training course at the Metropolitan Police Detective Training School just before Christmas. Having taken some leave he returned to duty the day she had gone missing. The following day, Sunday, he and other officers from Stroud joined the search on the snow-covered ground above Painswick Beacon, which looks down onto Gloucester. They walked the area from late morning until darkness fell, and then carried on the next day.

The local press covered the story and soon a witness was found that had seen Mary at the bus stop in Bristol Road at around 8.15 p.m. She was never seen again.

Enquiries continued throughout the following week and when a number of Monopoly pieces were found not far from where she would have waited for the bus the decision was made to call in the Yard.

With Marchand's arrival the investigation intensified. Every aspect of Mary and her background was gone into. There were house-to-house enquiries in the Bristol Road area and in Hardwicke. Officers with dogs searched the surrounding countryside, which still had a light covering of snow and was frozen hard. Thanks to Marchand's influence, a helicopter joined the search – a rare sight in those days – and as a founder member of the Gloucestershire Constabulary Underwater Recovery Section, Bennett was pressed into action to search beneath the bridges that crossed the Gloucester–Sharpness Canal.

They began at Hempsted Bridge, a short distance from where Mary was last seen and the Monopoly pieces found. They searched the icy cold water 20yd either side and then did the same at other bridges, but they found nothing apart from the usual cycle frames, tyres, mud and rubbish.

Later they plumbed the docks at Gloucester and other waterways, and searched more of the surrounding countryside, but learned nothing more of Mary's disappearance.

Some months later the investigation was scaled down with the file left open.

Just under five years later, on Thursday 27 December 1973, Lucy Katherine Partington went missing.

Lucy was an intelligent, industrious, caring and bespectacled 21-year-old whose family lived in Gretton on the outskirts of Cheltenham and who was in her third year at Exeter University studying medieval history. A recent convert to Roman Catholicism, she was spending Christmas at home.

That Thursday evening Lucy visited a disabled girlfriend who lived in Culross Close near Pittville Park, a short distance from Cheltenham Racecourse. It was a bitterly cold night and she left shortly before 10.15 p.m., having first written a letter to apply for an MA in Medieval Art which she put in her canvas satchel before walking to the nearby bus stop in Evesham Road to catch a bus home. When they realised she had not arrived as expected, her family contacted her friend and then reported her missing the following day.

A massive but fruitless search began. The Head of Gloucestershire CID, Detective Chief Superintendent Bill Turner, led a major investigation involving more than 100 officers. Fields and estates were trawled; there were house-to-house enquiries in Cheltenham, Gretton and the next nearest town, Winchcombe, along with posters and appeals in the media, but all they came up with was someone who saw Lucy hurrying towards where she should have caught the bus – a bus that was 10 minutes late that night and which, it was established, she did not get on.

By now Bennett was a detective sergeant at Stroud but once again joined the police frogmen searching lakes in Cheltenham's Pittville Park close to where Lucy had visited her friend and where she should have caught the bus. They disturbed lots of ducks and rats but nothing to help them find Lucy.

As part of their investigation, they looked at the Bastholm file and contacted Worcester Police about a girl named Carol Cooper who had gone missing the month before, but apart from the obvious similarities of the time of year and that the girls were either on or about to catch a bus when they were last seen, there was nothing. Worcester was more than 30 miles from Cheltenham, Gloucester nearly 10. There was nothing to link the three cases – and when Shirley Hubbard went missing from Worcester in similar circumstances in November the following year, the cases were compared again, but still there was no connection between any of them, nothing to give them a lead.

Just like that of Mary Bastholm, Lucy Partington's file was never closed. Although unresolved, both investigations had been thorough. They had also been reviewed more than once over the years, though in light of what was now known the police continued to look for any connection between Mary Bastholm and Fred West. Their dilemma was that West had not admitted abducting or killing Mary and the investigation had to maintain its focus on what *he had* admitted, as Bennett kept reminding the rest of the team whenever Mary's name was raised at briefings. Mary's brother, her only surviving close relative, had been told the same.

Lucy Partington, though, was a different proposition. West had admitted killing her and her file would now have to be carefully scrutinised. Identifying her remains and establishing exactly how she died was already a priority. What was known about how she had disappeared would have to be checked against West's explanations.

From the moment his signed note of confession had been delivered, West had maintained he and Lucy were having an affair and that he first met her in Pittville Park when he was there with Rose and the family. He claimed they met there regularly and began a sexual relationship almost immediately and, just like his other victims, it wasn't long before she wanted to move in with him. West called her 'Juicy Lucy' and said he warned her – and the many other women he had sex with – not to interfere with his family life, it was just sex, but, again like the others, she had ignored his warning.

The night she disappeared he had waited for her and when she came to him they had an argument in his van because she wanted him to meet her parents and for them to live together. West's answer was to strangle her, take her back to Cromwell Street and put her in the cellar.

That was one version. In another he claimed Lucy told him she had his phone number and was going to tell his wife about their affair. So, he strangled her in the park before putting her in the van. In yet another, they had agreed to meet and, after having sex, she told him she was pregnant and wanted money for an abortion.

West's accounts were always challenged but once he had settled on a storyline there was no budging him. His wife, marriage and family were always his justification for murder, though he always insisted Rose knew nothing about it.

The notion that West ever had an affair with Lucy Partington was fanciful in the extreme but he kept it up. While it was just possible he might have seen her in Pittville Park, she was definitely at university in Exeter at the times he claimed they were together. As for knowing quite a lot about her, her disappearance was widely reported in the local newspapers, television and radio and stayed in the news for weeks. Learning about her through the investigation would have been easy. He probably enjoyed watching the progress or lack of it.

Every enquiry they had made, now and down the years, had confirmed Lucy's devotion to her new-found Catholic faith, while West's motive for killing her was similar to those he offered for most of the other killings and he had still not offered an explanation for any of the items found with each of the remains.

That day, Sunday 13 March, was another milestone in Bennett's life and career. It was thirty years to the day since he had been sworn in as a constable at Cheltenham Magistrates Court, along with another cadet, Dave 'Ginge' Carter, and Brian Waldron, who was also new to the service.

Three months later, after finishing their initial training, they made a pledge that in thirty years' time – when they had 'come to the end of their time' – they would meet for a meal and whoever held the highest rank should pick up the bill. Brian Waldron was now a sergeant and Ginge Carter a police constable dog handler but Bennett was more than happy to honour their agreement, hopefully the next weekend.

He had never had any intention of leaving the force when his thirty-year contract was up. At 49 he was too young to retire and enjoyed his work too much. And even if he saw something that took his fancy, he would not be going until after he had seen this investigation through to trial.

That could be anything up to eighteen months to two years away, possibly even longer.

By the time he reached his lunchtime deadline, Bennett was more up to date with the Bastholm and Partington investigations but still behind with West's background. Even so, it was time to keep his appointment with Mother's Day. When he reached the steak house at Quedgley on the outskirts of Gloucester, his wife's car was already there. As he made his way to the front door a man and woman with two children came up to him.

'Aren't you that detective from Cromwell Street, it must be awful?' asked the woman.

Bennett was taken off guard, it was the last thing he expected. 'Yes,' he answered as politely as his surprise would allow.

But they didn't leave it there and as they followed him into the restaurant it was the man who asked, 'How many more do you expect to find?'

This time Bennett's response was unequivocal. 'I'm off duty now and do not want to and cannot talk about it. I'm sorry.'

The couple moved away without apology or any sign of embarrassment.

Bennett spotted his mother, wife and sister at a table in the window and joined them, positioning his chair with its back to as much of the room as possible but they could not shake off the feeling they were being stared at and talked about. It spoilt the occasion and as soon as they had finished their meal they left. It was an experience Bennett knew he was likely to encounter again and he didn't like it. He loved his job but also valued his privacy.

There was still time that day to take a look at what was known about Carol Ann Cooper, another missing person whose file had been found by West Mercia Police.

Also known to her friends as 'Caz', she was in care at the Pines Children's Home in Worcester when she went missing. She was 15 years old and had been there a couple of years. She came from a broken home and lived with her mother until she died. Throughout her time in care she was unsettled. Her strong personality and frequent mood swings made her a difficult proposition and she absconded regularly, often staying away overnight and sometimes for days on end when she mixed with local bikers and got involved in shoplifting.

Carol Cooper was certainly no angel and very streetwise for her age but she had behaved herself for a while and at the time she went missing, on the weekend of 10/11 November 1973, was on her way to her grandmother's at Warndon on the outskirts of Worcester where she had permission to stay overnight.

She had spent most of the Saturday in Worcester with a number of friends, including her boyfriend, and gone to the cinema. Around 9.10 p.m. she got on a bus to Warndon. At the time she had a burned left hand as well as self-made tattoos on her hands and 'Caz' imprinted on her left forearm. She was never seen again.

It was possible that Carol Cooper had met Fred West at some time. She could even have been to Cromwell Street, for in the 1970s many girls in care seemed to find their way there, though just like Lucy Partington he claimed to have known her for some time.

West said she was a prostitute he had picked up in his work lorry. When she asked for money for sex then threatened to cry rape if he refused to pay, he killed her.

Fred West did not pay for sex!

Once again, there was no mention of the bindings that had been found with the remains. It was another indication, if any were needed, that West's interviews were worthless except to confirm that nothing he said could be relied upon as anything near the truth.

TWENTY-ONE

At last there was encouraging news on the identity of some of the remains. Dr Whittaker was confident he knew who four of the victims were and was able to give the approximate age of four of the others. Professor Knight had sent him the skulls from the eight sets of remains, which, in the absence of any other means of identification, were still referred to as Remains 1–8. Whittaker's analysis showed the skull from Remains 1 was that of Heather West, Remains 3 Shirley Robinson, Remains 6 Lucy Partington and Remains 8 Lynda Gough.

As for the others, Remains 2 was a girl approximately 17–18 years old, Remains 4 a woman in her early twenties – but not Juanita Mott – Remains 5 were not those of Carol Cooper but a girl aged about 16, and Remains 7 a girl aged approximately 17–18 who might be Juanita Mott. Then again, either Juanita or Carol could have been Remains 9. He would consider both possibilities in due course – there was no room for guesswork.

Dr Whittaker's research was based on a combination of the information supplied by Professor Knight and available dental records. If there were no dental records or only old or partial ones then he would use his photographic imaging comparison system, though that too depended on the strict criteria he had previously outlined. For him to commit himself to giving a name to a set of remains, or at least a skull, he had to be 100 per cent sure and he updated the police as the percentages changed and identification drew nearer. He had explained all this to Bennett and Moore, who, with tongue in cheek, asked when, percentagewise, they could feel a victim would ultimately be identified to his satisfaction and that of the Gloucester coroner and the courts.

'When I say I am comfortable, 60 per cent or more,' was his reply. It was a real breakthrough.

The police had a lot of information about Juanita Mott and Carol Cooper, including dental records, but still very little was known about Alison Chambers and virtually nothing of Shirley Hubbard that would take their identification further.

As for the 'Dutch girl', 'Tulip', or 'Truck' as West was now calling the hitch-hiker he had picked up near Monmouth, there was even a possibility he was referring to two girls rather than one. Either way, there were already over 130 possibles, all of them foreign nationals whose details had come from various sources including Interpol, other police forces, direct from families, the Metropolitan Police Missing Persons Bureau, the National Missing Persons Helpline charity, Salvation Army and the media. The number had been whittled down from more than 500 simply by removing males and others who were outside the age ranges given by Professor Knight or Dr Whittaker, but the search was no longer restricted to Holland as it was now evident West had no real idea what language this victim spoke. He thought it was Dutch so he called her the 'Dutch girl'. The other nicknames appeared equally random.

Was it yet another example of West not telling the truth, playing games to exert control, or had he simply forgotten? After all, he was certain Juanita Mott was buried where Remains 4 were recovered, though Dr Whittaker said differently. With Fred West it was impossible to tell what was going on inside his devious, evil mind.

As the clock approached noon on that Monday, the Chief Constable Tony Butler beckoned Bennett and Hilary Allison into his office. Joining them for the briefing he had requested were the Deputy Chief Constable, Assistant Chief Constable and Detective Chief Superintendent. The Chief had taken to referring to the inquiry team as 'the A team', which Bennett found embarrassing, especially when anyone not directly involved with the investigation was present. It was, however, another sign of his support and interest in the inquiry, both as a policeman and a manager.

The question of leaks to the media was again high on the agenda. Information was finding its way mainly into the *Sunday Mirror* but also now the *Daily Mirror*. The rooms where West was interviewed had been swept for listening devices, along with the rest of the police station, but none were found. Some of the other measures Bennett had taken he kept to himself, like checking all of his team's personal and mobile phone bills to see if any of them had been calling the media – and there was no evidence there either, though he doubted anyone would divulge confidential information in such an obvious way. What bugged the Chief was the way the media seemed to be completely ignoring the Attorney-General's warning. Speculation over the number of victims, tales of the Wests' lifestyle and sexual perversions had continued in the weekend's newspapers as if nothing had been said.

Apart from all that, the Gloucestershire Constabulary was also planning for its busiest week of the year. In a matter of days Cheltenham would be hosting the National Hunt Festival and with it the Gold Cup. Every hotel within a 50-mile radius would be full as hundreds of thousands of visitors descended on the county.

The huge crowds and daily mix of royalty and other VIPs made it a security nightmare. Many of the officers specially trained for such an occasion were already involved at Cromwell Street and the Chief Constable had made it clear the West investigation took priority over the races and that other arrangements would have to be made. What he didn't know was that the Gloucester and Cheltenham Support Groups, or Gemini teams as they were also called, who had been doing all the digging, had already discussed it, both among themselves and with Bennett, and made it clear they would like to carry out their race-week duties, not least because it would give them a welcome break from their grim routine. Bennett was more than happy for that. After all, he had been trying to slow things down since day one. A break now would allow him to prepare properly for the searches at 25 Midland Road and Kempley. The Chief agreed that digging at Cromwell Street would be suspended until after the races.

Even though they had got what they wanted, it was not without potential pitfalls, for some of the men would see colleagues they had not been in contact with for weeks who would no doubt want to know what was going on and ask them questions they would not be able to answer. A warning would be issued to each of them before they left.

Of equal concern to Bennett was promotion, not his own but of staff who had passed promotion boards or been selected for specialist duties and were waiting for placements to come through. With the inquiry likely to continue for some months, those he could spare he would release but there were some whose skills made them virtually irreplaceable and others who were heavily involved in sensitive liaison work. So, when vacancies occurred, his proposal was to move them on paper but keep them on the investigation for as long as necessary, a plan to which the Chief Constable agreed.

Media criticism had picked up on both the failure of missing persons' records and the fact that West had been left free to kill for over twenty years. The Chief was well aware of the good relationship that had developed between the police, Gloucestershire County Council and its social services department and was determined it would not be undermined by the media setting one against the other. He resolved to see the council's chief executive about setting up a special executive group that would tackle issues raised by the media both during and after the investigation.

Bennett left the briefing clutching a further batch of goodwill letters and messages received by the Chief Constable. Together with the replies, they were placed in see-through files to be put on a table outside the MIR where everyone was encouraged to read them. Letters came from the public and people in high places, from home and abroad. Some contained cheques, others cash. The words were often humbling and the sentiments they expressed were a source of great pride to those who saw them.

As they drove back to Gloucester, Bennett once again voiced his concerns to Hilary Allison at the media's insatiable appetite and the damage that might be caused not only to the investigation but also future court proceedings. It was surprising, therefore, that when she told him that reporters were still asking to film or photograph inside the MIR, he suggested the press office produce a pack that would include a free video along with information about the computer software and other equipment being used.

Sensing the time was right, she told him of a conversation she had had with another group of police press officers involved in the Jamie Bulger case – the abduction and murder of a young child from a shopping precinct by two youngsters on Merseyside. It was a harrowing investigation that had attracted huge publicity and media involvement over a long period. Just as in Cromwell Street, reporters had arrived from all over the world and there was a likelihood coverage would get out of hand. The solution there was to invite one representative from each branch of the media – reporter, photographer, cameraman, writer, etc. – to form a 'pool'. The pool was given access to material on the strict understanding it was then passed on to everyone else. In this way the police could be seen to be cooperating but were better able to control the flow of information and numbers, while at the same time giving the media the task of distributing the material. It had worked well on Merseyside, as had the provision of a press pack – a booklet containing information about the investigation that would help with background stories.

Bennett said he would give both ideas some thought though he already liked the sound of each.

Not everyone, though, shared his enthusiasm. At the evening briefing, looks of mild surprise turned to outright astonishment when he told them he was arranging for the media to film and photograph the MIR and that they would be supplied with free video clips and an information package.

Even the Doc's success and the Chief's compliments failed to produce anything except the usual query, 'When are we going to arrest Rose?'

It was just before 11.30 p.m. and time to call it a day.

Bennett had been in touch with Standish Hospital and his sister to find his mother had come round from her operation and was comfortable. He'd done some more reading and dictated replies to letters addressed to the investigation. He'd had a last look at HOLMES. The policy log was signed and up to date. Terry Moore had left and he had phoned home to say he was on his way.

Some 40 minutes later, his car rolled onto the drive and pulled up in front of the garage. Bennett got out and clicked the ignition key to lock the door and set the alarm. The front door was well lit but that didn't stop him fumbling for his house key before inserting it in the lock. He turned the key but nothing happened . . . and through the confusion came the stark realisation he was trying to enter a house he had moved away from three years before!

Transfixed for a second or two – though it seemed much longer – he turned and went back to his car. As he reached the door, he tried to get in without first unlocking it. Fortunately the alarm did not go off but it did nothing to slow his pumping heart or calm his state of mind.

When, eventually, he made it into the driver's seat and started the engine he paused to see if he had disturbed the new owners. Fortunately, no one inside had heard his ham-fisted attempt to enter their home!

He was only 4 miles from home but for the entire journey he

drove with his nose almost against the windscreen, his shoulders hunched over the steering wheel, a picture of intense concentration.

Ann was waiting for him and came to the door as she heard him put the car in the garage. She could see straightaway that something was troubling him and thought it must be his mother.

'What's wrong – is your mum all right?'

When they sat down over a coffee in the kitchen he told her what had happened and that he could not remember driving to work or driving home for the last ten days or so. He could remember leaving home, even arriving at work, leaving work and going to bed, but nothing of the journeys. His mind had been totally on the investigation when it should have been on the road and the thought of driving on autopilot and being involved in an accident disturbed him, for he had never experienced anything like it before. From then on he would use a driver, at least until the pressure reduced. He would tell Terry Moore what had happened first thing, enter his decision into the policy log and inform the Chief.

Moore was not surprised. He had mentioned more than once the toll the investigation was taking on his boss. Both had been working virtually non-stop except for sleep since it began and while they both agreed they had to take rest days, with so much going on they also knew that was easier said than done.

The man who got the job as the Senior Investigating Officer's driver was Detective Constable Phil Chattersingh, who was already on the investigation. His first trip was to Cromwell Street so that Bennett and Moore could review progress.

The section of the extension abutting the bathroom, which had previously been fixed to the wall of the Seventh Day Adventist church, had all but been removed and what was left would soon be demolished. The work in the cellar was also progressing. Holes that had already been searched were being filled with concrete to enable the rest of the floor, more than half, to be excavated. The part of the ground floor close to where Remains 2 and 3 had been found was also exposed and would soon be excavated down to Severn clay in line with the search parameters set for the investigation.

Before the briefing, Bennett paid his mother a visit in hospital. She was as pleased to see him as he was to see how well she had recovered, though also concerned at how tired he looked.

As Bennett left the hospital he was approached by a middle-aged woman who had seen him arrive and recognised him from news reports. She apologised for intruding but just wanted to express her good wishes. She said she had prayed for the families and the officers from the day it started and having written to him had been amazed to receive a reply. Unlike the family in the steak house, it was the sort of intrusion that warmed the heart.

Little came out of the briefing that evening, which left time to make arrangements for the next day's annual visit of Her Majesty's Inspector of Constabulary who had asked to see the MIR. They also had to prepare for the media's 'pool' visit.

There was mixed news from Nick 'Finder' Churchill on missing persons and it was news that troubled Bennett. Churchill had managed to trace a number of absconders from care homes in Gloucester who had been to 25 Cromwell Street and could now be ticked off as 'safe and well'. He was, however, having difficulty getting hold of police missing person's records and, more importantly, establishing how up to date they were.

As far as he could see, most forces' records were inaccurate. Some noted people as outstanding when they had in fact returned home. Being side-tracked, however well-meaning the cause, was the last thing he needed.

TWENTY-TWO

For all that they had been through and all they knew, Stephen and Mae West still seemed to love their parents and want to believe in them. That much was apparent from conversations overheard within the safe house. If ever proof were needed that blood is thicker than water then this was surely it.

Now, though, that bond with their dad faced its sternest test. Fred West's confessions to murder, in particular of their sister Heather, had shaken them. The family 'joke' was no longer a laughing matter.

As for Rose, whenever the subject of the murders was brought up she simply raged about what she would do to Fred if ever she got hold of him.

Stephen and Mae's liaison officer had discovered that while they talked between themselves about whether their mother had been involved in the killings before they had been moved out of Cromwell Street, Mae had made it clear she did not believe her mum was involved in murder.

Bennett had met Rose, Stephen and Mae before and early that Wednesday afternoon saw them again at Gloucester Police Station. Surprisingly, given the circumstances, Mae brought along a girlfriend. There was very little new to tell them; that soon the fields at Kempley and the flat at 25 Midland Road would be searched and that he would also be seeing Anne Marie – Fred West's daughter by his first wife Rena, Stephen and Mae's step-sister – but it gave them the chance to ask him anything and while they were there the bugs at the safe house could be checked in secret, though, as he explained, with the media closing in they could soon be on the move again.

Throughout the meeting, Bennett aimed his words at Rose, her features fixed in that familiar cold, morose expression. From behind her big, horn-rimmed glasses came a penetrating stare that betrayed hatred either of him or all he stood for. It really didn't matter which. She barely uttered a word, leaving what little was said to Stephen and Mae.

As he spoke, it occurred to Bennett that she must have been aware by then that he knew her most intimate secrets, her immense sexual appetite and preferences – depraved by most people's standards – and how she and her husband had acted within the family. He also wondered, now that Fred had confessed, if she thought the police would accept what both of them had been saying, that she was not involved and knew nothing about any of it. If she did, he made sure there was nothing in his voice to suggest differently and that it was only a matter of time before she was arrested again.

As obstinate and argumentative as Rose appeared, in Stephen and Mae, Bennett could sense only sadness and disbelief, as what had been found at their home and what their dad had admitted sunk in. Mae, with her mother's jet-black hair, looked more like Rose than Fred, as did Stephen, but it was the look in their eyes that portrayed the desolate circumstances in which they now found themselves.

He had a similar feeling when he met Anne Marie. Her quiet, gentle voice and soft handshake betrayed a fragile personality and Bennett could feel her anxiety, too. She dressed smartly and spoke in a contrite, respectful manner. Unlike her brother and sister, she looked like her father, though her skin was paler than his and she wore little make-up. Bennett was as aware as anyone how she had been abused, how long it had gone on and what she had been subjected to, but they were just the facts. Only she knew the full extent of it and nothing could mask the sadness in her eyes.

By any standards Anne Marie's life had been difficult, made worse when her marriage failed, but after that she got back with an old boyfriend. By now she was in a stable relationship

Ann McFall.

Catherine (Rena) West.

Charmaine West.

Lynda Gough.

Carol Cooper.

Lucy Partington.

Thérèse Siegenthaler.

Shirley Hubbard.

Juanita Mott.

Shirley Robinson.

Alison Chambers.

Heather West.

Front of 25 Cromwell Street.

Rear of 25 Cromwell Street: view from alleyway to St Michael's Square.

25 Cromwell Street: view from rear towards St Michael's Square.

Excavations at Letterbox Field (Kempley B), 1994.

Front of 25 Midland Road.

25 and 23 Cromwell Street, demolished.

Walkway from St Michael's Square, 2005.

Model of 25 Cromwell Street and Victim Information display.

The prosecution committal file.

HRH Prince Charles's private visit, 19 December 1995. From left: DC Russell Williams, DC Stephen McCormick, HRH, DCI Moore, D Supt Bennett.

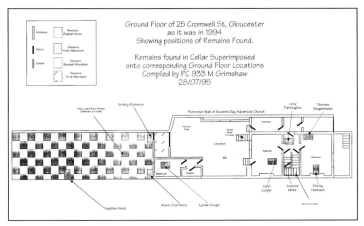

Ground floor of 25 Cromwell Street with positions of remains found.

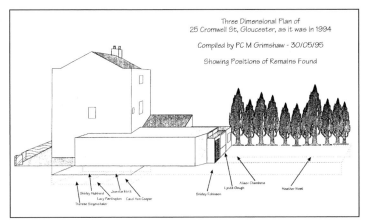

3-D plan of 25 Cromwell Street.

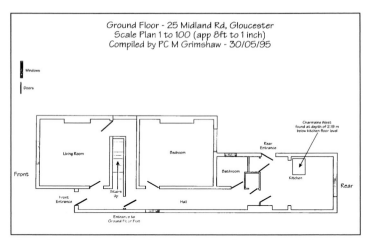

Ground floor of 25 Midland Road showing the position of Charmaine West's remains.

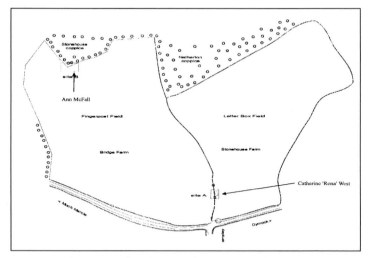

Sites A and B at Kempley showing the positions of Ann McFall's and Catherine West's remains.

and went by the name of Anne Marie Davis, retaining her married name.

Bennett told her as much as he could, just as he had Rose, Stephen and Mae, and even before she was asked, she had offered to help the police investigation in any way she could, including giving evidence if ever that was necessary.

Again and again she expressed her sorrow for what her dad had done and yet despite it all, and what he had done to her, she loved him still. Bennett knew from experience that people abused by relatives often retain that affection, even though in Anne Marie's case it was her father and she now knew he had admitted killing her mother, her sister and stepsister. Yet, anyone who later witnessed her testimony in court, heard her giving evidence in the trial against her stepmother, listening to details of the ordeal that passed for her childhood, knew that within that timid, nervous exterior was an extremely courageous, resilient young woman and that her enduring love for her dad was a remarkable act of forgiveness.

They talked over the 1992 investigation, in general rather than in detail, and the abuse she had suffered. Bennett was especially interested in hearing first-hand where and how her stepmother Rose fitted in. Finally, she told him she was involved with the media and while he would have preferred she had left it until after any trial he accepted she had every right to look after her own future and that of her children.

As they shook hands and parted, Bennett felt compassion for what she had gone through and concern for her health, especially with what was ahead if she did have to give evidence. He tried to reassure her that her liaison officers were there whenever she needed them and that if she had a problem or needed help or advice, all she had to do was call, whatever the time of day or night.

Most of the care home files had now been found and both Bennett and Moore had kept Fred Davies up to date with their enquiries. The question of how all these crimes could have been committed within a family that had been involved with the caring agencies for so long had already been raised but would soon come under more intense scrutiny.

It was of little comfort to them that reporters had the benefit of hindsight and that if information gathered then, came to light now, modern methods of communications and bodies like the Area Child Protection Committee would provide a swifter, more coordinated response.

Then, it was all so very different. Police and social services did not talk to each other as much as they did now. Today's values and technologies did not exist in the 1970s and finding out whether mistakes were made would also be difficult. Clearly, there would have to be a review, at least in respect of the deaths of Charmaine and Heather West, who were both under 17 when they went missing, but it would have to come later.

Trying to get Fred West to describe his victims for the police artist was not working, so it was decided to try another approach. Dr Richard Neave at Manchester University made plaster casts of skulls and then, guided by the muscular structure, added facial features in clay. By the time they were painted and had glass eyes and hair they looked very realistic. Dr Neave had also worked with Dr Whittaker before so it seemed a good idea.

The Doc also had some welcome news of his own. He had now compared the skull of Remains 9 with the dental records of Carol Cooper and was 'comfortable' it was her. Furthermore, dental records pointed to Remains 2 being Alison Chambers, while Juanita Mott might be Remains 7, though that was still to be confirmed. This meant that seven of the nine victims would soon meet the Doc's criteria for naming, leaving only Remains 4 and 5 unidentified. One of these was said to be the 'Dutch girl', the other, the second 'Worcester girl', who could be Shirley Hubbard though they had very little information about her and no photograph.

This meant the forensic focus would soon switch from concentrating on identification to finding evidence of how the girls had died, what the items found with them were and what they had been used for. While this may have appeared obvious, it was essential to try and establish where they had come from and what their real use was. If they were used for binding, as masks or gags then the evidence had to be collected professionally and scientifically.

The next day, as arranged, Paul Britton returned. A lot had happened since his last visit.

Bennett had kept him up to date with West's note, the recovery of more victims and what had been found with them, and the fact that quite a few bones were missing. Now the investigation was moving towards searching new locations, West appeared to be toying with his interviewers. Frustrating as it was, there was little they could do about it until all the victims found so far had been identified.

West had admitted eleven killings and knowledge of a twelfth – Ann McFall. Now he was there, Britton could discuss it all in more detail than was possible on the phone. To Bennett's surprise, Britton's first move was to hand over the reports he had been waiting for for several months.

Bennett was again anxious for Britton to take another look at the interview teams. Although they were getting regular breaks and days off, dealing with West was difficult and draining and was likely to get worse when they started to concentrate on what was found with his victims.

'You have asked about your interviewers,' said Britton, 'but can you cope with more?'

'More victims – are there likely to be more?'

He replied softly, 'Of course. I can't be certain but there could be. If you can find the key, he could open up like he did with the note.'

Bennett told Britton of the problems they had had with

identification and their attempts to trace anyone who had ever visited Cromwell Street – as well as establishing they were all 'safe and well'. Britton seemed impressed, and when Terry Moore joined them, he added that they should consider searching everywhere that West had worked or spent any time, as it was possible more victims could be scattered around.

Bennett's response was swift and to the point.

They had created a category in HOLMES to cover potential future search sites that included places where West had worked but, realistically, they would have to have a better reason to search than just that. Leaving aside the cost, there would have to be some evidence, either from a member of the public or even West, before a warrant to search could be requested. To say that they had to search everywhere was impractical and, even if desirable, could not be justified.

'Imagine going to someone's home that West had worked on and telling the occupier that the police were going to remove what building work had been done, just because he had put down a patio, dug a trench or whatever?'

To emphasise the point, Bennett added that West had spent some time putting in the foundations for Prinknash Abbey, home to a sizeable community of Benedictine monks just outside Gloucester. Often he had been on site on his own, as he had at scores of other properties. Was Britton seriously suggesting that such places should be searched? That the foundations should be dug up? How many times did Bennett have to say it? If somewhere was to be searched there was only one way to do it and that was properly. The ground-penetrating radar would be of little use there. It was just a pointer not a panacea. Britton accepted the mild rebuke but persisted: 'I can only say that it must be a possibility that he could have put other victims where he worked. He would have had the opportunity and may have taken it.' For now, at least, he accepted that they would concentrate the search on areas already identified for Charmaine, Rena and Ann McFall, and consider other places if and when tangible evidence came to light.

Then the discussion turned to the artefacts found with the victims and the missing bones. West, said Bennett, seemed unwilling to talk about this, except in the case of Lynda Gough, whom he said had died by accident when indulging in some sort of fetish involving bondage. It was this that led the police to have a closer look at the hook and holes in the beams in the cellar. Britton reminded him that both Fred and Rose West were predatory and sadistic sexual psychopaths who more than likely would have indulged their depraved ideas throughout the abduction of their victims and that there was no limit to what they might have done to them, alive or dead. For the Wests, this was something special and personal. Fred, he predicted, would not want to talk about it other than to his wife.

As for Rose, Britton was as sure as Bennett and Moore that not only did she know all about the murders, at least those at Cromwell Street, she was actively involved. It might even have started with her there. The investigation had already shown her to be the more violent and sexually insatiable, certainly as time went on, for despite the fantasy explanations he offered in his interviews, Fred's sexual prowess was limited by comparison and he had often been more of a voyeur than anything else. It was also the psychologist's view the couple had almost certainly agreed on a plan for Fred to admit the murders and exonerate her and that she would deny knowing anything, come what may. Through it all, her husband was as important to her as she was to him. They were a team in every way.

Before he left, Britton paid a visit to Cromwell Street and having checked out the interview teams as requested, confirmed they seemed to be coping well.

That evening it was decided to charge Fred West with the murder of Carol Ann Cooper between 9 November 1973 and 27 February 1994. She was the last victim to be found at Cromwell Street and Dr Whittaker was now 'comfortable' the remains were hers.

Even by their standards, it had been a busy day.

Apart from Paul Britton there was the visit by Her Majesty's Inspector of Constabulary – who had commented how impressed he was by the work they were doing, a rare tribute – and they had allowed the media into the MIR under the 'pool' arrangements as planned.

Just after 9 p.m. that night Bennett decided he had had enough. Tomorrow, there would be a news conference to announce the new charge against West, bring the media up to date and again appeal to them to be responsible, consider the feelings of the victims and not intrude into the police investigation.

Though Friday 18 March was Bennett's birthday, he had no special plans. He was taking the following day off anyway. There were family things to do, not least to try and find a hotel they liked to host his son Andrew's forthcoming wedding reception, as the bride's parents were away working in Hong Kong. Later that evening 'Ginge' Carter, Brian Waldon and he, together with their wives, were having their reunion.

As for his birthday, it was not an occasion that needed to involve the investigation or the team. It was a family affair and he was happy to keep it that way.

Except it didn't quite turn out like that.

The morning's news conference was arranged for 9.30 a.m. at the Brunswick Road Campus of Gloscat, the city's arts and technology college. There was an accompanying statement giving details of the new charge against Fred West and the circumstances of Carol Ann Cooper's disappearance. The statement also included an update on the search at Cromwell Street, the plan to use a police artist for facial reconstruction, and the information that no further sites would be searched until at least 28 March when the investigation would move to Kempley. It also emphasised there was still no formal identification of any of the victims, as that was a matter for the coroner, and like every release from then on, it also carried the warning from the Attorney-General like a health warning on a cigarette packet.

For Bennett, these set-piece conferences were becoming a bit of a chore. He knew he had to do them to support the press office, but this 'upside down' investigation left him with a limited role. He didn't need to make appeals for information from the public; when he had, it was only to diffuse speculation from the media over Rena and Charmaine, whom the inquiry team were already investigating. His only real appeal, and one that was heartfelt, was for reporters to act responsibly and with sensitivity, not that it had had the desired effect yet.

That morning the room was full almost to capacity. There were more microphones on the tables where Bennett sat between Moore and Allison than before, and more camera crews. As they sat down there was the usual jostling for position. The room quietened and holding the typed press release Bennett looked up and began as he had on every previous occasion.

'Good morning, ladies and gentlemen . . .', but before he could say another word a voice from the floor interrupted him.

'Can we say something?'

Bennett's face contorted in a mixture of anxiety and controlled anger. He glared at Hilary Allison and Colin Handy. This was not supposed to happen. They had been told that questions would be answered afterwards. What did they want to say? Why hadn't whoever interrupted him waited?

'Yes?' was all he could muster. And immediately a resounding chorus of 'Happy birthday to you' broke out and filled the room.

There was no doubt it was well intentioned but it was not what he wanted to hear and he was embarrassed. He wasn't just being dog-in-the-manger, there were practical reasons. Some of those singing to him he didn't like, most he didn't trust and he couldn't help thinking it was being done just to test his reaction. From the position of the camera crews and their stance, as well as the microphones, it was clear it was all being recorded. The last thing he wanted was a smiley, happy photograph of him that could be dredged up and used out of context later.

He managed to keep his composure but underneath he was seething. Whenever he had faced the media, he had tried to portray the sadness and tragedy of what they were involved in; it was how he and the team genuinely felt about every aspect of their work. There was nothing joyous in anything he had to say and that morning he was to tell them about the identification and murder of another young girl.

It may have been his birthday but the way it had begun had not made it a happy one and even if their best wishes were genuine this was neither the time nor the place to show it.

There were no further interruptions and Bennett ensured that when he did the one-to-one interviews later, he kept fastidiously to the two questions rule and made his answers as short as possible. He just wanted to get out of the room as soon as possible and get on with his real work.

The investigation was still attracting worldwide attention. Some of the reporters could speak little English, though the majority were home-based and included some of the best-known faces in television news. Every British national newspaper, agency and television network was represented and there was a healthy competition between them and the Gloucestershire media, who were all well known to Allison, Handy and Bennett – though to Bennett's disappointment, even some of the locals were beginning to adopt the tactics of their more unscrupulous colleagues, which was distressing the victims' families and disrupting the investigation.

Tabloid newspapers and TV companies were offering large sums of money to witnesses and potential witnesses, setting up contracts and book deals that in some cases promised six-figure payouts.

Sending items for forensic examination was not the almost casual matter cinema and television made it appear. It was a costly affair and there were many tests that could be applied to exhibits. Some were obvious given the circumstances of a case, others were more relevant to connecting a witness or offender to a scene or item. No two cases were the same and what might be relevant from the examination of an item was something that only someone on the investigation and, more often than not, the senior investigating officer and his scenes of crime officers could appreciate. Consequently, Bennett had to be specific about what to send for analysis and what he was expecting to find. Later that morning he had a meeting with the crime scene manager Bob Beetham and forensic scientist Dr Wilf Basley, who would be doing the work.

Any strands of hair present in what appeared to be masks or bindings would be compared with any hair that was found with the victim. In the case of the wound tape masks, they would first be examined intact and then unwound to see if there were any fingerprints or evidence on the inside. Any sizeable hair exhibits would also be examined. The same process would be followed for the other masks, the plastic and cord to enable the police to try and build a picture of what they were used for.

Withy Cole had visited the MIR regularly since his appointment, as had the Gloucester Crown prosecuting solicitor Rita Crane. As well as bringing them up to date, Bennett discussed West's detention and their interview strategy. Bennett knew that questioning West about what was found with the remains – rather than sticking to the issue of whose the remains were – could get him into trouble with defence lawyers later, but insisted he was 'trying to remove ambiguity'. He also considered the prospect of some of the interviews not being accepted as evidence on legal grounds but had decided it would make little difference. West's initial interviews, his admissions and the note would all be allowed and after that 'the facts would speak for themselves'. They discussed Paul Britton's visits and the psychologist's opinion that Fred and Rose were in it together, even if not all the murders had involved both of them, and they went over the case of Caroline Owens, who Bennett described as a 'sample', someone who at a time when the Wests were carrying out their sexual experimentation and going a stage further happened to be in the wrong place at the wrong time, just like all the others who followed.

The enquiries into Fred and Rose West's previous convictions for indecent assault and assault on Caroline Owens were continuing. In keeping with force procedure, the file had been destroyed long ago and the prosecuting police inspector was now dead. There was little detail of the case in the court records and the magistrate who had dealt with it only had a vague recollection. Caroline Owens had contacted the inquiry almost immediately and within 48 hours of the start of the investigation had made a statement. Soon afterwards, the *Sun* had reported that in 1972, a girl from the Forest of Dean, about 15 miles from Gloucester, had been sexually and physically assaulted by both Fred and Rose West, for which the couple had been convicted and fined at Gloucester Magistrates Court.

That Bennett had first become aware of the case through a newspaper report not only irritated him and was an early sign they might have a mole, it was also proof of the time it took in the early days of the investigation to process information. While detectives checked it out, the potential significance of the case remained obscured.

Caroline Owens, then Caroline Raine, briefly worked as a nanny to the Wests' children but then left. One evening, when hitch-hiking home, she was picked up by them in a car that Fred was driving. During the journey Rose, who was sitting in the back seat beside her, indecently assaulted her and soon after that she was punched unconscious by Fred. The couple then used her scarf to tie her up and bound her head in brown tape so she was unable to see. When they reached 25 Cromwell Street she was untied and after she had agreed not to struggle they removed all her clothing, tied her up and gagged her again. The Wests had talked of carrying out some sort of crude surgery that would enhance her sexuality and make her more responsive but made do with hitting her genitals with a belt buckle. Then, with her victim still tied up, Rose performed oral sex on her while having intercourse with Fred. When Rose went out Fred raped her. Later, on Rose's return, they bathed her – to get rid of the marks of the tape – but in the morning she managed to give them the slip and escape.

When the case came to court, Fred and Rose pleaded guilty to offences of assault and indecent assault and were both fined £25 for each offence, £100 in total.

Bennett had read Caroline Owens's statements but had seen no official detailed description of the offences, as they had all been destroyed. To get that detail detectives went to the offices of the local newspaper (the *Gloucester Citizen*) and found a full report of the case. This corroborated what Caroline alleged. Despite this there was some confusion over whether she had accused Fred West of raping her when she made the allegations or if there was some agreement that in exchange for her not pursuing a rape charge, they would plead guilty to assault. Later, other statements were being taken to clarify this, for it was obvious there had been a lot of violence and sexual deviance in these offences. Even without the rape allegation, abduction and false imprisonment were much more serious than assault and indecent assault and could only be tried at the Crown Court. Something did not add up.

However, the extent of the couple's depravity as long ago as 1972 was evident. That Caroline Owens had been bound and gagged seemed to correspond with what was buried along with later victims.

The criminal records of Fred and Rose at Scotland Yard included a note of the case and although details were scant, it did at least name the officers involved. One had retired and was unable to remember anything, while the other, Detective Constable Kevan Price, was still serving.

He had searched his old pocket books and found the entries

for the arrest and interviews of both Fred and Rose West. These were revealing. After both had continually denied the allegations, Fred eventually admitted sexual and physical assault and implicated Rose. When she was told, Rose simply responded that if her husband had said that was what had happened, it had!

Price also remembered photographs were taken of Caroline Owens's injuries and the marks the tape had left when she was bound and gagged. He was sure she had not mentioned being raped and could offer no explanation for the relatively minor charges that were preferred. He could only say that the decision in this respect was made way above him, as the file for proceedings would have been authorised at senior officer level.

A search through a large number of old police photographic negatives sent to headquarters for archiving when offices in Gloucester Police Station underwent a facelift in 1990 uncovered the original negatives for the offence. These included photographs of Caroline's injuries and the marks left by the tape, as well as the side of 25 Cromwell Street showing how, at that time, a car could be driven in between the house and the church, along with photographs of the car she had been picked up in.

Caroline had escaped and gone to the police only to be badly let down from then on, but for the Wests it was a warning they would not forget. They knew they could not afford to get caught again so when the need to satisfy their depraved desires resurfaced, which was when Lynda Gough was with them, they knew the only sure way of preventing her from ever telling anyone what they did was to kill her.

In light of all that, and the size of the house in which Rose West brought up their children, Bennett reasoned it was improbable that any of the victims could have been dismembered there without her finding out. West had talked about doing it in the bath and while that was certainly possible, there would have been copious amounts of blood. While Bennett accepted that there was still a lot of conjecture, common sense with regard to the similar stories of being tied up coming from the West children and Caroline Owens and the taping, which Rose West had instigated, meant the net around her was tightening.

And what of all the lies?

Rose had denied knowing Shirley Robinson, a blatant lie that could be uncovered in numerous ways. The differing accounts of when Heather left and her reasons for going, as well as the money Rose now claimed she had given her, were at odds with what she had said in 1992.

Bennett had already privately decided to arrest her. First he wanted to identify all of the Cromwell Street victims and start the other searches, then gather more evidence from anyone who had been at Cromwell Street.

The CPS solicitors listened intently then pointed out what Bennett already knew, that much of what he was saying was completely circumstantial and relied upon similar fact evidence, always difficult to get admitted as evidence. Bennett assured them that whatever evidence there was against Rose West would always be considered alongside anything that was found in her favour – except that up to now, there was nothing. Everything they had was to her detriment.

Withy Cole could see the merit in Bennett's thinking and said he would bring forward the legal complexities of using similar fact evidence and research current law on the subject, which would highlight the difficulties that might lie ahead. Bennett made it clear that he intended to have Rose West arrested again, possibly before her police bail expired, though for the moment there was too much else to do.

The master analysis diagrams and charts of Cromwell Street that adorned the walls in the Senior Investigating Officer's office had been brought up to date. The names of victims they thought they had identified were now listed as 'believed to be . . .', with gaps alongside Remains 4 and 5. Was one another

Worcester girl? Were they both Worcester girls, because West said he picked up the Dutch girl he called Tulip in Evesham, which is in Worcestershire? Was she even Dutch?

Each of them was depicted on the charts by an icon rather than a photograph as Bennett had decided that until an inquest had confirmed their identity they would remain as 'believed to be . . .'. A photograph would give a false impression. The artefacts that had been found and their exhibit numbers were displayed as well as the dates of birth, the date when they were last seen and descriptions for each of the remains, lines leading to the place where they were found like irregularly spaced spokes on a wheel.

The chart was nearing completion but there were still important things to be added, such as the names of witnesses to their disappearance or any scientific evidence. This would include information from Professor Knight on which bones were missing and, in time, the results of the forensic examination. It was a chart that contained all the information the team had gathered and, when the time came, all they and the Crown Prosecution Service would need to know and use.

Bennett was hoping that evening's briefing would bring forward some new evidence or ideas to help them identify Remains 4 and 5. Once it was over he could get away and call into the hospital to see his mother before getting home early to enjoy what was left of his birthday with his wife.

With the briefing approaching, Bennett was alone in his office dictating reports and replies to letters, but Terry Moore was nowhere to be seen. Normally the two detectives spent 5 minutes or so before a briefing outlining what they wanted to bring up. Bennett had always been a stickler for punctuality. Everyone who had worked with him knew it, and so Moore's absence was unusual. When he had still not arrived a few minutes before 6, Bennett decided to go on ahead, expecting to find his number two already there.

There seemed to be more of the team there than normal, but still no sign of Moore and it was now 6 p.m. exactly. Accepting that something must have cropped up that he would explain later, Bennett began the briefing but could not help noticing the team's focus of attention was somewhere beyond and behind him. At the same time, a few feet from his chair, he heard the rear door of the club opening and, as he turned, Terry Moore entered holding a large envelope in one hand and carrying a spade with a bow tied around it in the other, and a spontaneous chorus of 'Happy birthday' burst forth. Bennett got to his feet to receive the gifts and a broad smile creased his face, the feeling of slight embarrassment hidden by a smile that turned to laughter. This time and in this environment, he not only appreciated the sentiment but also felt humbled that they had gone to so much trouble.

The card was full of comments and good wishes from the team. The spade was a symbol of why they were all there. As he started to thank them, Moore turned and left the room again, this time returning with a gift-wrapped parcel containing bottles of a favourite claret. When he left and came back the final time, Moore handed over two smaller packages, one containing a petrol lighter engraved 'The West enquiry 1994', the other a box of cigars. Just for good measure, the fruit machine chipped in with a tune, which for once Bennett was happy to let run through to the end. It was, he remarked, 'better than Christmas'.

Before sitting down again, he told everyone to finish at 8 p.m. when he would buy them a drink in the bar. For those who couldn't make it he would 'leave one in'. Now, though, it was time to get back to work and the normally sombre atmosphere was restored.

The focus remained on identification but they were still no nearer naming Remains 4 and 5, while the number of possibilities for the Dutch girl continued to grow as parents whose daughters had come to the United Kingdom and not kept in touch, contacted the investigation. Until now they had never been regarded as 'missing'. It was further proof of the shadow cast by 25 Cromwell Street, both at home and abroad.

They had managed to find out more about Shirley Hubbard but there were still no usable photographs or dental records, which meant Dr Whittaker had no starting point to begin his analysis. Even so, there was a growing feeling based upon what West had said and the similarities between her disappearance and the others, that Shirley Hubbard was one of the 'Worcester girl' victims.

It also seemed that the secret of the safe house was out, so Rose, Stephen and Mae would have to be moved. They always thought it might happen but it was annoying nonetheless.

Bottles of whisky from a well-wisher and a £100 cheque for goods from the management of Tesco supermarket, which had been donated to the diggers, would be raffled and the proceeds donated to the Victim Support charity in Gloucester.

When the briefing was over, Bennett visited his mother in hospital and was pleased to see her making a better than expected recovery. He called his wife and she drove over and joined the gathering in the social club. It was an enjoyable evening, made all the more so because it wasn't planned. It gave everyone some momentary light relief and enabled them to put Fred and Rose West to the backs of their minds – if only for a couple of hours – for the fact that the team was virtually a prisoner to the investigation was something that was mentioned throughout the evening, as was the need for social gatherings in the future.

TWENTY-THREE

The cat was out of the bag. The media had found Rose West's safe house. So, together with Stephen and Mae, she would have to be moved to another secret location.

Irritating though it was, it was not unexpected, and that Friday, with the minimum of fuss, the operations division transferred them, and all the eavesdropping equipment, to a former police house at the back of the police station at Dursley, a town more than 10 miles from Gloucester. This time there would be no landline phone with its area dialling code to give the game away, only mobiles. Because Stephen West appeared to be in regular contact with the media they decided not to tell him the new location straightaway. He would have to find somewhere else to live.

The next day, Saturday, was only the second day since the investigation began when there was no work at Cromwell Street, as rest days were now an important part of the schedule. The MIR, though, remained open around the clock as the search continued for photographs that would help Dr Whittaker identify the last remains.

Although Shirley Hubbard was considered a real possibility, every lead towards finding more about her came to nothing. Born Shirley Lloyd on 26 June 1959, she was also known as Shirley Owen after her father. She was taken into care at the age of 2 when her parents separated. When she was 6, she was fostered by the Hubbard family and lived in Droitwich. She took their name in 1972 just before entering her teens. Shirley had always been strong-willed and grew into a confident adolescent. She seemed to enjoy her life with her foster parents though she had once run away from home and been missing for over five days before the police found her.

Less than a month later, on 14 November 1972, she was on work experience at Debenham's in Worcester. It was half-day closing and when she went to work she took all her belongings with her. When the shop closed at lunchtime, she met up with a boyfriend and they spent the afternoon and evening together in Worcester before he walked her to her bus stop. After agreeing to meet the next day he saw her onto the bus and watched as it set off for Droitwich.

But Shirley never made it home. She was reported missing and the Worcester Police mounted a major investigation, comparing her disappearance with that of Carol Cooper, who had vanished almost a year before to the day. Yet no evidence to connect what had happened to the two missing teenagers was ever found.

West's interviews were not much help either. The focus was still on getting him to name Remains 4 and 5 but he continued to refer to them as the 'two Worcester girls' or 'Dutch' or 'Tulip'. Whether he intended to confuse his interviewers or had genuinely forgotten who they were was hard to tell. Sometimes he referred to them as the same girl and when the mask was introduced he reckoned it was the 'Dutch' girl, only to change his mind again soon after.

As the inquiry teams traced more girls who had been in care homes in Gloucester, principally Jordan's Brook House, they found more evidence of a trail that led to 25 Cromwell Street. Two claimed the Wests had committed serious sexual offences against them and one of them said she had gone there with Alison Chambers, who was a good friend.

Alison, the girl said, was infatuated with promises the Wests had made to her about her potential future with the family. It was something she often fantasised about and had secretly told her she intended to run away that summer of 1979, when she was on a youth training scheme at a solicitor's in Gloucester. Alison asked her to cover for her with staff at the home and to bring her clothes to her after she had left. The girl did as she was asked but Alison failed to make the meeting. In September 1979, two months on from when she was reported missing as an absconder from care, Alison wrote to her mother and stepfather. It was a well-composed letter and in it she told them she was all right and happily working for a family looking after their five children. She apologised for causing them concern but told them not to worry and she would write again.

Nothing more was ever heard from her and later, when she would have been 17 years old, the letter was partially responsible for West Glamorgan County Council considering Alison Chambers as no longer missing. Fifteen years later she was about to be named as the Wests' latest victim.

The investigation had recovered her dental records and Dr Whittaker was now 'comfortable' that Remains 2 were those of Alison Chambers, the girl West had alternately referred to as 'Shirley's mate', her 'lesbian lover' or 'lesbian friend'.

It turned out that Alison had been in care in Wales and was only transferred to Jordan's Brook House in December 1978. She had no connection with Shirley Robinson; there was little likelihood of them having met as Shirley was three years older. West's version of why she had come to Gloucester and the threats she had made were more lies designed to cover up the truth.

The face staring out from the cover of the country's biggest-selling tabloid dashed any hope Bennett had had of an uninterrupted Saturday off. Dave Griffiths rang to inform him the *Sun* had published on its front page a full-face picture of Fred West, complete with his newly assigned prison number.

Of course, there had already been many photographs of Fred West in the newspapers but this was different. This was an up-to-date print and could only have been taken by someone in the prison service while he was in their custody the week before – and that had been for less than an hour. It was a breathtaking breach of security and one that showed jaw-dropping contempt for the Attorney-General's warning. Should identification be an issue during West's trial the defence could argue a witness was identifying the picture rather than the defendant. It called for an immediate investigation, not only by the police but also by the prison service.

The constabulary would have to conduct yet another investigation that would stretch its tissue-thin resources still further, while the Attorney-General would have to be told his caution was having little effect.

Some of the Sunday newspapers also seemed to want to test the patience of the Attorney-General and the strength of the Contempt of Court Act. There was further speculation about the number of murders West had committed and the scope of the inquiry. Stephen West had given an interview to the *News of the World* in which he talked of living in a safe house – the first of a series of articles.

The media hype was unrelenting, yet Bennett was determined the investigation would not carry the can. If there was any blame it lay somewhere between the failure of the Attorney-General to act and the inadequacy of the law governing contempt of court. Any submission from West's defence that he could not have a fair trial would be resisted. When Bennett told Chief Constable Tony Butler what was in the newspapers that weekend he was also far from happy that his warnings had not been heeded and summoned reporters to another meeting on Monday.

West was taken to 25 Midland Road to show the police where he had buried the body of his 8-year-old stepdaughter Charmaine. He maintained it was a waste of time – he had already tried and failed to find her when working on an extension. He reckoned she had been carted away with the earth and rubble.

He was taken to a nearby allotment he had used, a ploy to see if it jogged his memory about other possible victims. Then when he was driven along Bristol Road where Mary Bastholm was last seen, her disappearance was raised but he denied all knowledge of her and remained indifferent. There was no flicker of recognition, no outward sign he might be lying.

They were still no nearer to identifying Remains 4 and 5 and until they had, officers could not be moved to other lines of enquiry, such as a deeper investigation into the background of Fred West and his first wife Catherine 'Rena' West, formerly Costello, or further allegations of sexual offences by both Fred and Rose West and others.

Charmaine and Rena were next on the list of priorities. Their relatives had been contacted but there was still much more research to be done, not only into their time with Fred and Rose West but also to establish as accurately as possible when they were last seen. As for Ann McFall, whom West said had been murdered but not by him, a decision on whether to dig where West said she might have been buried would be taken later, though not before the searches at 25 Midland Road and Fingerpost Field had been completed. In the end, it was a piece of dogged detective work that proved the turning point in the quest to name Remains 4 and 5.

Terry Moore had been reviewing all of the HOLMES information on Shirley Hubbard from the moment her name attracted their attention. He came across a statement that mentioned her being a bridesmaid, and not long before she had gone missing. When he checked to see if this had been followed up it was apparent that more than one member of the MIR had overlooked it, a grave oversight, as she would almost certainly have been photographed. There may even be one of her smiling and showing her teeth as Dr Whittaker had requested.

Moore set the ball in motion and the couple whose wedding it was were soon traced, along with their photo album and photographer. Even better, he still had all of the negatives of the pictures he took including those of a particularly photogenic bridesmaid. It was Shirley Hubbard, and one of the photographs showed her peering from behind a tree, her pretty face fixed in a broad smile that clearly showed her front teeth and fulfilled every requirement on the Doc's photographic identification wish list.

The Deputy Senior Investigating Officer made sure the photograph and all the necessary information was sent on to him immediately. If Remains 4 or 5 were those of Shirley Hubbard, they would soon know.

It was now apparent that virtually all of the people who had passed through 25 Cromwell Street, either as lodgers or visitors, from the time the Wests took up occupation in 1972 right up to the day the digging began on 24 February 1994, had now been traced. As for the few who had not, it was decided now was not the time to make a public appeal as this would only crank up the speculation. If necessary, that could be done later.

Although Dr Whittaker still had doubts about Remains 5, he was quite certain the dental work on Remains 4 stemmed from mainland Europe rather than the UK. This meant that if Remains 5 *was* Shirley Hubbard, Remains 4 had to be the 'Dutch girl' as West had first called her.

In the MIR, Nick Churchill was not only trying to trace other missing persons listed in HOLMES, he was also handling requests from colleagues about other potential witnesses. Under pressure to get their information first, his exasperated trademark cry of 'It's not as simple as that' could often be heard above the general hubbub.

Staring at the chart on his office wall late that evening and once more reflecting on the sadness of it all, Bennett could not shake the feeling he was missing something, the key that would enable them to unlock the puzzle that contained the name of Remains 4. Then, as he stood and looked out over Gloucester Cathedral, he scolded himself for allowing such a thought to enter his head. Things like that only happened in films, not real police investigations. It worried him that perhaps he too was getting carried away with all the hype though, in fact, he was about to have his own 'Road to Damascus' moment.

As he sat down he looked at the chart again and all his misgivings were swept aside as he realised there *was* something missing from the chart, something so simple yet potentially vital in helping to establish the last identity.

From the moment they first realised there was more than one victim at Cromwell Street, Bennett had made a policy decision to call them 'remains' and number them in the order they were found. That's why Heather was *possibly* Remains 1, Alison Chambers *possibly* Remains 2 and so on. This, though, may not have been the order they were murdered. Reaching for a yellow highlighter pen, he put on his reading glasses and stood over the chart. Looking first at the garden, it seemed the remains found there were, in fact, the last ones to be buried at Cromwell Street. On a separate piece of paper, he noted down the last provable sightings of the 'possible' victims, concluding that although Heather West was Remains 1 she was actually Victim 9. Alison Chambers, though Remains 2, was Victim 8. Shirley Robinson was Remains 3 but Victim 7. Continuing this exercise he looked at all the information they had on each of the girls buried inside the house and came to the conclusion that Remains 8, found underneath the bathroom and 'possibly' Lynda Gough, was actually Victim 1.

Studying the cellar victims in the same way, he worked out the order in which they had gone missing. Leaving aside the unknown Remains 4, it appeared that after Lynda Gough had been buried in the bathroom, the five victims in the cellar were next, to be followed by the last three in the garden.

He could hardly get it down fast enough.

Excitedly, he transcribed the calculations onto the chart with his highlighter pen. From his frantic scribbling, a picture emerged that suggested the cellar victims had been buried clockwise. This made Carol Ann Cooper Remains 9 but Victim 2. The same process made Lucy Partington Victim 3 and if the theory was correct, Shirley Hubbard was both Remains 5 and Victim 5, Juanita Mott was Remains 7 but Victim 6, and Remains 4 would, by coincidence, be Victim 4.

What this simple calculation meant was that Remains 4, which Professor Knight and Dr Whittaker agreed was that of a heavy-boned female who at the time she was buried was aged anything between 17 and 22, but with a dental age of over 20, had gone missing between Lucy Partington's disappearance on 27 December 1973 and that of Shirley Hubbard on 15 November 1974.

Cautiously working from the outside ages first, this gave him a speculative profile for the victim of a quite heavily built foreign female aged 16 to 23, who had gone missing between December 1973 and November 1974. If this were right it would dramatically reduce the number of possible IDs. Though Bennett was tired he checked his calculations again and pondered his conclusion. It just seemed so simple and he could not understand why he or someone else had not thought of it before.

Mark Grimshaw was still in the MIR so Bennett asked him to come back to his office and have a look at the chart. Within minutes, they had returned to the MIR to run the information through HOLMES and the analyst software. Using Bennett's criteria, Grimshaw was able to bring down the number of possibles from over 130 to under 40, and when he based it on the age range of 20–22 given by both the Prof and the Doc, it brought the number down again, to less than 30. Of these, only 9 were of real interest, among them one young woman reported missing to the police in Lewisham, London. Thérèse Siegenthaler, a Swiss national, had been hitch-hiking to Dublin and was last seen on 14 April 1974. She was 22 years old when she went missing.

There was nothing more that could be done that night but finding out everything they could about Thérèse Siegenthaler would be a priority when they returned in the morning.

A meeting had been arranged at Gloucester Police Station for 5 p.m. on Wednesday 23 March involving Her Majesty's Coroner for Gloucester David Gibbons, his assistant Alan Slater, Professor Knight, Dr Whittaker, Bennett and Moore.

Human remains were the coroner's responsibility from the moment they were found until he agreed to release them for burial or cremation. In murder cases, the remains of a victim could be held for months or years just in case they needed to be re-examined. Bennett and Moore had kept the coroner up to date with progress at Cromwell Street. Now that it looked as though they knew the names of at least eight out of the nine victims, it was time to put some of it on the official record.

Nick Churchill was ignoring all the usual requests coming his way to work with Detective Constable 'Paddy' Hannah, one of the officers responsible for Remains 4. They were concentrating on the new, narrowed-down list of probables put together the night before. By mid-afternoon, they had discovered there was a file that included details of the disappearance of Thérèse Siegenthaler at the Metropolitan Police Missing Persons Bureau, which, only the week before, had changed to the Police National Missing Persons Bureau (PNMPB). The file was at Lewisham and contained photographs and a dental record.

Bennett wanted to look at the nine files as soon as he could to further narrow his options, though Thérèse Siegenthaler was now of most interest. The photographs and dental records would be faxed down that afternoon. Dr Whittaker could have a look at them when he arrived for the coroner's meeting.

When the fax from the PNMPB arrived, the information was readable but the transmission quality of both the photographs and dental records was poor. The complete file would have to be fetched.

The Prof and Doc arrived some time before the scheduled meeting and were greeted by Bennett and Moore. They went to the Senior Investigating Officer's office and got straight on to identification but before they could even mention suggestions for Remains 4, Dr Whittaker said he was now 'more than comfortable' that Shirley Hubbard was Remains 5.

If Bennett and Moore were pleased with that, their faces probably turned a redder hue at what followed, as the Doc went on to say that in all his experience, which covered more than thirty years, he had never come across such quality and standard of work as that produced by this investigation. Recovery of the remains, he said, had been more than exceptional. Teeth had been found from all the sites even though they had become dislodged after death, during decomposition or while they were being recovered. Their response to his request for the information he needed to go with the photographs was so detailed he could not have asked for more and, given the time that had passed since the photographs were taken, he was amazed at what they had managed to do. He wanted to meet the team and tell them this personally.

Professor Knight not only endorsed everything the Doc had said but also added that he, too, could not have asked for a better search or method of carrying it out as evidenced by the number of small bones, nails and teeth they had found in the most appalling conditions imaginable.

Bennett and Moore listened with a mixture of pride and embarrassment. It was a huge compliment to receive, especially from two such eminent scientists, and the Prof and Doc were invited to the briefing that evening.

Getting back to business, Dr Whittaker was told of Thérèse Siegenthaler and handed the fax of the dental record from her file. Almost immediately a smile lit up his face. He recalled similar dental work on the outstanding set of remains, adding cautiously that if she was who they thought she was, she had undergone other treatment than that shown on the fax.

No sooner had Bennett's hopes started to sink than they were raised again by the Doc's explanation that in mainland Europe it was often the practice to only record work that was done during a course of treatment rather than what had been done previously. This differed from the UK where records were updated at each session to record all dental work done, past and present.

Without further delay, Bennett decided he would have the full file on Thérèse Siegenthaler collected that evening by police motorcyclist and got on to the MIR to make the arrangements.

The coroner for Gloucester, David Gibbons, who chaired the meeting, remarked, too, how quickly they had reached a stage where the opening of an inquest could be considered. He suggested 14 April 1994 as the date for the opening of hearings into all but Remains 4 – unless they were identified in the meantime. It would be in the council chamber at Shire Hall in Gloucester.

Dr Whittaker took a video of some of his work to the briefing. The word had got around and nearly everyone on the investigation was there. As he began his lecture, you could have heard a pin drop. He told them that even in a plane or train crash, when there were manifests and records, he rarely got information from investigators that gave him a more than 50 per cent chance of success in carrying out his work. Repeating what he had told Bennett and Moore earlier, he said they should be proud of their work so far. It was an achievement he would never forget and an example other investigations would find difficult to match. The Prof nodded in agreement and added his own personal congratulations.

The video centred on their most recent success. The image of Shirley Hubbard was now seen in the context of his remarkable technique. As the pictures ran his audience hung on the Doctor's every word, hooked on every frame. It was a truly spellbinding demonstration.

It showed, among other photographs, a happy young girl in a bridesmaid's dress peering around a tree, her innocent features fixed in a glowing smile. As the sharpness of the photograph faded before their eyes, through it emerged the image of a skull, its outline coinciding almost exactly with that of the photograph. The video showed how the process was repeated again and again until the proportions were spot on, and explained just why the Doc needed so much information about the photograph and lenses used – to appreciate what distortion there might be in the photograph.

Then, through a small square that moved like a cursor on a computer screen, features from the skull were transposed onto the photograph and gradually a picture emerged where the eye orbits on the skull and photograph matched perfectly, followed by the ear canals. When the teeth were tracked in the same way, they showed through on the skull in exactly the same positions they were on the photograph. In size and shape, they matched perfectly with the smile in the photograph.

There was no need for dental records. What they had seen was so graphic, no one could doubt the skull was that of Shirley Hubbard. It also vindicated Bennett and Moore's earlier decision to accept the Doc's cautious 'comfort level' rather than waiting for him to say he was certain.

It had been a powerful demonstration and a haunting experience no one there was likely to forget. Bennett certainly felt that way and could see it in the faces of everyone else, for what they had seen depicted was a young girl whose life had been ended almost before it had begun and, perhaps even more poignantly, this was the girl whose face was wrapped in that appalling mask with its crude breathing tubes.

A short time later the briefing was over, though unknown to Bennett his directive to have the Siegenthaler file brought to him that night would bring with it fresh problems.

Shortly after 9 p.m., the press office alerted him to the news that a reporter was on to the Siegenthaler lead and was about to catch a plane to Switzerland to contact the girl's relatives. Was there any comment?

Bennett told them to say nothing nor issue any statement. This time he was sure the leak had not come from their end but that was of little consequence. No point either in venting his anger. That would not achieve anything. Even so, he could not let the media get to the relatives first.

According to force control, the motorcyclist was due back with the file within an hour. It would have details of next of kin, which were probably out of date. The correct procedure was through Interpol but that would take too long, for Interpol was just a network of offices belonging to police forces across the world that relayed requests to their local officers. Scotland Yard was the UK branch. They had no operational officers on the ground – that was another myth spawned by thrillers and films.

Any request to Interpol would not be resolved that night, perhaps not even that week! Bennett was still in a quandary when the motorcyclist delivered the file, still wrapped. It did contain addresses and some phone numbers but there had been no contact with the family for some time. Then, as he looked through the file, he remembered a lecture at the Police College which told how Swiss police had helped a British investigation. Bennett knew the lecturer – he had worked with him before and could contact him at any time. Could the Swiss police who had helped before help again? The call made, he discovered that the principal officer involved worked out of Berne, not far from where Thérèse Siegenthaler's relatives lived, and was easy to contact. He would get in touch immediately and ask him to contact Bennett direct.

Within minutes, the Senior Investigating Officer's phone rang. Bennett could hardly believe it; not only did the officer speak perfect English but the address was on his way home and in an area he knew well. He would go there straightaway.

In no time at all, the officer was on the line again, this time with a member of the Siegenthaler family. Bennett was able to confirm what they had just been told and that he and other officers on the investigation would get back to them as soon as there was more definite news.

Once again the media had caused the investigation added work, though this time their race to get the story first, without any thought for a victim's relatives, had been thwarted – albeit thanks to outrageous good fortune.

TWENTY-FOUR

Janet Leach had been present every time Fred West was interviewed since the moment it was decided he should have an appropriate adult; she was the only person with a 100 per cent attendance record. Bennett had been concerned about this for some time and having read the interview transcripts and listened to the tapes he detected a change in her attitude. It was difficult to put his finger on it, but while she was in no way obstructive, she no longer seemed to react to what West said in quite the same way. Had she been advised on this? Was she becoming too much of a confidante to West? Was she even a victim of 'Stockholm Syndrome', where a person in constant touch with someone who has committed serious crime develops feelings of friendship, compassion or perhaps even something stronger?

Now, if only to give her a rest, Bennett decided it was time for a change and for her to step down. Terry Moore would break the news so that if West took umbrage it could be blamed on him – though as West settled into his new routine at the police station most of his time was taken up with video cartoons.

To ensure Leach was still aware of her obligation, a document was drawn up and backdated to 24 February when the investigation began. It spelled out her legal responsibility to keep everything she had seen and heard confidential until she was officially released from her undertaking, in writing, by the constabulary, which would at the earliest be the conclusion of any court proceedings. It underlined what she had already agreed verbally and covered every conceivable aspect of her role as an appropriate adult.

Janet Leach signed the agreement on 24 March with the proviso she might be asked to come back at a later date.

Arrangements were made with the probation service to find a replacement.

The euphoria at Dr Whittaker's praise was only slightly dampened when, having been contacted to see how his work was progressing, he asked for yet more photographs – as many as possible of the victims, with some more important than others.

The Doc had always stressed the need to be 100 per cent certain, especially when testifying to a coroner or in court and continued to cross-check his conclusions against all the information and methods at his disposal. While he was already at 100 per cent for some of the remains and had reached very high percentages for the others, he would rather dismantle his own research himself than have someone else do it. It was this constant quest for perfection that made him an expert in his field.

Even so, in the minds of the rest of the team, all nine of the Cromwell Street victims were now virtually identified and they were keen to broaden the investigation. The possibility of other victims, including Mary Bastholm, was cropping up more and more at briefings. Then, there was Rose West. When would she be rearrested? As far as Bennett was concerned, it was still too soon to think about that. Rena, Charmaine and Ann McFall were the next priorities along with building the case they already had.

Inspector Richard Bradley and the operations department had put together a plan to search for Rena's remains at Letterbox Field at Kempley. Arrangements to look for Charmaine's at 25 Midland Road were under review.

The search at Kempley would be carried out by members of the constabulary's underwater search team under the guidance of a police search adviser. The team was specially trained to search on land as well as underwater, but it was about to be disbanded after twenty-two years, priced out of existence by the cost of health and safety.

To do their job they would need a large quantity of mechanical and other equipment, the best available in communications, storage tents, prefabricated buildings, and somewhere to eat and rest. Gloucestershire Fire Service would provide a mobile kitchen and the staff to run it.

It was hoped to begin the search for Rena during the next week and although they wouldn't start until they were ready, the media would be told at least two days before, as promised.

The search at 25 Midland Road would be conducted by another team of search-trained officers, this time from the Cotswolds Division, and would be a different operation from that at Cromwell Street. First the garden would be searched while preparations were made to excavate the floor area in the kitchen extension which was built above where the cellar once had been. They would have to think about searching the cellar too, for the Wests had access to it when they lived there. Search warrants would be taken up and kept in force until they were ready to start. That, though, would depend on progress at Kempley and the availability of officers.

It was possible that the toll would be at least twelve murder victims with the possibility of other victims of serious sexual offences as well as witnesses whose circumstances were complicated by their involvement with the Wests. This meant more and more liaison officers were needed when they were already fully occupied on other aspects of the investigation. The solution was to use more volunteers from the Victim Support charity where the two highly dedicated, overworked and caring coordinators of the Gloucester branch, the motherly Hazel Beckett and fatherly Phillip Lowery, would both work on this and coordinate the wider responses from then on.

The network of people affected by the Wests' crimes now spread across the entire country. Supporting them would stretch the charity to the limit. As well as regular meetings with the MIR and the police liaison officers, Bennett, Moore and

Gloucestershire Social Services in the form of Fred Davies promised to support any claims for extra funding.

Sat in his office, Bennett answered his phone. The telephonist asked if he would take a call from his eldest son's fiancée, Jenny. This concerned him as she was working at a primary school in Gloucester as a nursery nurse and had never called him at work before. Apologising for the intrusion, she said she felt he should know something, but first asked if it was true that some of the victims had been tied up and had masks on when their remains had been recovered. Apparently, it was the hot topic among some of the mums. When Bennett said he couldn't discuss it, she identified the source of the playground gossip as the wife of one of the officers involved in the search at Cromwell Street. Jenny thought it strange that the woman was talking freely about the investigation when he never did. After all the warnings, his own and the Deputy Chief Constable's, such a breach of confidentiality was both disturbing and disappointing. All the men at Cromwell Street had worked under the most arduous and stressful conditions and no one could have asked more of them.

He knew some of the younger officers were bound to have been quizzed both by close family members and their friends and, in the circumstances, it would be very difficult to keep it all to themselves. It was different for him. Close as his family were, they never asked about his job. The children had been brought up to understand that and his wife had accepted it soon into their marriage.

He decided to have a firm but quiet word with the officer concerned and keep him on the investigation. There would also be another warning at briefing, though subtle enough to avoid identifying him.

Two other incidents helped him get the message across.

First, Bennett's youngest son David, working as a chef in Cheltenham was stopped on a stairwell at work and asked if he was the son of Detective Superintendent Bennett. When David said he was his questioner identified himself as a reporter and asked if he could talk to him. David gave him short shrift and walked away.

Then Bennett himself took a call from the Royal Oak at Prestbury, for many years his local. The manager warned him that the previous Friday three men, who eventually said they were journalists, one of them with a camera, had come into the bar and asked if he had been in lately and when he was likely to next pay a visit! They left when they were told he had not been in for some time, the reason for which must be obvious.

He could not believe it. Which part of the warnings did these reporters not understand? Did they never take no for an answer? For although he found this continuing intrusion into his private life a real pain, if he was getting it then it was likely other members of the team were as well. So when he related these latest incidents at the next meeting it did nothing to improve the atmosphere. Indeed, some wanted the press office closed down altogether and their involvement with the media restricted to written statements only.

Bennett was torn. He valued the team's loyalty above all else and their opinions mattered to him. He had some sympathy with their sentiments but closing the press office was not an option.

It was just as well for the phone lines into the press office were rarely quiet from the moment they opened before 8 a.m. each day until they shut 12 hours later. Every call brought a request and for each request the press office couldn't deal with, a form containing the details arrived in the MIR to be answered whenever possible. Often, the press office was asked questions for which an answer should have been refused. Instead, it came back from the MIR and was given out. This, too, was something Bennett had never experienced before and it concerned him.

Though he blamed himself for not addressing the issue before, he was now worried the media was taking advantage of the press office's willingness to assist. He also knew their demands would keep on coming, especially when he learned of the pressure under which some reporters were operating, pressure which they, in turn, put on the investigation.

Having been tipped off that some reporters were scanning police radio and phone frequencies he had similar equipment set up so he could listen in to them. He rarely used it and only switched it on when there was a huddle of reporters outside the police station. He had hoped it might reveal where the leaks were coming from. One evening, the scanner was crackling away when a voice he recognised as that of a national reporter burst through. He seemed to be talking on a radio transceiver or a mobile phone either to his boss or someone senior.

The conversation was not going well and drew to a close with the boss informing the reporter in no uncertain terms to 'get one of those Swedes, those country bumpkins, down to that field [Kempley] to talk to you tonight!' When the reporter said he had tried and no one was available, he was told amid a volley of expletives 'well if you *** can't I'll *** get someone down there to *** replace you who *** will'.

There was no wrath like a media scorned.

The Senior Investigating Officer then did what he realised he should have done earlier, write a prescriptive media strategy confirming how and when interviews would be given. The media were not going to dictate when and where interviews were to take place, especially when there was no foreseeable gain to the investigation and no change to report. They could do it using their reporters.

When an early morning national television programme was refused a live interview – because the police had nothing new to talk about – it filled the slot with a report on how residents in Cromwell Street were cashing in on the investigation – mostly by charging news organisations for the use of their property.

Hilary Allison and Chief Inspector Colin Handy had striven to build a good working relationship between the press office and the media and became minor celebrities in their own right. In one newspaper feature, Allison was referred to as 'The Angel of Cromwell Street'. Despite this, Chief Inspector Handy was needed for other duties and was replaced by another officer, Inspector David Morgan, who had also worked as a force press officer.

As the start of work at Kempley drew nearer, aerial photographs were taken of the two fields they had targeted. Along with Ordnance Survey maps, they were used to enable Bennett to set the search parameters that would be entered into the policy log.

Catherine Bernadette Costello, 'Rena', was born on 14 April 1944 in Coatbridge, Scotland. She was the fourth of five daughters and like so many others to emerge during the investigation had an unhappy background. Her parents split up when she was a child. She was taken into care in her early teens; went to the big city, Glasgow; got mixed up with the wrong crowd and ended up in borstal for burglary at 17. It was soon after that she first met Fred West when she accompanied another borstal inmate to stay with her mother near Much Marcle in Herefordshire where West lived.

At the time she was on the run and pregnant but that didn't bother West and with his brother John as a witness, a role he repeated later for Fred and Rose, the couple were married at Ledbury Register Office on 17 November 1962. Shortly after that, they returned to Coatbridge where Charmaine was born on 22 March 1963.

Charmaine was obviously a mixed-race child and to hide the fact that Fred was not her biological father, Rena said she had miscarried and they had adopted a daughter instead. More likely, as Rena had been working as a prostitute, her pimp was the father, though when Rena gave birth to another girl on 6 July 1964 there was no doubt she was West's. They named her Anna-Marie Kathleen Daisy, which she changed to Anne Marie in later life.

They stayed in Scotland, but more than sixteen months later, while working as an ice-cream man, West ran over and killed a young boy. Among his various excuses, he claimed his marriage was on the rocks and in December 1965 he left Rena and took the two girls back home to Much Marcle where Herefordshire County Council soon put them into care.

Although West favoured Anna-Marie, he seemed to have genuine feelings for Charmaine as well – unless this was a show to get them out of care. To achieve that, he bought a caravan on a site at Sandhurst, a village just outside Gloucester, and worked as a driver for a tannery. He also persuaded Rena to join them, though as part of the deal she was allowed to bring two friends. One of them was Ann McFall and they arrived early in 1966. By the end of February they had the girls back but within two months Rena wanted to return to Scotland.

As ever, West's versions of why and how varied, but it was clear that he and Ann McFall had become lovers. What happened to Rena was less obvious. In one account she came back for the children and he let her take them. Yet they were all still together when Gloucestershire Social Services paid a visit later in the year. West and Ann McFall also had the girls when they moved to the Watermeads Caravan Site, which was where they were when Rena returned that autumn. Ann was moved out but Rena did not stay long. She stole from another caravan on the site and hit the road.

It turned out that in the investigation that followed, when Rena was arrested in Scotland, a young woman officer named Hazel Savage had been sent to bring her back to Gloucester to face a charge of housebreaking.

Rena appeared at Gloucester Quarter Sessions on 29 November 1966 and was put on probation. She then left Gloucester again. Ann McFall became pregnant by West. Gloucestershire Social Services paid them a visit. Rena returned, briefly. Ann was supposed to move out while Rena was there and return to West when she had gone.

Eventually, Rena came back and settled down with West and their two daughters.

West's accounts of what happened to Ann McFall were all too familiar. All were based on Rena killing her former friend for having an affair with her husband and becoming pregnant by him, and were liberally laced with accounts of her violence and drinking. Of course, he denied any involvement in her death or even knowing how she died. He did, however, have a 'feeling' she might be buried in a field at Kempley near a cow pond, and that she would never be found.

As far as the investigation could establish, Ann McFall was last seen in the summer of 1967 when she was six months pregnant, and had never been reported missing, though West claimed in his interviews he had reported her missing himself.

West, Rena and the children moved to another caravan at Bishop's Cleeve in the shadow of Cheltenham Racecourse early in 1968, where he found work first as a driver then as a labourer. His relationship with Rena was as turbulent as ever and she left him on a number of occasions. It was during this time he met a 15-year-old named Rosemary Letts, who lived nearby with her parents and the rest of her family.

West continued his minor criminal activity of theft and traffic offences and was caught regularly and convicted by the local police, often, coincidentally, by a young police constable named Terry Moore. Rosemary Letts's parents did not know of her friendship with West then. When they did find out they didn't like it but seemed powerless to put a stop to it.

Rena continued to drift in and out of the picture, though less frequently when she discovered he was seeing this young girl. Rosemary's parents tried to stop their burgeoning relationship with an injunction but she became pregnant and was put into care. When she agreed to an abortion she was allowed home but she kept the child and continued to see West.

Charmaine and Anna-Marie, on the other hand, went into care and back out again when Rena reappeared. When Rena left again, West was able to persuade social services he and Rose would be able to look after them after setting up home in a flat in Cheltenham. Rose's father was not convinced and tried once more to get his daughter away from West. When that failed, Fred and Rose fled unannounced to Gloucester and took the children with them.

At first they lived in a flat in Park End Road. Then they moved to another less than a quarter of a mile away at 25 Midland Road and that was the address they gave when Rose, who now called herself Mrs Rosemary West, gave birth to the couple's first child together. Heather Ann West was born at Gloucester maternity hospital on 17 October 1970. By a strange quirk of fate, that same day 9 miles away in Stroud Maternity Hospital Bennett's wife Ann was giving birth to their first son Andrew.

Soon after that, West was back inside. He was given a total of ten months for a series of thefts and sent to Leyhill Open Prison midway between Gloucester and Bristol. Rena had stayed in touch and probably knew of Fred's imprisonment, though, according to her family, she now had a new man in her life and was planning a new life in Saudi Arabia. She was even considering taking her children with her.

Rena was last seen in 1971, about the same time Charmaine disappeared. The identity of Charmaine's real father was never fully established and together with her half-sister Anna-Marie she had lived with Fred and Rena and then Rose, drifting in and out of care until Fred and Rose finally set up home in Gloucester sometime around July 1970, when she was about 7 and Anna-Marie 6.

In October, when her other half-sister, Heather, was born, Charmaine was a pupil at St James's School in Gloucester. Anna-Marie, or Anne Marie as the investigation knew her, could remember a lot about those days at 25 Midland Road. She told the police how Rena had visited them there and that Charmaine did not like Rose and often wound her up. When that happened it was Anna-Marie who usually got the worst end of the stick – often literally.

A number of people who were in contact with Rose while Fred was in Leyhill recalled seeing Charmaine during that time though her school record of 21 July 1971 showed she had 'moved to London'. There was no mention of who had given them this information but by then Charmaine had not been in school for some time.

West's accounts of the killing of Rena and Charmaine and his 'dreams' concerning Ann McFall had already changed, much like his other stories. If the police could find remains for the three of them, they could compare what they found with what they had already uncovered at Cromwell Street. Perhaps then they could get to the truth, or at least a little closer to it.

TWENTY-FIVE

A news conference was arranged for Monday to tell the rest of the world what the investigation had been virtually certain of for several days – the names of four more of Fred West's victims.

Bennett was keen to get the names out ahead of the inquest to prevent further speculation and unnecessary upset to families whose daughters were unaccounted for, and the coroner was happy to leave it to his discretion. The Senior Investigating Officer, on the other hand, didn't want to pressurise Dr Whittaker by making any premature announcements.

The Doc knew that adding names to the charges would help Bennett. So far West was charged with the murders of Heather West, Shirley Robinson, Carol Cooper and six other unnamed young women. When the two men spoke on the phone, Bennett promised that if any of the new names turned out to be incorrect, he would take the blame, but the Doc gave his blessing and that weekend four more families were officially given confirmation of the news they had feared but deep down had known was inevitable.

When the media next assembled, it was to be told that as well as his three named victims, Fred West was now charged with murdering Alison Chambers, Lucy Partington, Juanita Mott and Lynda Gough plus two other unnamed young women. As ever, reporters were asked to respect the privacy and welfare of the victims' families and told that from now on interviews would only be about what was in the official release.

This also included news that the police were about to start digging in Letterbox Field at Kempley. As promised, the information was given at least 24 hours before the work was due to begin, along with a reminder to respect not only the crime scene but also the landowner's property. In no time, officers guarding the field at Kempley reported a huge influx of vehicles as reporters, photographers, cameramen and assorted outside broadcast vehicles arrived and vied with each other for the best vantage points. The national networks even chartered helicopters and light aircraft to capture the scene from above.

Letterbox Field, the first site there to be excavated, was referred to as 'Kempley A' and had been mapped out and photographed on the ground using the same systems as at Cromwell Street. A vehicle exclusion zone some 200yd in all directions was marked out by 'police no waiting' cones. Reporters got around it by each paying the landowner £50 to park in an adjacent field on the other side of the road. A not inconsiderable sum of money went to local charities as a result – so much for local people 'cashing in' on the unfolding tragedy.

Acknowledging that this was the start of a new phase in the investigation, Bennett gave a formal news conference at the gate to the search site and then agreed to the ground radar machine being filmed on a pool basis. When the work began in earnest it would be completely hidden from view. Providing the media adhered to all the warnings, there would be an opportunity to film and photograph inside the search area later. MIR staff were told to keep away for fear that unfamiliar faces turning up would fuel fresh speculation – especially as it might be necessary to take West out to the area again.

It wasn't just a field near Kempley on which camera lenses trained. The *Today* newspaper, then a relatively young middle-ranking tabloid, had discovered that Rose West and Mae had been moved to a new address in Dursley and had staked out all the roads leading to the police station. They snapped her on a rare trip to a local supermarket. It meant she would have to be moved again – provided she wasn't arrested first.

Detective Constable Phil Chattersingh drove Bennett, Moore and Hilary Allison to Kempley. It was the morning of Tuesday 29 March. Bennett spent much of the journey trying to memorise the statement he was about to release, wondering how many times he would make the trip and whether they would find what they were searching for, the remains of Rena West. Although the release confirmed they were looking for 'human remains' Bennett would not divulge it was Rena's even if asked directly.

The Senior Investigating Officer's arrival prompted the usual flurry of activity. As the officers on guard opened the gate to let the red Rover saloon into the field, cameramen, photographers and reporters hurried into position as if scrambled by an alarm. After the familiarity of Cromwell Street, fresh surroundings brought a heightened level of expectation. The hedgerow, behind which the battery of cameras was lined, provided a natural boundary between the news crews and the road that skirted the search area. Bennett repeated his warning about what would happen if anyone breached it without permission.

Once the media conference was over it was time to review the organisation.

The Gloucestershire Fire Service mobile canteen and incident support unit was in full swing providing hot meals and drinks. Nearby was a temporary building that acted as a changing room, store and office with a telephone line. Boxes of high-calorie drinks, biscuits and sweets were piled against a wall; wet-weather gear hung all round.

The ground-penetrating radar had already identified a number of 'hot spots' beneath the surface of the proposed search area, signs that the ground structure had been altered. These were marked out with wooden pegs. Further up the slight incline, close to the left-hand line of hedge and trees where West indicated he had buried Rena, a temporary slatted pathway was laid leading to a large blue and white striped tent that was kept inflated by a generator. Beneath the canopy, West's wooden peg marked the centre of the search parameters Bennett had agreed. A clock hung from the entrance so that digging shifts and rest periods could be carefully timed.

All the excavated soil would be carried along a motor-driven conveyor belt so it could be thoroughly sieved and examined before being carried away by hand in wheelbarrows and dumped in an ever-growing pile further into the field. The plan was to dig around West's marker first, then excavate a trench along the tree line 4ft either side of it. If nothing was found another adjoining trench would be dug to the same dimensions. This would continue systematically until they found what they were looking for. At the slightest indication of bone, the digging would stop immediately and Bennett and the crime scene manager Bob Beetham informed. It would then be up to them to decide whether to call Professor Knight, just as it had been at Cromwell Street. As they knew reporters were scanning mobile phones and radio communications they decided to use a code if anything was found. Because of all the propane gas bottles in use, it was agreed someone would ring Bennett and 'ask for another gas bottle'.

With everything in place, the search adviser Sergeant John Pickersgill invited Bennett to start the operation by digging the first sod. As the spade went in to its hilt, and he levered it to and fro, he was surprised how firm the stony red earth was and how awkward it was to manoeuvre – and he was asking the men to dig through this to a depth of 4ft. The difficulty of the task that lay ahead sank in much quicker than the spade.

Leaving the tent, Bennett walked towards the brow of the incline where his gaze wandered across to the field on his right where West thought Ann McFall might be buried. For a moment he stood and pondered the problems they faced and hoped it would all be worthwhile.

Digging on that first day continued until darkness fell. Nothing was found and the area was left under guard overnight. Already, a trench 20ft long, 4ft wide and 4ft deep had been dug that stretched 10ft on either side of West's marker.

The Easter Bank Holiday meant a welcome break for everyone on the investigation except a small number of staff required to man the incident room and guard both crime scenes. There was no need to use up resources on unnecessary overtime.

When Terry Moore came into the Senior Investigating Officer's office that Thursday morning he was carrying a box of small chocolate Easter eggs under his arm. His intention was to hand them out to the men and Bennett suggested they get some more for their 'faithful media followers' – or those who were at Kempley that morning.

When the two detectives arrived, there was the usual flurry of media activity. It was a bright morning and there were fewer reporters than normal but with camera crews and photographers the numbers were still more than thirty.

Standing behind the gate to the field, Bennett quickly delivered what little he had to say: 'The searches would be continuing until lunch time . . . reconvened on Tuesday 5 April. . . . Nothing had been found . . . the pool facility can now visit the search . . . but before that, we would like to wish you a Happy Easter', and on that cue, Terry Moore handed out the eggs. Had Bennett announced Fred West had confessed to several more murders they would not have been more surprised. Later, the diggers and everyone else on the inquiry, received the same token.

Work resumed after the break and in no time the trench had expanded to almost 100ft and still nothing had been found. Maybe they were not digging close enough to the hedge and tree line? It must have grown thicker in the last twenty years; could it have been moved? West would have to be brought out again in the hope it would jog his memory and at least one tree would have to be felled. The farmer wouldn't like it but there was no other option.

In the event, West's covert visit only added to the confusion. He was convinced his marker was roughly where he had buried his wife though inevitably his account of when, how and why was as changeable as the spring weather.

If digging at Cromwell Street was grim, the back-breaking work of the teams at Kempley was no less arduous and whereas the search of West's garden had produced relatively quick results, far away in the countryside success was proving much more elusive.

Still, everyone was given a lift that Thursday.

It was the day West was once more due to appear before Gloucester magistrates. For the first time seven of his alleged victims were put on the record and there was no surprise when the court remanded him back into custody for another twenty-eight days. What had not been anticipated was the call from Dr Whittaker, who had continued to work on the remains of Shirley Hubbard and Thérèse Siegenthaler and was now sufficiently 'comfortable' for their names to be included in the charges. This meant that all nine of the Cromwell Street victims would be included in the opening of the inquests in a week's time. West would be served with the amended charges the following morning and another press conference arranged so that Bennett could thank the many people and organisations that had helped the investigation.

With no finds at Kempley and planning for the inquest to consider, it was still not the time to rearrest Rose West. Instead, that weekend, she and Mae would be moved to another house in Cheltenham with a property on standby in case that address was compromised, too.

During the press conference that Friday, Bennett announced there would be no search work on Saturday and later that day visited Kempley again. The digging had continued at a pace. The trench had been widened and lengthened, its depth maintained at 4ft. Some of the hot spots had now been examined but surrendered nothing. Yet again they had to confront the possibility that West was making it all up, and for the first time Bennett was beginning to have doubts.

By contrast, the morale of the men remained high. There

were no moans or groans and the pile of earth from the trench was growing by the hour and now appeared to dwarf the tent. Sergeant Pickersgill reckoned they would finish the search area within the next week, probably sooner. What would happen if nothing were found was a question to be put off until then.

The following morning, Sunday 10 April, Bennett was in his office preparing his statement for the opening of the inquests. As well as hearing from the Senior Investigating Officer, the coroner also wanted evidence from Professor Knight and Dr Whittaker in order to cover all the necessary points that would enable him to make a judicial decision on identification.

Each of the victim's families would be invited to attend. If they did, getting them in and out of Shire Hall and keeping them away from the media glare would be a delicate operation that would fall to their liaison officers with the help of Victim Support.

At 11.40 a.m., the phone rang. It was the MIR. Kempley had called and, not realising he was in the office, had asked for an urgent message to be relayed to him: 'Could he bring out another gas bottle?'

If the message appeared strange to the MIR it was the one he'd waited thirteen days to hear. Even so, he did not want to get his hopes up just yet. After all, they could have found animal bones so he phoned the search office to check.

Identifying himself he asked, 'Do you really want gas bottles now? Are you sure?'

John Pickersgill took the call. His reply was short and to the point, 'Yes sir, definitely.'

Bob Beetham was off that day. It was the day after his twenty-fifth wedding anniversary and he had visitors. Bennett phoned and asked if he could make himself available for a quick visit to Kempley. There was no need to call out the Prof, he just wanted to make sure everything was under control. Beetham agreed, but would need a driver as he had celebrated a little to excess the previous night. Bennett collected him himself and together they drove to Kempley. For once their arrival hardly registered among the few reporters there.

The blue and white canopy covered an area much higher up the field than where West had indicated. One tree had been felled just below it and the trunk cut a sinister silhouette against the skyline.

Sergeant Pickersgill took Beetham and Bennett beyond the tent and as they walked explained that for the first time that morning they had been using a mini mechanical digger with a scoop to remove some of the more solid soil. While doing so they spotted something out of the ordinary, which on closer inspection looked like part of a skull, though the red earth appeared to have heavily discoloured it. When they examined the trench itself, they thought they could see bones.

Bennett made his way into the tent with Beetham following and there, showing through the red stony soil some 3ft or so in the ground was what they both agreed looked like human lower leg bones – a fibula and tibia. These, together with the skull fragment on the pile of moved earth, undoubtedly justified the call for a 'gas bottle'. The find may not have been exactly how Bennett would have wanted it but it seemed to be what they were looking for. Before Bennett and Beetham left for Gloucester, the search team was instructed to carefully sieve all the soil removed by the scoop. It seemed that the sizeable pieces of bone already recovered had decomposed much more than those recovered at Cromwell Street and were extremely brittle.

After contacting the coroner and informing the Prof, who said he would be available the following morning, there was little else that could be done apart from informing the officers responsible for the 'Rena' part of the inquiry, so they could pass on the news to her family, and preparing a statement confirming the discovery of more human remains.

Later that evening, Bennett returned to Kempley to give the news in person to the relatively few reporters gathered there. It was the smallest news conference yet but it took away the need for another one the next day.

The discovery of remains reasonably close to where West had indicated made the decision to move into the next field and look for Ann McFall much easier. It made no sense taking all the equipment away just to come back at a later date. The police had already established that this field had changed. Old Ordnance Survey maps showed a cow pond next to a thicket called Stonehouse Coppice. In reclaiming it for planting, the farmer had drastically altered the lie of the land, laying down drainage pipes, infilling with all sorts of farm material and covering the area with soil. To overcome this, Police Constable Andy Ewens scanned the area with his electronic theodolite, reduced it to the scale of the OS maps and using the old maps was able to mark exactly where the pond had been over twenty-seven years earlier.

Weighing it all up, Bennett figured this would be even more difficult than the search they had just completed in Letterbox Field. Yet Ann McFall had not been seen since May 1967 when she was six months pregnant. They had no option. This would be 'Kempley B'.

That was the advice he gave the Chief Constable the following morning before heading back to Kempley to rendezvous with Professor Knight, who this time was accompanied by a young woman student from Malaysia. Just like Cromwell Street everything was videoed.

The Prof climbed into the trench, leaving his camera and notepad on the soil above him. Stooping down to look at the bones protruding from the dry, red stony soil he slowly removed them, carefully scraping away the soil with a trowel. When larger amounts of earth needed to be moved Bob Beetham lent a hand.

As the excavation continued two thigh bones were recovered. The Prof confirmed they were female and like the skull and other bones they had eroded and were in poor condition. As he tried to establish how the remains had been put into the ground it was clear the gravesite was similar in size and depth to those at Cromwell Street. Examining the femurs he pointed out faint, fine marks where they would have joined the pelvis. A tell-tale sign this body, too, had been dismembered.

Among the other bones he found a small rectangular piece of cloth and a piece of corroded metal that looked like a broken knife blade. Close to a piece of skull was a bright-red plastic boomerang with the words 'Woomerang Boomerang' in gold lettering – a catchphrase from a 1960s children's television programme. And, mixed in with more jumbled-up bones, a small piece of metal tube that looked as though it was chrome-plated. A sample of soil was taken and what was left was dug out and sieved until the Prof handed over to Beetham to finish off.

Arrangements were made for the remains to be taken to Gloucester for cleaning and from there transferred to the Prof's laboratory. The skull appeared to have corroded and come apart during decomposition, and broke into more pieces during recovery. It would present a further challenge to the Doc but at least they had a number of good photographs of Rena and plenty of information to help him. First, he would have to put the skull together again and relocate the teeth that had fallen out, though once again DNA was unlikely to be of any help. Still, from what they had seen so far, Bennett and Moore were confident the Doc's expertise would triumph.

As the professor and his student colleague bade their farewells, Bennett told him there would be at least two further searches – in the adjoining field and at 25 Midland Road in Gloucester. Moving towards the exit, the professor was aware of the clamour from the other side of the road for a comment. Having received the nod from the Senior Investigating Officer, the professor calmly faced the cameras and confirmed that he had recovered the remains of a female and that he would have to make further examinations before he could make any more comment.

With that, the gate was opened and his car reversed out into the road and left.

TWENTY-SIX

The search of Kempley B, known locally as Fingerpost Field, would soon begin and so, too, the search at 25 Midland Road. The inquiry now believed friends of the Wests and two other family members may have also committed sexual offences and had to be interviewed, and there was the opening of the inquest. Careful, sensitive planning would be needed to prevent it from turning into a media event.

A warrant to search an area next to Stonehouse Coppice was obtained on Monday 11 April. Extra plant and equipment was hired and plans drawn up.

Some of the new allegations involved Fred's younger brother John and a couple of long-term friends of the Wests. There was no suggestion they were involved in any of the murders but there was a strong possibility they may have committed serious sexual offences and if they thought the passage of time had left them in the clear they were wrong. Their arrests, however, could wait until later.

The extension at Cromwell Street was now just about ready for demolition but nothing else had been found there. Bennett was now more concerned with Kempley B and the escalating cost of the whole operation.

Arrangements were also being made for officers who had worked on the original investigations into the disappearance of Lucy Partington and Mary Bastholm to come into the MIR to see if they could add anything in the light of what was now known. Detectives Barbara Harrison and Stephen Harris were being briefed to interview Rose West, whose arrest was now imminent.

The interview strategy for Fred, however, was changing. Now the police knew who his victims were, they no longer had to sit through his fanciful accounts of how he met them and how they died. Of more importance were Rose's sexual activities, for although West seemed unconcerned about her lesbian tendencies, and even encouraged them, the investigation had discovered she had had other sexual encounters he knew nothing about which had upset him. If they were not so joined at the hip in their sexually depraved partnership as Paul Britton had suggested, and were he told she had sexual secrets which she had hidden from him, he might be prepared to divulge more of her role in the killings.

Mary Bastholm's disappearance would also be put to him again, along with any other sexual offences or even killings they knew of. Speculation was rife that he had been responsible for a number of attacks on women in Gloucester at the time Mary disappeared and witnesses said they might have known one another as both used the Pop-In Café, though this was never proved.

From the moment Bennett had managed to enlist him, Withy Cole had bedded in well with the team. He was in almost daily contact with the MIR and got on particularly well with the new HOLMES receiver, Detective Sergeant Dave Griffiths.

Cole had carried out extensive research into similar fact evidence. He knew how convinced the team were of her guilt and could see how the evidence of her involvement was growing, but like his colleague Rita Crane he was anxious about how much of it would be allowed in court. He would continue focusing on the laws of evidence to see how best they could turn what they already had into a case against Rose West.

The press office was still being swamped with calls, mainly asking if, when and where there would be any more searches.

This investigation by a rural police force in the United Kingdom now seemed to be top of the news agenda on all news services and in all languages. The latest find had whetted the world's appetite for the story even more, if that were possible. Among the new influx of reporters and photographers were many who could neither read nor speak English. It all added to the press office's problems and the chaos they brought did little to lighten the atmosphere around the gate to Fingerpost Field on Wednesday 13 April when Bennett formally announced the start of the search for Ann McFall's remains.

Right on cue, he heard the sound of motors and turning round was amazed to see a small column of officers, all wearing blue overalls, safety clothes and baseball caps. Each of them was pushing a motor-driven wheelbarrow and they were led by a quad bike that was making its way along the side of the field to the new search site. He hadn't realised they had this new equipment but it was impressive even though it looked like a parade. Overhead, an ITN helicopter added to the din.

The search parameters were set to encompass the outside edges and beyond where the cow pond had once been. Posts marked the outer boundary and inside were more markers to indicate the exact location of the pond. Once again they were excavating an area less than 4ft from the line of the hedge and trees, and would begin at the spot where West had *felt* Ann McFall's presence.

When Bennett looked at the proposed area it seemed larger than he had anticipated but it still only just reached to where the pond had been and fully enclosed West's marker. Once they had excavated to near the previous level of the land, all mechanical work would stop and digging by hand would take over, just like everywhere else.

As expected, Dr Whittaker was having difficulty using his technique to positively identify Remains 10, 'possibly Rena West', but he was hopeful he could piece together the skull and had plenty of photographs with which to work. Hearing this Bennett contacted the Gloucester coroner for permission to include the name of Catherine Bernadette West – Rena's full name – when charging West with her murder. It would help stave off further media speculation and the coroner agreed.

When West was next interviewed and told of the latest find at Kempley, including the plastic boomerang and pieces of metal, he said the toy must have been with Rena and fallen from her clothes. He still maintained he had killed her after an argument over her giving Charmaine barley wine during a visit to a pub. Of course, before he killed her they had intercourse, then afterwards used a knife and spade he carried in his van to dismember and bury her naked body. Her clothes he threw into a field fire of burning stubble. When he returned to the van, he had forgotten Charmaine was asleep in the back and because he did not know what to do he strangled her while she slept, took her back to 25 Midland Road and hid her in the coal cellar fully clothed and wrapped in a tartan blanket.

It was another story the investigating team had gone over many times and just did not believe, not least because it so neatly explained how Rena and Charmaine were murdered without Rose's knowledge or involvement. Whatever the truth, West had admitted murdering his first wife and given pretty accurate information as to where he had buried her. Charging him with her murder was a formality.

Generally, though, West did not seem as settled, either in his remand environment or his interviews, as he had when Janet Leach had been the appropriate adult. It had not gone unnoticed either that she still attended all his remand hearings even though she was no longer required to – and he always looked to see if she was there when he arrived in the courtroom.

When the arrangements for the inquest were finalised, only a small number of relatives decided to attend, but those who did asked if they could come and go with the minimum of contact with the media. It was explained that reporters would be allowed into the inquest but nothing more. The plan was to have their liaison officers bring them to Gloucester Police Station where they could be taken into Shire Hall through a connecting passage, away from the glare of the cameras. When it was all over they would leave the same way.

In the period since all the remains had been recovered, Bennett and Moore had either spoken to representatives of the victims' families or met them. There was much more the detectives had found out about their lost relatives and how they had died than they could share with them at that time. They probably knew more about the victims and their past than many members of their families would ever know or have been able to discover, such had been the depth of the investigation.

At 9.30 a.m. on Thursday 14 April, the morning of the inquests, Bennett announced that West had been charged with the murder of Catherine West née Costello between 1 January 1969 and 27 February 1994. He also used the news conference to issue his sternest warning yet that the police would do everything they could to ensure the privacy of families attending the hearing. He also asked the media to respect their wishes and not approach or try to film them, though his words had little effect.

By 10.30 a.m., half an hour before the inquests were due to begin and Professor Knight, Dr Whittaker and all the relatives were assembled at the police station, Bennett looked out of his office towards Shire Hall and saw news crews and reporters on every street corner, so that every public entrance to the building was covered. When an officer was sent to check the front he radioed back to say there were even more camera crews there. The area was surrounded.

Bennett told the Prof and the Doc what he had arranged for the relatives and asked if they wanted to go in that way too, or would they be prepared to act as a decoy and walk in through the court entrance. It would give the crews something to film and at the same time distract them from the station or Shire

Hall building. Both agreed and around 10.45 a.m., as the Prof and the Doc headed past the cameras, Bennett and Moore took the relatives quietly along a corridor and into a waiting room just outside where the hearings would take place.

The atmosphere was sombre and in the few minutes before the proceedings got under way the Senior Investigating Officer was asked a number of times when the remains would be released. The question was not unexpected, the families had asked it of the liaison officers many times, but the answer was not the one they wanted. It could be months, even longer. Bennett promised to speed things up as best he could but the decision rested on agreement between West's lawyers and the coroner.

Just before 11 a.m., once the reporters were settled, the police officer guarding the door opened it and escorted the victims' relatives to their reserved seats.

The large amphitheatre-shaped council chamber was occasionally used as a court. Coroner David Gibbons sat in what on another day would be the council leader's chair, raised up in front of a huge wooden carving of the county crest on the wall behind him. Evidence was given from a lower level, to the coroner's right. There were microphones at every seat, though for this occasion most were switched off. Only Bennett, Professor Knight and Dr Whittaker were required to give evidence. Apart from them and the relatives there was a larger than normal police presence and the press seats were full.

This was just the beginning of the process, 'the opening of the inquests for identification'. The coroner explained how he wanted the evidence to be presented then called Bennett to the stand to give an outline of what he had witnessed during the recovery of the nine sets of remains from Cromwell Street between 26 February and 6 March.

First he outlined the recovery of Heather West's remains and was followed into the stand by Professor Knight and Dr Whittaker, who explained how they were able to identify her. It was the same procedure for each of the eight victims who followed and each time he returned to his seat Bennett's feelings began to well up, growing in intensity through each account until for the first time in his service he found it difficult to deliver his evidence without his voice giving way to the emotion he felt.

As a coroner, David Gibbons was warm and compassionate and no one could have conducted the proceedings with more sensitivity or shown more respect to the relatives and yet it all seemed so matter-of-fact. Nine young women whose lives had ended in the most horrific circumstances imaginable were now being dealt with in such a piecemeal fashion.

Even with all his years of experience Bennett had found it a struggle and yet could not begin to imagine how the families were feeling – and they still did not know the full extent of the depravity to which their loved ones had been exposed or, indeed, what West was saying about them.

The coroner confirmed the identification of all nine victims, added his condolences to the bereaved and then adjourned to a date to be fixed. He also added his praise to the work of the investigation and that of Professor Knight and Dr Whittaker though the words went over Bennett's head, as he was still lost in his own melancholic thoughts. Reporters were held back as the families, Professor Knight, Dr Whittaker, Bennett and Moore left the chamber and returned to the police station via the private route.

Less than two months since the investigation had begun, and against all the odds, nine murder victims spanning more than twenty years had been recovered and positively identified. Before leaving that day, Dr Whittaker reassured Bennett that he should be able to confirm Remains 10 as Rena, but not just yet.

The work at Kempley B was under way but the weather had changed to frequent downpours and squalls of rain that blew across the fields with little protection from Stonehouse Coppice. This, in itself, had not hampered the work unduly. The 'diving diggers', as Bennett affectionately referred to them, had adequate wet-weather gear. The real problem was drainage. Moving the pipes that had been laid meant the water had to go somewhere else and the natural lie of the land was directing it into the hollow they were searching. They could pump it out but as summer approached they were banking on an improvement in the weather.

Once the area was dry and levelled, the ground-penetrating radar could be used and the results considered alongside the advice of an archaeologist, but there was still much to do before then.

When Bennett actually visited 25 Midland Road for the first time, he was surprised at how similar it was to 25 Cromwell Street. The rear garden was a little wider and shorter but that was because of the shape of the extension, built this time with proper foundations. Underneath was the coal cellar where West said he put Charmaine when he brought her back from Kempley after killing Rena. To get through to the ground and foundations a hole would have to be cut through the floor, which consisted of more than 6ft of impacted rubble with a layer of steel on top. The work would have to be done by pick and shovel, and would be another very difficult and physically demanding operation that this time would be carried out by the Cotswold Division Support Group or 'Gemini team'. The rear garden would also have to be strimmed clean of weeds and anything found there taken away. The ground-penetrating radar would then be used there and in the cellar. The garden area would definitely be excavated. A decision on the cellar could wait.

The extension at 25 Cromwell Street was now down and the inside of the house secured by new brickwork. A large amount of concrete had been poured into the holes to shore up the building.

At Kempley B things were different. There, not even the pumps could cope with all the rain that was flooding into the watercourse, even though they had been running throughout the day and all night. Within the excavation, an area of more than 25 ft square had begun to fill with water. One side of the huge pit had to be reinforced with a metal lining before any more digging could be done in that section.

The problems were plain to see when cameras were given access on a pool basis. When the filming was over and Bennett was on his way back to the gate at the top of the field an American woman journalist caught up with him.

'Which one of you is already writing a book?' she asked.

Bennett looked at her quizzically. What could have given her that idea? She insisted she was certain one of the officers on the case was writing a book. Bennett was adamant she was mistaken. It was not possible while the investigation was active, at least not until all the court proceedings were over. The journalist, who was going home to continue research for her own book, insisted she was right and promised that when she returned from America she would tell him who it was.

When Moore and Bennett were on their way back to Gloucester, Bennett mentioned what she had said, passing it off as just more speculation.

Later, when they made a joke of it to Hazel Savage, who was with some other officers on the stairwell outside their office, it was met with shrugs of laughter.

TWENTY-SEVEN

The relentless, energy-sapping work at Kempley B, and for that matter the digging at Kempley A and Cromwell Street, could hardly have been described as glamorous, but it was the visible side of the investigation. Away from the prying eyes and lenses of the media, equally important tasks were being carried out in the MIR.

The files that would form the basis of the case for the prosecution had to be ready within a time limit laid down nationally by the Crown Prosecution Service – a tall order even on much less complicated investigations, but achievable if they could maintain their current rate of progress.

Preparing the files was one of the most responsible jobs on the inquiry and was given to Dave Griffiths. He was already excelling in his work as the MIR's receiver and had struck up a good working relationship with the CPS adviser Withy Cole. At first he was taken aback, later confiding that he sat in a pub and over a pint questioned whether he was up to it, but with the backing of Bennett and Moore he rose to the challenge. An example of his thoroughness came with the mysterious plastic boomerang found buried with the remains at Kempley A.

He remembered that when he was a young boy there was a slot on children's ATV – one of the original independent channels – featuring two stuffed koala bears called Tingha and Tucker. It was called *The Tingha and Tucker Club* and was fronted by a presenter named Jean Morton, 'Auntie Jean' to members of the club, and 'Woomerang Boomerang' was the club's catchphrase – the words inscribed on the side of the plastic toy. Griffiths managed to trace Jean Morton, who by then was living in retirement abroad, and discovered it was probably a free gift in a comic that was a spin-off from the series. Although he was unable to find the precise copy, he established it was published sometime in the late 1960s or early 1970s, the time when Rena disappeared. The story became Griff's party piece and was another example of the thoroughness of the investigation.

Elsewhere, Mark Grimshaw, working with the companies that produced the software he was using, had virtually created a new method of retrieving information from the HOLMES database. It streamlined the whole system and meant the interviewing teams and researchers could be updated much more easily. Grimshaw's systems were invaluable, too, for checking the exhibits database against statements from members of the West family and other potential witnesses. The police had recovered a large amount of cheap jewellery which had to be compared with descriptions of items that may have been with any of the victims when they were last seen. If that failed, the relatives could come in and look at it in the hope it might jog their memories.

With everyone stretched to the limit, tension inevitably rose. When information was not up to date or entered into the wrong section of HOLMES it was the MIR staff that copped it from the inquiry teams – even though it was often their fault. To keep the peace there were regular 'JB amnesties' when the inquiry teams' personal file trays were searched and missing papers retrieved.

There was humour, too, in the cartoons that appeared on the noticeboard, the balloon comments from photographs taken from press cuttings and suggestions as to 'who would be who?' when the film was made. Even the Sequence of Events file that Grimshaw had produced for all aspects of the investigation was now referred to as 'the film script'.

It was the sort of banter that marked them out as a team, though when the Assistant Chief Constable passed on the latest media idea for a 'fly on the wall' programme it was rejected out of hand. Bennett even said that he would ask to be immediately removed from the investigation if it went ahead on the grounds it would increase the pressure to an unacceptable level and lead to mistakes. The idea was discarded and never discussed again, but while requests like that were direct, other attempts at getting inside the investigation were not so transparent.

Within the first week of the inquiry, Bennett had asked the Police National Computer management to introduce a system for letting him know whenever anyone from another force tried to access the criminal records of either Fred or Rose West. Of the many 'hits' that came to light, some were legitimate, others appeared to have come from outside the police but using officers or civilian staff to gain access. Whether they were more examples of reporters infiltrating the force was never proved despite internal investigations, though it was considered highly probable.

On the other hand, the media did not always rely on the police for information, for example when a journalist contacted the press office to ask about a well in the garden at 25 Cromwell Street. The first Bennett knew of any well was when his wife rang to say their son had heard about it on the news and that as a former diver Bennett would be going down to search it himself. Considering her husband had been out of that line of work for years she was not very happy at the prospect. Bennett reassured her he knew nothing of a well and that if there were one, which he doubted, he certainly would not be getting into it.

That, though, was not the end of it. Beneath the floor of the extension which was now demolished, they discovered a concrete-and-stone-covered, brick-lined, bottle-shaped well with about 10ft of water in the bottom. The Senior Investigating Officer could hardly believe it. Others speculated on its potential as another of Fred West's burial grounds.

When the well was searched, on Friday 22 April, members of the underwater section were brought in from Kempley to do the job. It was covered live on 24-hour news channels and as Bennett watched wistfully via a camera linked to a monitor, he couldn't help thinking it would probably be the last proper operational use of the force's divers before the section was disbanded. As a founder member of the unit, he had taken part in the first dive at an ice-covered gravel pit in 1967. Twenty-seven years later he was there at the end, too.

It was all over in next to no time. There were no dramatic discoveries on live television and soon the diver, Police Constable Martin Skinner, and other members of the unit were heading back to Kempley and the monumental task they faced there.

There was disappointment when Bennett refused the request for a 'team night out'. They wanted to include colleagues who were working on other parts of the investigation in other parts of the county whom they never saw, but the Senior Investigating Officer was worried the media would find out and report it as unprofessional and, perhaps even worse, irreverent.

Their spirits rose, however, when he announced that Rose West would be rearrested on Wednesday 20 April, five days before she was due to answer her bail, though their joy was short-lived when he added that no decision had been taken on what charges she might face other than assault occasioning actual bodily harm and indecent assault. The evidence they had so far was uncorroborated and they had to keep looking for more conclusive data. It was there, they just had to find it. Establishing a timescale for the crimes Fred West had committed would be a start. For example, if he had abducted Mary Bastholm, it would have been before he met Rose. Ann McFall would also have died before he and Rose had got together.

It was rumoured that Fred West's mother was aware her son had killed Ann McFall and that Rose West's mother said her daughter had once said something like Fred could do anything, even murder. On top of that, there were the still undetected sexual attacks that took place in Gloucester around the place and time of Mary Bastholm's disappearance. Witnesses described someone who looked like Fred West and used a similar method of picking up his victims – stopping in his vehicle, leering out of the window, offering lifts.

More and more women had got in touch, either through the MIR or the media, accusing West of accosting them many years before. They had recognised his photograph from the newspapers. Old friends from West's days in Bishop's Cleeve and Gloucester talked of his sexual conquests and that he said he had used tools to perform abortions – and they had seen them.

Much of this seemed to work in Rose's favour as it appeared West was the dominant partner, first inviting her along then introducing her to more deviant activity. Examination of Fred West's medical history was also revealing, though it brought with it more circumstantial evidence and provided more questions than answers. It revealed that West had received treatment at the Gloucestershire Royal Hospital for a bad cut to his hand shortly after midnight and a week after Lucy Partington's disappearance. A knife was found alongside her remains. If West had injured himself while dismembering her – and while there was no evidence to say this was so, it had to be a possibility – then where had Lucy been and what had happened to her during the previous seven days?

And where was Rose West during that time?

Every enquiry that had been made of family, friends and neighbours confirmed that Fred and Rose had always been very close, though it was hardly evidence.

A major obstacle in securing potential witnesses lay in their being identified. No one wanted to admit they had been sexually involved with the Wests, though it was believed some probably faked their involvement in order to sell their stories to the tabloids. When that was proved, the names and information were passed on to the CPS but they were never used as witnesses.

One woman who came forward was Elizabeth Agius who was living abroad and had contacted the media before the police, apparently because she could not get through on a police phone. When she did it posed a dilemma.

Elizabeth Agius claimed she had been living in Midland Road in 1971 and had got to know both Fred and Rose West well.

While her husband was working away Fred had tried to coax her into having three-in-a-bed sex with the couple. Eventually she agreed but she made it clear she would not put this in any statement and would deny it if ever she was asked in court. The difficulty for Bennett and Detective Constable Gerry Watters, who interviewed her, came in what she said next.

Apparently, Elizabeth Agius regularly babysat for Fred and Rose and saw first hand their very close relationship. She recalled how they had told her they used to drive around looking for girls to pick up and that having a woman in the car made it easier.

The couple admitted travelling quite long distances, sometimes to Bristol, on other occasions to London, and preferred picking up homeless runaways. At the time, she gave little thought to this, just as she had when they moved to Cromwell Street and she visited them there. That was when Fred showed off his cellar and said that he was going to combine it as a children's playroom and a torture chamber.

When Detective Constable Watters heard this he telephoned Bennett direct. He told him what Mrs Agius was saying, including her need for reassurance that no mention would be made of the three-in-a-bed sex – she was frightened her husband would leave her if he ever found out.

Bennett thought long and hard, holding the other detective on the phone as he did. He knew this could bind Fred and Rose together. Foraging for runaways made them equal partners in their evil scheme. He could see her problem but he needed a signed statement. Watters would have to lie. He could give her the reassurance she sought, take down her story in writing but miss out the part she wanted. By telling the Senior Investigating Officer Watters had already broken her confidentiality anyway, though she did not seem to understand that.

Bennett had genuine concern for the care of the witnesses, but in this instance he had to consider the broader picture. When Watters returned he would tell him to submit an officer's report alongside Mrs Agius's statement that clearly outlined everything she had told him and what she had left out and the reasons why. Also, that he had given her the assurance she wanted on Bennett's directions. This would all be disclosed to the Crown Prosecution Service and the defence. The CPS would not like it and Bennett was all too aware of the possible repercussions – that Elizabeth Agius could be portrayed as an untrustworthy witness who faced the risk of perjuring herself, and the police could be accused of acting deviously, thus threatening the integrity of the investigation – but he had no choice.

The thread of Rose West's sexual deviance with her husband ran throughout their time at Midland Road and on to Cromwell Street, as did an increase in her violence towards Charmaine and Anne Marie at Midland Road and the couple's sexual and physical abuse of some of their other children. Just as important was evidence of her insatiable sexual appetite and use of sex toys.

A variety of large dildos were found in the 1992 search. Women who had had sex sessions with her, including most notably Kathryn Halliday, were to mention them. One that had been photographed by the 1992 investigation was so big it completely filled a wooden box that once contained a bottle of Bladnock malt whisky. It was Rose's taste for such fearsome implements that frightened off some of her lesbian lovers.

Then there was the tying and the taping that was used to restrain her children and Caroline Owens, so similar to the artefacts found with the victims, and the rape and violent sexual assault of other witnesses.

It also appeared that during their time at Midland Road and Cromwell Street both Rose and Fred had had sex with partners the other knew nothing about, and although it was unlikely Fred's infidelity would upset Rose, the same could not be said for him. In fact, for the first time since his arrest, his smug, self-satisfied air had been replaced by anxiety and frustration. First, he appeared to fall out with his solicitor and clerk, and then he changed his story saying Charmaine was not buried at 25 Midland Road and that she would never be found.

While Rose West was also becoming noticeably more truculent and disturbed in her safe house, anxious that she had still not been released from her bail, Detective Constables Barbara Harrison and Stephen Harris's research into her sex life was making them experts in all manner of sexual depravity and mutilation. The books that Steve Harris carried with him made him the butt of much mickey-taking.

The strategy for Rose West's arrest and how they would question her was already laid down. She would be arrested for assault, indecent assault and rape. Whether she was charged would be decided after she had been interviewed. She would then be arrested on suspicion of the murder of Lynda Gough. Mrs Gough's visit to Cromwell Street and her claims to have seen Rose wearing her daughter's clothes and slippers would be put to her. By then they would know what her tactics were likely to be. If her previous interviews were anything to go by she was unlikely to say anything at all.

All the lies she had told would be put to her, focusing on her involvement with Caroline Owens, her own daughter Heather, Shirley Robinson and Lynda Gough. Her deviant sexual behaviour and what she was alleged to have done within her family would also be raised, for she had to be given the chance to admit she had lied or been prevented from telling the truth either through fear of her husband or someone else.

She would be reminded of the sexually explicit agreements she had made in writing with her husband – she had referred to herself as 'Fred's cow' and described in detail when, how and what she would do sexually with him or anyone else he nominated. In another note she promised 'she would obey him without question for three months'. This would give her the opportunity to say how much under his influence and control she really was. If that was the truth, they wanted to know. She might be under arrest but she had to be given every opportunity to defend herself and never be able to claim she had not.

She would also be asked what she knew of each of the victims and where she was when they disappeared. She would be told all about what was found with the remains and specifically asked if she was involved in sexual acts or depravity or mutilation with them before or after death. If there were any objection from her solicitor he would be told that they had the right, given the circumstances, to ask the questions to try and establish whether she was involved in any way.

It was an unusual strategy but they were confident they were within their rights. Steve Harris, with his soft Welsh lilt and deadpan expression that hid a wry sense of humour, and Essex-accented Barbara Harrison with her pleasant, disarming manner were both tenacious, unrelenting interviewers when the situation called for it, as it did now. Colleagues who knew them were about to see a different side to their characters.

Barbara Harrison and Steve Harris called at the Cheltenham safe house and arrested Rose West just before 9.30 a.m. on Wednesday as planned. Clearly surprised and annoyed, she was taken to Cheltenham Police Station. Her solicitor Leo Goatley was informed and arrangements made for her to be interviewed. Her arrest also meant the teams involved in the bugging operation could now stand down. From three safe houses they had 885 tape recordings of incidents and conversations. If anything, their efforts should have helped Rose, for throughout the entire period all they heard were denials of anything to do with murder and threats of what she would do if she ever laid her hands on Fred again.

Once Rose was taken into custody it was to no one's surprise that she chose not to answer any of the questions put to her. Whether she decided this herself, was advised by her lawyer, or whether it was a combination of the two, each question was met with 'No comment'. Even when she agreed to be held under similar conditions to her husband at Gloucester it made no difference.

While two Afro-Caribbean men, both friends of the Wests, were arrested, interviewed and later charged and bailed by Gloucester Magistrates Court with offences that were later to be dropped by the Crown Prosecution Service, Rose West was first arrested and questioned about her involvement in the same crimes and other offences of assault and rape. She was later remanded to police cells for three days, which enabled the next phase of her arrest and questioning to take place.

It was while she was in custody that Rose West was arrested on suspicion of the murder of Lynda Gough. The two detectives, Harrison and Harris, put the evidence to her calmly and professionally but they were also probing her most intimate secrets, delving into her world of depraved sexual excess. It is quite possible that in the entire history of crime, no other officers had ever been required to ask such explicit questions of one person. Time and again they asked if she was acting under any form of duress from her husband. Every time the answer was the same, 'No comment'. No matter the unremitting catalogue of depravity put to her, it was always 'No comment'.

Withy Cole was brought up to date with Rose's attitude and the results of the bugging operation. He still believed prosecuting her would be difficult, but he was, as ever, supportive. Not only were the police relying on circumstantial and similar fact evidence, it would have to be backed up by witnesses who would have to go into the box and talk openly about some of their darkest, most shameful secrets and he wondered how many would be up to it. Then there were all the witnesses who had already been signed up by the media.

Bennett's views had not changed. Try as he might, and he had, he could see no reason to believe Rose West was not involved in the killings. She would be charged with the murder of Lynda Gough jointly with her husband. He would be informed and the charge amended later.

Rose West was served with the joint charge of murdering Lynda Carol Gough on the evening of Sunday 24 April. After being cautioned she replied, 'I'm innocent.' She was later charged with the remaining eight murders, the last of which, on 26 May, was that of her first child, Heather. To each of the charges, except for the murder of Shirley Hubbard when she made no reply, she answered, 'I'm innocent' or 'I'm innocent by the way.'

When Hazel Savage broke the news to Fred West the following day he seemed to just accept it – there was no other reaction. Either he had guessed it would happen or he knew already. Later, Howard Ogden suggested West be interviewed again on the Friday morning, this time with Janet Leach as appropriate adult. He believed he then might have something 'important' to say, by which time he would already have seen a psychologist and a barrister.

Hopes were high that Fred West was about to make another crucial intervention, just as he had when his handwritten note admitted nine murders. Maybe he would once again open his 'Pandora's box', implicate his wife, admit more murders – anything was possible.

Bennett and Moore sat pensively in their office as the scheduled 9.30 a.m. interview time passed. Then, a few minutes later, an exasperated Hazel Savage appeared in the doorway. Rather than making a clean breast of his crimes, she told them he was now denying committing any of the murders, that he had completely retracted his earlier confessions. Howard Ogden had another West note:

> I have not, and still not, told you the whole truth about these matters. The reason for this is that from the very first day of this enquiry my main concern has been to protect other person or persons, and there is nothing else I wish to say at this time.

When Ogden saw Bennett later that morning he appeared a little embarrassed and even apologetic. He said that after seeing his psychologist West had discussed what to do with his barrister and 'had taken advice'.

Even so, West's time was now running out. He would have to be asked about this latest statement. Who was this other person or persons? Why and who was he trying to protect? If and when the remains of Charmaine and Ann McFall were recovered, all that would have to be gone over, too, and once he had explained the rope, tape and other items found with the remains they would no longer need to have him kept in police custody. The interviews with Rose West would soon be completed and the same would apply to her. Then, they would begin preparing the evidence for the Crown Prosecution Service and the committal proceedings, what some regarded as the real work of the investigation.

The legal clock was already ticking.

TWENTY-EIGHT

There was no holding the tabloids, either in their coverage of the case or their involvement with important witnesses. Where the 'House of Horrors' was concerned the normal reporting restrictions ahead of a trial just didn't seem to apply. The Crown Prosecution Service could not stop it and even the Attorney-General appeared impotent.

Angry and frustrated, but mostly concerned the amount of publicity and the number of witnesses whose stories had been bought would wreck the case the police were building, Bennett contacted the CPS head office in London himself. It was not meant as a slight to Withy Cole and it would probably irritate many others, but he had to think of his own team.

Right from the start media interference had been an issue. Insensitive speculation, callous indifference towards the victims' families, the blatant disregard for the law and normal working practices, all fuelled an anti-media bias within the inquiry team that came to a head in many of their briefings. Bennett was sympathetic, but more than that, as Senior Investigating Officer it was his responsibility to ensure all their outstanding work did not go to waste, which could happen if the witnesses became tainted by their dealings with the press.

The case against the Wests was growing but it was still only a house of cards that would fall if the wrong one were pulled out. Bennett had to get that message across to the CPS bigwigs. Whether they would take it from a country copper like him he wasn't so sure.

At least the Attorney-General had authorised contempt proceedings against the local newspaper, the *Citizen*, its editor and owners the Northcliffe Newspapers Group. Would he now target some of the other bigger titles? Would it curb some of the more outrageous reporting?

Rose West was now in custody at Cheltenham where she was being held in similar conditions to Fred at Gloucester. There, the custody officer's security check uncovered a mobile phone in clean clothes that had been brought for her.

With the police preparing to search 25 Midland Road, it was like Cromwell Street all over again as reporters descended on neighbouring properties that overlooked it, making deals with residents to watch the operation from their premises. Then, at 9 a.m. on Monday 25 April, Bennett called a news conference to announce the work would begin the next day, though he successfully avoided questions about who or what he expected to find. However, as the gathering broke up, an angry, well-dressed, middle-aged man accosted him.

In another echo of Cromwell Street the man, his eyes bulging with rage, pointed his finger in Bennett's face, accusing him of 'hyping up the investigation' and 'bringing the press in droves'. It turned out he was trying to sell his house in the area and with no buyers so far was worried the price would plummet. It was all Bennett's fault, he raged. There were no bodies in 25 Midland Road anyway and if the police had to waste taxpayers' money – his money – doing the search, he should have kept it quiet until they had found something – not that they would.

Bennett decided that a polite but firm response was needed. He told him the end would justify the means and that he was powerless to keep the media away. Indeed, he warned, it would probably get worse before it got better. It was not what the man wanted to hear and he stormed off, promising to write to him and send a copy to the Chief Constable. The man was as good as his word. A few days later Bennett received a lengthy letter written in the same vitriolic tone.

With work beginning at Midland Road, the media was fighting a battle on two fronts and to make sure they did not miss anything, more crews arrived to ensure a full complement remained camped out at Kempley.

By mid-morning the scene around Midland Road compared with almost anything that had gone before. The spectacle of camera crews hanging out of windows, climbing on roofs and lining the walls of adjacent gardens was something to behold. And that wasn't all. When the search team began to strim the garden and remove debris from both Nos 25 and 26 there were continual requests from cameramen and sound recordists to either stop, or quieten it down, as the noise was affecting their filming. Bennett shook his head in disbelief.

Now that the search at Cromwell Street was almost over the property was being made safe enough to hand back to Howard Ogden and Leo Goatley on behalf of the Wests, though Rose had made it clear she would never live there again whatever happened. Bennett rejected Goatley's idea the property should be considered an exhibit in its own right until any trial was over, though he did agree that even when it was locked up and secured, the police would continue to keep an eye on it.

On Thursday 28 April, just over two months from when the search had begun, it was a very different property that was handed over. Where previously the sandy-coloured rendering and wrought-iron address plaque marked it out from the rest of the street, now it was shabby and deserted. The many bunches of flowers placed outside in memory of the dead had wilted and died. The windows were boarded up, the outside walls scarred by all the remedial work. There had been fourteen deliveries of ready-mixed concrete – 72.2 cubic metres – to prop up the structure as the search had progressed.

In order to help investigators, lawyers, even members of a jury, to visualise it all – the tight living accommodation, external extensions, internal modifications and how it all related to the nine graves – Bennett decided they needed a scale model of the property, a three-dimensional replica to supplement the plans and drawings they had already. It would give a better impression of the scale of the house and garden, and help to reinforce their conviction that Fred West could not have murdered, butchered and buried nine young women without his wife being involved.

Police Constable Eric Williams, the force exhibitions officer and a model maker, who had previously created accurate models that had been used in major crime investigations, was given the job. Made to a scale of 20:1, it would provide a panoramic view of the house and garden and could also be taken apart to show various stages of the extensions and the grave sites. There were plenty of accurate measurements, photographs and video footage to help him get it right. Coincidentally, Williams's wife had lived at 24 Midland Road before their marriage and had met both Fred and Rose West during the 1970s.

When Paul Britton came again on 26 and 27 April, he was brought up to date with how Fred and Rose West were reacting to the changes in their circumstances. He was also told of the new approach to interviewing Fred. Another new team would be introduced who would be more formal. His interrogators would be a different rank, they would dress differently, their questions would concentrate on different areas, even the furniture in the interview room would change, all in an attempt to break down his smug resistance. Of course, they still had to follow the legal rules on questioning suspects but if the bodies of Charmaine or Ann McFall were found, they would be able to question him about that.

Britton could not foresee any problems with their strategy and agreed it may succeed in getting him to explain some of the unanswered questions, though he held no hope that Rose's attitude would change.

The intensely physical, back-breaking work at Kempley was slow. A number of very large tree roots, used to infill the ground, had been uncovered and were hanging on stubbornly. The wet conditions did not help either. Even so, they were on their way to getting it back to how it was in 1967; the ever-expanding hole in the ground that now looked more like an archaeological dig was proof of that.

At Midland Road, the diggers were already through the floor and down to the rubble underneath. Soon they would know whether Charmaine was buried there. Bennett was in no doubt she was dead but if she wasn't there, as Fred now claimed, he had no idea where else to look.

When he and Moore were told after briefing on 4 May the kitchen had been excavated down to earth level and the diggers had come across evidence of coal dust they decided to pay a visit. They arrived at 7 p.m., long after the media had packed up for the night, and were taken around the back of the property to the kitchen. Unlike Fred's attempt at Cromwell Street, it was part of a well-built extension, though everything inside had now been stripped out apart from the sink and adjoining work surface. An area of metal floor some 8sq. ft just inside the room had been removed, leaving a hole more than 6ft deep at one end and around 4ft deep in the rest, deep enough to need a ladder to get in and out. To the side was some of the original wall and evidence of where the rubble had been removed. The earth in the bottom of the pit was dry and varied in colour between brown and red, with patches of black that looked like coal dust in the deepest part.

Police Constable George Sharpe, one of the search team, was slowly scraping the soil from the surface of the deepest area when he uncovered a small object and handed it to Bob Beetham. It was small, not more than 1in wide and like a butterfly in shape. After examining it closely, Beetham climbed up the ladder and handed it to Bennett and Moore, saying it looked like a pebble or piece of stone or maybe a peculiar-shaped fossil. Bennett studied it pensively. He was sure it was a bone but could not think from which part of the body. It definitely rang a bell; he had seen this shape before. In any event it did not feel like a stone. The search had to continue but even more carefully now, in case there was anything else there.

Beetham climbed back down into the pit and as Bennett joined him, another identical shape was found. As he continued to scrape this one, another round, similar-coloured shaft began to show through. There was little doubt that this was bone and it had been uncovered almost directly below where Fred West had said Charmaine was buried. It looked human, too.

They must have found the remains of Charmaine. Remains 11. The coroner was informed and so too was the Prof. It was part of their now well-practised routine. The area was secured to await his arrival the next day. It also meant the whole of the cellar would have to be scanned by the ground-penetrating radar and then excavated down to the hard clay, just as at Cromwell Street.

Bennett made the formal announcement of the discovery of yet more human remains at a news conference the following morning. When Professor Knight arrived, he was first shown what they had found the night before and quickly confirmed they were the ends of a young child's femur, the parts of the thigh bone that fused together as the child got older. It was then that Bennett remembered the Prof showing him this in a previous investigation.

As Bennett and Moore looked on, the professor, with Beetham close by to assist, slowly scraped at the earth in the area where the bone had been found, gradually exposing two lower leg bones – the tibia and fibula. Deftly dusting away the earth, he seemed puzzled at the way the remains had been left, the position in which he had found them. Alongside the notes he was keeping he began making sketches. The two femurs, from which the knee ends were uppermost, suggested that when she was buried she had somehow been folded, with the rest of her body off to the left. Looking at the bones as best he could in the circumstances he could find no evidence of disarticulation anywhere, yet the legs could not have been in that position while connected to the trunk.

It was clear from their size the rest of the bones were those of a child, which the professor confirmed was a girl.

Eventually, the remains were recovered and arranged in their anatomical position, including the skull. As they were brought out, everyone there paused in silence, each alone with their thoughts. Finding what they were looking for was a measure of their success but this was no cause for celebration. What they had was evidence of another young life ended before its time, another family member, and another unforgettable reminder of what they were involved in.

The silence was broken when the Prof remarked he was missing both patellae – kneecaps. There was no evidence of any clothing either, something else these remains had in common with the Cromwell Street victims. Just as before, the remains were placed in an exhibit box draped in black cloth and carried out to a waiting police van. The uniformed policeman on guard outside bowed his head as a mark of respect and made a sign of the cross as they passed.

When Professor Knight completed the examination at his laboratory later, he was still unable to find any evidence of cuts or disarticulation, while the bone count revealed more than just the kneecaps missing. As well as the patellae, the lower part of the breastbone and a large number of wrist, ankle, finger and toe bones were also absent. If they had been there, they would have been found.

A lot of work had already been done to try to establish exactly when Charmaine was last seen. The police had some photographs of her but there were not many showing the front of her face. They were also of poor quality and had little of the information Dr Whittaker needed to make the job of identification easier. As a result, he asked for photographs of other young girls around the same age as Charmaine so he could see how the skulls compared, to check whether the one they had, fitted the right age profile. Not only was he striving for accuracy, he did not want anyone to suggest he had made Charmaine's photograph fit the skull rather than the other way round.

Charmaine was around 8 years old when she disappeared, sometime in 1971. Mrs Shirley Giles, who lived in a flat above the Wests at 25 Midland Road, recalled seeing Rose with Charmaine and Anne Marie. Charmaine, said Mrs Giles, was a difficult child to handle. Her own daughter Tracy was a friend of hers. Although she couldn't say Rose had ever harmed Charmaine, she did remember once seeing the little girl standing on a chair with her hands tied behind her back, apparently being threatened by her stepmother with a wooden spoon. She also remembered Fred West being sent to prison in November 1970, leaving Rose to look after Charmaine and Anne Marie on her own, which was still the situation when she left Midland Road in January 1971.

Sometime later, she could not be sure when, Shirley Giles visited Midland Road so that her daughter could see Charmaine, only to discover she was no longer there but had apparently gone back to live with her real mother. Significantly, at the time of the visit – and Mrs Giles was sure she only made one visit – she saw a caravan made out of matchsticks that Fred West had made in prison. She was so taken with it she wrote to Fred in prison and asked him to make one for her. If this was true, it meant he was still inside when Charmaine had left.

Enquiries at Leyhill Open Prison were complicated because the authorities there were at first unable to find the right records. Bennett asked them to look again and sent detectives from the investigation to help. As a result, they discovered that Fred West had been due for release on 24 June and that Rose had applied to visit him nine days before, on the 15th. Although Leyhill was an open prison, West would not have been allowed to go home before his release date and there was no record of him absconding. Furthermore, the note in Charmaine's school records showed she had left before the end of the summer term on 31 July.

When all these dates and information were analysed, then compared with what Fred West had said about how he had killed Charmaine and what they now knew about her burial, it raised a number of questions.

West had always maintained that Charmaine was not interfered with and had been buried fully clothed and wrapped in a blanket. In fact she was naked and there was no sign of a blanket.

While there was no evidence she had been dismembered, similar bones to those missing from the Cromwell Street victims were missing – significantly both kneecaps. Given the way the excavation had been carried out and the conditions in the grave, Professor Knight was as certain as he could be that the bones would not have decomposed and they had definitely not been missed in the recovery process.

Given all the information they now had – dates, sequence of events – it had to be a possibility that Rose West was not just involved in Charmaine's murder but had committed it when her husband was in prison. At this stage it was still just a possibility, nothing more, for West clearly knew where she was buried. Much would depend on precisely how old Charmaine was when she died and only the Prof or Doc would be able to establish that, which could take some time, perhaps months.

When Fred West was told that Charmaine had been found and he was charged with her murder his eyes welled up and he appeared close to tears. Could it be for the first time there was just the hint of pity for a victim? Or was it self-pity at his predicament? Only he knew.

When the interview team was changed, as planned, West was asked to explain why, when they had found Charmaine's remains, the circumstances differed from his account. His response was to refuse to answer any more questions or help with the search for Ann McFall. As for the missing bones and the other items that were found, he had nothing to say – literally. Staring dispassionately into the middle distance, any pretence at emotion evaporated; now he appeared unrepentant, lost in his own thoughts, apart from the odd denial and occasional aside that he was 'not prepared to say who he was protecting'.

Everything was falling apart. All his plans had gone awry, there was no time to think things through. Whatever he tried to confuse the investigation and wrest back control the opposite happened, which gave him more problems to overcome. It was never meant to be like this. After all, he had always considered himself much smarter than 'them coppers'. There was no point in dragging it out any longer. West wanted an end to the questioning and the police were not going to get anything more from him. On Friday 13 May, he was handed over to Winson Green Prison at Birmingham as a maximum-security category 'A' prisoner.

He would only return to Gloucester to appear in court when he would stand alongside his wife to face the joint charges laid against them.

If Ann McFall was found or there was any need to question him further, it could be done at the prison or when he was at Gloucester again.

TWENTY-NINE

Finding Charmaine did not mean it was now time to move on. Not yet anyway. Not before they had answered the question everyone was either asking or thinking. Was Midland Road another Cromwell Street? Were there more bodies buried there?

Everyone played the numbers game. Supposition became fact. Among the more extreme theories was the suggestion of a sinister link between the two house numbers – 25. That Fred West was obsessed with it and that it must be the number of times he had killed.

With reporters now camped outside Midland Road from dawn to dusk there was no hiding the ground-penetrating radar machine. That scanning floors was now part of the routine did nothing to dampen the speculation. True, it had uncovered a number of hot spots in the cellar but that just meant the ground had been disturbed, nothing more conclusive. To some, hot spots meant bodies so when the police issued a progress report they were careful not to mention them.

Even so, word got out that the police had found 'more victims, more bodies' – only the numbers varied – which furthered Bennett's belief there was a leak within the investigation. Worse still, he was becoming more anxious this type of speculative reporting could play into the hands of the Wests' defence.

Eventually, all the speculation proved just that. The search at Midland Road was completed after the cellar had been excavated and filled in with concrete just as Cromwell Street had been. With nothing new uncovered the property was made habitable once more and handed back to its occupiers on 7 June.

Fred West's younger brother John had been under investigation for some time and despite all his protestations of innocence was arrested and charged with two offences of rape, one of a girl aged 7 or 8 and the other of a girl aged 11 to 16. When he appeared before Gloucester Magistrates Court he was remanded on bail to be dealt with after the trial of Rosemary West.

On 18 May, Inspector Ted Kania, who had been on the investigation since 24 April, took over the role of search adviser at Kempley B, known locally as Fingerpost Field. An improvement in the weather brought with it an archaeologist to help them identify the precise parameters of the cow pond and any potential grave sites. She advised that the best way to uncover areas that had been disturbed in the past was to scrape the surface with trowels, gradually removing the firm soil on the top to reveal what was underneath. Laboriously slow, it was nevertheless such an effective technique that those who used it said it would show them where fence posts and stakes had been and would certainly identify the site of a grave.

Bennett and Moore had been to Kempley B on a number of occasions and seen this technique in action. As far as they were concerned, the area where the pond had been was now as visible as it ever would be, while the massive pit that surrounded it was still nowhere near the level they wanted and it had to be there before they could begin the real work of looking for Ann McFall.

What with Fred West's vague directions, now countered by him saying she would never be found anyway, plus the cows trampling over the field for years, scraping such a large area with trowels was not Bennett's idea of getting the job done, not when time equalled taxpayers' money.

The archaeologist did not like it but the Senior Investigating Officer's mind was made up. Bennett told Kania he did not want to see any scraping by trowel unless they uncovered something of significance.

As May continued, the spring weather was as changeable as ever, sunshine mixed with heavy squalls of rain and prolonged downpours. Despite their attempts to divert the natural drainage or pump it out, the excavated area regularly filled with water, turning it into a bog of red mud and clay that never completely dried out.

Coping with the conditions as best they could, they stuck to the plan of beginning the search from a point furthest from the line of trees and hedge – to avoid any unnecessary tree felling. Nearest the tree line would be the last area to be searched and was some 30ft from where West had put his marker.

By the middle of the month, it was estimated that well over 400 tons of earth had been moved and they had still only excavated half the area under surveillance.

Kempley B was now the only place they were searching and Bennett and Moore visited regularly. Often they would arrive and peer into the massive crater and see officers struggling to do their work, their clothes covered in mud, their wellington boots being sucked from their feet as they manhandled the sodden earth onto the conveyor system. Often, the search had to be stopped until the weather improved. It was the only respite the men had.

There were times when Bennett wondered whether they should have started this search in the first place, though he kept those doubts to himself.

The 'diving diggers', whose farm labourer complexions now glowed from working outdoors, their muscles honed, their needs supplied with everything from equipment to food by the Gloucestershire Fire Service, had no such reservations. They knew why they were there and were convinced they would find Ann McFall. Their unwavering morale and unstinting effort, just like everyone else on the investigation, was infectious and banished all Bennett's doubts – at least until he returned to Gloucester and reflected on what he had seen.

An unexpected phone call to his office one evening didn't

help either. It came from his eldest son Andrew, who had just seen a report of the excavation on television. He wasted little time in getting to the point of his call. 'Dad, enough is enough. I've spoken to Dave [his brother] and to mum. They know I'm phoning. We know you and what you're like, but it's time to stop this – there's no need for the foundations to be dug for a car park or block of flats at Kempley!'

Laughing, Bennett thanked him for his advice and concern, if not support. It may have been delivered as a joke, but he knew Andrew meant it. No doubt his son meant well but it was not the time to pick away at his floundering self-belief.

The media had been given several opportunities to take a closer look at the work and it was apparent from their reports they, too, were amazed at the scale of the task and the working conditions. It still did not stop some reporters and their 'snappers' from branching off into Stonehouse Coppice in search of other suspected burial grounds. When police dog handlers caught them they found children from the village with them, no doubt taken along to camouflage their real intentions, probably after agreeing a fee with their parents.

With no sign of a breakthrough, the weekend of 11 June was regarded as crucial. By then, it was reckoned they should have excavated the whole of the area earmarked and either have found Ann McFall or would have to consider extending the parameters of the search. Bennett knew it was a decision he might have to face, but had not anticipated facing it quite so soon.

Then again, his mind was already made up. The search would not be extended as there was no evidence to justify it and that's what he would tell the Chief Constable.

Tony Butler listened, then informed Bennett it should not be his decision alone whether the search should proceed. That did not just apply to Kempley B but included other possible sites that had come to the attention of the investigation – areas they had been tipped off about by the public or places where West had worked. He could not just disregard them; all had to be treated on merit. As for Kempley B, the Chief accepted that having seen photographs and the media reports no one could doubt they had done their best to establish whether Ann McFall was there.

Bennett confided that he thought the search would be finished by the end of the week and that when he broke the news to the media he was expecting some difficult questions, not least about the cost of the operation. That being the case, the Chief said he would join him at the site and they would face the music together.

Bennett was first to arrive; the Chief, anonymous in jeans rather than his uniform, followed soon after. His deception worked as none of the reporters noticed him. By contrast, the search team knew he was coming and were all kitted out in navy blue Gloucester Constabulary Underwater Section tee-shirts, no doubt to make a point.

With Bennett alongside, Tony Butler walked along the edge of the huge hole in the ground that was now more than 600sq m and 2m deep. Clearly impressed, he thanked them for their efforts so far and noted that in the circumstances it was as well they were trained for underwater searches.

As he and Bennett turned to leave, undoubtedly affected by what he had seen, the Chief told Bennett that if he wanted to extend the search he would back him. Bennett, though, was adamant. Pointing out the spot West had indicated and the vast area they had searched around it there was no new evidence to justify carrying on – though he would like to explore a small area in the coppice pointed out by some of the locals.

A pool facility for the media was organised for 11 a.m. on Tuesday 7 June. Bennett and Moore met the chosen representatives at the gate to Fingerpost Field and escorted them to the site. The winter wheat that was shooting when work began on 13 April was now knee high.

To prevent unnecessary speculation, they had been told to expect an announcement about when the search was to end but there was still a buzz of anticipation.

With the group hanging on his every word, Bennett began his short statement: 'Our search at Fingerpost Field is beginning to draw to a close. . . . We will move to another site in the immediate vicinity – highlighted by a number of local people and this should not take long at all. . . . At this stage we do not plan to search any other areas . . . I am not prepared to say why we have searched in the locations so far, but I can assure you that if my plans change in the future I will let you know.'

When it came to the one-to-one interviews, he took up a position on the side of the excavations from where he pointed out the last area to be searched in Stonehouse Coppice. He was expecting some probing questions, but not the rancorous tone.

'Do you accept you have been searching in the wrong place; you have dug out an area bigger and deeper than an Olympic swimming pool?'

'What do you say to the Gloucestershire taxpayers about the enormous cost of this operation, the money for which could have been put towards fighting crime that is on the increase while the detection rates are falling?'

'Who is going to look into whether the decision to make this search was justified – don't you think the public have a right to know as well as who you are searching for?'

The questions kept on coming and Bennett decided he just had to stay there and take it on the chin as best he could. Low as he felt, they were only asking what he had asked himself many times.

The early evening news brought almost universal criticism, not only of the way the search was undertaken but also questioning whether it should ever have taken place. At 6.30 that evening, the earliest he had finished for more than two months, he decided it was time to go home, have an evening off, a meal in with his wife and try to get away from it all.

He had to pick himself up, for all he could think of now was that he had let down the force, the Chief and everyone else on the investigation. He had never felt this low in all his years in the service, yet he had to shake himself out of it as there was still so much more to be done.

As he made his way along the Golden Valley bypass towards Cheltenham, still reflecting on how it had all turned out, he felt his pager vibrate. Pulling in to the verge, he looked down and took it from his belt. It was 6.40 p.m., less than 10 minutes since he had left his office. He stared in disbelief at the words on the screen: 'FROM TERRY, THEY APPARENTLY WANT A LARGE GAS BOTTLE.' It was not quite the agreed code but there was no doubting what it meant. There had been a find, one that was almost certainly what they had been searching for.

Setting aside the pager in favour of his mobile, he phoned the MIR. When Moore came on the line he tentatively asked him if they 'definitely wanted one now'.

'Oh yes,' he replied. 'The largest we have got, they said.'

There was no doubt. Their coded conversation confirmed that the coroner was being informed and that Professor Knight and Bob Beetham were also being called out. Before heading back towards Kempley, Bennett phoned home to cancel his early night.

He could barely contain himself. As he accelerated back towards Gloucester he realised he was travelling at over 80 miles per hour until common sense and a more professional approach prevailed. There was no point in speeding. The search team would be in control and if they had found Ann McFall, she had already been dead for twenty-seven years and nothing could change that.

Up on the fourth floor a beaming Terry Moore greeted him with the news that Beetham had contacted the Prof, who would join them at Kempley that evening. The two detectives travelled the 15 miles at a more sedate speed, still trying not to get too carried away just in case it was a false alarm, though they were convinced the message would not have been sent if there were any doubt. As they passed one pub along the way Bennett recognised journalists' cars parked outside. He liked to think he was above such petty thoughts as 'I told you so', but after the grilling he had received earlier that day he felt a sense of satisfaction at what he now knew and they did not.

A smiling Ted Kania – the look was infectious – brought them up to date when they arrived just after 7.20 p.m. It turned out that Police Constables Robinson and Skinner had been working close to the tree line near the edge of the search area when they discovered part of a skull and other human remains.

Any lingering doubts were now dispelled and Bennett could wait no longer. As he and Moore walked down the slope they saw the search team sitting away from an area that had been cordoned off in textbook crime scene management style with a walkway to it clearly defined. The grave was less than 2m from the tree line and 10 to 12m from the final corner of the search. As Beetham pointed out the part of the skull and bones protruding from the red soil, the 'diving diggers' edged towards the tape they had put in place.

Kania then made one simple request, 'Can the team stay and watch when the Prof arrives?'

Bennett turned, congratulated them and said that 'it went without saying', adding that what they had achieved was outstanding and that like many other parts of the investigation it was something he would never forget.

Professor Knight arrived about an hour later. Pausing to take it all in, he remarked on what a massive undertaking it had been. The procedure was the same as before. The professor, assisted by Beetham, was watched by the Senior Investigating Officer and this time the entire search team, who were seated on a raised amphitheatre fashioned from the earth they had excavated.

Inside the pit, the bones seemed to be jumbled and there were signs of cloth or clothing. As the work progressed slowly, darkness began to close in and it was agreed they could achieve nothing more in the fading light. Instead, another trademark blue and white striped tent was erected to protect the site, a guard put in place and everything left until the professor could come back to finish the job.

It was the only topic of conversation on the way back and they could not make up their minds whether it was bad luck or a bad decision to start the search away from the tree line rather than near it. They wanted to avoid cutting down trees, but had they started there, once they had got down to the original contours of the pond, the search would have taken much less time.

The following morning the press office notified the media there would be a short but significant news conference outside Gloucester Police Station at 10.30 a.m. Quite a large number of reporters and camera crews turned up but not as many as usual.

Bennett made it brief: 'At 6.15 p.m. last night the police search team at Kempley were working in the search area when they discovered what they thought were human remains. The work stopped and Professor Bernard Knight went to the scene late that evening and confirmed they were human remains.' Identification, he said, was a matter for the coroner. Professor Knight would be back to finish the job later.

There could hardly have been a greater contrast between the news reports that night and those of the day before, as criticism and questioning gave way to admiration and footage and photographs of an 'incredible' search and a job well done. Such a blatant U-turn with no apology did not go down well at that night's briefing and although Bennett accepted it was the media's way, there was no doubt it had upset him deeply.

When Professor Knight returned to Kempley on the Thursday, the media presence was back to its former strength. The work took a little longer than expected, mostly because the ground was harder in places than others. He quickly established the bones were female and contained the remains of a foetus that would have been 6 to 7 months old. In addition, there were a number of other artefacts including a discoloured cardigan in a polythene bag, a number of pieces of material, including one that was quite large, discoloured and floral, like a curtain or quilt. There were also long and short pieces of rope, one of which was knotted, and a length of cord that bound the wrists together and was laid over the ribs.

When the Prof had finished he could see marks on both femurs that, along with how the remains were positioned, indicated the body had been dismembered. The only sizeable bone not recovered was part of the left fibula and a right twelfth rib. Again, there were a large number of finger and toe bones missing. The professor confirmed the find to the waiting media as those of a female in the advanced stages of pregnancy and shortly afterwards the remains were taken away for further forensic examination.

The area in Stonehouse Coppice that had aroused local suspicions was searched but nothing more was found.

Soon Dr Whittaker would begin the painstaking procedure that would prove whether Remains 12 were those of Ann McFall. Taking everything into consideration, he was unlikely to reach any other conclusion.

THIRTY

Twelve sets of remains had now been recovered. Twelve young women and girls whose lives were ended brutally, sadistically and long before their time.

It was eleven murders more than Fred West had originally admitted and three more than in his later handwritten confession.

Rose West was in custody once more and the case against her was building.

As the investigation moved into a new phase Withiel Cole was anxious they should appoint the lawyers who would prosecute the case as soon as possible. The names he coveted were Neil Butterfield QC as lead counsel and Andrew Chubb as junior. Both worked out of the same chambers in Exeter, less than 100 miles from Gloucester, both were known to Bennett and Moore and both had made their names in a number of high-profile trials. Butterfield already enjoyed a reputation as the eminent barrister in the region and the word on the legal grapevine was that he would soon be offered the position of High Court Judge – hopefully *after* the Wests' trial. Chubb, too, was a leading barrister and Cole wanted to get them for the prosecution before the defence snapped them up.

By mid-April both men had been approached and accepted the brief, though brief was hardly an apt description of the work that lay ahead.

The file was split into sections:

- *sexual proclivity* – the Wests' penchant for sexual deviance, violence and masochism, as well as their insatiable sexual appetite;
- *similar fact evidence* – the similarities in circumstances and

events over the years stretching back to before Midland Road through to Cromwell Street. The violence used, tying up, taping, travelling to pick up runaways, the attack on Caroline Owens who was taped and tied up, the sexual violence inflicted on Anne Marie and other witnesses, the implements they used, the voyeurism and violent lesbian relationships, the victims – how they disappeared and the bindings and masks found with them – all completed the similar fact circle. The lies and subterfuge would weld it all together, as would the size of the property and the impossibility of human bodies being dismembered and buried without the knowledge and involvement of the owners – both of them;

- *interviews, forensic evidence and other police evidence.*

Cole regarded it as the most logical way to break down the case. It would be ready for the committal proceedings well within the legal time frame.

It was hard to see how Fred West would not be committed for trial, though Rose's solicitor Leo Goatley maintained he would fight to have the case against her dismissed and was even considering applying to get her out on bail. By the time she was charged with the murders of the nine Cromwell Street victims, the police reckoned they had all the evidence against her they were likely to get, though some interesting witnesses had come forward whose statements showed she knew some of the victims and had severely sexually assaulted some with her husband.

While her husband was starting to waver in his insistence that he had done it all himself, hinting that 'others' might be involved, he did not name her. The cornerstones of the case against Rose were the same as they had been since early March, a combination of common sense, circumstance and lies, though there was still insufficient evidence to link her to the murders of Rena and Charmaine.

There was some suspicion that Charmaine could have died when West was in prison, based upon what Shirley Giles had said, and the school note, but it was no more than that because the prison records were still missing and no one knew exactly when he was released. Dr Whittaker was trying to determine precisely how old Charmaine was when she had died. As for Rena's murder there was nothing to link Rose at all. The suggestion that Rena had come to collect her daughter – not knowing the couple had already killed her – and was then murdered herself to cover it all up, was a good story, but with no evidence to back it up, no more than that.

At least there was no doubt about Ann McFall. Fred alone would be charged with her murder because Rose had not arrived on the scene when she disappeared.

The first conference with prosecuting counsel was arranged for the late afternoon of Friday 24 June at Exeter. Neil Butterfield and Andrew Chubb were seated at the head of a baronial-length table, Bennett and Moore sat at the other end, Griff, Cole, Rita Crane and David Stott, manager of the CPS overseeing the Gloucester area and the one to whom Withy Cole was responsible, sat along one side.

A smiling Butterfield invited Bennett to outline the case, which as far as Fred West was concerned was relatively straightforward. Rose's, on the other hand, was not. Stott had already voiced his concern at the lack of hard evidence against her and the QC was equally sceptical, asking rather theatrically, 'Is there no smoking gun – no whiff of cordite?'

It may have been a throwaway remark but it reminded Bennett that not everyone was as convinced of her guilt as the inquiry team and that they could not afford to be complacent. Everything they had done so far would have to be checked and rechecked.

The integrity of the investigation must be above reproach and there must be no weaknesses for the defence to exploit.

Almost a week later, both Fred and Rose West were due back in court – the first time they had met since Fred walked out of 25 Cromwell Street and gave himself up to the police just over four months earlier.

From the moment he arrived at the police station, Fred West looked apprehensive. As well as meeting up with Rose again, he knew he would face more questions about Ann McFall. Rose appeared as sullen and indifferent as ever, reluctantly complying with whatever she was told to do.

Wearing a blue cardigan over a beige crewe-necked jumper, she climbed the stairs that led from the cells into the courtroom and took her place in the dock where she sat with her head bowed throughout the 10-minute hearing. When her husband was brought up there was hardly enough room to accommodate both defendants and their security guards, for Rose West always a combination of Tina West, Debbie Willats and Chrissie Mannion, there specifically to note any attempt at communication and prevent it.

As his eyes fixed on the back of his wife's head a faint smile lit up his face and he shuffled along the bench towards her, patting her on the back a number of times before his guards pulled him back. But there was no reaction from Rose, not a flicker, and the smile disappeared. Bennett pondered, was her indifference real? Or was it the first outward sign of her strategy to distance herself from the crimes, an initial public expression that his deeds were as abhorrent to her as everyone else? Either way, West was visibly deflated by the snub and switched his focus to the body of the court, where he found first Janet Leach and then his son Stephen. He nodded in recognition but there was little enthusiasm in the gesture.

Both husband and wife were jointly charged with the murder of the nine Cromwell Street victims. Fred West was also charged with the murders of Rena and Charmaine, Rose West with two charges of rape and one of assault. There was no application for bail and the magistrates remanded them until 28 July.

During the next three days Fred West was questioned over the murder of Ann McFall, and continually denied all knowledge of what had happened to her. Indeed, he seemed sad to hear her name mentioned and that she was six to seven months pregnant, though he was already well aware of this.

By the time he was charged with her murder on the Sunday evening, eight officers working in teams of two had interviewed him on 151 occasions since 24 February, altogether more than 110 hours in total, with Hazel Savage and Darren Law conducting most of the early interviews. The evidence to be presented at the forthcoming committal proceedings was contained in thirty-one lever-arch files.

There was more praise for the inquiry team, this time from the Chairman of the Gloucestershire Police Authority, Richard Somers, who described their work as 'A shining example to others of how a police force should conduct itself in today's environment . . . they have been extremely professional during this major inquiry, the like of which has never been seen before.'

Fine words and compliments kept their morale high, though Bennett could not help thinking it increased the pressure, not only to maintain the high standard they had set but also when their work was scrutinised by the legal process and ultimately the media.

By now the Senior Investigating Officer had carried out the Chief Constable's instruction to review all the potential burial sites entered into HOLMES and was still of the opinion there was insufficient evidence to justify any more searches. The news disappointed Central Television, the local ITV station, which was leading the clamour for the Pop-In Café to be excavated in the belief it held the key to Mary Bastholm's disappearance.

With this phase of the investigation drawing to an end, the size of the team was being scaled down as some of the inquiry officers and diggers returned to their normal duties. Stress counselling continued for those who wanted it and was tailored to suit individual categories like search teams, MIR staff and other groups.

Long before the searches had ended, Bennett had come under pressure to lift his ban on a team night out. They wanted a chance to get together socially and let off a bit of steam, though Bennett was worried how it would look if news got out. Eventually he changed his mind but only under the strict guidelines he laid down.

He had discovered a pub in Gloucester Docks, close to the city centre, that was being done up. Its regulars would be told it was shut for the night because of the work and the Cromwell Street team and their guests would have it to themselves. Under Bennett's guidelines, officers not attending the party would stand guard outside and if any reporters turned up everyone inside would drink up and leave without comment. No one would drink and drive and it would be an orderly affair that would be open to wives and partners of anyone who was involved in the investigation in any way, though if the media got the slightest inkling it would be called off.

If there was a mole within the investigation, there was no breach of security this time. There was a disco and dancing and the atmosphere was heady, so that when the search team's spontaneous rendering of the Seven Dwarfs' song 'Hi ho, Hi ho . . .' reached the chorus of 'We dig, dig, dig, dig, dig, dig, dig, dig, dig the whole day through . . .', accompanied by digging motions, it almost brought the house down. Bennett knew he had taken a risk but as he watched the evening unfold he also knew he had made the right decision. The last few months had brought them face to face with acts of unbelievable human behaviour, bestiality that no known animal would have been involved in and way beyond most people's imagination. This was not a night for celebration but an opportunity to lance a festering boil and for some was probably better than any counselling.

Even so, he was glad it never got into the newspapers.

There was still no sign of the remains being released to their families. The coroner was equally keen to have the issue resolved but his hands were tied until the defence gave its consent.

Bennett was in regular contact with Howard Ogden and Leo Goatley and suggested another pathologist could carry out a second set of post-mortems and produce their own independent report. If the findings were the same as Professor Knight's the coroner could authorise release. If anyone else were arrested there would be two reports available.

It seemed a workable solution – to everyone but the defence solicitors. The families were not happy, for they knew there was little left of their loved ones to examine, certainly not their bodies, just the bones that had survived. Eventually, two further pathologists carried out examinations on behalf of the defence, leaving the relatives to await their conclusions.

The investigation into how the *Sun* had acquired the photograph of Fred West inside Gloucester Prison had been unsuccessful. It could have come from any one of a number of prison staff and the police could not be sure from whom. The newspaper, too, was in the clear. It had received a call to say that a photograph of West with his prison number was for sale and sent a reporter and photographer to see a man, whom they were unable to describe, in a car park. When he showed them the picture they paid him for the privilege of photographing it, though first he had to put it on the bonnet of a car so they could do so without touching it and therefore get what they wanted without handling stolen property.

Howard Ogden spent many hours with his client in the cells at Gloucester Police Station, often after interviews had ended. He was entitled to do this though West had mentioned to the police he had signed some form of agreement authorising Ogden to write a book about him and the case, and now he was worried his solicitor was concentrating more on the book than preparing his defence.

None of this bothered the police unduly; after all, West could always change his solicitor if he wished. Ogden knew this only too well and often complained himself that other lawyers were lining up to take West from him. Janet Leach had also let it slip that she too had been offered a similar sort of agreement by West.

Early in August West sacked Ogden and appointed Tony Miles of Bobbetts and Mackan, Bristol solicitors well known for their criminal defence work. When Miles asked for another pathologist's report it meant the families would not have the remains released to them for at least another month.

It was no surprise either when a week later, two investigative reporters on the *Daily Mail*, Paul Henderson and Stephen Wright, who had been working on the case almost from the start, reported that Ogden had been offering the tapes he had made of conversations with West, as well as photographs of Cromwell Street, to filmmakers and agents. According to them, his asking price for the material was £500,000.

West instructed his new solicitors to take out an injunction preventing Ogden from using the information and the courts ordered him to hand over the tapes, letters, clothing and photographs in his possession. The Law Society mounted its own investigation and Ogden was eventually barred from practising for a year.

Within days of Fred West dispensing with Ogden, Leo Goatley brought in new lawyers for Rose. Richard Ferguson QC was to lead for the defence, with Ms Sasha Wass his junior. Ferguson was an Irishman who had been involved in a number of terrorist trials in Northern Ireland and had a reputation as a highly skilled and astute counsel. He would be a formidable opponent.

Yet while the inquiry team immersed itself in preparations for what was already being hyped as the 'Trial of the Century', others had no such concern for the legal niceties.

Among the more bizarre allegations of contempt to land on the Attorney-General's desk, and therefore likely to prevent the Wests from receiving a fair trial, was a scurrilous anthem composed, printed and sung at the ground of non-league Gloucester City Football Club that went to the tune of 'Go West'. The comedian Billy Connolly produced a video, of which around 2½ of the 90 minutes were devoted to jokes about Fred and Rose. Faxes alluding to the couple and their pornographic lifestyle arrived in offices nationwide. There were even some, advertising the services of Gloucester CID for 'building work and demolition'.

Individually they may not have amounted to much, some might have been mildly amusing, but they provided fuel for stories that somehow found their way onto television and into the newspapers and Bennett was concerned that when it was all lumped together by the defence, the volume of material would make a compelling argument for the case against the Wests to be thrown out before it had even started.

THIRTY-ONE

By mid-July, the investigation was more than £935,000 over budget, more than £1,000,000 if the extra cost to the divisions of covering for staff working on the inquiry was added. From the outset a tight rein had been kept on expenditure. Once the scale of what had to be done became apparent Bennett had sought the help of the Gloucester Division's finance officer Mike Cresswell. He set up a separate system to deal with the estimates and accounts, assisted by Sergeant Richard Green. Bennett was to use this at every briefing of the Chief Constable, who had put a temporary halt to recruitment in an effort to fund the investigation with the savings made as a result.

Eighty-four officers were assigned by the end of the first few weeks, with a similar number of regular officers, members of the special constabulary and civilian staff providing back-up. In total, more than 10 per cent of the constabulary's strength was fully concentrated on the West case, with many more involved or affected by the drain it placed elsewhere throughout the county. But the true cost of the investigation would only be known when the trial was over, anything up to eighteen months away.

At least there was an opportunity for Bennett and Moore to take some of the leave they were owed, for neither had taken a day off since it all began. Bennett hitched up his caravan and headed for Normandy with his wife and youngest son, yet even in France there was no escape. He had only been on the site just over a day when another English family recognised him and wanted to talk about the case. Like a boxing referee in the ring, Ann Bennett stepped in immediately and ruled the subject off limits – much to the other family's surprise.

And it did not end there. On the way back, they stopped at a hypermarket at Le Havre where he was approached first by a French couple who in good English wished him and his officers well, and then as he was leaving by another English holidaymaker who asked to shake his hand and patted him on the back.

He was not the only one. It transpired that when other members of the team on holiday were asked where they were from and replied Gloucester or Gloucestershire, they were quizzed about Cromwell Street, even without mentioning their occupation – though they did get the odd drink bought for them as a result.

On his return, Bennett went to visit his mother, who had made a good recovery from her operation and was now back home. That day, though, she took a turn for the worse and was taken back into hospital where she stayed for the next six months, for much of it critically ill. Many times Bennett was called at work and told his mother was close to death.

Handing over the papers for the committal was the first step to trial; now they had to decide upon a venue for these proceedings. The prosecution was hoping for a 'paper' committal where the defence would accept the Wests had a case to answer and the hearing would all be over in minutes – it could therefore be held at Gloucester.

Rose's lawyers had other ideas. They wanted an 'old style' committal where the evidence against her would be tested in front of a stipendiary magistrate – a lawyer who could decide on legal arguments such as the admissibility of evidence – who would decide whether she had a case to answer. It was likely the hearing would last three to five days and because of the inevitable media interest and security issues, could not be held at Gloucester.

Dr Whittaker had now completed what examinations he could of Remains 10, 11 and 12 and was 'comfortable' they were

Catherine West née Costello, Charmaine West and Ann McFall, though he was still unable to be precise about the date of Charmaine's death. It now seemed unlikely her exact age would ever be established.

The coroner fixed the inquests that would confirm their identities for 27 July at Dursley Magistrates Court. It was a small, fairly modern building dating from the 1960s and attached to the town's police station, close to one of the safe houses where Rose West had stayed. As ever, reporters and cameras were there in force and although sure to be shorter than previous inquests, it was another experience Bennett was not looking forward to. He tried to keep the sadness of it all at the back of his mind by telling himself it was just procedure, just another court appearance, but it was not and nothing could erase the thought that he was talking about the end of the lives of a mother and young daughter and a young pregnant girl, the manner of whose deaths he was very unclear about. For sure, Fred West was involved in it all somehow and his wife likely figured in the deaths of Charmaine and Rena, but right now he could not see a way to prove it. As the coroner concluded the paperwork, adding his condolences to the families, Bennett mused on whether either of the Wests would ever tell the truth about the murders – probably not, was his realistic assessment.

The police now had time to concentrate on the missing teenager Mary Bastholm, who, it appeared, might have known Ann McFall, as both girls used the Pop-In Café in Gloucester.

Within the weeks and months that followed more than 250 further actions or lines of enquiry were pursued and over 100 people questioned. These were either people first seen during the original investigation or others uncovered by the current inquiry, though the passage of twenty-six years since Mary disappeared and the deaths of others in that time who might have been able to help, held them back.

Fred West was interviewed again and still denied any

involvement in her disappearance. There was never any firm evidence to link him to her, though she may have known Ann McFall. Stephen West later claimed he confessed to him. Although no longer acting as West's appropriate adult, Janet Leach continued to visit him in Winson Green and receive telephone calls from him.

West seemed to be settling into his new prison routine. His relaxed, compliant approach went down well with the staff, who found him happy to talk about himself and Rose, slipping in that there were at least two more victims. West was well aware his family was in contact with the press and loved reading about himself in the tabloids, lapping up his notoriety. It led to Stephen claiming his dad had mentioned burying many more victims at a farm. He didn't name the farm, but just described it.

To Bennett, it all smacked of West the chameleon, but when talk of his funeral cropped up, the Senior Investigating Officer began to question West's mental state. It was West's daughter Anne Marie who raised the alarm by disclosing her dad had asked her to take care of the arrangements, not Rose. Neither mentioned suicide but it was enough for Bennett to alert Winson Green straightaway and fix up a meeting.

It was arranged for 25 November. Also there to discuss Fred West's security and anything else relating to him were Terry Moore, the Constabulary's Prison Liaison Officer, Detective Sergeant Jan Blomfield, and Home Office Prison Liaison Officer, Detective Inspector John Kerr.

Winson Green was a forbidding place built by the Victorians, its outside walls mainly of dark red brick. Bennett had not been for eight years and little seemed to have changed. The corridors that echoed to their footsteps, the high walls topped with barbed wire, the lack of natural light, it was all very oppressive and depressing. Even the exercise yard outside offered little respite. Their meeting was with Deputy Governor Polkinghorn. Bennett raised a number of issues about West and his custody before moving on to his conversation with Anne Marie and their concerns over his mental state. The Deputy Governor assured Bennett that West was a model prisoner. He had settled down well, was the 'best pool player on the landing' and went by the name of 'Digger'. As if to provide further reassurance he reminded them the prison had previously held Michael Sams, another high-profile abductor of women, without any problem and invited them to see West's cell while he was exercising.

But Bennett was not reassured and when the Deputy Governor mentioned that a special team of prison officers was in charge of West and the landing it only added to his unease. When West was in custody in Gloucester, Bennett explained, his guards were regularly changed to prevent him gaining control over them through cunning and his disarming personality, character traits that had enabled him to conceal his crimes for nearly thirty years.

As soon as Bennett was back in his office, he made a list of things to do and who to contact in the event of Fred West taking his own life.

The Church in Gloucester had wanted to hold some form of service of commemoration for some time to give local people a chance to express their respect for the dead. There was even talk of a memorial plaque, possibly in the cathedral. The Bishop of Gloucester headed the list of clergy who approached Bennett but he was unsure about the timing. After all, the remains had still not been released, there had been no funerals and if the families were in favour, they were likely to want it in private. In response, the Church said prayers for the victims would be said at Evensong on All Souls' Day, a service to remember departed loved ones. An invitation was extended to the families and any members of the investigation team who would like to attend.

From that Bennett took it to be a normal service and was dismayed to learn the diocese had issued an official press release and reporters were asking whether he would be attending. He was planning to go, and so were other members of the team, but not in the full glare of the media. It was not what they had in mind at all. Bennett told the team he would still attend, though with the media there in force, he was worried All Souls' Day would turn into 'All Ghouls' Day'.

Ironically, another murder in another part of Gloucestershire almost kept him away. A 40-year-old mother was found stabbed to death in her home in Tetbury more than 20 miles away and as he was the only senior detective available, he would have to hold the fort. Professor Knight had also been contacted and was on his way. Another lengthy murder investigation was the last thing Bennett needed.

Even before the Prof had completed the post-mortem examination Bennett knew he would be late for the service but at least by then the reporters and cameramen were off their guard and he was able to slip into the cathedral unnoticed. It was another sombre occasion and the Bishop, the Right Reverend David Bentley, encapsulated the mood with his opening remarks: 'Our city and county seemed full of pain and darkness earlier this year and the saga has not, as yet, come to its end . . . many here today were deeply touched and moved by those events and much more support and comfort was given and received.'

It was just what Bennett was thinking and he was sure all of the families and officers involved as well. It was a moving service and when it was over all of the police officers there found a side door and managed to slip away in the darkness without being spotted.

The next day, Bennett handed over the murder of the Tetbury mother to another senior detective.

The pressure of work and more extra demands exerted on the MIR continued as every aspect of Fred and Rose West was looked into from their birth. Now as the creation of the file for committal proceedings progressed, a dynamic process in itself as further potential evidence continued to come to light. More witnesses were being found and items taken from the search of 25 Cromwell Street. In particular, documents and letters exchanged between Fred and Rose when he was in prison revealed more of the closeness of their sickening relationship.

The preparation of lists of documents and exhibits for disclosure to the Crown Prosecution Service and defence became an additional priority. Most of the information obtained from the outset of the investigation would now have to be copied and distributed; this would be an ongoing process right through to the end of any trial. Little would be considered worth being kept confidential to the police investigation, that is not being disclosed to the defence under the rules of public information immunity (PIR). Those that Bennett thought he could retain that would come into this category would have to be agreed by Withy Cole for the Crown Prosecution Service; if not then they would be disclosed. This was yet another area where things had to be right – there was no room for error. A number of high-profile investigations that had resulted in convictions in the distant and more recent past for serious crimes, including murder, had been overturned on appeal as unsafe because material that might have been useful to the defence had been kept back, the defence at the time being totally unaware of its existence. These convictions were overturned despite the prosecution having complied with the rules of discourse of the day but the Appeal Court more often than not decided to use the newer rulings retrospectively, no doubt considering those in place previously to have been unfair. Despite all the documents and exhibits having been uniquely marked by Roger Kelland as Disclosure Officer and as frequently by Dave Griffiths, from the time they had entered the MIR so they could be easily identified on the HOLMES system, the lists had to be reviewed and if necessary the status of items changed by the SIO. Just like the need to mark and finalise other aspects of the HOLMES database, it was an essential but time-consuming chore.

So far the police had traced more than 170 people who had either lodged with the Wests or just passed through Cromwell Street or Midland Road and the numbers continued to rise as they, in turn, remembered others. There were similar enquiries covering former residents of Gloucester care homes.

Among the stories they uncovered were two horrific accounts from girls who alleged they had suffered extreme physical and sexual abuse at the hands of Fred and Rose, which corroborated what other witnesses had related, including Anne Marie and Caroline Owens. Again, it seemed to Bennett that not only would they face legal obstacles to introducing such explicit evidence in court but also asking young women to describe their most intimate secrets in a courtroom packed full of lawyers, reporters and any number of other strangers was very different from having a private conversation.

Where the trial would be held was another bone of contention. While the defence favoured the Old Bailey the prosecution preferred Winchester on the grounds that getting witnesses to and from there would be easier, finding accommodation for anyone who had to stay would be cheaper and providing security at the Crown Court there would be easier.

At least a decision had been made on the committal. It was fixed for February 1995 and would take place at Dursley Magistrates Court in front of the Chief Metropolitan Stipendiary Magistrate Peter Badge, the country's most senior JP.

With the cost of the investigation rising by the day, and another expensive operation just around the corner, the Chief Constable applied to the Home Office for help to pay for it all. The figure he quoted was £651,000. He received nothing.

Within the MIR the charts had been updated and now included small photographs of each of the victims with their name, date of birth and the order in which they were killed and discovered. There were additional boxes containing the names of witnesses able to give evidence about their disappearance and identity, and other areas listing what was buried with them and which of their bones were missing.

Among the forensic details now established it was known that:

- Heather's hair included fibres that appeared to come from a carpet;
- Alison Chambers's leather belt that had been round her skull had hair on it;
- the tape found with Lucy Partington had hairgrips and hair attached;
- the brown tape found with Lynda Gough and the headband of Carol Cooper also had hair attached.

The tape mask of Shirley Hubbard had hair on the inside but no fingerprints. It was a truly grotesque exhibit which to be examined had to be unwound to its original form, which was a length of tape that was now old, discoloured and crumpled. Of all the artefacts found it was the one that disturbed its finders the most, but just like the others it only hinted at its horrendous use without giving up any of its secrets. Items of clothing and rope used for binding had also been examined along with items found with Rena and Ann McFall, but they seemed to shed very little new light on how they had met their deaths.

There were other charts, too. One showed the ages of the West children when each of the victims had gone missing, another setting the disappearances against when Rose was pregnant, one comparing the similarities between the victims – how they were buried and what was buried with them; who was living in what room and when, together with their various nicknames. Many of these themes sprang from Bennett's shower time and were useful in proving or disproving various theories.

As everything in the house was systematically gone through, the police found a small urn and jar containing burnt material which, when examined forensically, proved to be most likely the remains of underwear, some of which was written on and dated. According to Fred West, it was the couple's way of remembering past sexual experiences, something to look back on in years to come.

Among their private papers, the police also found a copy of the *Citizen* containing a report of their appearance in court for the Caroline Owens episode – a notable discovery considering Rose claimed she could remember nothing of it. Added to all the other letters they exchanged when Fred was in prison, these could have been some of the 'trophies' or 'souvenirs' which Paul Britton had earlier remarked psychopaths were known to keep. It might also explain why bones were missing, but West was to deny this, saying they had been taken to prevent identification, refusing to comment further.

There was also a vast amount of cheap jewellery, much more than in a normal family, which Detective Constable Tina West had catalogued and put on display for the victims' families to try and identify, though without success.

Tuesday 13 December was the last day Fred and Rose West would appear at Gloucester Magistrates Court together. The committal date was announced that morning as 6 February 1995, at Dursley Magistrates Court.

The Gloucester court building was again packed to capacity and there were many more who wanted to get in but could not – reporters and members of the public. Those who did began queuing before 7.30 a.m. for a hearing that was scheduled to begin at 10 a.m. Soon after Bennett and Moore had taken their usual seats, a grim-faced Rose West appeared, having already made it clear to her guards she did not wish to speak to her husband or for him to touch her – not that they would have allowed it anyway.

A moment later Fred West joined her in the dock and immediately fixed his eyes on his wife's back and shuffled towards her, but before he was within reach Detective

Constable Tina West intervened and gently pushed him to the side. West looked around the courtroom and picked out Janet Leach and Stephen, acknowledging them with a nod and a shallow smile.

West appeared to have lost weight, his face was thinner, his cheekbones more pronounced, and while he looked tidy in his open-necked shirt, Rose looked as if she had put on weight.

The nine joint murder charges were put to them and the other three to Fred, whose eyes rarely left his wife, but while she stubbornly looked to the front, head slightly bowed, there was hardly anyone else there whose eyes were not fixed on them both, reporters in particular noting their every mannerism.

It was another milestone in the investigation and without any objection both were remanded back into custody to await the committal hearing early in the New Year, the next time they were due to appear together. West paused momentarily in a last, vain attempt to catch his wife's attention, but perhaps realising this, her gaze never left the floor.

What she did not know then was that she would never see him again.

When Rose had come into court, Tina West had tried to draw Bennett's attention to a length of wool that was tied in a large bow in the buttonhole of her cardigan. When the two women were out of sight of the court the police officer asked what it meant.

'It's to help me remember something!' was all Rose West would say but it led to speculation that it might have been a sign to her husband that she had not betrayed him and to remind him to stay faithful to her.

While no one knew for sure, it remained a topic for debate, as the couple were known to communicate by sending signals to one another.

THIRTY-TWO

Until now, the families had been told nothing except their daughters had been murdered and buried. They had been spared the detail of dismemberment, tape masks and rope. Soon that would have to change.

Bennett had always promised, either in letters or through the liaison officers, he would tell the relatives when the time was right. With the committal a matter of weeks away, that time was approaching.

Fred West's children Anne Marie, Stephen and Mae, though, posed a particular problem, because as family they were entitled to find out from the police what had happened to Heather and Charmaine, and, just like all the other relatives, would have to be told what was found in the graves. It was known that there had been media contact, and Bennett could not risk that information getting into the newspapers before the committal. If it did it could prejudice any future trial.

His solution was to see the three of them the day before the hearing at Dursley. The others he would get to in early January – and he would do the job himself. He had considered sharing the responsibility with Moore but he didn't want them both to be away from the MIR at the same time and it would ensure everyone was told the same things.

The Siegenthalers were due to visit Gloucester soon; the rest – save one who was living in Germany and whom he would visit later – though scattered around the UK, he would make arrangements to visit at home. Thus they would receive this most distressing news in familiar surroundings and have whoever they wanted there for support.

There were still doubts concerning the strength of the case against Rose West. David Stott of the Droitwich CPS was particularly anxious that if any of the witnesses refused or were unable to give evidence, an already fragile case would collapse. Some detectives saw this as negative; Bennett reasoned he was merely applying the CPS's standard of a better than 50 per cent chance of winning before going ahead.

When the prosecution met for a conference in mid-December, the detectives were able to advance the case for charging Rose and Fred with the murder of Charmaine. It stemmed from a number of letters that Rose had sent to Fred while he was in prison the year the little girl died. One of them read: 'I think Charmaine likes to be handled rough but darling why do I have to be the one to do it?' It went on: 'I would keep her for her own sake if it wasn't for the rest of the children. You can see Char [Charmaine] coming out in Anna [Anne Marie] now and I hate it.'

It at least seemed to support Anne Marie's claims about the way Charmaine was treated by Rose and the physical abuse she suffered, and established 24 June as the day Fred was released. There seemed no way that he could have been home earlier; an early release would have been in the prison records.

As for Fred West's confession, which the CPS was happy to accept, all he seemed to know was the spot where she had been buried. Having seen the thoroughness of the police search at Cromwell Street, he must have known they would find her, and as for his claim she was fully clothed and wrapped in a blanket when she was buried, it was possible he just did not know. Bennett knew it was circumstantial and far from perfect but with the Doc now favouring the time of death around mid-1971 rather than later he was convinced Rose had a case to answer.

Of course, if Rose was charged now it would be jointly with Fred, but if the Doc was able to show Charmaine died when Fred was in prison then the charge against him could be dropped and she would face it alone. It would be one less murder to put to Fred but he would still face the other eleven charges. Apart from his confession, everything now pointed to his wife, but for now they would have to face a joint charge. As for Rena, all Bennett could say was that Rose claimed Charmaine had gone off with her and she either considered Rena dead or to have divorced Fred because she had actually married him.

Opinion was divided. Neil Butterfield with his wry smile looked around the room, as did Bennett, who could see that Stott was by no means convinced. Withiel Cole seemed more in support, and so too Andrew Chubb. After a long conversation, which kept coming back to Fred West's confessions, it was decided that Rose West should be charged with murdering Charmaine but not Rena – even though Bennett made it clear he believed she was somehow involved in that, too.

As Christmas approached Bennett wanted to thank everyone who had helped over the past ten months. A card on behalf of the force and inquiry team with a picture of Gloucester Cathedral seemed the most appropriate way, except that when he worked out how many cards he would need he could not justify the expenditure. Instead, he sketched the city's most famous building in pen and ink himself, used card from the MIR, got Grimshaw to copy it into the computer and print them off and, with the inscription 'From the West Enquiry Team', sent them out at a fraction of the cost. As a mark of goodwill, some even went to the media.

Tina West's suggestion for a 'Christmas do', made way back in March, was also taken up and held on 9 December. Staff who had leave and rest days outstanding were encouraged to take them – the Senior Investigating Officer included.

The team had been scaled down considerably by now and consisted of MIR staff and inquiry officers who were also liaison officers to both families and witnesses. Keeping a check on the welfare of the families and potential trial witnesses was now the most time-consuming and intense aspect of the investigation.

The final briefing before Christmas was on 19 December. There was an end of term atmosphere and Bennett sent them off with more of his Churchillian rhetoric, that '*The Team* was a formidable force that had reached and achieved all its objectives so far . . . they had found all known victims and identified them . . . served committal papers . . . but there was still a long way to go.' At that point the banter began:

'But sir, where exactly are we?'

'What bridges have we crossed?'

'Are we digging in over Christmas?'

Enough was enough. Wishing them the compliments of the season, he knew that for them life had gone on as it did for everyone but they had put the job and the investigation before their families in a way he could not have asked or expected. For some there had been sorrow, disappointment over exams and promotion boards, for others achievement and celebration. There had been deaths, births, illnesses and problems at home that they had shared and dealt with as best they could.

The MIR closed down for Christmas on the afternoon of 23 December and would reopen on 3 January. The Senior Investigating Officer would take a few days off, leaving Moore at the helm.

Bennett had always enjoyed Christmas even if the call of duty meant it was not always celebrated on the day or even the day after. Christmas for a policeman was one of the busiest times of the year and he had spent many of his in hospitals and mortuaries dealing with the fallout from drink and violence. This year he planned to do what he liked best, spend it with his wife and family, though as his mother was in hospital and his mother-in-law suffering with advanced Alzheimer's, Christmas Day would be spent taking meals to Stroud then visiting Gloucester Hospital before settling down in the evening. The true family day would be Boxing Day. On New Year's Eve friends invited him and Ann to a fancy dress party. Normally he liked such occasions but this time said no, for he was still worried that photographs of him letting his hair down would end up in the newspapers and he did not want to spend the evening fending off questions about the investigation that were bound to crop up in conversation. His wife took it on the chin, even though she hated the way the Wests had dominated their lives like no other job before. Instead, they looked forward to the next day, when his sister and her family were coming round for lunch, the first time they had all met up since the inquiry began.

The aim was to gather at 12.30 and to sit down at around 2 p.m. The menu consisted of canapés, starters of smoked salmon and prawns, then stuffed roast leg of pork and vegetables, an assortment of sweets, followed by cheese with plenty of wine and other drinks. The day was entirely down to JB. He had enjoyed cooking since before he was married and was quite adventurous, but today it was a good old English roast. By late morning everything was going to plan. The dining room was ready and the whole family awaited his sister Gill, her husband Richard and their family, who arrived just after midday. The Christmas spirit began to flow. With a glass never far from his hand, and regularly topped up by whoever was nearest the bottle, Bennett had just taken the meat from the oven and was about to call everyone into the dining room when the phone rang.

Ann took it in the hall and instantly called her husband. 'It's the headquarters control room inspector,' she said, handing him the phone and heading off into the kitchen.

Slightly bemused because he was not on call, he answered, 'Hello, what's the problem?'

'Sir, I've had a Prison Governor Polkinghorn from Winson Green on the phone; he wanted your phone number as he wants to speak to you urgently. He's given me a number for you to call him back – he wouldn't say what it was about but said if I couldn't get you, to phone back as soon as possible.'

Bennett thanked the inspector and put the phone down on

the kitchen worktop. He knew why Polkinghorn was calling and it wasn't to wish him a happy New Year or extend Fred West's seasonal compliments either – West was dead.

Collecting his thoughts, and his glass of wine and mobile phone, he headed along the hall to the bedroom. When his wife asked what had happened he told her only that he had a brief call to make. Opening his briefcase, he took out a notepad and the plan of action he had roughed out over a month before in the event of Fred West's death. With pen in one hand, the notepad resting on the bedroom window and the telephone receiver wedged between his head and shoulder, he punched in the number the inspector had given him. The voice that answered did not identify itself and it wasn't one Bennett recognised, but he gave his name and asked for Governor Polkinghorn. Almost immediately the Deputy Governor came on the phone. In a rather contrite tone of voice he said, 'Mr Bennett, I am sorry to tell you West is dead. It appears he has committed suicide. We need to let his relatives know – will you do this for us?'

Numerous questions raced through Bennett's mind and the short silence before he replied must have registered his shock even though he had guessed correctly. Before he could speak the Deputy Governor added, 'He's been certified dead and the police and coroner have been informed and will be investigating.'

In a tone that reflected not only his disappointment at the news but also queried the prison's ability to deal with the situation, Bennett asked when it had happened and whether the cell area had been sealed: 'Wasn't he on suicide watch?'

The Deputy Governor replied that everything was under control. West had not been considered a danger to himself, had appeared fine earlier in the morning and had been out for a walk in the exercise yard. Somehow, though, he had managed to make a rope and, it seemed, had hanged himself.

Bennett's mind was racing. He needed to get off the phone. He had calls to make. It would not be long before the news got out, if it hadn't already. Apart from West's relatives, the victims' families had to be told.

There would never have been a good time to receive this news but on a bank holiday, and New Year's Day at that, getting everything sorted out was going to be difficult. He had to get the MIR opened and into HOLMES to get details of the families but he had been drinking and could not drive. The force control room could not help that much until they had addresses and contact numbers – what a mess it all was.

He called to his wife and as she entered the bedroom he bellowed, 'Fred West's dead. He's killed himself. Don't ask any more, you'll have to take over the dinner. I need your mobile phone and mine, I'll stay in the bedroom.'

Ann Bennett recognised that look and tone. They only surfaced rarely and then in emergencies, but she knew she had to do exactly as he asked – immediately.

Equipped now with three phones – two mobiles and a landline – he was ready to go. He would use the landline to make the calls on his list and give out the other numbers for incoming calls. Taking control, he reasoned, would enable him to get the MIR up and running much quicker than waiting for someone to pick him up and take him there, which would waste more than an hour. Griff lived in Gloucester and could open up the MIR and start notifying West's relatives first, followed by the other families. Moore could go in and take control there. When he told them, neither could believe the news.

As he paused to log everything he was doing, his home phone rang. It was the West Midlands Coroner's Office informing him that an investigation had already begun and that given their interest, someone from Gloucestershire Police ought to be there for the post-mortem that evening. As he went to make another call the home phone rang once more; this time it was the Chief Constable.

Tony Butler had only got as far as 'John . . .' when Bennett realised he was seething. He had never been on the end of one of his tongue-lashings before, though he had heard them from afar. Now he was about to experience one first hand, for not only had the Chief been informed of Fred West's death by the Assistant Chief Constable of West Midlands, he was also told that some of his officers already knew, including Bennett – who had obviously not considered it necessary to inform him.

Bennett cursed his luck. He had been about to phone him and realised he should have had the control room do it while he was getting everything else organised. It was a bad mistake, even though he had not expected him to find out that way, but after all the Chief's support he felt he had let him down. Nor did Bennett's apology and explanation placate his boss, who demanded to know what had been done and what else was planned.

As Bennett outlined the rest of his plan – to call out Hilary Allison, arrange for a car to take them both to the West Midlands, have a press statement prepared based on that evening's post-mortem – the Chief calmed down, though he made it clear he expected to be kept fully informed and would contact Ken Daun and get him to go to the MIR.

Putting the phone down, it occurred to Bennett it was the first time in all his years in the force he had had a dressing down like that, and it would not have happened if the West Midlands Assistant Chief Constable had waited another 5 minutes before making his call. Still, there was no point brooding over it, as his next task was to trace West's solicitor, Tony Miles. Rose West and Leo Goatley were being dealt with through the MIR, as were Anne Marie, Mae and Stephen.

By now the meal with the family was drawing to an end. Bennett went in and apologised before announcing he would soon be on his way to Birmingham. His long-suffering wife raised a glass and muttered, 'What's new?', though his brother-in-law, a builder, plumber and property developer, seemed fascinated by the excitement.

'Fancy being here when all the action was taking place,' he said, adding to Bennett's utter astonishment, 'Isn't it strange

Fred West sometimes used a builders' merchants in Stroud. I've seen him about there and in Cromwell Street – you know I own number 24, which I let.'

It was the first Bennett had heard of this, another unbelievable coincidence on an unforgettable day.

The media were on to the story long before Bennett and Allison arrived in the West Midlands. They had already decided Gloucestershire Police would comment along the lines that 'All deaths are tragic and our condolences go to the West family at this time, who should be allowed some privacy.' As for the death having any effect on Rose West's prosecution, Bennett would say, 'The death is under investigation by the West Midlands Police on behalf of the coroner. People die in police custody as well as prison custody; there is always a detailed investigation into such deaths and if a person intends to take his life then it is very difficult to prevent it.'

Any attempts to draw criticism of the prison would be avoided at all costs, though the initial account of how West met his death was hard to grasp. Somehow, it appeared that he had acquired part of a razor blade, which he had stashed away in his cell along with a needle and thread that he had used to sew a button on his clothes or do some repairs to his laundry. The needle and thread were never returned and no one had asked for them back. The blade he used to cut strips of material from one of his prison blankets, which he rolled up tight and neatly sewed in blanket stitch to give himself two ropes, one long, the other short. These he tied together and attached to the airvent above his door to form a noose and somehow managed to kill himself.

It did not even seem as though he had hanged, as the vent he used was not that far off the ground. He was found slumped behind the door, which was blocked by the weight of his body, forcing the prison officers to push their way in. West was fully clothed and there were a few short letters and his notes for a book he was writing in the cell. Some of the letters were meant for Rose and had been written over a period of time rather than on the day, suggesting he had been thinking of taking his own life for some time. They included one that may have been meant for his wife's birthday on 29 November: 'Well Rose you will be Mrs West all over the world. That's wonderful for me and for you. Keep your promises to me you know what they are I have no present all I have is my life I will give it to you my darling. When you are ready come to me I will be waiting for you.' A gravestone was drawn below inscribed 'In loving memory Fred West Rose West', and printed underneath: 'Rest in peace where no shadow falls. In perfect peace, he waits for Rose his wife.' Another note read: 'Rose and I will love for ever in heaven I will wait for you darling so please come to me.'

Inside the Birmingham City Mortuary, Fred West lay on a trolley in the passageway. He was still clothed in his rough brown prison trousers and blue and white striped shirt. Bennett looked at his face, which was fixed in that sickeningly smug grin that was his trademark. Bennett could imagine him smirking as he made the final preparations, his features fixed as he went into oblivion, his final thoughts along the lines of, 'Well Rose, plan A didn't work so now it's time for plan B!'

According to the post-mortem Fred West died from cerebral anoxia – asphyxiation. The hangman's noose he had placed around his neck and the weight of his body, possibly leaning rather than hanging, had squeezed his neck and cut off the supply of blood and oxygen to his brain. He was almost certainly dead within a couple of minutes. The doctor also revealed that had he lived he might have been crippled in later life as a result of the arteries in his legs closing.

On the way home the same thoughts kept recurring: what did this mean to the investigation, to Rose West and her trial now? Bennett's wife was asking the same questions and he could only reply that he was not really sure. It was never thought Fred would give evidence against Rose, even though it seemed he might have been suggesting in his last interviews she was involved, so his death changed very little. Ann Bennett was not convinced and believed that Rose West would now get off.

But Bennett did not want any more discussion that night, though he accepted her view might be shared by others who relied on reports in the media – especially those who for some reason protested Rose West's innocence.

THIRTY-THREE

If Fred West thought committing suicide would take the heat off his wife, it also shifted the focus away from the investigation and onto the prison service. Already the media was baying for blood and they were not the only ones.

The Home Secretary, Michael Howard, called for an inquiry and did not appear satisfied when told there was one under way. The Chief Inspector of Prisons, Judge Stephen Tumin, was quoted as saying West should have been under 24-hour surveillance and the Prison Governors Association chipped in too, along with psychologists, psychiatrists, fellow prisoners, and solicitors. Everyone, it seemed, from Gloucester to Glasgow, was being asked his or her opinion.

One newspaper reported that West was responsible for as many as sixty murders, conveniently ignoring the fact that before his death he and his widow were jointly charged and that now she would face the same charges alone. Others quoted relatives who claimed he had admitted killing Heather; in one article Stephen suggested his dad had 'killed them all'. Leo Goatley got in on the act, arguing that the case against his client, always flimsy, was even flimsier now than ever. The former Deputy Chief Constable of Greater Manchester turned TV pundit, John Stalker, used his television programme to examine how West's death would affect the legal process and questioned whether, in light of all the coverage, Rose West would get a fair trial. Lord Denning, the former Master of the Rolls, was widely quoted and also appeared on television to argue that all charges against her should now be withdrawn.

Bennett could not believe such an eminent lawyer was advancing such a view without being aware of the evidence, though it occurred to him that after months of coverage that was hostile to the Wests all of this was in part redressing the balance in favour of Rose. The real frustration for the police was that West had gone leaving so many questions unanswered, for his death made little difference to their case against his wife. The Director of Prosecutions Barbara Mills called for an urgent meeting with Butterfield to be personally reassured of this and although he needed little support, Chubb, Cole and Bennett attended for good measure.

Fred West had a low opinion of the police, or rather, he had a higher opinion of himself. Concealing his crimes for so long gave him an inflated feeling of invincibility and convinced him he was much cleverer than them. On D landing, he must have seemed the model prisoner, mostly keeping his own company, enjoying a game of pool, quietly relishing his notoriety. The other inmates could not work out this short, stocky, barely literate man who did as he was told and was not at all their idea of a mass murderer. That of course was his skill, for he had spent his life understanding how to merge into his surroundings, how to become transparent, a figure of fun – especially when there was something in it for him. As far as he was concerned, it had enabled him to outsmart Gloucester Police, for it was his family who had brought him down, not they.

West's last months in prison were spent writing a book he planned to dedicate not to Rose but to his 'Angel', Ann McFall. This seemed to be apparent from throwaway lines to prison officers, odd comments to his lawyers, prison psychologists, probation officers, tales they would mention later, but beneath it all his devious mind was at work. Whatever Rose had done – and he had now learned things he had not known before – she was still his, as were the kids. He had always protected Rose but maybe he had said too much. Perhaps it was her he was referring to just before he was sent to Winson Green.

In his last interviews he seemed to be hinting he would plead not guilty to all the murders and blame someone else or even a number of people. He never mentioned his wife, but did not say it was not her either, as he had insisted previously. Perhaps the thought of sitting in the same courtroom betraying Rose was just too much for him. If he killed himself then all the charges against her would be dropped. Rose would know he had done it for her, it would be in his notes, and she would understand about the book.

His death, though, cleared the way for the police to ask Janet Leach about what West had said to her when the tape recorder was not switched on, during their meetings and phone calls, though to Bennett's surprise, she first sought advice from a lawyer.

At least there was some good news for in among the saturation coverage of Fred West's suicide, it was also reported that Hazel Savage had been made an MBE in the New Year's honours list.

Fred West's extended family were also considered victims of the investigation and had been harassed daily by the media. Their liaison officer, Detective Constable Stephen McCormick, had kept them as up to date as he could, but it was clear that they too found it difficult to accept that West was as evil as he was being portrayed by the press, though it was not possible then to tell them otherwise.

Arrangements were now well in hand for Bennett to visit the victims' relatives, 'JB's Grand Tour' as it was often referred to in the MIR, though no one doubted its importance or the daunting nature of the Senior Investigating Officer's job. The plan was for Bennett and Detective Constable Russell Williams, one of the liaison and inquiry officers, to call on each family in turn. Gloucester Victim Support would also organise for a local volunteer to precede the officers and stay for as long as the family wanted after the two policemen had left. If they were in another police force area, a local officer would also be there if requested. With the exception of the West family, who were being left as late as possible, arrangements were made for those living in the Gloucester area to be seen towards the end of the first and second week in January, with the others fitted in between. The 'tour' would take them to the Midlands and North of England, Central Scotland, North and South Wales.

Deciding *what* to tell them was not a problem, the real difficulty lay in *how*. First he would go through when the victim was last seen and the circumstances of her disappearance. Then he would tell them what West had said and anything that involved or was known about Rose. Finally, he would go into what was found and then answer any questions. It would be the same for all the families; Williams was there for support and to make sure he got it right. Bennett had never been one to wish his life away but after the first visit he wished it was the last and that it was all over. Instead, the two detectives talked it over and decided the format was the best they could come up with and they would stick with it.

Bennett had intended taking the Sunday off before the tour proper began on Monday but an early call from Dave Griffiths put paid to that. From the tone he knew it was more bad news. Griff was going through the newspapers when he came across an article in the *Sunday Express* alleging that Hazel Savage was trying to sell her story for up to £1,000,000. According to the report, a go-between had approached Chelsea literary agent Gloria Ferris and although the details of the conversation were secret, Ms Ferris had apparently confirmed 'She [Savage] is our client' and the manuscript could be worth a considerable amount. It even appeared that a reporter had spoken to Hazel Savage. Bennett was devastated.

He had dismissed earlier rumblings against her as malicious rumour; now there was mention of a book, an agent and quotations that seemed to give it substance. There would never have been a good time for such an exposé but the day before he was to set off to see the families was one of the worst possible. As far as he was concerned, her continued involvement in the investigation was untenable but this was not the right time for an inquiry. He made sure Terry Moore knew, as she was an officer from his division. If the report were in any way true it would be a huge embarrassment, for not only had she just received the MBE, a rare honour in itself, but many stories credited her with unmasking the Wests in the first place. It was a real can of worms that could undermine the inquiry and damage the relationship they had worked so hard to forge with the victims' relatives.

Any hopes Bennett had that Savage might refute the claims ended the following day when she accepted the story was basically true, though at the same time making it clear she had neither entered into an agreement nor divulged any information. As a result she was transferred to other duties and an internal investigation began. The rest of the team still clung to the hope the *Sunday Express* story was a fabrication, another hyped-up account based on speculation. When Savage apologised for any distress she may have caused them, while at the same time expressing her bitterness at being removed from the inquiry, many regarded her as a media martyr. Bennett was then far from that view. The team had suffered an unnecessary, self-inflicted 'casualty', one never expected. He did not know there would be others who would fall in the months to come, and while some would not bring the investigation more problems, one would.

In due course, the investigation conducted by Wiltshire Constabulary confirmed that quite early in the inquiry, Savage and her solicitor had met an agent on two occasions for preliminary talks, but cleared her of passing on confidential information. When she appeared before a disciplinary hearing for falsehood and prevarication and discreditable conduct and pleaded not guilty, the allegation of falsehood was thrown out but she was found guilty of discreditable conduct. Chief Constable Tony Butler described this as 'an error of judgement', one that while not intending to bring discredit on the force had shown a 'degree of naivety' that warranted an official reprimand. Savage maintained she had done nothing wrong and Bennett could not believe it when she appealed, though without success. To him it was a sad blemish on an otherwise outstanding career. Even so, it did not alter the fact that at an early stage of a high-profile, highly complex investigation she had taken the first tentative steps towards writing a book about it. At the very least it would have come to light and caused them embarrassment at trial.

'JB's Grand Tour' was undertaken and completed on schedule. Bennett and Williams were received with a warmth that was humbling. The families knew why they were there and what was in store and no matter how awkward the detectives felt, it could not compare with the anguish experienced by their hosts. Only once were they asked to leave, but by the time Bennett was back in his office there were messages of appreciation from that family, and others he had seen, waiting on his desk. It had been a physically tiring and emotionally draining journey but Bennett knew only too well it would take the families many more months, possibly years, to come to terms with what they had heard and would hear at the trial.

Whatever the doubts expressed in the media or by other commentators at the credibility of the case against Rose West, the prosecution was unperturbed. The lawyers agreed she should still be charged with the murder of Charmaine along with the nine other charges of murder she already faced. As Neil Butterfield explained, 'If it was wrong to charge Mrs West with the murders it was always wrong, it never relied upon evidence provided by her husband. There has been no loss of evidence against her by his death.' Rose West was formally charged, at Pucklechurch Remand Centre near Bristol on Friday 13 January, with the murder of her stepdaughter between 1 May and 31 December 1971 and made her standard reply, 'I'm innocent'. Her solicitor reckoned the prosecution was in disarray and was pulling charges out of the air.

Reporters were told at a news conference, when Bennett also

confirmed the date when committal proceedings would begin as 6 February. Even some of the journalists thought this a gamble and that there was now little chance of her standing trial at all. What they did not know was that the decision to charge Rose with Charmaine's death had been made before her husband committed suicide. This all meant yet another delay in the release of the little girl's remains for burial, for whereas she had previously been of little concern to Rose West's defence, her bones now had to be re-examined as a matter of urgency.

Those funerals that could go ahead were to be largely private affairs, with discreet police support, through Bennett, Moore and the liaison officers, where families requested it. They were moving occasions and to show their appreciation most families included praise and prayers for the work of the police. Even reporters who got to know of some of the ceremonies respected the families' desire for privacy – with the exception of the funeral of Fred West, whose remains had not yet been released. The police had been told their services would not be required and Bennett hoped it would stay that way, but it was already an emotive issue. According to some reports, West's remains would not be welcome at Much Marcle and Bennett doubted if they would be anywhere else.

As the committal date approached, no one knew how many prosecution witnesses would be required to appear. Although the hearing was not a trial, examining a sample of the evidence was all part of establishing whether Rose West would be sent to the Crown Court. Among the most likely to be called were Caroline Owens, Anne Marie and the witness who, for legal reasons and to protect her identity in the light of her evidence and what she alleged, would become known only as Miss A. Bennett was assured that Caroline Owens would not waver but there were concerns over the other two as their evidence was even more sexually explicit and covered a much longer period, in Anne Marie's case, years. According to their liaison officers both women were anxious at the thought of what lay ahead, though both were determined to see it through. To add to their trauma, they would have to be on permanent standby from the time the committal started to the moment it ended, for they could be called at any time and only the defence knew if and when that was likely to be.

Fred Davies and social services were also to have staffing problems. A temporary social worker who tried to sell details of where the West children were in care to the local newspaper failed to convince his employers it was a 'red nose day prank' and was sacked.

Quite apart from its legal importance, the committal was seen as a useful dress rehearsal for any subsequent trial, which now looked most likely to be held at Winchester. Getting everyone there who needed to be, keeping out those who did not, making the building secure, keeping the media satisfied – the whole operation was mapped out with military precision.

No court in the country would have been able to house everyone who wanted to be there, let alone a small country courthouse. The Lord Chancellor's office representative Mike Wickstead had worked with the Gloucester magistrates' clerks' office and the police, so extra seating and an audio system to relay the proceedings were installed in what was normally the witnesses' waiting room. Reporters would not be allowed to use typewriters, computers or recorders but a strict rotation system was introduced so they all had some time in the courtroom. Both sets of lawyers and the presiding magistrate each had their own private rooms, the police had a control room and conference room, and there were separate areas for witnesses and the victims' families. Access to the building was through the main entrance, via a small, tented porch where everyone was scanned, airport-style. A 4-ft-high ring of linked steel crowd-control barriers was thrown around the perimeter of the police station and court.

The side entrance to the police station where Rosemary West would come and go each day would be covered so that no one could photograph her. At pre-arranged rendezvous points her prison van would be handed over by motorcycle outriders from Avon and Somerset Police to a pair from Gloucestershire who would escort her in. The journey from Pucklechurch Remand Centre would take less than 30 minutes. MIR staff would be responsible for her security during the proceedings each day and there were separate plans in case of fire or any other disruption.

An area was marked off for satellite vehicles and all other parking was located outside an exclusion zone marked by 'police no waiting' cones. Some enterprising schools made space available in exchange for a contribution to their funds.

The operation began 24 hours ahead of the actual committal when the whole area, including buildings, was thoroughly searched. The same procedure would take place every day, when the search team would include a dog specially trained to sniff out explosives.

If a witness were called they would be collected by a liaison officer and a member of Victim Support who would stay with them until after they had given evidence and at no time leave them alone with the police. This would avoid any suspicion they had been told what to say.

Bennett ensured that Anne Marie, Stephen and Mae West were brought up to date that Sunday morning with what he had told all the other victims' families, when it was too late for anything more to get into the media. Journalists were about to hear much of it themselves anyway, but would be restricted from reporting it by the rules of court.

By the first morning everything was in place but as Bennett, Moore and selected MIR staff climbed into the minibus that would take them to and from the courthouse, its windows blacked out for extra security, their adrenalin-fuelled confidence was beginning to waver, for ahead of them lay the first public examination of the investigation. The evidence, how much of it would be admissible in the higher court, whether Rose could expect a fair trial, the openness and integrity of the inquiry, would all be scrutinised as never before over the next few days. And it would not just be the criticism of a speculative, ill-informed media but careful dissection by lawyers.

Bennett had no doubts over the legal expertise of Withy Cole or the prowess of Neil Butterfield and Andrew Chubb, but they were only as good as the evidence the team had provided and any cracks or flaws would surely surface now.

As the minibus neared Dursley, Tina West leaned forward to Bennett who was in the front and asked: 'Dad, are we there yet?' And as laughter broke the tension: 'Can I have an ice cream when we arrive?'

On entering the restricted area more than 100 reporters from all over the UK, mainland Europe, the United States, Canada, the Far East and India were lined up to record the event. Every room in every hotel and guesthouse for miles around had been booked for weeks. For perhaps the first time in its history, Dursley was at the centre of a world news event and people going about their daily lives and children on their way to school paused to witness the arrival of the woman at the heart of it all. Some booed and hissed, most were just bemused.

The courtroom itself had few distinguishing features and was similar in size to most other courts servicing a small, mainly rural area. The Stipendiary Magistrate Peter Badge sat at the bench directly above the clerk, with counsel and solicitors facing him in rows in front. The dock where Rose West was held was to his left; the witness box to his right. A copy of the master chart from the MIR was on a stand for both sets of lawyers to use as required.

Reporting restrictions were not lifted and the magistrate reminded reporters of the perils of ignoring this instruction.

When Rose West arrived in the dock with Tina West at her

side it was evident beneath her long white blouse and navy cardigan she had put on weight. She listened impassively as the charges against her were read out, and then took her seat.

The defence's opening gambit was to apply for a stay of proceedings. Sasha Wass argued that Rosemary West was the subject of an abuse of process that meant she should never have been charged at all because she would never have a fair trial. Her argument was based on the media publicity surrounding the case, the length of time between the offences being committed and her client arrested and, because of the delay, the potential loss of witnesses, their memory and evidence, all of which may have helped her client.

To the members of the investigating team listening in court it all sounded reasonable, except that it was not the fault of the police Rosemary West had not been charged earlier; that was more to do with the methods she and her husband had perfected over more than twenty years to escape detection. Neil Butterfield's response demonstrated why he had been their first choice as prosecutor. In the respectful, measured, though devastating tone that lawyers use, he set about dismantling her argument. Her submission, he said, had no real substance, the prosecution had not contributed in any way to the delay, there was no substantial prejudice caused to the defendant who 'by her own conduct had contributed to the delay', and as for prejudicial publicity, that was not a matter for the examining magistrate anyway.

At the end of the first day, nothing unexpected had emerged and Peter Badge decided to sleep on his decision. Rose West lumbered slowly out of the dock and was soon on her way back to Pucklechurch.

No one expected a mere legal submission would be enough to get the case thrown out at this stage and the following morning the magistrate ruled that was how he saw it too, and there was more good news when the defence indicated they would not need any witnesses to give evidence in person. Caroline Owens, Anne Marie and Miss A could all be stood down.

After Peter Badge's opening the atmosphere rose from expectant to electric. Throughout the building, whether in court or the ante-room, this was what reporters had been waiting for, an outline of the evidence that formed the basis of the case. It was bound to be sensational and if Rose was let off the story could be told now; if she went to trial it would give them a solid grounding.

Again, Butterfield did not disappoint. Outlining why the police had gone to 25 Cromwell Street – now almost a year ago – and describing how, after two days of digging, they had recovered the remains of Heather West, he painted a truly chilling picture.

'Twenty-five Cromwell Street', he said, 'had more than one dark secret to yield to the searching police teams. Over the following days the remains of eight other young women were recovered, making nine in all. One of these victims was carrying a foetus of six to eight months' gestation. Cromwell Street had become a charnel house, a graveyard in which, say the Crown, over a period of something like fourteen years young girls were sexually abused in depraved and appalling circumstances.'

So began a spellbinding tour de force that took everyone there on a journey into the dark, sadistic world of Fred and Rose West, where young girls were used as sexual playthings then discarded, dismembered and dumped in holes to prevent them reporting what had happened to them. Butterfield described in detail how each of the victims had been lured to Cromwell Street, how they were found and what was found with them. How the Wests controlled and abused their children and others, and how the couple's voracious and deviant sexual appetite had brought them together and then led them along a path to murder.

Rose West sat unflinchingly through it all and, even though her features were partially obscured by the large plastic frames of her glasses, Bennett was in no doubt as to her complete indifference. He wondered, too, what the media made of it all and, more importantly, the impact on key witnesses like

Caroline Owens, Anne Marie and Miss A who, though not needed at this hearing, would have to divulge their darkest, most intimate secrets at trial in public. Caroline and Anne Marie were already tied to newspapers and losing their testimony because of it would seriously weaken the prosecution. Their integrity had to be protected at all costs.

That evening Bennett returned to the MIR. He had to keep up with his reading and respond to the continual flow of letters. Mark Grimshaw and Nick Churchill were also there at work. As he entered the room, a worried-looking Grimshaw called him over and pointed to his computer screen, 'Boss, I think you need to see this.'

The analyst had been marking up press reports he thought might be of use at trial and had logged on to the internet, then in its infancy. Bennett's eyes scanned the screen and saw a Reuters news agency report on Compuserve that anyone with a personal computer and a modem could subscribe to for £5 a month. To his horror, there in full was Neil Butterfield's opening speech to the committal – practically word for word: 'Twenty-five Cromwell Street . . . charnel house . . . graveyard . . . young girls sexually abused in depraved and appalling circumstances.'

Mark Grimshaw scrolled on and on but by the time Bennett reached the description of the mask around Shirley Hubbard's skull – 'she was kept living but restrained so that her body could be used at will. How long she survived, how her body was abused, how exactly she died, the prosecution cannot say' – he had read enough. If Grimshaw could access the report in Gloucester, so could every other computer user – perhaps more than 200,000 in the UK and 2,000,000 worldwide. The CPS, the Attorney-General, and the Stipendiary Magistrate would all have to be told, along with the defence, who would have a field day.

Bennett had to get it off the internet. It was going to be another long night.

That, though, was only part of the problem for it was now past seven in the evening and getting hold of the people he needed would be difficult. A call to Withy Cole started the chain and after that David Stott, followed by attempts to contact the Attorney-General, Sir Nicholas Lyell's representative, Sir Michael Havers' office, Neil Butterfield and Peter Badge.

Sir Michael was on holiday in the South of France where a call from the Senior Investigating Officer on the West Inquiry was among the last he expected. Both Sir Michael and Stott then considered nothing more could be done until morning.

Bennett's next target was the internet. Perhaps motivated by the fear of a huge contempt action, Reuters' evening manager took the detective's call and promised to get straight on to the news editor who in turn promised to alert Compuserve in New York. Within half an hour Compuserve's New York man was trying to reassure the MIR they were trying to get it off the net – but were having difficulty.

The telephones lines were smouldering and when Bennett checked the website at just after 11 p.m. the material was still there, though Reuters were confident it would be off by the morning. That just left him and the other two detectives with the task of filing a report on what had happened. As Grimshaw prepared the file cover and index on the computer, Bennett dictated and Churchill typed. By 3 a.m. it was done – with the ending left open until the morning.

Returning after just a few hours' sleep, Grimshaw checked the website to find Reuters had been true to their word and the report had been wiped. The file was updated and Grimshaw enlisted to give a brief demonstration of what had happened to the magistrate and lawyers.

Once again, their vigilance and equally swift response had saved the investigation from potential disaster, for this was something that could never have been foreseen.

After its unscheduled delay, the proceedings resumed, though Rose West seemed no more interested than before as she sat, head bowed as ever, doodling on a notepad. Now that Caroline Owens, Anne Marie and Miss A were not required to appear, their statements were read out. By now Neil Butterfield had deferred to his junior Andrew Chubb, who like a preacher reading from a Bible over half-framed glasses, recounted what they and others had been through. His clear, refined English seemed to coat the words with a forensic respectability, though sanitising the crude, vicious attacks now disclosed for the first time was impossible.

Again, Bennett's eyes fixed on Rose West and when Heather's name was mentioned he watched as she raised a hand to wipe under her glasses then fumble with them as if to make sure this rare show of emotion did not go unnoticed. Bennett was not fooled. He was close enough to see there were no tears. Perhaps she thought it right to cry, after all this was her first child they were talking about, the child whose disappearance she had spent eight years covering up in an attempt to avoid precisely what was happening now.

That afternoon, Bennett took Griff's advice and instead of returning to the court listened to the proceedings in the media ante-room. It looked more like an exam room for reporters, their heads motionless over their notebooks, pens and pencils moving swiftly across the pages as their shorthand struggled to keep up.

Andrew Chubb's voice filled the room as if he were there, but there were no smiles, no asides, just the occasional head shaking and expression of astonishment. One female foreign reporter who spoke perfect English and had followed the investigation from the very beginning sat with tears running down her face. She wiped her eyes and face regularly but the tears would not stop. Unlike Rose West's, Bennett thought her sadness sincere. In the end she could listen no more, stood up, collected her things and hurried out, never to return.

Unusually, she was not the only one whose emotions showed through; even hardened tabloid reporters displayed signs of welling up as the details they had sought for so long percolated through. Griff had been right. It was a sight and experience Bennett would not have wanted to miss, though he had little sympathy.

After the previous night's internet scare, the close of proceedings that evening brought a fresh problem as newspapers printed in English and normally available abroad contained full reports of committal proceedings and could be bought from newsagents in some parts of the UK. So far, the most graphic and detailed accounts were in newspapers from the Irish Republic.

Again, the problem had come to light outside office hours. Tired and exasperated, Bennett did not relish another night of phone bashing, so while the CPS chased up the Attorney-General's office, he got on to the six main newspaper distributors, who all agreed to either remove the report from newspapers on sale at home or withdraw the papers altogether, depending on the amount of coverage.

In the days that followed, recordings of some of Rose West's interviews were played and for the first time the media experienced her harsh, soulless voice, her poor use of English and foul-mouthed tirades. Her lack of feelings for either Charmaine or Heather and her blatant hostility towards Anne Marie were obvious. None of this was apparent in court, where she sat silently listening to the evidence. Her self-restraint only disappeared during breaks for lunch and at the end of the day when left alone by her guards – the muffled sound of her anger and rage could be heard through the cell walls.

When the prosecution had finished it was the turn of the defence and Sasha Wass systematically went through every piece of evidence that had been put forward. She may have lacked the gravitas and panache of Neil Butterfield but it was nevertheless a well-structured, detailed and plausible response. Bennett, Moore, Griffiths and Withy Cole hung on her every word, making notes, for, probably unintentionally, she was giving away what the defence case would be – if Rose was committed.

The loss of memory, the media intrusion, payment of witnesses, destruction and non-availability of papers and evidence, the possibility that the murders were committed elsewhere and the remains merely buried at Midland Road and Cromwell Street were all covered. Each of the victims and what Rose West knew or did not know about them, how they had been dismembered – unlikely to have been done by a woman – and the missing bones were all explored, as was Fred West's habit of picking up women alone.

Rose West, she said, was not involved in and knew nothing of the murders; in essence, the Crown's case was based upon surmise, speculation and no evidence.

The court adjourned on the afternoon of Monday 13 February with the Stipendiary Magistrate saying he would consider the matter overnight and give his judgment the next day.

The following morning, dressed in a long, beige cardigan over a white open-necked blouse, her blank expression as ever concealed by the glasses that seemed to get bigger with every appearance in court, Rose West stood before Peter Badge for the last time and listened dispassionately as he committed her for trial on the ten charges of murder put to her. Two further counts of rape and two of indecent assault were added, though the previous rape charges against her and two other Gloucester men were withdrawn.

Another hurdle and attendant complications facing the investigation had been overcome and as the court cleared, leaving Bennett and Butterfield alone, the QC produced a packet of cigars and offered him one. Both knew that much of the similar fact evidence could still be thrown out at trial and there was no room for complacency, but at least they could enjoy another battle won – if not yet the war.

After thanking all the ancillary staff Bennett went to the police station for a mug of coffee and a slice of celebratory cake. Something a bit stronger was planned for later that night.

Outside, Leo Goatley faced the media, his face somewhat contorted as he searched for the words to convey his client's innocence. 'She strenuously denies all the charges that have been put against her and we will be defending this matter when it comes to trial. We have not disclosed our defence but we will certainly be putting forward a very strong defence,' he said, adding that he would be seeking a judicial review, as she could not receive a fair trial.

Despite his words, the prosecution team were elated that his client's defence had been revealed to them in a way that would have been impossible had they settled for the more usual form of committal.

When Bennett arrived back at the MIR he went straight to his office and there on his desk was an envelope containing a card with a picture of roses and the word 'Congratulations' on it. Inside it said, 'To John and Terry – So far so good'.

It was from Fred Davies and his staff at Gloucestershire Social Services.

THIRTY-FOUR

The committal success did not mean they were home and dry, nor did it lead to a reduction in the workload – quite the opposite.

What they had learned of the likely defence strategy had given the inquiry a new focus, though Bennett now had fewer officers at his disposal and many of them were due a holiday. Quite apart from preparing for a trial that would be held 100 miles away, more and more women were coming forward claiming to have had contact with Fred West, particularly in the late 1960s and early 1970s. The problem for the police was distinguishing which claims were true, exaggerated or completely made up. They already knew 25 Cromwell Street had been a draw for runaways and residents of Gloucester's care homes and one of them, Sharon Compton, traced early in the investigation, looked as if she could be an important witness. She claimed to have been a friend of Alison Chambers but could not be sure if she had ever been to the Wests' home. When the police took her to Cromwell Street she picked out No. 25 as the house she had visited but made no mention of being abused there – though she did remember it later. Because this gradual recall is regarded as relatively common among victims of sexual abuse she was only ever seen and interviewed by the most experienced officers in this field.

As the months of 1994 passed, this potential star witness began remembering more and more of what had happened to her at the hands of the Wests. Everything she said was fastidiously recorded as her recollections became more vivid and horrific. Among the descriptions that emerged, either as an accessory to the abuse or even a participant, was that of a person she first described as someone smart who wore a raincoat

– 'raincoat man'. Her description gradually became more detailed until it was suggested he was a policeman and after that she was able to recall his uniform number. Initially some of this seemed quite plausible to Bennett as the police had often been to the house during that time. Against that, her descriptions of the inside were often variable and other leads like a farm where she claimed murder had been committed, when checked out, were unreliable. She also changed her story often and refused to sign her statements.

It became a question not so much of whether what she said was true but how much? Despite Bennett's misgivings, Sharon Compton was still seen as an important witness even though he regarded her as just the sort of witness he and the CPS were worried might not have the stomach for court.

During the committal, Sasha Wass had dwelled on suggestions that the Cromwell Street victims may have been murdered elsewhere and simply buried there. That's what Fred West had claimed and it was a possible explanation for the missing bones. Professor Knight was put on notice to consider this theory in more detail. Recollecting the blue deposits found in the dig at Cromwell Street, Bennett recalled that these had been scientifically examined and found to be vivianite, a mineral not normally found in the area, but that as it had also later been found in other places nearby it would be of no use to the defence to advance an argument that the victims had first been buried elsewhere.

As for Wass's contention the media coverage was preventing Rose West from getting a fair trial, Bennett was now probably as relaxed about that as he had ever been, for it was obvious the defence would try to exploit it. The prosecution just had to be sure they could counter their arguments.

What he was not expecting was the call on the afternoon of 1 March from Withy Cole to tell him that Neil Butterfield had been appointed a High Court Judge with immediate effect and would not be prosecuting the case. Everyone knew Butterfield's appointment was coming, they just did not expect it before the trial. His removal meant a huge hole to fill and left everyone on the team deflated, for now they had to find someone to replace him and who could tell what extra pressures and work that would bring? Cole's response was swift and the name he came up with was that of Brian Leveson, a QC on the Northern Circuit who had been involved in a number of high-profile cases himself, notably when prosecuting the long, complex Strangeways Prison Riots trial, which he won, and the Ken Dodd tax evasion trial, which he lost. All the CPS had to do was persuade him to take the brief. Bennett made a call to a fellow SIO who had worked with the QC and learned that he was a highly respected and sought-after leader, renowned for his ability to assimilate large amounts of material, his attention to detail, and pride in his representation whatever the case, civil or criminal, and for whatever side. Hearing this removed some anxiety and Bennett and Moore just hoped he would take the case on.

The Bennetts spent his fiftieth birthday in Vienna with their closest friends, whom they had seen little of in the months before. In the course of the weekend they dropped the bombshell that Caroline Owens was their niece. They had not mentioned it earlier as they did not think it right to do so. It was simply another in the series of extraordinary coincidences. Bennett returned to work in the hope that this time the team would ignore his birthday. Instead, as he climbed the stairs to his office, he was confronted by a banner and bunting proclaiming '50 years today'. Among the cards was one made by the team with a rose on the cover and the inscription '25 + 25 = 50' – an alternative take on the Wests' house numbers!

It also ushered in another period where emotions were tugged first this way then that, for by the end of the month Bennett's mother-in-law lost her prolonged battle with Alzheimer's and died. She had always been particularly fond of her 'Benny', and he her, so the preparations for his son

Andrew's wedding a few weeks later only dulled the pain. But his mother, who had been in hospital for six months, came home at last. Terry Moore also had to contend with the deteriorating health of both his in-laws, further evidence that life did not stop for the Wests.

Janet Leach now had a solicitor but was still holding back on what Fred West had told her and was certainly not prepared to put any of it down in writing. Bennett could not understand it. Was it because of the confidentiality agreement she had signed preventing her from talking to the media? If so, he was not about to get it lifted. Or was she acting out of some misguided loyalty to West? Whatever the reason, he was not prepared to wait much longer.

Pondering over photographs of the ropes and bindings unearthed with the victims' remains and comparing them with the ligature Fred West made in prison, Bennett remembered another senior investigating officer talking about an expert in knots. Since the use of restraints was relevant to much of the similar fact evidence they had amassed, he decided his opinion could be worthwhile – instead it took them up another blind alley. With two senior officers present, the so-called expert examined the exhibits and reckoned they could provide some significant evidence – and when Bennett received his report even he had to admit the conclusions were appealing.

How the knots were made was described in detail and compared with one another. According to the expert, they seemed to have been tied in a similar fashion but, more importantly, the later ones appeared to have been tied by two people. When Bennett shared this apparent breakthrough with the rest of the team they were ecstatic. To them it was another piece in the jigsaw that proved Fred and Rose were in it together from beginning to end. The Senior Investigating Officer, however, thought it just too good to be true. The evidence that could be gleaned from a crime scene never ceased to amaze him, but how could a few knots produce such clear and specific information? It did not help, either, when he delved into the man's qualifications and found his background was not in forensic science.

He needed a second opinion and went to Roger Ide, without mentioning his other 'expert'. When Ide's report came back, there could hardly have been a bigger contrast. According to him, the only similarity was between the knotted sheets in Fred West's cell and one other knot found with the remains and there was nothing to indicate the numbers involved or their sex. When Bennett showed him the original report, not only was he astounded at the claims it made without forensic or scientific support, but also some of the knots were wrongly described. Bennett's solution was to bring the two men together to see if they could reconcile their differences. Within no time the first 'expert' had backed down considerably and made a statement to that effect. There was no chance of the prosecution using any of it but the defence was told what had happened anyway.

It was now official. The trial of Rosemary West would take place at Winchester Crown Court before senior presiding judge Sir Charles Mantell, the Honourable Mr Justice Mantell, with a provisional start date fixed for 3 October 1995. These, the barest details, were fixed at a pre-trial review at Bristol Crown Court. Filling in the gaps for what was already being hyped as 'the trial of the century' would take a little longer and would involve the Lord Chancellor's Department, the court clerk, the CPS, the Winchester Witness Support Scheme, Hampshire and Gloucestershire Constabularies but most of all the West Inquiry team itself, who as well as doing its own work would oversee everything else.

Among the most difficult and sensitive problems they faced was ensuring the privacy and security of the witnesses and any victims' family members who might want to attend. Finding somewhere to live for members of the inquiry team who would be there for the duration of the trial or those who attended from time to time, was another priority.

Inside the court they would need rooms for counsel, the CPS and police who would be working for them. They would need a place for exhibits and somewhere else to access the HOLMES computer. They would need extra telephone lines, a fax, a copier and extra shelves to take the piles of files that would be brought up from Gloucester, and there would have to be another room with an audio link to accommodate all the journalists who would not be able to get into the courtroom – just like at Dursley.

It was estimated the trial would last six to eight weeks. Booking the team into a guesthouse was ruled out because of the risk to security; bedding them down in the local army barracks was also rejected for fear of disrupting the military's security. With just about every spare room within the town and its surrounding area snapped up by the media weeks before, they were in danger of being squeezed out. Instead, they found the answer at Hampshire Police headquarters at Netley, about 20 miles out of town. There, in the grounds of a former Royal Naval Psychiatric and Mental Hospital, were a number of barrack-style blocks that, although barely habitable, were deemed ideal by the Senior Investigating Officer. The one they would occupy had just two toilets and one shower for ten bedrooms, a small, ill-equipped kitchen, no lounge or anywhere to relax and a restaurant that would be closed when they left in the morning and shut by the time they returned in the evening.

Spartan it may have been but Bennett did not think twice about taking it, after all they were not there for a holiday and the hardships they would encounter would strengthen their fellowship and unity of purpose – if that were possible. They could bring a few home comforts to help make it a little more habitable and there were plenty of places around where they could eat. Netley would only be a base after all, somewhere they could get their heads down when the opportunity arose.

Brian Leveson had accepted the brief, but his first meeting with the Senior Investigating Officer did not go well. He had arranged to visit the MIR, to meet everyone and get up to speed with the investigation, and Bennett and Moore decided that to break the ice they would drop in on him at his hotel the night before. Andrew Chubb was already there and took the two detectives to the barrister's room, where they met for the first time a small, serious-looking, rather short man who was bald on top and wore round, dark-framed glasses.

There was not much space in his room but Leveson covered every bit between the window and his bed, walking this way and that, backwards and forwards, sometimes pointing, occasionally stroking his chin, but always on the move. He was, he confessed, a pacer. It helped him think and concentrate, and he did not mince his words. Why had he not received the background papers the CPS had promised him? He needed to review everything that had been done and had not had the chance to make a start. If there was more work to be done, and that was a real possibility, there would be little time to put this in hand, let alone get to grips with it all. His review would start the following day.

Bennett was taken aback and it was as much as he could do to bite his tongue. For a start he knew the papers to which the QC was referring had been prepared long ago and sent to the CPS. While he understood he had not worked with any of the members of the team before and accepted the need to review the case, he doubted whether there was much more to be done, as their work had been good enough for Neil Butterfield and little had changed since the committal and his elevation. While accepting that all barristers, especially QCs, had their individual preferences for how they dealt with a brief, through gritted teeth Bennett suggested he first undertake the review he intended and if more work was necessary it would be immediately actioned.

The impromptu meeting ended with the two detectives wondering what they were in for. Perhaps they had misunderstood what the QC had said and were too sensitive and proud of what the team had done so far, though both knew from experience how prosecuting counsel could upset the applecart and there was no room for any of that here. It was hoped the new leader for the prosecution would come to appreciate the quality of what had been done the more he learned of the case.

The quest to establish precisely when Charmaine had died continued. Leo Goatley asked for her remains to be re-examined by another odontologist working for the defence. David Whittaker was desperate for more photographs and when a new one appeared in the *Sun*, the police had mixed feelings – anger that the picture had slipped through their net, delight that it could be just what they were looking for. It showed all of Charmaine's face front on, with a broad grin, ear to ear, that revealed not only all her teeth but also, just as important, the gaps where her baby ones had fallen out and her second teeth were starting to come through.

Incensed that the *Sun* had acquired what was clearly a professionally taken photograph where they had failed, Bennett contacted the newspaper and after much haggling managed to get them to hand it over, along with the negatives and details of when it was taken. It turned out it was taken by a local photographer whom the police had previously questioned about a picture of Fred West and Shirley Robinson he had also sold to the *Sun*. Seen again now, more than nine months later, he admitted finding pictures of children he had taken for a family called 'West at 25 Midland Road' and selling them to the newspaper because he did not think the police would be interested.

Whittaker certainly was, it was just what he wanted. Comparing the photograph and when it was taken to Charmaine's skull with its two missing baby teeth and barely formed second ones, he was able to say she could have died almost immediately but certainly not more than two or three months after it was taken. This was as precise as he could be and in terms of the case against Rose West it was hugely significant for it added to Anne Marie's account of how her stepmother had abused her sister and other evidence, including

Rose's own letters to her husband, Charmaine's school record, Shirley Giles's visit when Fred West was in prison and, perhaps most crucially, West's release from Leyhill on 24 June. Even Dr Whittaker's maximum calculation of two to three months increased the likelihood of Rose West killing her stepdaughter while the little girl's father was in prison. After that, just as at Cromwell Street, her naked body, minus both kneecaps and many finger and toe bones, was buried beneath the couple's flat.

Just like the other murder charges she faced, it was inconceivable she was not involved in a killing that almost certainly preceded that of Charmaine's mother, Rena.

Throughout the daily grind of preparing all the paperwork for the trial, Nick 'Finder' Churchill had managed to trace more than 100 people reported missing, all of them safe and well. It was one of the largely unsung achievements of the investigation, perhaps because not all of them wanted to be reunited with their families.

Brian Leveson's review of the case also continued, though his anticipated 'shopping list' remained conspicuous by its absence. Indeed, many of his ideas had been anticipated, like the photograph album with its small-scale photographs, charts and diagrams to show who, how and where everything fitted in. The QC recalled his idea of 'witness packs' that he had produced for the prosecution in the Strangeways riots investigation. These had been invaluable and he wanted them prepared for every potential witness in this case. The packs covered how the witness entered the investigation, tracking every aspect of their involvement and contact with officers and the reasons for it – essential where witnesses had been seen many times and a number of statements taken. It would highlight the integrity of the investigation (or otherwise) in the important area of the witnesses and their management, which might become an issue.

If the QC had been initially apprehensive then it had clearly passed by the time he announced that his opening speech would centre on the professionalism, quality, integrity and openness of the police investigation. Of course, if that subsequently turned out to· be wrong he had little doubt the case would fail, but his words gave everyone a lift – and meant they would have to be on their toes to the very end.

Like Butterfield before him, Leveson suspected that not all the evidence would make it into court and that witnesses like Caroline Owens, Anne Marie, Miss A and Sharon Compton were key to the outcome. Of the four, Caroline appeared the most stable, Anne Marie was devastated by her father's suicide, and after managing to stay out of the spotlight for so long, Miss A was experiencing more trouble in her life and like others was now in touch with a national newspaper. That left Sharon Compton, who was not only agitated that Rose West had not been charged with any of the offences she had allegedly committed against her, but her story also seemed to vary depending on whom she was telling it to, with one version for her friend and another for her liaison officer.

More worrying for Bennett, the more they checked out what she said the more doubts arose, and having two reporters from the *Daily Express* as minders did not help. To make it worse, at least one of them had been in touch with Miss A. Even so, Leveson wanted to use her, for apart from her own experiences, her evidence put Alison Chambers inside 25 Cromwell Street and being abused. So concerned was Bennett at Sharon Compton's state of mind and her value as a witness, he made a direct appeal to the *Express* reporters. They listened to what he had to say but continued their involvement with her regardless.

Janet Leach eventually revealed what Fred West had told her and put it in writing. She claimed that Rose had killed the Cromwell Street victims and that Rose's father, her brother-in-law John West and her black friends were all involved. Fred had not even known where they were buried until the night before he was arrested and after that he was protecting his wife. Rose, according to this version, had killed Charmaine when he was still in prison. The couple had a pact and he was upset when she was arrested because the plan had not worked. According to Janet Leach, Fred had described a farm at Gloucester where other victims were concealed, where their hands had been removed to prevent them being identified, and that Rose was involved in mutilation, too.

It was all very interesting and seemed to support what the rest of the inquiry team thought probably happened, but it was all hearsay and could never be used by the prosecution. What Janet Leach did not know was that by then Fred West was beginning to question her loyalty and that some of the stories he had told her were very similar to what he told others, and in particular his son Stephen – especially about the farm and the other victims. It looked like another example of Fred West revelling in his notoriety and trying to see which story got out.

Rosemary West's barrister was an imposing figure. Tall, slim and grey-haired, Richard Ferguson was an eminent Ulsterman with a reputation as a ruthless defence advocate, a penetrating interrogator and a destroyer of police evidence. A former Unionist MP who had represented the Birmingham Six, his disarming manner contrasted with the more studious, clinical style of Brian Leveson and he was a formidable opponent. Bennett and Moore came across him for the first time at the Old Bailey at another pre-trial hearing. Watching the two lawyers in the corridor afterwards, deep in conversation, they noted both were 'pacers'. Maybe it was the possibility of a view of 25 Cromwell Street that exercised them. Leveson wanted the jury to see how claustrophobically small the house was, how cramped the conditions were inside. Ferguson was not opposed to the idea but wanted all the other charges against his client, of rape and assault, to be heard another time when the murder trial was over.

By now Leveson not only appreciated the thoroughness of the investigation, he had also come to consider himself part of the team, while always maintaining the detachment his role demanded. Any fears they might have had about him had also been dispelled; those who were principally involved were often in awe of his industry and grasp of the evidence. He even showed the detectives his opening speech and asked their opinion, something Bennett had never come across before.

The police were still trying to corroborate the allegations made by Sharon Compton. When they were put to Rose West, along with all the other witness statements, she stuck to a prepared statement claiming that Sharon 'like all the others, was linked commercially to the media'. Bennett became ever more anxious as Sharon's claims continued to broaden and involve more and more people, even suggesting there was a leak within the investigation, which was where the media was getting all its information from. To try and get to the bottom of it, the Senior Investigating Officer made an appointment to see her at home, along with her liaison officer, Detective Constable Dave Stephens. It was the first and last time Bennett would meet Sharon Compton, though it would be a long time before her legacy was overcome.

They met in a quiet, friendly atmosphere and, with her children out of the way, chatted easily, though she declined to share any new allegations with Bennett on the grounds the media would get to hear of it. When Bennett explained it was the only way to get to the truth she changed her mind but then started to make fresh claims, at times composed, at others agitated. It was not what they wanted to hear and as Bennett was driven back to Gloucester his mind was almost made up. Brian Leveson would not like it, nor would anyone else, but Sharon Compton was not a 'witness of truth' and although they would continue to investigate her claims he would recommend they drop her. The detective still thought she might have been abused by the Wests, and he wanted her treated with the same sensitivity as all the other witnesses, but where the truth ended and her fantasies began, he could not say.

In the weeks to come, her unsubstantiated claims also included her house being burgled, being abducted and claims of improper police conduct. To try and separate fact from fiction, Bennett obtained permission to covertly record all her telephone calls to the MIR and whenever anyone from the team visited her.

By now it was apparent that most of the key witnesses had been tracked down by reporters and many of them had either agreed to sell their story or been offered money to do so. Although Bennett knew what they had told the investigation, he had no way of knowing what they had told the media, what they had been promised or paid or if the two versions were different. The problem was discussed with Brian Leverson and it seemed imperative that the truth should be established before the trial rather than brought out by the defence in front of the jury. If the prosecution could bring the issue into the open first, they could limit the damage caused by the inevitable defence claims that witnesses were making it all up to get more money. It would then be up to the jury to decide who was telling the truth.

It was agreed that each witness should be seen by their liaison officer and further statements taken from them, showing exactly how much they had been paid and by whom, along with the details of any contracts they had signed or were negotiating, with signed permission for those who had made the payment or offer to fully disclose the details of the arrangements and what they had been told. When the statements were in it was hard to believe the five-figure sums of money on offer but easy to understand why, in the light of what they had been through, they probably felt they deserved every penny.

Rose West appeared before Judge Mantell for the first time on 12 May at the first pre-trial review, a routine hearing where lawyers and court staff map out in broad terms how the trial will be organised. Still as sullen as ever, her weight ballooning, it was there she formally pleaded not guilty to each of the ten murder charges she faced. About a month later, Richard

Ferguson successfully applied to have the charges of rape and indecent assault temporarily removed from the indictment, though like his junior at the committal, he failed to get the trial halted.

Organising a viewing of 25 Cromwell Street was beginning to look a non-starter, not least because the judge appeared less than enthusiastic. Leveson, however, thought it crucial because the model that had been specially made, though accurate, seemed to make the house look bigger than it really was. As a fallback he asked for a scale plan of the court on acetate to the same scale as the plans of the room so it could be used as an overlay to compare sizes while contingency plans for a viewing were prepared.

The police accommodation at Netley was just as Bennett had envisaged. There was a bedroom opposite the kitchen that could be turned into a living room, a bed would act as additional seating and he would bring a large camping table, some chairs and a portable television. They could either bring enough food for breakfast from home or stock up at the supermarket nearby. In the evening, they could go to one of the many eating houses around. Travelling to and from the accommodation would be mostly on the motorway and would take about 45 minutes in the morning and less in the evening. It was ideal.

Leveson and Chubb, on the other hand, were renting a flat within walking distance of the court, Withy Cole would travel daily, David Stott and Fred Davies less frequently. The police and county council's legal advisers and the council's press officer were all staying in Winchester to be on hand when the need arose.

The police at Winchester had made their own security arrangements for getting Rose West to court from the local prison where she was being held during the trial, and where necessary witnesses and victims' relatives. An inspector, Paul Stallard, a sergeant, Alan Jackson, and a number of constables had also been set aside to work with the inquiry team – 'JB's mad Gloucester lot' as the locals referred to them.

During what was left of that summer, members of the inquiry team took what leave they could, knowing the true test was just around the corner.

Two small furniture vans, packed from floor to ceiling, were needed to transport all the paperwork and exhibits to Winchester Crown Court. Anything else that cropped up during the trial would be assessed in the MIR and driven to Winchester if necessary. At the final briefing on Monday 2 October, the day before the trial was due to begin, it was revealed that the defence was planning an application to have the charges of murder in respect of Heather West, Shirley Robinson and Charmaine West separated from the other seven so that, in effect, Rose West would face two trials, a move Leveson was determined to resist.

There was a surprise, too, for Bennett, and Sharon Compton was at the heart of it.

The *Daily Express*, who were still courting her, had promised to reply to the Senior Investigating Officer's questions about their involvement but had complained to the Director of Public Prosecutions instead. Typically, it was all very woolly, with the witness claiming her statements had not been taken properly, that the police had failed to draw comparisons between Lucy Partington's disappearance and some of the others, with her former husband getting a contract to service police helicopters thrown in for good measure. Bennett was incensed.

Not only was this not the way to complain against the police, it also called into question both his professionalism and integrity as well as everyone else's on the investigation. Only his most experienced officers had interviewed Sharon Compton and everything had been done by the book. How did the *Daily Express* know what comparisons had been drawn between the victims and where did her ex-husband fit into it all?

What was apparent to him was that the reporters behind the complaint had neither checked their facts nor had any knowledge of dealing with victims of abuse.

Even so, Leveson still wanted to keep his options open and suggested someone outside the investigation, ideally from another force, should handle it. Bennett was in no position to argue. He now felt more strongly than ever that she was an unreliable witness, an Achilles heel who could do untold damage if she took the stand. As for the *Express*, it could say what it liked, it had still not divulged the information he had asked for.

After all the months of hard work, of toiling to ensure everything was done correctly, it was a low point on which to set off for Winchester. As Bennett and Moore headed out of Gloucestershire neither knew what pitfalls still lay ahead, though the Senior Investigating Officer was confident that if Leveson was able to coax the witnesses' stories from them, and the court accept some of the similar fact evidence, then Rosemary West would be convicted of at least some of the murders.

The evidence against her was strongest in respect of Heather, Charmaine and Shirley Robinson. Ferguson recognised that; it was why he wanted to split the trial in two. Yet if Rose West was only convicted of one murder, say that of Heather, she would still get life – but the team would have thought they had failed.

THIRTY-FIVE

It was billed as 'the trial of the century' and as Bennett and Moore arrived just before lunch on the day before proceedings began, they sensed an air of expectation to match the hype.

Winchester Crown Court is an amalgam of the old and the new. The modern, concrete courthouse with its high glass windows and equally high security adjoins the ancient Great Hall of Winchester where the infamous 'hanging judge' Jeffreys presided, Sir Walter Raleigh was tried for treason and the famous Round Table of King Arthur hangs.

Reporters and producers were already scouting out the best vantage points. A Sky Television satellite truck was parked in an alleyway that ran down one side of the complex, ITN had erected their own Portakabin in a yard nearby and the BBC had taken over the entire first floor of a clothes shop overlooking the entrance to the court and converted it into a number of studios for national and local television and radio coverage.

The police had their own small room inside the court building and were linked to the MIR in Gloucester by phone, fax and computer. HOLMES was also up and running. With numerous courtrooms leading off one vast waiting area and a public address system calling witnesses and announcing courts in session, it looked and sounded more like an airport waiting lounge. The Crown versus Rosemary Pauline West was scheduled for Court 3, a huge, oak-panelled arena – more than big enough to accommodate 25 Cromwell Street – with blast-proof windows, a necessary precaution for the terrorist trials that were staged there. Admission for journalists and public alike was by ticket only and just like Dursley, reporters who could not get in could listen to an audio feed of the hearing in a nearby annexe.

419

Everything it seemed was set and ready to go.

In the small robing room above the court Leveson was putting the finishing touches to his opening speech. When it was done all present read it. That it was less colourful than Neil Butterfield's opening at the committal reflected the difference in the two proceedings. There, the sole aim had been to convince the presiding magistrate that Rose West had a case to answer; here, every sentence, every word even, put before the jury had to be justified. Overstating the facts now might lead to problems later. Tailored to counter the likely defence, it was no less persuasive. From that shaky, rather confrontational first meeting, the QC had evolved into a highly respected member of the team. Yet as lawyers and detectives looked forward to the day ahead, the old doubts remained, the same niggling questions still unanswered.

How much of the similar fact evidence would they be able to use and, more importantly, how were all the witnesses? How would they stand up in court? Were they still willing to give evidence and if so would they be able to talk about such terrible experiences in public? Would they relate to him? There was no doubt that the key witnesses would be cross-examined ruthlessly and some of them would be accused of making things up. The defence knew Lynda Gough's mum had made a mistake over the date she had gone to Cromwell Street and seen Rose West wearing her daughter's slippers, so she was sure to be targeted. It would not be pleasant for any of them but had enough been done to make the ordeal as painless as possible?

These are some of the questions all barristers ask before trials but Leveson knew that the loss or discrediting of any of the witnesses would be catastrophic. The integrity of the witnesses and how they had been managed had been considered from the beginning of the investigation. The Senior Investigating Officer had ensured that arrangements were in hand for this, which would be maintained throughout the trial. Each of the main witnesses would be conveyed or accompanied to the court by their liaison officer, but always with someone from Victim Support or the probation service, so that it could be shown that their evidence was not discussed. Once at Winchester the witnesses would be handed over to Caroline Martin and the volunteers of the Winchester Crown Court Witness Support Service, who would look after them until they had given their evidence and been released from court.

Ever since the committal they had tried to keep one step ahead, going over and over what they thought the defence might be. Even requests for documents took on an added significance. Leo Goatley had spent a lot of time that summer looking at the Mary Bastholm file, even though, as Fred West had never admitted any part in her disappearance, it would not have played a crucial role in any case against him, let alone Rose. It could only be that the defence was trying to make a comparison between her abduction and the others, for as Fred and Rose were not together at that time, it would suggest he had acted alone throughout and that just as he had said many, many times, Rose was not involved.

Goatley had also been delving into Hazel Savage's discipline hearing, along with the way prosecution witnesses had been handled, while the *Daily Express*'s letter to the Director of Public Prosecutions also suggested the integrity of the investigation would be questioned. As they tossed around what was likely to crop up, no one there thought Rose West would give evidence. Having listened to her interview tapes, there was no way she could be trusted not to revert to type under the pressure of cross-examination. The defence, it appeared, had also decided against playing some of Fred's interviews.

The next time they arrived at court it was for real.

The pavements on Trafalgar Street were lined with reporters and camera crews getting ready. Others were stationed on the upper walls overlooking the cobbled courtyard that led to the court. The Hampshire Police had never experienced anything quite like it, certainly not the hordes of media that had dogged the investigation from the start. They had already had to move some cameras from the courtyard, which had not gone down well. Leveson and Chubb were also taken aback, and when press officer Inspector Dave Morgan implored Bennett he reluctantly agreed to take his men back outside and walk them into court, because the cameras had missed them driving in earlier; it was like a scene from the film *Reservoir Dogs*.

When Rosemary West's prison van, with its motorcycle escort and blacked-out windows, swept down the hill and into court, the pictures went all around the world. It was not only the start of the trial, but also a ritual that signalled the beginning of each day's proceedings for the next six and a half weeks, and although there were a few spare seats in the public gallery that first day, it never happened again.

At just before the appointed time of 10.30 a.m. the patrician figure of the Honourable Justice Mantell entered the court. Heralded by the clerk, he bowed solemnly to counsel, who followed suit, and took his seat. It was an imposing sight, the judge enthroned in his scarlet robes and white plaited wig, looking down on the counsel in their black silk gowns and white wigs. Bennett and the other police officers sat on the judge's left, next to the witness box, while on the opposite side of the court sat the jury.

Escorted by two women prison officers, Rose West entered the dock, which was hidden from the public but was directly facing the judge and slightly elevated. She was wearing a navy suit with a green waistcoat and white blouse and bowed nervously.

The jury of eight men and four women were sworn in and the judge smiled down on them, explaining paternalistically that the defendant had already pleaded not guilty to the ten charges of murder. He then warned them of the heavy responsibility the oath they had taken placed upon them and not to be affected by anything they had already heard or seen about the sensational aspects of the case. He told them they could watch television or read newspapers but that was not 'evidence'. They should only consider what they heard in court and not talk to anyone outside, including their families.

With that he stood them down until Friday because the next day was the Jewish Day of Atonement, Yom Kippur, and the following day was taken up with other business. Then he turned his attention to the first round of legal argument that would at last resolve all the angst over similar fact evidence and what the jury would and would not hear. It was a potentially defining moment, as his rulings would affect the way the trial was run and possibly even its outcome.

In a much less formal atmosphere, Ferguson went first, asking for a ban on any interviews with witnesses until after the trial was over, a relatively straightforward request that was not disputed. Then, much more crucially, he set out the argument why the similar fact evidence should not be allowed. This included the testimony of Caroline Owens and others whose experiences, the prosecution maintained, were the templates for the murders that followed. The judge was unconvinced and in a colourful analogy cited the legend of Bluebeard the Pirate who chopped off the heads of his wives. If one had escaped, he reasoned, surely she could have given evidence about what happened to her. It was precisely what the prosecution would argue happened to Caroline Owens.

Ferguson did not give up, suggesting there were no similarities between some of the murders and that Rosemary West was not involved in two of them. The prosecution, he said, had speculated and were asking the jury to do the same. If the similar fact evidence was allowed and his client convicted, it would almost certainly lead to an appeal.

Leveson countered every claim and the judge, often leaning forward and smiling, clearly enjoyed the cut and thrust of legal debate. Aside from the grimness of the main event, they were an engaging treble act. The civilised lawyer-speak and good-natured way they went about their business were features of the trial.

The judge decided to consider his ruling overnight, which meant an anxious wait for the prosecution. When they returned, Chubb and the team appeared confident, Leveson and Bennett apprehensive. They need not have worried for the judge ruled that the evidence, though prejudicial, was too important to leave out. It was a significant victory as it meant the jury would hear everything the police had learned about Rose West's voracious appetite for sadistic, lesbian sex. Ferguson was no more successful in his application to split the trial seven and three, the judge assessing that the first trial would be widely publicised, making it impossible for a second one to be heard fairly.

So, the prosecution had won on both counts. What they did not expect to lose was an application to allow Bennett to remain in court even though he would be called as a witness. Everyone thought it a formality until Ferguson objected on the grounds that allegations were likely to be put that might involve the Senior Investigating Officer. The remark sent a shock wave through the media benches, while in the annexe, where the atmosphere was less restricted, Bennett could imagine dark mutterings and thoughts of what it meant and how they could get the story – whatever it was. There was little Leveson could do except have the officers who were not witnesses admitted in the Senior Investigating Officer's place, but it gave their confidence a huge jolt and started a whole new period of self-analysis.

When the court adjourned, Bennett was conscious of reporters staring at him more than usual. Leveson was equally quizzical but there was nothing the Senior Investigating Officer could say. He was totally bemused, too, and his mood was not helped when a tabloid reporter sneered 'Has JB been a naughty boy then?' Of course, he knew he had not, but the ruling barring him from watching at first hand all their work of the last eighteen months reach a conclusion gutted him.

Maybe that was why his first, rather petulant, impulse was to return to Gloucester and get on with his other work, for he could not justify staying in Winchester under the circumstances. Further talk about Sharon Compton and the *Daily Express* did not help either and at last Leveson agreed she would not be called. Eventually, Moore, Cole and the other officers managed to persuade him that going back was not only irrational it would lead to even more media speculation. When eventually he saw things their way, Bennett apologised for losing sight of the bigger picture and vowed that it would not happen again, even though neither he nor anyone else had any idea why he had been barred.

Still, it did not alter the fact that it had been a very good day for the prosecution, better than they could have hoped. All the evidence could now be put before the jury. It was up to the witnesses to stand up and Leveson to do his job.

After one false start, the trial proper began on Friday 6 October. Already there was more public than seats as people clamoured to get in to hear Leveson open for the Crown.

The tabloid journalist who had asked Bennett if he had been 'naughty' confided in the Senior Investigating Officer that the defence were playing 'cowboys and Indians', and that 'they had got rid of the chief, so now the Indians would run away', adding, while laughing, that disappointingly they had got nothing on him. Bennett passed it off; as a strategy it did not stand up and as a joke it was not funny. Neither did it alter the fact that once Leveson had finished his speech he would have to leave the court.

As the room filled up Rose West arrived in the dock. This time Bennett could see that underneath her familiar dark jacket and white blouse she was wearing a crucifix. It sickened him, knowing as he did every disgusting detail of the treatment she had inflicted on her victims down the years.

Before the judge arrived, Leveson beckoned him over. Sympathising with his predicament, he whispered, 'You have wound me up and now you have got to let me go and hope that I will do justice for what you all have worked on so hard.'

425

Bennett reassured him that no one had any concern at passing on the baton, for he was now the leader in every respect and they would all do whatever they could to make his job easier.

The QC's opening was a performance in itself that ran to more than sixty pages and took all of that day and some of the following Monday. Although essentially not as vivid as Neil Butterfield's account at the committal, its understated, forensic description of how the police had gone to 25 Cromwell Street looking for Heather West and stumbled upon secrets 'more terrible than words can express', the remains of young girls dismembered and decapitated then dumped in holes in the ground without dignity or respect, was powerful and moving.

His delivery was precise, and strings of words, soon to become catchphrases, that he used to start sentences or emphasise a point, like 'I say at once', 'Let me say immediately', 'I will tell you immediately', were heard for the first time. It was, he said, 'an investigation unparalleled to the Gloucestershire Police, and perhaps for any police force'. Outlining the evidence, which he described as 'harrowing' and 'more horrific than words can describe', he meticulously related each of the victims, what was known of the murders, the recovery of their remains and what was known of the Wests and their depraved partnership. Some of it was in book-like bundles containing plans and photographs and distributed among the jury, though he implored them that 'emotion must play no part in this case'. No one, he said, saw either Frederick West or Rosemary West commit any murder, but they were 'in it together – they did everything together'.

In both length and content it was a stunning piece of oratory, yet as he listened Bennett knew that if Leveson could coax the witnesses into telling their stories, their first-hand accounts would be even more powerful and convincing.

For the most part, Rose West remained impassive, though when Heather's murder came up she dabbed her eyes. This time Bennett was too far away to assess whether her tears were real but he doubted they were after hearing her dismiss the girl so harshly in interviews that the jury would soon be told about.

In the MIR, all they could do was watch and read what was happening on television, radio and in the newspapers. They also had plenty to do making arrangements for the forty-six witnesses, who were not only stressed by the wait but also becoming more and more anxious as each new sordid revelation made the news.

As the trial wore on, days ran into nights for those camped out at Netley, leaving each morning around 7.15 and not returning until after 8 p.m. The sparse but habitable rooms had been customised to suit the new residents. The lounge was a converted bedroom with a single bed moved sideways to become a settee, the dining room had camping tables, folding chairs and whatever was available. A portable television that purely by luck had a good picture, and a portable radio, completed the room's luxuries. The fridge had everything they needed from milk to beer and wine. A shower rota appeared on the bathroom door, for use in order of rank with priority at all times for superintendents – though no one took it seriously.

Finding somewhere relatively private and decent to eat after work was becoming a problem, so after taking more stick than normal about his love affair with Italy, 'Marco' Grimshaw promised to knock them up some Italian food. He brought all the ingredients from home and despite the limited facilities at his disposal rustled up quite a spread, right through from antipasta to dessert with wine and grappa that would have graced many a restaurant. Afterwards Bennett, who preferred French cuisine, promised a similar culinary treat. His pâté starter was no problem but when he reheated the main course of his favourite boeuf bourguignon, duchesse potatoes and boiled fresh vegetables, the heat in the tiny kitchen set off the fire alarm. Sirens sounded, lights flashed and the PA system summoned everyone to the exit. The chef, though, stood his ground and with the fire exit door open so everyone could see him, red faced with embarrassment he had to apologise when the security guards arrived on the scene. It was a French farce that helped break the tension of the trial, all washed down with a few glasses of Corbières. The evening meal problem was soon resolved when the manageress of The Ship, a pub with a restaurant where they had eaten a couple of times, realised who they were and with the minimum of fuss found them a quiet corner where they could eat and drink each night in relative privacy.

The case followed the list of prosecution witnesses with the difficult task of coordinating the arrangements for getting them to court, often at a moment's notice, undertaken by the MIR. Unusually they would later do the same for the witnesses called by the defence as all had been traced by the police investigation and the defence had asked for the police to do this. Rose West's aged mother had not had much to do with her daughter for many years but said she had mentioned something about Fred being capable of anything, even murder. It set the tone for many of the witnesses who followed.

Although the judge had made it clear he was against a viewing of 25 Cromwell Street, the jury had specifically asked to go. Reluctantly he agreed and put Bennett in charge of the arrangements, with the security of the jury and the premises, which for the duration of the visit would become part of the court, his priority. The stakes were high, for the judge made it clear that any breach could jeopardise the proceedings with little chance of a retrial. The good news was that the police were ahead of the game, for the Gloucester end of such a plan had already been drafted. For them it was just like organising a royal visit and with so many members of the royal family living in the county they had plenty of experience. All they had to do was make sure Cromwell Street was secure and organise the travel arrangements.

A bigger problem was presenting the house as it was when the Wests were living there. With no illegal extensions and all the doors and windows bricked up and shuttered it was a very different property from what the police saw when they arrived on 24 February 1994, not least the cellar ceiling, which was now much higher and had to be reinstated to the level it was when the investigation began. With everything to do it was now clear that even without the ban, Bennett would not have been able to spend as much time in court as he would have liked.

The trial was progressing well, and after fearing her evidence might not be allowed, Caroline Owens's testimony was among the most poignant. An early victim of the Wests, the tabloids tagged her as 'the one who got away' and when Leveson asked her, 'Mrs Owens, is commercial advantage anything to do with why you have come to court today?' she broke down in tears.

'Nothing at all. I want to get justice for the girls who didn't make it. It's like it was my fault.'

When Bennett heard, he knew her sincerity would override any damage that might have been caused to her credibility by the *Sun* paying for her story.

As well as being responsible for Rose West's travel arrangements, the Hampshire Police contingent was also helping to safeguard the witnesses and had spotted a motorcycle with the words Central Television following the blacked-out minibus that took them to and from court. Detective Constable Dave Stephens, who was driving the vehicle, had also seen the machine but managed to give it the slip. A similar thing happened on another evening only this time the woman motorcyclist overtook the minibus, acknowledging its driver and police outriders in the process.

When it happened again, Stephens was determined to get to the bottom of what was going on and managed to outmanoeuvre the bike and stop it. It turned out to be an ITN despatch rider with instructions to find out where the minibus was going. When Bennett found out he hit the roof and instructed the press office inspector to take statements from everyone involved and have a file and copies ready for the court the following morning. When the news reached the judge he also viewed it as 'very serious harassment' and although he took no direct action, it never happened again.

On hearing the defence was trying to discredit Lucy Partington's background and her conversion to Roman Catholicism, Bennett knew they must be getting desperate. The huge volume of evidence in support of her character far outweighed the unbelievable fantasies of a rambling Fred West. Even so, the judge was prepared to allow the jury to decide. Bennett believed the defence was putting up a smokescreen to hide West's knife wound the week after she disappeared, but the prosecution agreed to call a new witness just to enable Ferguson to cross-examine her – an unusual arrangement but indicative of the prosecution's openness.

The woman went to the same school as Lucy and was there when she went missing. She also told how, in the late 1960s, when she was on her way home, a man alone in a car, who might have been Fred West, had tried to entice her into taking a lift with him and she had never forgotten it – the inference being that West was a lone operator, just as he had always claimed to be. It was a desperate ploy, seemingly seeking to cancel out witnesses who followed, who all fostered the image of the Wests' relationship as one founded on and fuelled by their obsession with sex. It also prepared the ground for Miss A, a sad-looking woman with considerable mental health problems whose presence in court owed much to her liaison officer, Detective Constable Russ Williams and Victim Support. Having been brought up in children's homes, Miss A had looked up to Rose West as a big sister until she was savagely abused, tied up and raped. It was another grim account that paired Rose West and her husband in the abuse of young women.

As expected, Miss A's sad existence was picked to pieces in the witness box but just being there was a sign of a newly found strength and Bennett hoped it might signal an upturn in her life, for although he had often agonised over whether she would be mentally strong enough to give evidence and survive cross-examination, he was in no doubt she was telling the truth. It did not even bother him that she also was now contracted to a newspaper, for he believed that in the light of what women like her had been through, they deserved every penny that came their way – it was the media's timing that was the problem – though whether they received all they were promised was another matter altogether.

Arrangements for the 'viewing' were well in hand. It would be another media occasion but there was nothing they could do about that except make it impossible for anyone to photograph the jury or pierce the security of the 'court for a day'. Jury members would travel in a coach with blacked-out windows and everyone, the judge and counsel included, would have to wear hard hats and safety clothes. The garden would be covered so no one could see them get off or on, or take pictures from above. Inside the house, restoring the level of the cellar floor was in hand, though depicting where other walls had been or where victims were buried was trickier. Ferguson's original opposition to the idea had hardened and the judge was a reluctant visitor too, so once again the police planning would be on trial.

The viewing was to take place on 19 October, two days after what would have been Heather West's twenty-fifth birthday and which by coincidence was also the day her half-sister Anne Marie was due to give evidence. Anne Marie, perhaps more than any other, had faced more pain and suffering in having to delve into her sordid upbringing in front of complete strangers. The effect of all that, the death of her father, and what had been uncovered in the investigation, including the murder of her mother and another sister, had been devastating. It left her depressed and resulted in attempts at suicide and being arrested for drink-driving. Like Miss A, Anne Marie's presence in Winchester owed much to others, in her case her partner Phil and liaison officers Detective Constables Nick Barnes and Steve Harris. The court timetable, though, appeared less sympathetic, for if everything went to schedule her evidence would be interrupted by the visit to Gloucester and there was no telling what effect the strain of that and having to go back into the witness box would have on her.

Anne Marie's delivery that day, though there was nothing made up about it, was the most dramatic and courageous of all. Dark-haired and heavy set, she was the image of her father and referred to Rose throughout as 'Rosemary' or 'my stepmother'. Her voice was soft, almost dreamy, and barely registered above a whisper, yet it was not the sound but the content that made her story difficult to listen to. Her first sexual experience, she remembered, had been at the age of 8 and after that she was raped by Fred and Rose, who said she should be grateful; instead she wished she was dead.

When the session ended that Wednesday afternoon, Bennett was on the landing with a cup of coffee in hand and watched as the courtroom emptied. The reporters seemed in even more of a hurry to get away to prepare their stories but their conversations were more muted, their faces more sombre. Few looked up to acknowledge him, some of the women had been crying and he knew instinctively why. Even in that hostile environment, Leveson's understanding and compassion had coaxed her into sharing her darkest, most intimate secrets.

When the QC and Chubb emerged they both admitted to being shocked and humbled by what she had said and how she had said it. No other witness had ever pulled on their emotions like that before and they would not have believed it had they not been there.

The prosecution had expected Elizabeth Agius to deny her sex sessions with the Wests when she gave evidence, and she did, even though it was put to her that her denial was so that her husband would not become aware. Detective Constable Watters's reports and the instructions he received from Bennett were brought before the jury, who were to decide the truth of it all.

As Bennett arrived back in Gloucester ahead of the court visit he was delighted to see the whole of the alleyway that led to the back of Cromwell Street under canvas and an entrance big enough for a coach to reverse into. It meant everyone could get in and out of the property without being seen or photographed. Hard hats and protective clothing were laid out inside, and there was even a toilet and police control room. It seemed that everything had been thought of. Bennett walked the course, made a few suggestions and thanked everyone, confident neither the judge nor the defence would be able to find fault with any of it.

All being well, it would be just like a royal visit.

THIRTY-SIX

How was Anne Marie?

Apart from the visit to 25 Cromwell Street, that question was uppermost in Bennett's mind. The police always knew their case might stand or fall by how well the witnesses coped with giving evidence and Anne Marie had surpassed all expectations. Forced once more to re-enact her worst nightmares in front of strangers hanging on her every word, hers had been the most harrowing testimony of all – and it was not all over yet.

How would she be in the cold light of the following day after a night in a hotel room to reflect on it all?

A phone call to Moore at Winchester brought the answer. Witness Support had sorted out accommodation and arranged for a nurse to be with her. However, it was now apparent the court would not reconvene after visiting Gloucester, so Anne Marie would have to wait around another day and night before she could return to the witness box to be cross-examined, further prolonging the ordeal.

St Michael's Square in Gloucester was completely coned off and police 'no waiting' signs lined the route along which the coach carrying the jury would come and go. The white canvas passageway leading to the marquee that covered the garden made it look like the entrance to a circus. Here, at the back of the house, the visit had been planned to the last detail and was a picture of organisation, quite a contrast to Cromwell Street itself, where the sound of music filled the air, neighbours had come out of their homes or peered out of windows, children hung around trying to find out what they could from reporters, the more adventurous of them bobbing in front of cameras in the hope of getting on television. Out front, it was like a carnival without the procession.

Unable to relax, Bennett walked the course once more just to check that everything was as it should be. Overhead, he could hear the sound first of a light aircraft that had already buzzed the site a couple of times, then the police helicopter called in to ward it off. As the court convoy approached, two more helicopters arrived, making three in all, and conversation on the ground became impossible until Bennett made it clear to operations control it had to stop.

Justice Mantell's party was the first to arrive and he approached the Senior Investigating Officer with a face like thunder. Despite all the precautions, he had been photographed and he was not happy. Worse than that, if it happened with a member of the jury the judge had already warned him the trial could be abandoned.

At least he appeared a lot happier after being shown around the house and seeing the arrangements that had been made.

Soon afterwards, Bennett heard in his earpiece that the jury had arrived. Inspector Paul Stallard, who was the senior officer in the Hampshire contingent, reassured him that everything had gone to plan and that the media presence along the way had to be seen to be believed – and that he would not have missed it, or the chance of seeing Cromwell Street for himself.

The eight men and four women of the jury were assembled for a pep talk by the judge, who reminded them of what would happen, what they could and could not do and what they would see. Where each of the victims had been buried would be marked out by tape with the name printed in black on white card with no embellishment. Walls and windows that had been bricked up would be marked out in yellow tape.

The jury listened intently. Some had changed into the hard hats and overalls provided, some allowed their attention to wander over what had been the patio and back garden they had heard so much about, though the canvas ceiling prevented them seeing up to the top of the three-storey building. The judge then stepped aside and Sergeant Pete Maunder led them off towards the back of the house. To the right was the rectangle of tape bearing the name of Heather West, the first set of remains recovered. As they encountered more tape marking out where the extension door once stood and where the remains of Alison Chambers were buried, they all slowed down and adjusted their stride to avoid stepping on it, just as if they were picking their way through the graves in a churchyard.

It did not take long and when it was over the judge gave the jury some time alone to talk about what they had seen. After a while the jury foreman asked if they could see the front room and cellar again and not long afterwards they were on the coach and heading back to Winchester. From Bennett's point of view, it could hardly have gone better.

After that the media pool was shown around, and after them members of the inquiry team who had never seen the house were given the same opportunity. Many remarked how much smaller the property was, something they had not appreciated from the model, plans and photographs they had seen – the very point that Leveson had been so anxious to get across to the jury.

That night Anne Marie decided she wanted to be alone. There was nothing anyone could do to prevent it, she was entitled to her privacy if that was what she wanted, but Bennett made sure the police had the name of her hotel, her room number and the police control room that covered it just in case. The wisdom of this became apparent sooner than expected.

Bennett had changed from a suit into more casual clothes ready to leave for The Ship when his mobile rang. It was Anne Marie's liaison officer, Nick Barnes. Anne Marie had been drinking and taken some medication prescribed for her. Now she was feeling unwell and had called for help.

The rumour spread among reporters that she had tried to

take her own life, but more likely she had just found the strain of the delay too much and mixed medicine with too much drink by mistake.

Barnes knew she was in her room and fearing the worst had called out the local police, who headed straight there while everyone at Netley awaited news. It was an anxious wait but eventually Bennett received a call to say she was on her way to hospital to have her stomach pumped and was likely to make a full recovery. Whether she would be able to attend court the next day no one knew, though the implications for the prosecution if not were too hard to contemplate.

When the court reconvened at 10.30 the following morning the judge announced that Anne Marie was indisposed and to avoid any disruption, Leveson called her former husband to give evidence. Soon news reached Bennett that she had left hospital and was being driven back by Mark Grimshaw under a police escort and that their departure had been photographed – though that proved less of a problem when the judge ruled the pictures could not be published. He also ruled in the prosecution's favour that some of the videos and sex toys seized during the 1992 investigation could be introduced, including the photograph of the dildo stored in the whisky box.

Repulsive it may have been, but it showed the size and nature of what Kathryn Halliday had experienced and the precise reason she had ended her relationship with Rose West. She was to describe emotively how she had considered herself to be like a moth drawn to a flame.

All in all, it was a better start to the day than Bennett could have imagined and it picked up even more when he heard that although pale, Anne Marie was well enough to return to the witness box.

Ferguson's cross-examination did not take long. Despite all the trauma of the last 24 hours, Anne Marie was composed and convincing, and clearly the defence had little to gain in unduly attacking a witness whose evidence had attracted such universal sympathy.

It marked the beginning of the end of the prosecution. Some of the taped interviews with Rose West were played and among the other exhibits brought into court was a door with a peephole. Professor Knight induced a few gasps of astonishment when, like a magician pulling a rabbit from a hat, he produced a femur from his blue cloth bag to illustrate a point and even Dr Whittaker's demonstration of how he used photographs to assess Charmaine's age at death went unchallenged.

Inside the waiting room, Bennett reflected on how witnesses like Caroline Owens, June Gough and Anne Marie, who had never given evidence before, must have felt before they were called. Even for him, with all his years of experience, it was an anxious wait. What did the defence have? Why had they had him excluded from court?

In the end, his appearance in the witness box passed off uneventfully as neither the attack on his integrity nor that of the investigation materialised, just a few routine questions on procedure that he was able to answer easily, including, as expected, the covert listening operations.

'The purpose of the operation, Mr Bennett, was to try to obtain further evidence if you could against Mrs West?'

'No, sir, it was for the purpose of seeking intelligence to gain the truth.'

The judge saw the joke and grinned. Ferguson, too, just about managed to suppress a chuckle and came back with 'Yes. If I could just endeavour to gain some further intelligence from you, Mr Bennett.' For some reason, this was not the first time that barristers had found it a source of amusement that his investigative methods were designed to seek the truth.

The Senior Investigating Officer's most difficult task was probably suppressing the look of relief as he took his seat in court alongside other members of the team.

At just after 3.30 p.m. on Wednesday 25 October the case for the prosecution came to an end and Ferguson asked for an adjournment until the following Monday to put the finishing touches to his defence.

In the absence of the jury, it included an application to play some of the taped interviews with Fred West – or, as the headline writers put it, 'the voice from the grave'.

While it was not a unique application to rely on the evidence of persons since deceased, no one could remember such a request being made to play police taped interviews of an alleged offender, let alone someone accused of mass murder. It also meant that if the defence was allowed to play a selection for the purpose of showing that he was the murderer and not Rose, then the prosecution could rebut this by showing he was not a reliable witness – and from most of the interviews on 132 tapes, that would not be too difficult.

Even if the judge agreed, the prosecution never expected the defence to play the tapes, but then again, they did not expect Rose West to give evidence either and expose herself to Leveson's cross-examination.

THIRTY-SEVEN

The trial was now entering the finishing straight, yet still events outside conspired against a smooth passage.

During the weekend, one of the younger men on the jury had been arrested for fighting and was bailed to appear at court, which meant the judge had to stand him down, reducing the jury from twelve to eleven. It was irritating but not terminal, and practically inconsequential compared to the twists ahead.

Richard Ferguson rose to his feet, turned to the jury and began his defence of Rose West.

In the course of the last three weeks, he reminded them, they had heard from many witnesses. Some of the evidence they may have found shocking, some of it undoubtedly harrowing, some of it perhaps irrelevant and much of it admitted but that was only to save time and money and was not a confession of guilt because Rosemary West, he said, was not guilty of any of the charges she faced. 'She neither knew of nor participated in any of the acts which led to the death of these girls, nor did she knowingly do anything afterwards either to hide or conceal them.'

It was a familiar theme that somehow seemed more persuasive in Ferguson's soft Irish brogue. Much more surprising was his promise that the court would soon hear from Rose West's own lips her version of what went on inside 25 Cromwell Street and that, more predictably, she was innocent of all the charges laid against her. Preparing the court, clearly anticipating that come what may it was bound to be sensational, the QC asked that it be kept in mind that it would be a considerable ordeal for her – even more than any other witness 'because this was her family and this was her home'.

Bennett had always known Rose West taking the stand was

possible, they had discussed it more than once in their briefings and conferences, but like everyone else involved in the prosecution he never thought she would take the risk. Now, at last, after all those 'no comment' interviews, she was about to give her side of the story, though whether the jury would respond to Ferguson's appeal for sympathy seemed equally improbable.

Returning after a short adjournment, Rose West left the dock and made her way slowly to the witness box from where she faced the jury. Her voice faltered as she took the oath and she was allowed to sit down.

As Ferguson gently probed her early days with Fred, Bennett was struck by the change in her voice and vocabulary. Whenever he had met her or listened to the covert tape recordings from the safe houses she sounded dog-rough. Now she was much more refined and as her QC teased out details of her life with her husband and her sexual relationships she appeared to grow in confidence and even chanced at humour in her answers.

Bennett was not fooled, confident this new-found smugness would only dig more holes and that it was a matter of time before she slipped back into her more naturally confrontational way, and yet when she returned to give evidence the next day, she continued in the same vein. Clearly taken with her own performance the day before, she saw no reason to change and even Ferguson seemed unable to rein her in.

This was not a Rose West that Bennett recognised, the Rose West who throughout all her interviews suffered alternately from 'memory loss' and 'selective amnesia'. Surely she was not going to try that here?

Sitting within 6–8ft of her, the Senior Investigating Officer watched closely as first she failed to recollect Caroline Owens in any detail then resorted to intermittent sobbing, dabbing at her eyes with a handkerchief. From his vantage point Bennett could see there were no tears beneath those trademark spectacles and wondered if she was capable of them anyway. And where did her use of the word 'consensual' come from? In 73 interviews under caution and nearly 700 hours of covert bugging in safe houses she never used it once, yet now there was hardly a reference to her sexuality and lesbian relationships that did not include the 'c' word; not only that, she seemed to be lapsing into 'tabloidspeak'.

When asked what she felt about her husband when she saw him in court after he had confessed to murder, she declared: 'I hated him. I didn't see the man that I had known all those years. He was just a walking figure of evil. I know it might sound daft, but I saw him with horns and complete with a satanic grin because he never looked sorry for what he did or anything. He just used to grin like it was all a joke or something.'

If Rose was pleased with herself, the looks on her lawyers' faces suggested anything but, yet still they appeared powerless to stop her. Bennett even thought Ferguson wanted to get more from her but when asked if she played any part in the deaths of her ten alleged victims, her reply showed why he could not take the risk. A simple 'No' would have been enough, instead she mopped her eyes once more and sobbed, 'No, sir, I had no part in murder whatsoever. I am not a murderer. I can't take somebody's life away from them. I wouldn't want it done to me and I wouldn't do it to anybody else, especially my own daughter.'

It sounded like the worst sort of amateur dramatics; all it lacked was 'on my baby's life' or 'honest, guv'nor'.

Fred, she claimed, had tricked her and everyone else down the years. 'I just feel such a fool. I just don't know how he managed it, to actually get those poor girls in and out of the house. I don't know how he did it without being seen. The houses were always full around our house, anybody could have seen him at any time.'

'Did you ever suspect that Fred West was a murderer?', asked Ferguson.

'Not for one minute, sir; if I had thought that, I could never have lived with a murderer. I would never have known when it was my turn. I would have been too scared. I would have had to have gone to the police, I couldn't have lived like that.'

And to the QC's final question, 'Did you ever do anything after the death of any of these young women either to hide or disguise the fact that they had been murdered?'

'No, sir, I didn't know, I wasn't aware of it.'

Ferguson: 'At any time?'

Rose West: 'At any time.'

When it was his turn, Leveson adopted a style of quiet inquisition rather than confrontation for although he knew the media would want him to be more direct, more forceful, what was the point? He knew she would not be able to hide her true colours forever so why risk alienating the jury unnecessarily or harass her into giving them a reason to feel the sympathy Ferguson had sought?

As he probed and her response became curter, the absurdity of her answers and selective amnesia became clearer. She never saw anything – the girls, their bodies, their clothes, the blood, etc., never heard anything from the cellar and certainly never said anything.

During one exchange, to clarify whether she had access to the cellar, the QC asked if she had a key to the door and she replied, 'We had a main key that opened a lot of doors, what we called the master key at the time because they were all the same locks.'

'So you could get into the cellar whenever you wanted to?'

'No, sir, they were bolted from the inside,' she hissed, not realising the ridiculousness of her answer.

'Well, they could not be bolted from the inside if there was not anybody in, could they?'

'I don't understand, sir,' was her limp riposte but there was no reason for him to explain.

As a clash of intellects, it was an uneven contest which produced sniggers from the press benches and a stern look from the judge to prevent full-blown laughter. Bennett and his men were seated in full view of the jury and he had impressed on them the need for blank looks and straight faces at all times, yet inside their hearts pumped at the mess she was making.

She managed to stop just short of revealing the foul-mouthed harridan of her early brushes with the law, but could never fully conceal her contempt for authority and her diminutive tormentor. As she became more argumentative the questions came back in sharper, more rapid fire, causing her to stumble through the QC's account of Mrs Giles's evidence about Charmaine.

'I remember her coming when Charmaine wasn't there and it was after Fred came out of prison, but she could have well come to see me before that as well.'

'We can dance around this all afternoon, Mrs West, the fact is that she came once and Charmaine was not there, is that not the truth?'

'No, she is mistaken, sir.'

'Because if it was only once and Charmaine was not there, she was already dead, was she not?'

' No, sir, I couldn't have killed a little girl at that time, or at any time.'

'And you kept her body for Fred to bury?'

'No, sir. Please, sir, where could I have kept a body in Midland Road? Could you explain to me where I would keep a body, a little girl's body?'

'Underneath your flat there was a coal cellar, was there not?'

Perhaps she did not see the question coming, or if she did could think of nothing better to say, oblivious to how absurd she sounded. 'I wasn't aware of it, sir – to me it looked like a vent.'

Leveson concluded his examination soon after and perhaps, fearing it might lead to more damage, Ferguson did not dwell on his re-examination.

The following day, three women witnesses all testified that Fred West had followed them, tried to abduct them or committed a lewd act in front of them when giving them a lift. The prosecution would have accepted statements from all three but the defence was desperate to inject some credibility into their faltering case.

Just how desperate became apparent when the court received a request to play extracts from four of the taped interviews with Fred West. The media had always hoped they would hear the voice of the dead, though the prosecution thought it would never happen as it left Rose West vulnerable to damaging evidence that otherwise would not have been allowed. For that reason alone it was doubtful that either Ferguson or Sasha Wass had suggested such a move, more likely the opposite, but if that was what Rose wanted they had to comply, hence the QC's coded application that he had received 'express' instructions.

Now wearing a Remembrance Day poppy, an adornment Bennett found as distasteful as the earlier crucifix, Rose West sat in the dock with her head down and along with everyone else there listened to her late husband's sickening accounts of how he murdered two of his daughters, his first wife and the other Cromwell Street victims and why. How Rose knew nothing about any of it, how he had killed them all to preserve his relationship with her, how he dismembered them, buried them and, for those he had not known before, how he had met them.

Some of the police and lawyers had heard it all before. There were others hearing his tales of lurid sexual fantasy and cold-hearted murder for the first time, mesmerised by the heavily accented Herefordshire drawl that filled the courtroom and came out of the speakers in the overspill rooms – all of them packed to capacity. Almost as startling as his vivid descriptions was the utterly dispassionate way he delivered them, as though his behaviour was perfectly natural and commonplace, except it was not, and although the jury did not know it then, counselling was available after the trial had finished for anyone disturbed by what they had heard.

Just as he had during the committal, Bennett spent some time sitting in the media annexe where, because of the acoustics, every word and movement from around the court could be heard even more clearly than in the court itself, somehow making West's voice more pronounced and chilling, and the officers conducting the interviews clearer and more direct.

No one spoke as no one wanted to miss a word, but because the atmosphere there was more relaxed than in the court the reporters occasionally glanced at Bennett with bemused looks on their faces, shaking their heads from side to side in disbelief. Some gesticulated that West was mad.

When the last tape had been played and the court adjourned, Bennett set off back to the police office and as he did, Simon Hughes of the *Sun* quipped, 'I can see the headline now, "When Rose goes shopping Fred goes chopping".'

After all the time he had spent with witnesses and victims' relatives Bennett did not want to see the funny side but he could not help smiling, as that, in its crudest form, was precisely the point that playing the tapes set out to achieve, though even the *Sun* reporter doubted whether much of the content could be reproduced in his newspaper.

Having played his last card – from a very bad hand – Ferguson gave notice he would finalise the defence on Tuesday 7 November, and as the prosecution prepared their response from the 128 *other* tapes of Fred West's interviews they knew there would be no early nights for them.

There was a vast amount of evidence to show that West had lied; they just had to pick out the best examples, like just before he was transferred to Winson Green when he withdrew his confessions and virtually pointed the finger at Rose and others. Like the letters found in his cell after his death, especially the one intended for his wife's forty-first birthday alluding to their pact and including, 'Keep your promises to me you know what they are . . . I have no present, all I have is my life. I will give it to you my darling. When you are ready come to me, I will be waiting for you.'

Then there was Janet Leach, the appropriate adult, who could now be called and asked about her private conversations with West. Uncontaminated by media money, she could yet be the prosecution's trump card – or so it seemed.

As Bennett and Moore completed the drive back from Netley they were buoyant. The week had gone better than they could have hoped, with every expectation of more to come, so they could not believe it when, as Moore approached the drive to Bennett's bungalow, they saw Ann Bennett come running out to meet them almost in a state of panic.

Instead of going to her husband, she went to the driver's side where Moore wound down the window and saw she had tears in her eyes. 'She's going to get off. It's been on the news all week and especially today. Rose didn't do it. It was Fred. All the work you have all done will be for nothing. Tell me JB's got something up his sleeve – it can't end like this!'

Bennett was shocked. He had never seen his wife like this before – certainly not over any of his cases – and he could not understand it. Even more disconcerting, she seemed to have formed the complete opposite opinion to that of the two detectives.

As he stepped inside she continued to relate what all the reports had been saying and even produced a couple of newspapers their sons had kept to back up what she was saying. As her husband tried to reassure her, it occurred to him that people in the MIR might also have the wrong end of the stick.

Nick Churchill took his call and to Bennett's dismay seemed just as depressed as his wife had been. Despite all the updates from Winchester, the overriding view was that Rose would get off. The Senior Investigating Officer's remedy was to get Churchill to pass the word around that he would be over the next day to explain what, because of the restrictions on court reporting, the news reports had not been able to – and to invite them all to be in court when the jury returned its verdicts. He also suggested Ann and Pat Moore, Terry's wife, should pay a visit.

Pat Moore, Ann Bennett and son Andrew could hardly have timed it better. They would be in court to see Janet Leach give her evidence – potentially the prosecution's *coup de grâce*. Surely that would put their minds at rest.

Excluded from another brief discussion on points of law, the jury returned to hear more damning statements from Lucy Partington's mother – whose detailed accounts of her daughter's movements in the months before her disappearance gave the lie to Fred West's obscene claim he and her daughter were lovers – and the equally damaging testimony from a former probation officer, who revealed that in the assault on Caroline Owens, West confided in him that Rose had been the instigator and prime offender. Even more importantly they heard from a Winson Green prison psychiatrist who had seen West when he was on remand. Not having spoken to the media, and not paid by them, he referred to his notes, telling of how West had said he had lied to Ogden and alleged his wife had abused his daughters, buried the girls without him knowing and used large vibrators.

Then it was the turn of Janet Leach. To avoid any irregularity, Leveson suggested she first sign a waiver for the duration of the proceedings that would enable her to breach her confidentiality agreement.

Janet Leach was 39, a mother of five and a trainee social worker. Thickset, with a mane of dark, shoulder-length, corkscrew hair that emphasised a pale round face, she appeared on edge from the moment she entered the witness box and took the oath, so when the QC invited her to sit, she eagerly accepted. This nervous demeanour should have surprised no one who had had dealings with her, for one of the reasons she had been so reluctant to make a statement about what West had told her was that she feared it would end with her in court.

As Leveson maintained his understated approach, she revealed in a wavering Midlands accent that Fred West had told her 'he had a pact with his wife' to admit to the murders even though she, and others, were responsible, not him. That was why he was pleased when his wife was released from custody but distressed when she was rearrested as it meant the plan was not working.

Janet Leach sobbed frequently as she related in detail what West had confided in her. How he had made up stories and changed them, how many other victims there were and where they were buried, and how Rose was involved in all of those as well. It was, she said, a heavy burden to bear as all of it was privileged information which her role as appropriate adult forbade her from divulging – at least while he was alive.

One question that had troubled the police was why she had kept in touch with West after she had been discharged from her duties, even visiting him in jail just before Christmas. If anything, she seemed even more nervous now and claimed it was in the hope he would eventually tell her the truth and lift the weight from her shoulders.

It had been a shaky performance and when, finally, as if to establish her credibility, Leveson asked if she had been paid by the media, or spoken to them, her denial was equally unconvincing.

As Bennett approached his office at the start of the lunch adjournment, he noticed his wife, son and Pat Moore briskly making their way towards the stairs. As Ann Bennett passed she made a point of not acknowledging him but said in a voice loud enough for him to hear, 'she's lying', and Mrs Moore nodded in agreement. While Bennett knew his wife had a good instinct for that sort of thing, neither he nor Moore, who also heard, paid much attention.

Then again, she was not the sort to let it drop and when 'JB' registered on her mobile shortly after, she was back on the scent. 'That woman told lies about something, it was obvious. She had no reason to be so upset and the reasons for her keeping in contact with Fred West just did not ring true. She was out to make money out of it.'

Bennett tried to explain Janet Leach's previous ill health but his wife was having none of it. Women, she said, could wind men round their finger for sympathy and she could not believe they had all been taken in by her.

If it had been false before, Janet Leach's state of anxiety now took a turn for the worse. She was complaining of pains in her arms and legs, and after suffering a stroke the year before, there was concern she might be about to have another, especially when her condition deteriorated and she could no longer walk or talk. An ambulance was called and as she was the last witness in the trial the jury was temporarily stood down.

Still her plight cut no ice with Ann Bennett, who was convinced that whatever was wrong with her was down to stress, probably because she had become involved with the press. John Bennett still held that as she had signed a confidentiality agreement, that simply could not be true.

When a doctor saw her later, it was still not clear whether she had suffered a stroke, though she would not be in court the following day, maybe not until the following week.

The atmosphere in The Ship that night was more guarded and was not improved when Bennett's pager went off, instructing him to phone Leveson urgently. With no mobile signal he had to use the phone in the bar, which was heaving, but then bad news at any time is just that, how it is communicated makes little difference.

Bennett felt the blood drain from his face as the QC related the conversation he had just had with a brother barrister who was representing some of the media on the issue of handing over information and had heard that Janet Leach had told the court she had not received any payment or been involved with the press – which he knew to be a lie. Ethically, the barrister had no choice but to bring it to Leveson's attention and the rest of the court. Leveson, in turn, had told the defence and would have to inform the judge as well.

In the doom-laden conversation that followed the two men considered the options, the worst of which was the abandonment of the trial. Bennett thought it best to keep the news from Janet Leach. This might hasten her recovery though her credibility would still be destroyed once the defence got to her. Leveson's more optimistic assessment was that in that case it would be up to the jury to decide whether all or just a part of what she had said was true.

Their brief discussion over, Bennett's mind was on damage limitation and he straightaway arranged for Janet Leach to have a round-the-clock guard to avoid any contact with reporters. While she remained in hospital, only her doctors and nurses would be allowed to see her.

Returning to the group, feelings of concern, frustration and resentment bubbled inside. Concern at what effect it would have on the trial, frustration with himself for not spotting what his wife had seen – and he knew when she found out she would not let him forget it – and resentment towards yet more media involvement and the woman herself for her disloyalty.

That was pretty much how everyone else felt when he poured out what Leveson had told him and they left feeling even more subdued that when they had arrived.

It was also a time for reflecting on all that had happened during the arrest and interviewing of Fred West and what would have been allowed in evidence. Bennett knew that he had gone to the limits of the Police and Criminal Evidence Act in having some lines of questioning pursued when there was sufficient evidence to charge him, and also afterwards, but he had been prepared to lose that as identification was his main concern. However, what would his defence have made of the evidence that had been obtained during the questioning in front of all or combinations of Leach, Ogden, Canavan and Savage? It would have been argued that no one was there to act in his interest, but rather their own. What effect that might have had on the case might be an interesting debating subject for lawyers in the future, but all there that evening agreed that fortunately they had been spared a court having to make such deliberations.

When Paul Stallard got in touch later it was to say that Leach's new security was in place and that she had not suffered a stroke after all, to which Bennett offered his own diagnosis, 'a severe bout of dock asthma' – an old police expression for when prisoners become unable to speak or collapse under the stress of lying in the witness box.

The details of Janet Leach's deal with the *Daily Mirror* were unravelled the next morning. It appeared she had contacted the newspaper through a friend in June or July 1994, three or four months after she became Fred West's appropriate adult and long after signing the police confidentiality agreement. Initially, she was sounding them out about a book but ended up telling her as yet unpublished story to reporters – which apparently was the same as she had said in evidence.

The amounts she was to be paid were certainly eye-catching. She had a verbal agreement for £100,000 for her book and newspaper serialisation, depending on the lifting of her confidentiality agreement. A sum of £7,500 had already been paid to her partner in August 1994, plus a further £100 in October and another £100 in December. In August 1995, just before the trial started, a chalet at a holiday camp was provided for her, her children and partner, with an additional £500 paid to her partner for the holiday. The following month, she was given £5,000 to pay for medical treatment for her partner abroad.

By the following Monday morning, when Janet Leach returned to court in a wheelchair, accompanied by a doctor, looking pale, withdrawn and as anxious as she had been when she left six days earlier, she was one of the few, perhaps the only one, unaware her secret was out.

Ferguson had little difficulty in nailing her and Leveson did his best to limit the damage by emphasising the measures taken by the police to prevent such duplicity, but the star witness who was supposed to provide the prosecution's *coup de grâce* had become a liability.

The closing speeches, once again characterised by the contrasting styles of the two QCs – the difference between a Canaletto and a Van Gogh was how the judge described it – led the trial towards its conclusion.

The jury had heard first-hand all the evidence, Leveson had promised in his opening and more. The courage of the witnesses, their support and the compassionate way the QC had coaxed them to tell their often sickening and torrid experiences had ensured that. As a bonus, Rose West had by her evidence and the playing of her dead husband's interviews caused them to hear more than it had ever been envisaged they would.

The integrity of the investigation had survived its sternest examination and was shown to be above reproach, which for Bennett, the result apart, was the ultimate accolade – even though the defence still argued the evidence against their client was to all intents and purposes pretty thin. What Rose West made of it all was still hard to tell as for the most part she stared straight ahead as if in a trance, occasionally looking down, but registering no evident feeling.

It took the judge the best part of three days to sum up and the jury was sent out at 11.45 on Monday 20 November. The long wait for a verdict had begun. At precisely 4.25 that afternoon, the jury was recalled and as they had not yet agreed on any verdicts they were sent to a hotel for the night.

After all the hype, the unforeseen twists and turns, the truly sensational evidence and cast of characters involved in the trial, the waiting period was charged with more anxiety and expectation than Bennett had ever experienced. Now, as reporters hung around the restaurant and corridors not daring to leave for fear of missing the call to Court 3, it seemed more like an airport lounge than ever.

As news deadlines came and went there was an obvious tension in the air and once again it was the *Sun*'s Simon Hughes who came up with the simplest image to express what most of them were thinking, 'Is she going to get off, because if so all I've written will go down the gurgler.'

Confused by his cockney drift, Bennett asked him what he meant, and laughed and shrugged his shoulders as the reporter held his nose and pulled an imaginary toilet chain.

Then, at 3.05 p.m., the suspense was broken as over the tannoy came the summons for everyone connected with the case of Rosemary West to go to Court 3. By now the Chief Constable of Gloucestershire, Tony Butler, had arrived and along with everyone else was somehow squeezed into the crowded court. Only Rose West and the judge had a place to themselves.

In the time-honoured fashion the court clerk asked the jury foreman if they had reached a unanimous verdict on any of the counts and he replied 'yes'.

Rose West was told to stand but only one voice at a time disturbed the absolute silence as the clerk and jury foreman continued their exchange.

Clerk: 'On Count One [Charmaine], have you reached a verdict on which you are all agreed?'

Foreman: 'Yes.'

Clerk: 'Do you find the defendant guilty or not guilty of murder?'

Foreman: 'Guilty.'

There was a faint, muffled gasp from some unidentified corner of the court then the clerk continued to read out the remaining counts all the way up to nine, all of which were still undecided until he arrived at Count Ten, Heather West.

Clerk: 'Do you find the defendant guilty or not guilty of murder?'

Foreman: 'Guilty.'

Bennett's eyes fell on Rose West as she was helped out of the dock. Now there were tears all right, real ones – but not for her victims, for herself.

When the judge sent the jury back out to continue their deliberations, Bennett looked around the courtroom. Ferguson and Wass had an air of resignation, Leveson and Chubb appeared calm, no doubt trying to take in what had just happened, and the police too, in line with the Senior Investigating Officer's instructions, were just trying to keep a lid on it. Back in the library, away from public and media scrutiny, there were hugs and handshakes all round for they were in no doubt justice had been done.

Even better, it seemed to the police that the jury were carrying out their task with the same forensic approach as Leveson's, for they had found Rose West guilty of the first murder the prosecution alleged she had committed and the last, raising hopes she would be convicted of the others, too.

This time they did not have so long to wait.

At 4.30 p.m. the jury signified they had reached another verdict and on their return declared Rose West guilty of the murder of Shirley Robinson. Their work done for the day they were sent back to their hotel on the outskirts of Bournemouth.

Rose West left the court looking stunned that in the eyes of the world she was now a murderer. Outside, reporters were impatient for a reaction from either the Chief Constable or the Senior Investigating Officer, but now was not the time. The liaison officers were already on the phone to the victims' relatives and some of the witnesses.

That night, they ate at The Ship as usual, only this time they were joined by the Chief and the lawyers, and when Leveson remarked he was 'greedy and wanted the lot' he did not mean the menu. There was no standing on station, no order of rank seating plan, everyone just mixed in, making it probably the most relaxed they had been since the night the entire investigation team took over the pub in Gloucester. The Chief Constable reckoned it was the best night he had had since his days as a detective sergeant.

On his way to court the following morning, Bennett popped into a hardware shop and bought a sink plug and chain, wrapped them inside a note he had signed that read 'I'll no longer be needing this, perhaps you can make use of it?', sealed it all in an envelope and handed it to Simon Hughes.

All the other reporters there wondered why the Senior Investigating Officer, who had barely exchanged a handful of words with any of them during the proceedings, should be communicating with the *Sun* in this way – until Hughes opened it up and seeing the joke laughed out loud. Shortly after that, one of the *Daily Express* reporters, Alun Rees, sought out Bennett to tell him they would not be running the Sharon Compton story after all.

The real unfinished business, though, was still just that, and a little after noon the jury returned and a note was passed to the judge. It asked two questions, the first of which was: 'Is the total absence of direct evidence, other than the presence of their remains linking a victim to 25 Cromwell Street, an obstacle to bringing in a guilty verdict?'

To this the judge replied, 'The answer is no, provided always you draw the inference, and feel sure about it, that the prosecution invite you to draw.'

The second question, 'Is the jury entitled to rely on a combination of the presence of the remains together with conclusions drawn from the evidence of other actions taken by the defendant with, for example, Caroline Owens, Miss A, etc.?', drew the following ruling: 'The answer is yes, once again, provided you can be sure about the inference you are being invited to draw. I think your question was intended to include, not only the remains, but the articles found with the remains?'

The foreman replied, 'Yes, my Lord.'

Justice Mantell explained his answers in more depth and the jury retired once again to consider the remaining verdicts, though there was now little doubt what they would be.

At 12.53, just in time to catch the BBC's regional television bulletin, which broke the news, the jury returned and delivered seven more guilty verdicts. There was a moment of silence followed by gasps and a cry from the public gallery as all eyes zeroed in on Rose West.

Justice Mantell did not waste words on her, his tone as cold and ruthless as she had once been. 'Stand up. Rosemary Pauline West, on each of the ten counts of murder of which you have been unanimously convicted by the jury, the sentence is one of life imprisonment. If attention is paid to what I think, you will never be released. Take her down.'

And with that Fred West's widow, the surviving half of Britain's most infamous serial killing couple, who for more than twenty years presided over Gloucester's equally grotesquely named 'House of Horrors', disappeared from view.

After a momentary pause, a mental bridge to a more salutary tone, the judge addressed the court. 'Mr Leveson, the Gloucestershire Police deserve to be commended for the meticulous way in which they have conducted the investigation of this case, as do Professor Knight and Dr Whittaker for the part they have each played.

'Members of the jury, you will never have had a more important job to do in your lives. I am fully aware of the sacrifices each one of you has made in giving your time and great effort in helping to decide this case. I am also aware of the great stress that it must have placed each of you under. You deserve my thanks and your country's for the part you have played.

'If it is what you wish, but only if it is what you wish, you are excused from ever serving on a jury again.'

The four other charges Rose West faced, two of rape and two of indecent assault, remained on the file.

The courtroom cleared quickly and back in the library, where the news was already being relayed to the witnesses and victims' families, the hugs and handshakes were even more vigorous than before, the judge's public commendation the perfect seal on what had been achieved.

As Bennett, Leveson, Chubb and Cole exchanged farewells, the QC asked the detective to keep him informed on how the families and witnesses were. Each then went their separate ways.

Looking forward as ever, the Senior Investigating Officer already had his mind on the news conferences to come, which were never his favourite pastime. All he wanted to do now was pack up his things, say goodbye to Winchester, and get home.

THIRTY-EIGHT

Within minutes of the jury returning its damning verdict on her, there were mutterings from Rose West's solicitor of an appeal and fresh protestations from Leo Goatley of her innocence.

The Director of Public Prosecutions, Barbara Mills QC, issued a statement praising the police for their meticulous investigation, a hallmark of which had been the close cooperation between the CPS, prosecuting counsel and Gloucestershire Constabulary. Bennett wished it were that simple for him, that he could just release a few words, add a few thank yous and depart the scene, though he had a feeling he was about to face as demanding a grilling from the media as anything he had experienced previously.

In truth, he need not have worried – not then, anyway – for Rose West's conviction, now for ten murders, and the judge's recommendation she should never be released, was still fresh and the newspapers, television and radio were now legally free to tell the story in full. That was more than enough to keep them occupied; trickier issues could be delved into later. Not only that, he had now had the chance to browse through the official reports into the affair, which basically posed the question, how could the Wests have got away with it for so long?

First the executive summary of the Children Act-driven but completely independent review by the Bridge Consultancy. This had been suggested by the Chief Officers' Strategy Group and commissioned by the Area Child Protection Committee (ACPC) to look into the deaths of Charmaine and Heather West. Then the separate report on runaways from Gloucestershire care homes. At first glance, it appeared that none of the caring agencies was being harshly criticised or blamed for the tragedies. There were concerns about missing social services and NSPCC files lost over the years, and recommendations. But everything the reports were now putting forward was in the context of working with today's values rather than those of twenty-five years before, and this was a true analysis rather than an excuse.

Remarkably, by the last week of the trial, of the hundreds of known visitors to Cromwell Street only nine had not been traced. A public appeal then would have led to fresh speculation and brought criticism from both the defence and the judge. There was nothing to suggest any harm had come to any of them but at least the information could now be released.

That information, along with his statement and copies of two huge, ring-bound press packs, one sixty-six pages long that was prepared before the trial and a second containing a further fifty-five pages of detail, including descriptions of the nine girls still outstanding, were in the briefcase that he took with him to the media centre – a grand name for a large hall with a stage.

Alongside Bennett on the podium were the Chief Constable, Tony Butler, and Michael Honey, the Chief Executive of Gloucestershire County Council. As the television cameras rolled and flashbulbs flashed the Chief Constable spoke first.

He praised the courage of witnesses who had themselves been victims of the Wests and without whose personal sacrifices the police could not have pursued the case. He paid tribute to the strength shown by the victims' relatives and the work of Victim Support, but reserved the highest praise for the man who had headed the inquiry from the beginning.

'It is impossible for me to overstate the dedication, leadership and compassion of Detective Superintendent John Bennett, ably supported by Detective Chief Inspector Terry Moore and a number of officers and members of the civilian staff. The work that they have [all] undertaken has been beyond the call of duty but underlines the compassionate nature of British policing at its best.'

Keen not to miss out anyone, the Chief Constable's credits went on to include Gloucestershire Social Services and the whole of the legal team. Although Bennett had some idea of what the Chief was going to say he had not read the finished statement and so was surprised and somewhat overwhelmed.

Then it was his turn. Looking out into the sea of reporters, he emphasised the resilience and dedication of all his staff and the excessive demands the investigation had made on their personal lives.

He touched on the considerable scientific help needed to identify victims dating back twenty-seven years and how their families' uncertainty had been replaced by the terrible circumstances of their deaths – not only that, they had been continually visited and harassed by reporter after reporter and that had only added to their distress.

'No one can appreciate the pain and suffering they have been through over the past eighteen months and I now appeal again that the families be left alone to rebuild their lives.'

As he approached the end of his statement, with the hope that everyone who had been touched by the case would now be able to put it behind them and move on, he felt his emotions well up inside and his voice started to falter, just like during the inquest. Then, he had put it down to the nature of the occasion but this was the first time his emotions had threatened to get the better of him when addressing an audience and he was relieved to leave the stage to the next speaker.

There was little respite, though, and Bennett was immediately escorted to the impromptu studio where the television interviews were taking place. He was quite used to the concept of being questioned by journalists on a one-to-one basis but this was not what he had expected. For a start there were three times as many reporters as he was told there would be and the way they were lined up meant they would be right in his face.

As he sat uncomfortably in his chair, he repeated his mantra that he would take only two questions from each of them and would not answer questions about his feelings or his family.

The chain was fairly swift, each asking relatively similar

questions, some even repeating what the reporter before had asked. Some asked about the nine missing girls, others how many more searches would be made. Were there any more victims? Were the nine missing girls victims? Did he think they would be found? A few erred towards probing his personal feelings and were politely rebuffed and told they had lost a question.

By the time it was all over, Bennett was physically and emotionally exhausted and got his driver to head for the rugby club, where Paul Stallard had arranged for the rest of the team to gather and watch the news on a wide-screen television. Cheers and handshakes heralded their arrival.

Later that night the Chief Constable was due at the BBC to be interviewed by Jeremy Paxman on *Newsnight*. Bennett, Moore and some of the others joined by Ken Daun had stayed on at Netley to watch – as the Chief had directed.

There was beer and wine in their makeshift kitchen but no one had more than the occasional glass. Considering they had just put away one of the country's most infamous serial killers there was no air of celebration. Instead, they squeezed onto the single bed that doubled as a settee and huddled in front of the portable television.

Paxman wasted no time on the investigation or the successful prosecution of Rose West; both topics had been covered in detail elsewhere. Instead he went straight to why the killing had gone on for so long and the failure of the authorities to act earlier.

Tony Butler had never expected any plaudits, quite the contrary, and that was why he wanted them to watch the interview so they could fill him in on how it went. Even so, he had not expected such a persistent and virulent inquisition that led him to respond that he had not come to take part in a quiz. Still, the Netley audience reckoned he had done as well as he could and paged him to that effect.

As Bennett, Moore, Griff and Grimshaw began the journey back to Gloucestershire the following morning, Winchester was noticeably quiet. There were no hoards of photographers and television crews lining the street and no satellite trucks, but although the media circus had moved on it had not finished with them just yet for there, in thick bold print on the front page of that morning's *Daily Express* was the headline:

Claim by witness as mass killer gets 10 life sentences:
ROSE'S HOME WAS A POLICE BROTHEL

Alongside was the photograph of Rose West issued by the police and underneath it was an introduction that read:

Policemen used the home of Rose and Fred West as a brothel while the evil couple were torturing and killing young girls, a witness claimed last night.

According to the *Express*, it was an 'exclusive' by Nicola Briggs and Alun Rees, the reporter who had told Bennett the paper would not use the story, based as it surely was on information given them by Sharon Compton – though the newspaper called her simply 'Sharon' – which everyone agreed was unreliable.

Bennett was incensed, as were the others with him and everyone else in the MIR who had tipped him off. Inside pages two and three were reports of the end of the trial and calls for a public inquiry by Gloucester MP Douglas French, while the story from the front page reported that 'Police must have heard screams inside number 25' and that although 'Sharon's' identity was being kept secret by the *Daily Express* she would be interviewed by the Police Complaints Authority.

There were allegations concerning 'raincoat man', who was wearing a police uniform, and many of the other claims she had first made to the investigating team – all of which had been painstakingly followed up and caused them to doubt her truthfulness.

There were quotes about police officers having drinks at the bar and seeing the same policeman there a number of times.

'I'm not sure if they were involved in anything other than sex. I don't see anything wrong if they were there for that alone, but they must have heard the screams. The house wasn't that big they can't have thought the cries were just people indulging in kinky sex', Sharon was quoted as saying.

As angry as he was at the unfair stigma this would leave on both the investigation team and the constabulary, Bennett was also saddened at the effect the reports would have on their relationship with the victims' families, who were not aware of the background and were now bound to question the police's past involvement with the Wests.

What also vexed him greatly was that he had gone as far as he could without breaking the law or betraying confidences to guide both reporters and ensure their work was accurate. Apart from anything else, he had made it clear that the description of 25 Cromwell Street that 'Sharon' was giving was not as it was when she was there and that both reporters had also had doubts about her information. He had always feared his warnings were falling on stony ground, now he had the proof.

There was little doubt what that afternoon's news conference at Cheltenham would focus on, as other reporters and news crews were certain to pick up on the story. There was no doubt either that it would all be referred to the Police Complaints Authority and an investigation mounted. While Bennett was sure what the outcome would be, it would cast a cloud over all their good work until it was finished, and having been involved with similar inquiries himself, he knew it would take months to complete.

The *Express* 'revelations' were the main subject of interest along with the nine missing girls, but the event had an air of after the Lord Mayor's Show about it. Bennett had had enough and the conference had been arranged to give reporters an opportunity to talk to some of the other key officers on the case, but few reports of this were broadcast or printed; the story had already moved on.

That evening Bennett took his wife to the nearby Rising Sun Hotel. It was their first evening and meal out alone together for almost a year.

After a drink at the bar, they made their way to the restaurant area and were seated near a centre pillar. Having both ordered mussels as starters and a bottle of Muscadet they turned to what the immediate future would bring – the internal investigation, whether further searches were likely, the trial of Fred's brother John West and the distinct possibility of an appeal by Rose West.

As they stacked the mussel shells neatly round their plates and awaited the main course, the conversation waned and Bennett's mind drifted onto his priorities for the following day until he felt his hand being gently shaken and it startled him.

'Is my company that boring?' quipped his wife.

Without realising, he had dozed off, almost as soon as his head had touched the pillar.

THIRTY-NINE

Although no one on the investigation was aware of it then, approval of their work was on its way from senior members of the royal family and in the weeks to come there would be praise aplenty, though, as ever, it did not come without a fair measure of angst.

On the other hand, and to no one's surprise, the *Daily Express* kept up the attack. Its front-page splash the following morning was:

Officers knew girls were being abused at West Home
ROSE SIX POLICE NAMED

Below followed more allegations that officers used the address as a brothel and drinking club and that girls were available for sex 'during the Wests' killing spree', adding piously that the information would be passed to the Police Complaints Authority.

There were more referrals to the story of the day before, of 'raincoat man', and even a quote from Bennett from the news conference in Cheltenham virtually pleading with the *Express* to pass on the information to the police.

The MP for Gloucester, Douglas French, joined in, repeating his call for a public inquiry, though the Chief Constable had already set in motion an investigation that would be carried out by West Mercia Police, who would have full access to the West HOLMES database and all the documents in the MIR.

As the *Express* stretched out the story into a third day, it informed readers it had promised the Police Complaints Authority it would 'forward the names of 6 police officers' allegedly linked to Fred and Rose West's home, given to them by Sharon X and an 'anonymous former Gloucestershire police officer'.

The report also carried more detail of what the mysterious 'Sharon X' – who most people involved with the investigation knew full well was Sharon Compton – was alleging, namely that the police had failed to investigate her claims about police visiting Cromwell Street when it was a brothel and that the West Inquiry officers had treated her so badly her health had suffered.

Bennett knew this would mean both he and her liaison officer Detective Constable Dave Stephens would come under the closest scrutiny, and although he was certain they would be fully vindicated he could not help thinking Stephens, Barbara Harrison and Debbie Willats would be devastated, particularly after all their good work. He always feared their involvement with Sharon Compton would end this way and yet he still had genuine feelings of sympathy for her, as he knew Stephens and the others did as well. As for the *Express* and the reporters involved, his thoughts were far less compassionate.

The question of whether the police should be searching anywhere else for remains had still to be resolved and after trawling through the HOLMES database yet again, Bennett remained of the opinion there was just no information that warranted it. One or two areas were revisited just to update the database but when he posed the question to Moore and Griff they, too, agreed they had no evidence to justify digging anywhere else.

A detailed report was prepared which, after due consideration, the Chief Constable rubber-stamped – just as he said he would.

Even so, it did not stop the *Daily Mirror* taking matters into its own hands.

Reporters hired ground-penetrating radar equipment similar to that used by the police and scoured the local council-owned Castlemeads car park just outside Gloucester. They had pinpointed it from a description Fred West had given Janet Leach and even though the newspaper was told he had given a similar description of another site to his son Stephen – no doubt as a ruse to see who he could trust – they were determined to go ahead.

That they went about the search when the area was still in use meant it was doomed from the start, not that there was any evidence to support either location anyway. Maybe the newspaper was just trying to force the police into action, but when the car park attendant and the council complained it gave them reason to bring the operation to a halt.

It was written up the next day along the lines of 'Cops halt Daily Mirror hunt for more missing bodies', though relations between the tabloid and the Gloucestershire Constabulary could hardly have been more strained.

Even though she was still bound by her confidentiality agreement, Janet Leach had acquired legal aid and was suing the constabulary for negligence on the grounds she should have been offered counselling, either during the investigation or soon after.

Right from her introduction as appropriate adult, Bennett had been worried how she might be affected by what she heard and what she was exposed to. He had spoken, and written, to her employers making it clear she could have the same counselling as officers on the case. He did not think there was much else he could have done.

In response to her claim, the constabulary argued that the independent nature of her role ruled out any duty of care they might have. Her special relationship was with Fred West and not the police. Although a judge at Bristol County Court threw out her claim, Janet Leach appealed. The Appeal Court in part agreed with the Bristol judge's decision, that it was never envisaged the police in such circumstances would owe a duty of care towards an appropriate adult. It also adjudged that on the issue of failing to provide counselling services, this would be allowed to proceed to trial, though ultimately the case was not pursued.

There was better news of the nine outstanding girls mentioned at the Cheltenham news conference, as all but one were found safe and well. Quite apart from those he was specifically looking for, Nick Churchill had traced an additional 110 missing girls, and as a direct result of the inquiry, the police eventually introduced new procedures for dealing with missing persons which even included a redefinition of the term 'missing' in an attempt to ensure fewer slipped through the net in future.

Of the nine, the exception was Donna Lynn Moore, believed to be the daughter of an American service member, who was also known as 'Yankee Doodle'. While there was no doubt that a girl of that name and vague description had visited 25 Cromwell Street at some time, continued enquiries over the years by both the police in the United Kingdom and the armed forces in America had failed to find either her or any other member of her family.

No doubt the public appeals had played a part in tracing the others but now it was time to focus on some of the media's more questionable involvement throughout the investigation. The scale and range of payments to some of the witnesses had already been exposed during the trial, but the boundary between privacy and public interest had been blurred. After earlier discussion with Neil Butterfield and latterly Brian Leveson, it was decided that detailed reports channelled through the Crown Prosecution Service, the Lord Chancellor's Office and the Chief Constable should be sent to all the media regulators. The documents would set out what had happened and include complaints and recommendations designed to safeguard future trials from being jeopardised, especially by potential witnesses being offered inducements to sell their stories before the end of proceedings.

Brian Leveson announced to Mr Justice Mantell that he had been invited to report the effect of the media's involvement with the witnesses to the Attorney-General. Looking on, Bennett knew that his Chief Constable would certainly be making his views known and hoped that it would have an effect, and that no other senior investigating officer would have to contend with such intrusion in the future.

To the disbelief of most people on the investigation, the various bodies found that the media had operated within its voluntary code of conduct – though it emerged the code was already under review and changes were in the pipeline. The review had been instigated directly as a result of the actions of the media during the investigation and the concern expressed by the reports the commission had received. Now there are much tighter restrictions on the payment or offer of payment to a witness, or anyone likely to be called as a witness, and whenever such payment or offer is made details have to be passed to the prosecution and the defence.

As exhibits officer, Paul Kerrod – whose wife, in yet another of the coincidences the investigation seemed to throw up, had once lived in the ground-floor flat of 25 Midland Road – now had the Herculean task of making sure that everything that was seized during the investigation was returned to its rightful owners. There was so much, it had taken removal vans more than three days to cart it all to a nearby military base, where it was stored in a hangar. As for all the books, magazines and other documents still in the incident room, someone had to decide what could be destroyed and what needed to be kept.

In terms of sorting out who was entitled to what, the West family was no different from any other, and Fred West's death had made it even more complicated as the Official Solicitor, Peter Harris, was appointed to act on behalf of the younger children. Usually they were able to agree who should have what, and when they could not there was always a court to adjudicate. The whole process went on for almost a year.

More controversial was the Official Solicitor's decision to include as part of West's estate material disclosed by the police to the defence, including all the tapes of his interviews. Although some were played in court, and their content widely reported, only a very small number of people within the investigation had heard the others. Quite apart from their prurient nature, the police were concerned the decision could embarrass witnesses whose involvement had, up to then, remained secret, with an obvious knock-on effect for future investigations. Despite their objections, access was granted under licence to selected authors and film-makers. Though the circumstances that made this possible may have been unique, more recent legislation has prevented it ever recurring.

It was not all doom and gloom, though, and calls and messages of congratulations were received by the Chief Constable or went direct to the investigation. Some of them, from other forces both within the UK and in mainland Europe, included requests to see the MIR.

If that sort of response was, perhaps, expected, a request from Prince Charles to pay a private visit took everyone by surprise.

It was quickly agreed and arranged for the morning of 19 December. All the officers who had stayed with the investigation from its early days were present, and photographs and the model of 25 Cromwell Street were dusted down and put on display. The Chief Constable introduced His Royal Highness to Bennett and Moore and left them to introduce members of the team and describe their roles.

From the outset, the Prince showed both his interest and compassion and surprised everyone with his knowledge of the investigation, adding that the Queen, too, had taken a personal interest. He listened intently and spoke individually to each of the officers, asking questions and empathising when their answers revealed more of what they had been through. The visit was scheduled to last 50 minutes but the Prince was so engrossed he overran by at least half an hour and made a big impression on everyone there.

A new year dawned and with it, on 17 January 1996, Rosemary West's leave to appeal. After all the post-trial rumblings the only wonder was it had taken so long, for there were no surprises as to the grounds for the plea, which were as follows:

- The trial judge had wrongly exercised his discretion in refusing to stay the indictment.
- The trial judge erred in law in admitting the similar fact evidence. Alternatively, he wrongly exercised his discretion in allowing this evidence to go before the jury.
- That having admitted the similar fact evidence, the trial judge wrongly exercised his discretion in refusing to sever the murders of Charmaine West, Shirley Robinson and Heather West.
- That the verdicts in respect of Lynda Gough, Carol Cooper, Lucy Partington, Thérèse Siegenthaler, Shirley Hubbard, Juanita Mott and Alison Chambers are unsafe and unsatisfactory in that the evidence of similar fact witnesses was tainted by the interference of the media.
- That the trial judge erred in law in failing to remind the jury of the defence case on 22 November when they sought further direction on the similar fact evidence.

The hearing was scheduled for March that year and although the inquiry team was sure it would fail, they had other matters to keep them occupied. There was the impending trial of Fred West's brother John on four specimen counts of raping and indecently assaulting Anne Marie and one other girl, and another trial of West's cousin John Hill for rape and indecent assault. Once again, the need for sensitive care of all the witnesses was paramount, though the outcome bore a chilling resemblance to previous events.

The trial of John West would not, however, take place until long after Rose West's appeal. It was once again prosecuted by Brian Leveson and began on Monday 25 November 1996 – two days after the first anniversary of Rose West's conviction. He pleaded not guilty to all the charges and by the end of the fourth day all the evidence had been heard. The jury retired to consider its verdict and West's bail was renewed as it had been on each of the previous days.

At about 9 p.m. that evening his wife found him hanging in the garage of their home in Gloucester. Just like his older brother Fred, he had taken his own life.

John Hill would have to wait until the middle of May 1998 for his trial, when he pleaded not guilty to rape and three charges of indecent assault. He was found guilty on each of the four counts and sentenced to four years' imprisonment.

Inquests into the deaths of Ann McFall and Rena West finally took place in Gloucester in February 1996 and were conducted along the same lines as all the others, essentially to complete the formalities as no one had been convicted of their murders, though they did include one startling revelation.

In his evidence, Bennett related for the first time in public how the investigation had traced a friend of Fred West's mother Daisy, who had died in 1968. According to the friend, Daisy knew her son had killed the pregnant Ann and buried her in Kempley woods because he had confessed to her in 1967, though the police were not told until after the investigation had begun some twenty-seven years later!

The coroner formally returned verdicts of unlawful killing.

The year of 1996 had become one for dotting i's and crossing t's, as in July another inquest formally concluded that Fred West took his own life, while the outcome of the investigation into the Sharon Compton affair was expected in the autumn.

Looming yet even larger on the horizon was the question of what to do with 25 Cromwell Street itself.

Opinions were divided, for while many were appalled by its presence, some argued its notoriety could become an asset to the city, a macabre tourist attraction. The notion that in years to come it would assume 'historic' importance was perhaps behind another suggestion that it should be converted into a museum with a plaque to commemorate the girls who were murdered there.

Although this was not a police matter, Bennett knew it was not what the families wanted. He was hoping the city council would buy the property, and perhaps the one next door, knock it down and give the victims' relatives a say in what replaced it. After a lengthy consultation process, that was exactly what they resolved to do.

The Wests' house would be raised to the ground and replaced by a pathway with no plaque or any other indication of what had happened or been there before. Bennett also recommended that Sergeant Pete Maunder should return to supervise the demolition and that the contractors would be told to take all bricks and other material to a landfill site where it would be ground to dust or incinerated so that nothing remained and no souvenirs could be taken.

If Prince Charles's visit had been a surprise, so, too, was the handwritten letter Bennett received from the Home Secretary, Michael Howard. It read:

> I have had a number of very complimentary reports about the way which you and your team investigated and assisted the prosecution case of Fred and Rosemary West and I wanted to add my personal congratulations to you and your team for your excellent work.
>
> The investigation must have been very difficult and demanding not least because of the scale of the enquiry, the logistical problems caused by the length of time some of the bodies had been buried, and the sheer horror of the crimes. You and your team did a wonderful job in bringing together the evidence, preparing the case for trial and assisting the prosecution during the trial process.
>
> Thank you for all your dedication and hard work.

Bennett was already in the process of preparing a report to the Chief Constable to ask him to consider commendations for the team and the letter added considerable weight to his case.

Rose West's leave to appeal was due to be heard by the Lord Chief Justice, Lord Taylor of Gosforth, Justice Mitchell and Justice Newman on 18 March, which was also Bennett's birthday – what was it about the West and Bennett birthdays? – though she was not required to be there.

Arriving at the Royal Courts of Justice, Bennett, Moore and Griff had no real purpose as they were only there to witness the outcome but the sight of camera crews and reporters jockeying for position outside took them back to Winchester. Perhaps their lack of direct involvement explained their buoyant mood, in contrast to the more subdued Brian Leveson whose mind was locked into the legal battle ahead, though he was still concerned to ask after the health and welfare of the witnesses, the victims' families and 'the team'.

Unlike the trial, Richard Ferguson went first, guiding the judges through each of the grounds of appeal, explaining why the jury's verdict should be overturned. Leveson countered, and even though a week had been set aside they had completed much of their work by the end of the first day, and by lunchtime on the second they had all but finished.

That afternoon, the Lord Chief Justice adjourned and in less than 20 minutes returned to announce that Rose West's leave to appeal was refused and their reasons would be published later.

Pausing only to congratulate Leveson and Andrew Chubb once more, Bennett went straight to the court's police office and scribbled out a press release which he faxed to the Chief Constable and the force press office:

Following the decision of the Court of Appeal refusing leave to appeal of Rosemary West on 10 counts of murder

Detective Superintendent John Bennett said, 'The legal process is now complete. It is hoped that now the media will allow the victims, their families and the witnesses to continue their lives in privacy, as far as possible to put the tragic events of the past especially the past two years aside.'

Outside the court, news crews and reporters were waiting and Bennett voiced the statement for the benefit of television and radio but did not take questions.

When, eventually, judgment was published on 2 April, the reasons for refusing Rose West's leave to appeal were unequivocal:

> Mr Ferguson argued that there was a dearth of evidence against the appellant. We cannot agree.
>
> At the heart of the case was the incontrovertible evidence of the bodies buried at 25 Cromwell Street, of the sadistic sexual abuse they had suffered in life and of the fact that the applicant [Rose West] and Fred West lived in the house together throughout the period. Given, as we have held, that the similar fact evidence was admissible, it showed that the applicant and Fred West were sadistically abusing young girls in the cellar of their house for their joint pleasure. There was the evidence of Fred West's admissions coupled with his late confession that he had been protecting the applicant.
>
> The jury had the advantage of hearing and seeing the applicant give evidence and be cross-examined. Clearly they rejected her evidence. We fully understand their doing so. The concept of all these murders and burials taking place at the applicant's home and concurrently grave sexual abuse of other young girls being committed by both husband and wife together, without the latter being party to the killings is, in our view, clearly one the jury were entitled to reject.

The evidence in its totality was overwhelming. For the reasons we have given in detail, we had no doubt that the verdicts were safe and accordingly we refuse the application.

Once again, Leo Goatley hinted at an appeal, this time to the Court of Human Rights, and the Criminal Cases Review Commission, though his client eventually decided not to pursue the matter.

On the basis of Bennett's recommendations, twenty-one officers who made up the main MIR staff, inquiry teams and liaison officers were highly commended and another ten, including Chief Superintendent Ken Daun, were commended. A further thirty-seven officers who conducted searches at Gloucester and Kempley or were otherwise involved were also singled out.

The final number had disappointed him as many more of the names he had put forward were removed because the Chief Constable's office felt the list was too long, though Tony Butler made sure the Senior Investigating Officer's name was added to the highly commended category.

The citation that was published in a special police bulletin borrowed heavily from Judge Mantell's remarks after the trial that: 'The magnitude of the enquiry, whilst having been supported by the entire force, placed a considerable onus on departments, staff and the officers principally involved in organising and pursuing the investigation itself. Even now, certain facets of the work of some officers and their true commitment cannot for reasons of confidentiality, be fully expressed. Although it is impossible to fully acknowledge all the staff involved in this case, the following awards are made to recognise the outstanding contributions made by these officers.'

The Chief Constable also made a personal award of commendation to Syd Mann of Gloucester City Council, who had been closely involved with excavations at 25 Cromwell Street. All of the awards were due to be presented at a private ceremony later in the year, but before then came news of another honour that arrived from Buckingham Palace via the Chief Constable.

Leaving home as Bennett did before the post arrived, it was a phone call from Tony Butler that brought the news the Senior Investigating Officer was to receive the Queen's Police Medal in the next birthday honours list. A letter was on its way but he had to keep it to himself until it was announced officially. He could hardly believe what he had heard. Joining him in the hall, his wife could see he was shocked and was equally overcome when he explained why.

From the outset, Bennett considered it as a tribute to the whole team rather than to him personally and was actually quite embarrassed at some of the gushing praise now coming his way, which included a press release issued by the Chief Constable: 'This honour for Detective Superintendent Bennett is richly deserved and not only underlines his distinguished career in Gloucestershire, but recognises the dedication and leadership he showed in the investigation of the Cromwell Street murder enquiry. His personal contribution to that investigation cannot be overstated.'

The investiture at Buckingham Palace, where the Queen would make the award personally, was scheduled for 17 July. The Chief Constable was planning to hold Cromwell Street commendation ceremonies on 16 and 17 July. Bennett wanted to attend both so he could add his own thanks and congratulations to the team but even he could not be in two places at once. He and the other highly commended officers would see the Chief Constable on the 16th, the following day he would keep his appointment with the Queen at the Palace.

There, standing in line with all the other royal award recipients, he had time to reflect on his career and in particular the last two and half years. How as a young boy he had always wanted to be a policeman, and how he had so enjoyed his career but never envisaged that he would rise so high in his profession or deal with such an investigation or receive such an honour. With his wife and two sons watching from the wings, it was a moving experience and one he would never forget, especially his brief conversation with the Queen.

'Dealing with such horrible crimes must have been a terrible experience for you and all your officers, I felt for you all,' she said as she pinned the QPM on his chest.

'Yes, thank you Ma'am' and he bowed, took one step back and the Queen moved on.

The investigation's reputation now extended far beyond Gloucestershire. As a result Bennett was constantly asked to lecture other forces on the lessons of Cromwell Street. There was more than a hint of déjà vu when the Chief Constable passed on a request from the Belgian police for him to travel to Brussels to assist in an investigation with striking similarities to the West Inquiry. The subject was the paedophile Marc Dutroux, though Bennett's involvement remained confidential until it was leaked by the Belgian Justice of Investigation.

The evidence of abduction, abuse and murder all recalled the darkest chapters of the previous two years, memories he had hoped to forget, and all of it complicated by the search for victims, the recovery of human remains and media intrusion. It was obvious why they wanted Bennett on board and even allowing for Belgium's different legal requirements, he was able to give them an idea of how the investigation might develop and how best to handle it.

It was a gruelling two weeks, consisting mainly of over 14-hour days at various locations while the almost Napoleonic system of justice did not make it any easier. Neither the local nor the national police force was in charge and certainly not a senior investigating officer. That role was undertaken by a justice or magistrate and Bennett was just thankful he had not had to operate under such a system.

To this day, the West Inquiry remains a source of help and advice to other forces, particularly in the way it was managed, how it carried out the searches and its relationship with the media. It forms a part of training courses for detectives of all ranks and some of its officers have been involved in high-profile investigations across Europe and given advice to those being undertaken as far away as Australia.

At shortly after 9 a.m. on 25 September 1996, Bennett picked up the phone in his office to hear the voice of Deputy Chief Constable Nigel Burgess who wanted to inform him that the Police Complaints Authority had at last received the results of the West Mercia Police investigation into allegations made by Sharon Compton as reported in the *Daily Express* and found no truth in any of them. Complaints against him personally had also been thrown out.

As a result, Burgess went on, an unusually long release would be issued by the Police Complaints Authority setting out its conclusions in detail, and he would be making a similar statement.

What it all amounted to was that the constabulary, its officers and the team had been completely cleared of any suggestion of improper or unprofessional behaviour, both collectively and individually, and although Bennett had never been in any doubt that would be the outcome, it was the final endorsement of their work.*

The report levelled some criticism at the *Daily Express* and *News of the World* who published the allegations, as did the Deputy Chief Constable. After further consideration by the police and the Crown Prosecution Service it was decided not to prosecute Sharon Compton for wasting police time.

By the time the internal investigation had been completed, the cost of the West Inquiry to the Gloucestershire Constabulary and the taxpayers of the county was more than £2 million over budget, which, following the Chief Constable's unsuccessful application, was paid for without any extra financial help from the government.

---

* See Appendix One for the full text of the PCA conclusions.

Gloucester City Council finally purchased Nos 23 and 25 Cromwell Street and in accordance with the wishes of the victims' families set in motion plans to demolish them both. A note was made to inform members of the West family, who wanted to pay their respects to Heather and the other girls, when work was due to begin.

Buying the two properties, grinding what they could to dust and burning what they could not, cost the council around £120,000, but no one who was asked complained for by now the address was considered a blight on the city, a stigma that had to be removed.

The cameras that returned to witness demolition, which began early on the morning of 7 October, were far fewer than at the height of the investigation two and a half years earlier. By the end of the week, the country's most notorious address was just a pile of rubble.

Today, there is no No. 25 in Cromwell Street.

In its place is a neat pathway leading to St Michael's Square with cobbled edging, shrubs, grass verges on both sides and cast-iron bollards at either end. If you did not know any different, you would think it had always been there and probably in time the marks on the wall of the Seventh Day Adventist church made by Fred West's unlawful extension will disappear as well.

And yet, most people who had anything to do with the place, like Detective Superintendent John Bennett, would never find it as easy to erase such distressing, deep-seated memories and for that reason alone he has not been back. He has seen film and photographs of how it is now but he has never returned.

Nor was he ever a believer in coincidence – let alone the sequence that arose during the investigation – but if fate had chosen him to deal with the tragic events that unfolded he could have asked for no more than the confidence his chief officers had shown in him and to be supported and aided by a team for whom no problem was insurmountable and whose loyalty and commitment knew no bounds.

For that he would forever be grateful.

SEQUENCE OF EVENTS

1941

29 September   Frederick 'Fred' Walter Stephen West born in Much Marcle, Herefordshire.

1953

29 November   Rosemary 'Rose' Pauline Letts born in Northam, Devon.

1961

1 November   Fred West found not guilty of incest at Hereford Assizes.

1963

22 March   Charmaine Carol May West born to Rena West in Coatbridge, Scotland.

1964

6 July   Anna-Marie 'Anne Marie' West born to Fred and Rena West in Glasgow.

1965

11 December   Fred West returns to Much Marcle with Charmaine and Anne Marie, without Rena West.

December   Fred West asks Hereford Social Services to take Charmaine and Anne Marie into care.

1966

23 February   Rena West joins Fred West in Gloucester, Charmaine and Anne Marie are returned to them.

July   Charmaine and Anne Marie West placed in care.

1 August   Charmaine and Anne Marie West returned to Fred and Rena West.

September   Fred West, Ann McFall, Charmaine and Anne Marie live together in Gloucester, Rena West having left.

1967

July	Rena West returns, Fred, Charmaine and Anne Marie in Gloucester, Ann McFall leaves.
August	Ann McFall, seven months pregnant, living in Gloucester goes missing. Her disappearance is not reported to the police.
September	Fred, Rena, Charmaine and Anne Marie West move to a caravan site at Bishop's Cleeve.

1968

6 January	Mary Bastholm, aged 15, goes missing from Bristol Road in Gloucester.

1969

October	Rena West leaves Fred; Rose Letts begins to act as nanny to Charmaine and Anne Marie.
18 November	Fred West imprisoned for 30 days for non-payment of fines, Charmaine and Anne Marie taken into care.
21 November	Rena West returns to Fred, Charmaine and Anne Marie are released to them, then Rena leaves.
28 November	Charmaine and Anne Marie taken into care.

1970

February	Rose Letts is pregnant by Fred West.
March	Rose Letts placed in care for about a month then she leaves her parents to live with Fred in Cheltenham.
March	Charmaine and Anne Marie are returned to Fred West, who says that Rena has returned and Rose Letts will help with the children.
March	Rena West last seen.
April	Fred West and Rose Letts move to Gloucester, without Rena.
July	Fred West and Rose Letts move to a flat in 25 Midland Road, Gloucester.
17 October	Rose Letts gives birth to Heather Ann West.
4 December	Fred West imprisoned for nine months for theft.

31 December	Fred West receives a further month consecutive imprisonment.
1971	
24 June	Fred West released from prison.
July	Charmaine West, aged 8, is recorded in her school register as having 'moved to London'.
1972	
29 January	Fred West marries Rose Letts at Gloucester Register Office.
1 June	Rose West gives birth to May June West. She later changes her name to Mae.
September	The Wests move into 25 Cromwell Street, Gloucester.
October	Caroline Raine (Owens) goes to work for the Wests as nanny to Anne Marie, Heather and Mae.
November	Caroline Raine (Owens) leaves.
6 December	Caroline Raine (Owens) is abducted, physically and sexually assaulted by Fred and Rose West.
1973	
12 January	Fred and Rose West plead guilty to separate charges of occasioning actual bodily harm and indecent assault on Caroline Raine (Owens). They are fined £25 on each charge, a total of £50 each.
19 April	Lynda Gough, aged 19, who had left home to live at Cromwell Street, goes missing. Her disappearance is reported to a police officer neighbour and friend.
April	Lynda Gough's mother visits 25 Cromwell Street to look for her daughter. Fred and Rose tell her she has left.
19 August	Stephen Andrew West born to Rose West.
10 November	Carol Ann Cooper, aged 15, goes missing on her way home. Her disappearance is reported to the police, who mount a major investigation.
27 December	Lucy Partington, aged 21, goes missing after

	visiting a friend in Cheltenham. Her disappearance is reported to the police, who mount a major investigation.
1974	
16 April	Thérèse Siegenthaler, aged 21, goes missing. This is reported to the police, who mount a major investigation.
14 November	Shirley Hubbard, aged 15, goes missing while returning to her Droitwich home by bus. Her disappearance is reported to the police, who mount a major investigation.
1975	
11 April	Juanita Mott, aged 18, who had visited Cromwell Street, goes missing. Her disappearance is not reported to the police.
1977	
April	Shirley Robinson, aged 17, comes to live at 25 Cromwell Street.
October	Shirley Robinson becomes pregnant.
9 December	Rose West gives birth to Tara Jayne West. Her father is not Fred West.
1978	
April	Shirley Robinson, six months-plus pregnant, goes missing. Her disappearance is not reported to the police.
17 November	Rose West gives birth to Louise Carol West.
1979	
September	Alison Chambers, aged 17, who had visited Cromwell Street, tells her mother she is working for a family as a nanny. She then goes missing.
1980	
16 June	Rose West gives birth to Barry John West.
October	Fred West convicted of receiving stolen property. He is sentenced to nine months' imprisonment, suspended for two years.
1982	
13 April	Rose West gives birth to Rosemary Ann West. Her father is not Fred.

1983

16 July

Rose West gives birth to Lucyanna Mary West. Her father is not Fred. Rosemary West is sterilised.

1987

19 June

Heather West, aged 16, goes missing from 25 Cromwell Street. Her disappearance is not reported to the police.

1992

3 August

Gloucester foot-patrolling Police Constable Steven Burnside receives a third-party disclosure alleging Fred West was sexually abusing one of his daughters, and makes a report.

4 August

Case conference held by police and social services, joint investigation agreed. Social services to deal with emergency protection order, police to obtain search warrant.

5 August

Search warrant obtained.

6 August

Search warrant executed. Five children removed, Emergency Protection Order (EPO) granted by Tewkesbury Magistrates Court. Fred West arrested from his work in Stroud.

7 August

Fred West subsequently charged with three counts of rape and one of buggery against one of his daughters. One of the West children mentions a family joke to a social worker, 'Heather is under the patio' at 25 Cromwell Street.

8 August

Fred West is remanded in custody. Discussions with Crown Prosecution Service about tracing Heather to see if she had been abused result in agreement not to pursue this, in light of investigation of other serious allegations.

11 August

Rose West arrested and interviewed. She is asked about Heather's whereabouts. Subsequently charged with cruelty and causing or encouraging the commission of unlawful sexual intercourse with a child, one of her daughters. She is released on bail.

12 August	Rose West attempts suicide at 25 Cromwell Street and is admitted to hospital.
14 August	Fred and Rose West interviewed about Heather's whereabouts; both say she has gone to a holiday camp in Devon.
September	Fred West is released on bail to a hostel in Birmingham.
December–June 1993	Social workers caring for the West children still in care become aware of 'family joke' about Heather being under the patio.

1993

7 June	Fred and Rose West face trial in Gloucester. The witnesses refuse to give evidence against them; Judge Gabriel Hutton enters formal verdicts of not guilty.
20 August	Social services hold planning meeting about West children in care. Police are not in attendance. Fred and Rose West are attempting to have the children returned to them. Brief discussion about the children mentioning the 'family joke'. Social services agree that police should be told. A solicitor leaves a message for Detective Constable Savage.
23 August	Detective Constable Savage returns call, after which she makes further enquiries to trace Heather.
12 October	Detective Constable Savage discusses lack of progress in finding Heather with Detective Inspector Tony James.
18 October	Detective Constable Savage submits written report to Detective Inspector James seeking advice. At an impromptu meeting Detective Superintendent Bennett considers the report and discusses it with Detective Inspector James and Detective Constable Savage, further enquiries are directed and a strategy to pursue them outlined. The investigation is not considered to be high priority.

1994

15 January	Results of further enquiries are negative. Detective Suprintendent Bennett instructs written statement to be obtained from social workers then arrangements made to interview children in care.
12 February	Detective Chief Inspector Terry Moore holds meeting with Detective Inspector James and Detective Constable Savage to arrange West children in care to be interviewed on video at Gloucester by police and social workers.
23 February	Section 8 Police and Criminal Evidence Search Warrant obtained to search the garden of 25 Cromwell Street for evidence of the remains of Heather West.
24 February	1.25 p.m.: search warrant executed at 25 Cromwell Street. The Cromwell Street investigation officially begins.
24 February	Rose West is interviewed voluntarily at 25 Cromwell Street. She calls Fred, who does not return until after 5.30 p.m. and then presents himself at Gloucester Police Station at 7.40 p.m., where he is voluntarily interviewed before returning home.
25 February	Fred West is arrested, having confessed to the murder of Heather, and shows police where she is buried. Rose West is arrested.
26 February	A femur is found in the garden of 25 Cromwell Street and in addition, the remains of Heather West (Remains 1, Victim 12, Cromwell Street Victim 9) are discovered. Fred West admits to the killings of Shirley Robinson and 'Shirley's mate' (Alison Chambers).
27 February	Rose West is released on bail. She returns to Cromwell Street.
28 February	The remains of both Alison Chambers (Remains 2, Victim 11, Cromwell Street Victim 4) and Shirley Robinson (Remains 3, Victim 10, Cromwell Street Victim 7) are

recovered from 25 Cromwell Street. Fred West appears at Gloucester Magistrates Court charged with the murder of Heather and is remanded in police custody. Arrangements made to rehouse Rose West.

March Neil Butterfield QC to be leading counsel, Andrew Chubb to be junior counsel for the prosecution.

2 March Fred West is charged with the murders of Shirley Robinson and an unknown female (Alison Chambers).

3 March Fred West further remanded in police custody at Gloucester Magistrates Court.

4 March Fred West admits to nine further killings, in a note to Detective Superintendent Bennett – including Rena, Charmaine, Lynda Gough 'and others to be identified', and is taken back to 25 Cromwell Street to show where the remains are buried.

5 March Fred West is taken to Letterbox Field; points out where he buried Rena. Investigation refers to location as Kempley A. The remains of Thérèse Siegenthaler (Remains 4, Victim 7, Cromwell Street Victim 4) and Shirley Hubbard (Remains 5, Victim 8, Cromwell Street Victim 5) are recovered from 25 Cromwell Street.

6 March The remains of Lucy Partington (Remains 6, Victim 6, Cromwell Street Victim 3) and Juanita Mott (Remains 7, Victim 9, Cromwell Street Victim 6) are recovered from 25 Cromwell Street.

7 March The remains of Lynda Gough (Remains 8, Victim 4, Cromwell Street Victim 1) are recovered from 25 Cromwell Street. Frederick West is taken to Fingerpost Field, Kempley, and points out where he believes Ann McFall may be buried. He denies killing her. Investigation refers to location as Kempley B.

8 March	The remains of Carol Ann Cooper (Remains 9, Victim 5, Cromwell Street Victim 2) are recovered from 25 Cromwell Street.
11 March	Fred West appears at Gloucester Magistrates Court on eight charges of murder.
17 March	Fred West is charged with the murder of Alison Chambers, amending a charge of one of the 'unknown females'. He is also charged with the murder of Carol Ann Cooper.
18 March	Rose West's accommodation compromised. Rehoused to Cheltenham. Covert listening operation continues there.
20 March	Fred West taken to 25 Midland Road, where he says the police will not find Charmaine, and then to Bristol Road, Gloucester. Denies any knowledge of the disappearance of Mary Bastholm.
28 March	Fred West has existing charges of murder of 'unknown females' amended to murders of Alison Chambers, Lucy Partington, Juanita Mott and Lynda Gough.
29 March	Search warrant executed and search begins at Letterbox Field (Kempley A) for the remains of Rena.
6 April	Fred West is taken to Letterbox Field, where he indicates again where he buried Rena's remains.
8 April	Fred West served with amended charges naming Thérèse Siegenthaler and Shirley Hubbard.
10 April	The remains of Rena West (Remains 10, Victim 2) are discovered at Letterbox Field (Kempley A).
13 April	Search warrant executed at and search begins at Fingerpost Field (Kempley B), where Fred West 'believed' Ann McFall had been buried.
14 April	HM Coroner David Gibbons opens inquests into identification of the nine remains found

	at Cromwell Street and adjourns proceedings *sine die*.
20 April	Rose West arrested for unrelated matters. The covert listening operation ends after 885 45-minute tapes have been recorded.
21 April	Rose West appears before Gloucester Magistrates Court charged with unrelated matters and is remanded in custody. These proceedings are later withdrawn.
23 April	Rose West arrested for the murder of Lynda Gough.
24 April	Rose West is charged with the murder of Lynda Gough.
25 April	Rose West is again remanded in custody.
26 April	Search warrant executed and the search begins at 25 Midland Road, Gloucester. Rose West charged with the murder of Caroline Cooper.
28 April	Rose West charged with the murder of Lucy Partington.
29 April	Rose West remanded in police custody. Fred West retracts his confessions: 'I have not, and still not, told you the whole truth about these matters . . . from the very first day of this enquiry my main concern has been to protect other person or persons, and there is nothing else I wish to say at this time.'
30 April	Rose West charged with the murder of Thérèse Siegenthaler.
4 May	Rose West charged with the murder of Shirley Hubbard. The remains of Charmaine West (Remains 11, Victim 3) are found at 25 Midland Road.
6 May	Rose West charged with the murder of Juanita Mott.
11 May	Fred West is charged with the murder of Charmaine West.
13 May	Fred West's 132nd and final interview at Gloucester Police Station.

18 May	Rose West charged with the murder of Shirley Ann Robinson.
23 May	Rose West charged with the murder of Alison Jane Chambers.
26 May	Rose West charged with the murder of Heather Ann West.
2 June	Nine of Fred West's eleven murder charges are amended to joint charges with Rose at Gloucester Magistrates Court.
3 June	All nine of Rose West's murder charges are amended to joint charges with Fred West at Gloucester Magistrates Court.
7 June	The remains of Ann McFall (Remains 12, Victim 1) are found in Fingerpost Field (Kempley B).
30 June	Fred West arrested for murder of Ann McFall. Fred and Rose West appear together at Gloucester Magistrates Court. He is charged with eleven counts of murder, she with nine and other sexual offences.
3 July	Fred West charged with the murder of Ann McFall, bringing the total number of murder charges against him to twelve.
27 July	HM Coroner David Gibbons opens inquests at Dursley Magistrates Court for identification of the remains of Charmaine West, Catherine West née Costello and Ann McFall.
28 July	Fred and Rose West appear together at Gloucester Magistrates Court and are remanded in custody to 25 August.
3 August	Fred West dispenses with services of his solicitor, Howard Ogden. Representation taken over by Tony Miles Bobbetts and Mackan of Bristol.
13 December	Fred and Rose West appear for the last time together at Gloucester Magistrates Court and are remanded in custody to their committal proceedings.

1995

1 January	Fred West found dead in his cell at HM Prison Winson Green.
13 January	Rose West is charged with the murder of Charmaine West.
6 February	Rose West's committal proceedings at Dursley Magistrates Court begin.
14 February	Rose West is committed for trial on ten charges of murder by Chief Metropolitan Stipendiary Magistrate Peter Badge.
29 March	Fred West is cremated at Cranley Crematorium, near Coventry.
1 March	Neil Butterfield QC appointed High Court Judge; no longer able to lead prosecution.
5 March	Brian Leveson QC appointed leading counsel for the prosecution, Andrew Chubb remains as junior.
10 May	On authority of Official Solicitor Peter Harris, defence and prosecution counsels visit 25 Cromwell Street. The house is then resealed.
12 May	Rose West attends pre-trial review at Winchester Crown Court and formally pleads not guilty to all charges.
3 October	Rose West's trial on ten counts of murder begins at Winchester Crown Court. *Daily Express* forward concerns about the investigation's dealings with Sharon Compton.
8 November	Sharon Compton writes to the Police Complaints Authority complaining of how she had been dealt with by the investigation.
21 November	The jury unanimously returns three verdicts of guilty (Charmaine, Heather and Shirley Robinson), and retires again to consider the remaining seven charges.
22 November	The jury unanimously returns a further seven guilty verdicts against Rose West. Justice Mantell sentences her to life imprisonment for each of the ten murders, recommending that she should never be released.

23 November	Details of nine girls so far not traced who had visited 25 Cromwell Street are mentioned in press conferences and press packs.
23 November	*Daily Express* reports 25 Cromwell Street used by police as a brothel and that Sharon X (Sharon Compton) claimed her complaints had not been investigated properly. Gloucestershire Constabulary arranges for West Mercia Police to investigate the complaint and voluntarily refers complaint to the Police Complaints Authority.
24 November	*Daily Express* reports further allegations of Sharon X (Sharon Compton) and that the names of six officers from an anonymous former police officer have been forwarded to the Police Complaints Authority.

1996

18 March	The Court of Appeal hears Rose West's application to appeal against her conviction.
19 March	The Court of Appeal refuses Rose West permission to appeal.
April	Eight of the nine outstanding girls are traced, leaving Donna Moore unaccounted for.
21 April	The *News of the World* alleges Sharon Compton complains of having been assaulted in the presence of a police officer.
11 July	The inquest into Fred West's death begins at Birmingham.
12 July	The inquest jury decides that Fred West killed himself.
26 September	Police Complaints Authority issues a three-page press release detailing how and why it found no evidence to support any of the serious allegations made by Sharon Compton in connection with the events at Cromwell Street, totally vindicating the constabulary, Bennett and the investigating team. Deputy Chief Constable Nigel Burgess of Gloucestershire Constabulary issues a

	three-page press release elaborating on that of the Police Complaints Authority and criticising the press reporting.
7 October	Police supervise five-day demolition of 23 and 25 Cromwell Street; the fabric is reduced to rubble and ground to dust and placed deep in a landfill site. Other items are burnt.
1997 July	Pedestrian walkway replaces 23 and 25 Cromwell Street.

APPENDIX ONE

*Police Complaints Authority Press Statement of
26 September 1996 Concerning the Complaints
of Sharon X (Compton)*

The independent Police Complaints Authority has found no evidence
to support serious allegations against officers from Gloucestershire
Constabulary in connection with events at 25 Cromwell Street.

PCA Member Mr James Eliott has now written to the complainant.

BACKGROUND

Sharon X had first come to the attention of Gloucestershire
Constabulary claiming she had been a victim of assault and rape by
Fred West. As part of the West murder investigation, the allegations
were thoroughly investigated.

No evidence was found to support Sharon X's claims and her
evidence was not used in the prosecution of Rosemary West.

Sharon X then made allegations against Gloucestershire
Constabulary. They appeared in the *Daily Express* on 23 November last
year.

Gloucestershire Constabulary voluntarily referred the matter to the
PCA and the allegations were investigated by a team led by Detective
Superintendent Ian Johnston of West Mercia Constabulary under the
supervision of PCA member Mr Tony Williams.

THE ALLEGATIONS
Sharon X alleged that:

- Gloucestershire Constabulary had not properly investigated her
  allegations against the Wests and had been unsympathetic in
  their treatment of her;

- She had been tied to a chair and assaulted at Cromwell Street before being rescued by a person – described as 'raincoat man' – whom she believed to be a police officer;
- That police officers used 25 Cromwell Street as a brothel and drinking club.

According to a subsequent article in the *News of the World*, she also claimed that she was tied to a slab and raped by Fred West with a police officer present.

THE EVIDENCE

Neither the initial inquiry by Gloucestershire Constabulary into the West affair, nor the investigation into her complaints by West Mercia Constabulary could find any evidence to support her story. Various independent witnesses cast doubts on the claims made by Sharon X.

No evidence was found to support her claim that 'raincoat man' was a police officer.

At the time of the alleged incident, Sharon X was living in a Gloucester children's home. Witnesses who were also resident there, at the same time, cast doubt on her involvement with Cromwell Street.

None of those who lived at or regularly visited 25 Cromwell Street, in 1979, identified Sharon X from her photograph. Nor could they recall anyone looking like her.

Her description of the fixtures, fittings and decoration in the property is not supported by the tenants. For example, her description of an undecorated and dingy cellar was similar to that published in a national newspaper, whereas the cellar was decorated as a playroom in 1979.

Sharon claimed to have been present when one of the West murders was committed, but her description of the event bore no relation to the medical evidence.

When interviewed by West Mercia officers about the *News of the World* allegations she denied that she had told the newspaper that Fred West raped her in the presence of a police officer.

The West Mercia investigation also established that the murder inquiry team had treated Sharon X with patience, sympathy and compassion.

Mr James Elliott reviewed all the evidence produced by the inquiry. He said:

> The work of the West Mercia officers has shown that the original Gloucestershire Constabulary murder inquiry team thoroughly and professionally investigated all of Sharon X's claims.
>
> Furthermore the thorough and painstaking investigation by West Mercia Constabulary has found no evidence to support subsequent claims that 25 Cromwell Street was used by police officers for sexual purposes and as a drinking den. There is no evidence to suggest that Sharon X was assaulted at Cromwell Street.

GLOUCESTERSHIRE CONSTABULARY PRESS RELEASE OF 26 SEPTEMBER 1996 CONCERNING THE COMPLAINTS OF SHARON X (COMPTON) ISSUED BY DEPUTY CHIEF CONSTABLE NIGEL BURGESS

In normal circumstances the Constabulary does not make public comment about complaint investigations or their results. This is because they are matters to be resolved between the complainant and the Constabulary, with the independent involvement of the Police Complaints Authority and, on occasions, the Director of Public Prosecutions, both of whom are, of course, free to make public statements if they choose.

There are, however, occasions when the nature of the complaint means that it is in fact in the public interest for the Constabulary to provide a detailed formal statement; the complaints made by Mrs Sharon Compton and the *Daily Express* newspaper fall into this category.

Three areas of complaint were made and were set out in a letter from Sharon Compton to the Police Complaints Authority dated the 8th November 1995 and disclosed in articles in the *Daily Express* on the 23rd and 24th November 1995.

The complaints alleged that Mrs Compton's health suffered as a result of the treatment received from the Gloucestershire Constabulary; that the police had not properly investigated her complaints about assaults upon her at and by people living at or visiting 25 Cromwell Street; and that her allegation that police officers were using 25 Cromwell Street when it was operating as a brothel was not investigated to her satisfaction.

Although not required by the Police and Criminal Evidence Act, because of the serious nature of the allegations, the Constabulary referred the complaints to the Police Complaints Authority for independent supervision. With their agreement, officers from the West Mercia Constabulary were appointed to investigate the allegations.

Following a thorough investigation and a comprehensive report scrutinised by the PCA, no evidence was disclosed to support the complaints.

Mrs Compton had potentially been a witness in the trial of Rosemary West but as a result of close scrutiny by murder inquiry officers, and acting upon legal advice, she was withdrawn as a witness owing to the extreme unreliability of her evidence.

The complaints investigation by the West Mercia officers confirmed this unreliability, with many of her claims made during the inquiry being found to be wholly inaccurate. Little or no corroboration could be found in relation to any aspect of the allegations and on some occasions she declined to co-operate in providing the corroboration which she claimed would substantiate the complaints.

The complaint that her health had suffered as a result of treatment by Gloucestershire Constabulary officers, and by Detective Superintendent Bennett in particular, was not substantiated. Investigating officers found that Gloucestershire Police followed recognised guidelines on dealing with alleged victims of abuse and that she was treated with 'patience, sympathy and compassion'. No evidence was found to suggest that Detective Superintendent Bennett had treated her in anything but a caring, professional manner and her complaint was deemed to be unfounded.

Her complaint that her allegations of assault and abuse were not thoroughly investigated was also found to be totally unsubstantiated. The complaint investigation revealed that every aspect of her earlier criminal allegations was pursued fully by the murder inquiry team and properly linked to all other relevant evidence being gathered in the Cromwell Street Investigation.

The complaint inquiry additionally found no evidence to show that officers were frequenting 25 Cromwell Street when it was alleged it was being used as a brothel.

For several months prior to making her complaint, Mrs Compton was linked commercially with the *Daily Express* newspaper.

Coinciding with the conviction of Rosemary West the *Daily Express* published articles on the 23rd and 24th November 1995 setting out allegations made by Sharon Compton and adding additional claims. The contents of the first article were based on information allegedly supplied by Mrs Compton, several aspects of which were subsequently denied by her. Her unreliability as a witness had already been established and the complaint inquiry team found that publication took place without any proper attempt at corroboration or scrutiny of apparently conflicting information.

It has been accepted by the *Daily Express* that the article of the 24th November was printed on the basis of untested information supplied by an anonymous caller.

An additional allegation not subject of the original complaints by Mrs Compton and not revealed during the West Mercia investigation, was reported in an article in the *News of the World* on the 21st of April 1996. This contained the suggestion that a police officer had been present on an occasion when Sharon Compton had allegedly been subject of a serious sexual assault. Sharon Compton subsequently denied the accuracy of the article and the newspaper failed to co-operate in providing any evidence of corroboration.

In reviewing the conclusions drawn by the West Mercia investigating team and the Police Complaints Authority, the Deputy Chief Constable of Gloucestershire, Mr Nigel Burgess, said:

> The decision to refer the complaint voluntarily to the Police Complaints Authority and to invite an external inquiry from another Force, was obviously prudent in view of the high public profile of the circumstances of the complaint and the specific nature of the allegations.
>
> The PCA's conclusion is that the Constabulary has been completely exonerated from any suggestion of improper or unprofessional behaviour on the part of any officer. Whilst these conclusions do not come as a surprise, I am obviously very pleased with the clean bill of health being given to the Force.
>
> What I find disappointing and far from satisfactory is the harm caused by the approach adopted by some reporters and newspapers, whose lack of objectivity and professionalism can give such a distorted and sensationalised picture to the public.

I am aware of the unnecessary pain which was caused to the families of the Cromwell Street victims by these particular publications in the *Daily Express* and the *News of the World* and I am pleased now to be able to confirm to all of those families the earlier reassurance we gave that the stories were unfounded.

APPENDIX TWO

Most Frequently Asked Questions

HOW MANY MURDERS ARE FRED AND ROSE WEST SUSPECTED OF COMMITTING?

There is no evidence to support claims that Fred or Rose West committed any other murders, although it must remain a possibility. Their joint addiction to sexual depravity in which Rose West appears to have eventually exceeded her husband and which was to end in murder has no consistent pattern as regards timing and no reason is apparent for the irregular gaps between the known offences.

While the disappearance of Mary Bastholm has distinct similarities to that of at least four of the victims found at Cromwell Street and Fred West frequented Gloucester's Bristol Road area from where she went missing in January 1968, he never admitted to the police knowing her or having any involvement in her disappearance, though others allege he did to them. Rose was just 15 years old when Mary disappeared and did not know Fred then.

West was clearly involved in murder before he met Rose Letts, who was only 13 years old when Ann McFall was killed. This was a murder charge he would have faced alone and one which he maintained until death he had not committed, though he is said to have mentioned knowing of it at about the time she disappeared.

Equally it seems that Rose West was capable of murder in her own right as the evidence gathered pointed to the likelihood of Charmaine being killed while West was still in prison.

Fred West is known to have told other people, but not the police, that he and Rose committed more murders but none of these claims can be authenticated. Neither can the similar and vague descriptions of these offences, or where they took place, which were not consistent. It is believed that he was purposely giving similar information but different locations to see which version reached the media and so establish in whom he could safely confide.

HOW DID THE VICTIMS DIE AND WHAT HAPPENED TO THE MISSING BONES?

It is not known how the victims met their death. Fred West's account of the murders and the circumstances he said surrounded them was inconsistent as he continually attempted to exculpate his wife, who remains in denial. The artefacts found with the remains, for most of which he never offered a rational explanation, did not corroborate what he said happened.

It is not known what happened to the missing bones, though had they been where the victims were buried they would have been found. Fred West vaguely mentioned that this was an attempt to prevent identification; in the circumstances, this does not appear credible. There are some similarities in what is missing, victim to victim, and it is therefore possible they were retained and taken elsewhere.

ARE OTHER HIGH-PROFILE INVESTIGATIONS LIKELY TO SUFFER THE SAME MEDIA INTRUSION?

While the media remains self-regulated it has tightened up considerably its codes of conduct to restrict its involvement with and payment of potential witnesses in criminal investigations, and is required to disclose this to the prosecution and defence. It is still the case that if it can be shown that 'it is in the public interest' such involvement might be justified. A more responsible attitude now seems to prevail but it must be likely that if these codes are regularly transgressed without justification that further legislation will follow.

COULD SUCH A SERIES OF OFFENCES AND MURDERS BE COMMITTED TODAY?

In the wake of the West and other recent high-profile murder cases, many lessons have been learned. The West murders spanned twenty-seven years during which communication, methods and technology which would have possibly identified the crimes was either non-existent or in its infancy. Today procedures and legislation for monitoring sexual offenders and identifying those who may have the potential to commit or graduate to committing such crimes have been put in place, combined with the sharing of information and the coordination of the caring and investigative agencies. Further, there have been changes in the way missing persons are recorded and investigated which increase the potential for early recognition of abuse and series crime, as well as major advances in forensic science and the use of DNA to aid identification.

While it is hoped that such crimes, the way they were carried out and the fact that they remained undiscovered for so long is a thing of the past, there can be no room for complacency. The deviousness and cunning of those like the Wests is universally known to be limitless.

APPENDIX THREE

Recognition

(Services, titles and ranks as at March 1996, unless otherwise stated)

The magnitude of the Cromwell Street or West investigation, as it is also known, was supported by the entire Gloucestershire Constabulary throughout its duration, from regular officers to special constabulary and civilian support staff. In addition, many other police services and agencies assisted in the diverse aspects that arose, ensuring and maintaining the thorough approach of the investigation, its openness, care and completeness. To respect confidentiality, not all agencies and individuals can be mentioned; neither can certain facets and details of the work some officers on the investigation and those agencies undertook. The coordinated and very willingly given support of all involved was pivotal to the outcome of the investigation.

Justice Mantell in his commendation and Chief Constable Tony Butler recognised this while reserving his personal commendation for those principally involved for their contribution to aspects of the investigation.

Some of those services, agencies, organisations, officers and staff involved to whom the Gloucestershire Constabulary are indebted follow, before the names of officially commended officers and staff.

The Crown Prosecution Service headquarters, The Home Office Prison Department, The Prison Service, The Lord Chancellor's Office, The Department of Health, The Department for Education and Employment, The Department of Social Security, The Inland Revenue, The Office for National Statistics, Gloucestershire Fire and Rescue Service, National Criminal Intelligence Service, Police National Computer, Police Scientific Research Service, Interpol, The Forensic Science Service, Police National Missing Persons Bureau, The Police College Library, The National Crime Faculty, National

Missing Persons Helpline charity, The Probation Service, Victim Support, Winchester Witness Support Service, Gloucester City Council, Gloucester Magistrates and Winchester Crown Courts clerks and staff, Gloucestershire County Council, British Telecom, Midlands Electricity Board, I2Ltd [investigative analyst software],Watson Analyst software by Harlequin, Catchem Database and Chuck Burton OBE, All Scottish Police services, The Hampshire Constabulary, Warwickshire Constabuary and Detective Constable Bob Wilcox, West Mercia Constabulary, Wiltshire Constabulary, Hertfordshire Constabulary, Metropolitan Police Service.

The University of Wales College of Medicine, Wales Institute of Forensic Medicine and Home Office Pathologist Professor Bernard Knight CBE, University of Wales Forensic Odontology Department and Dr (now Professor) David Whittaker and staff; South Western Forensic Science Service, Dr Wilf Basley and staff, Forensic Scientist Dr Roger Ide, HM Coroner David Gibbons, Mr Alan Slater and office, Mr Justice Butterfield (then Neil Butterfield QC), Mr Justice Leveson (then Brian Leveson QC), Andrew Chubb (now sadly deceased), Withiel Cole, special caseworker CPS, and the Gloucester CPS Office, especially Rita Crane and Eric Ware, Gloucestershire Social Services, especially Fred Davies, Deputy Director, Gloucestershire County Council Legal Services, especially solicitor Richard Cawdron.

GLOUCESTERSHIRE CONSTABULARY

Chief Inspector C. Handy, Inspector W. Freeth-Selway, Detective Inspector M. Wilson, Detective Inspector W. Murdoch, Detective Sergeant T. Onions, Police Sergeant R. Green, Detective Sergeant H. Barrett, Detective Constable G. Watters, Detective Constable M. Wood, Police Constable K. Price (Snr), Police Constable J. Hannah, Police Constable C. Guthrie, Police Constable D. Avery, Police Constable E. Williams, Police Constable R. Rumbellow, Ms H. Allison, Ms Elaine Smith, Mr Mike Cresswell, Ms S. Weratt, Ms W. Camm. Headquarters, Gloucester, Cheltenham, Cirencester and Stroud typists. Operations and Traffic Division and all other officers and staff who, although not mentioned by name, played a part directly or indirectly in the investigation.

HAMPSHIRE CONSTABULARY

Superintendent G. Stogden, Inspector P. Stallard, Police Sergeant A. Jackson and team

GLOUCESTERSHIRE OFFICERS

HIGHLY COMMENDED

Detective Superintendent J.W. Bennett QPM
Detective Chief Inspector T. Moore
Detective Sergeant D. Griffiths
Detective Sergeant B. Harrison
Detective Sergeant R. Kelland
Police Sergeant P. Maunder
Detective Constable R. Williams
Detective Constable R. Beetham
Detective Constable N. Barnes
Detective Constable N. Churchill
Detective Constable D. Fryatt
Police Constable M. Grimshaw
Detective Constable S. Harris
Detective Constable P. Kerrod
Police Constable C. Mannion
Detective Constable S. McCormick
Detective Constable J. Morgan
Detective Constable C. Stephens
Police Constable D. Stephens
Detective Constable C. West
Police Constable D. Willats

COMMENDED

Detective Chief Superintendent K.W. Daun
Chief Inspector D. Morgan
Inspector R. Bradley
Detective Inspector A. James

Inspector T. Kania
Detective Inspector R. Scrivin
Detective Constable J. Field
Detective Constable D. Law
Detective Constable J. Rouse
Detective Constable H. Savage MBE
Inspector D. Cooper
Police Sergeant A. Jay
Police Sergeant J. McCarthy
Police Sergeant J. Pickersgill
Police Sergeant P. Mohamed
Police Sergeant I. Robinson
Police Constable D. Powell
Police Constable R. Burge
Police Constable S. Cooke
Police Constable E. Hanna
Police Constable M. Wilkinson
Police Constable D. Barnes
Police Constable N. Jefferies
Police Constable R. Lecouteur
Police Constable A. Elsdon
Police Constable J. Garner
Police Constable J. Hammonds
Police Constable P. Wand
Police Constable N. Butt
Police Constable C. Skinner
Police Constable M. Skinner
Police Constable R. Holt
Police Constable M. Smith
Police Constable M. Evans
Police Constable S. Crook
Police Constable K. Richards
Police Constable L. Speer
Police Constable M. Jones
Police Constable J. Wiffen
Police Constable G. Sharpe
Police Constable C. Parrot
Police Constable M. Godsland
Police Constable A. Ewens

Detective Constable A. Fuller
Detective Constable K. Benson
Detective Constable M. Wood
Police Constable J. Wilkinson

CHIEF CONSTABLE'S AWARD

Mr S. Mann, Gloucester City Council

INDEX